The Tibetan Book of Everyday Wisdom

The Library of Tibetan Classics is a special series developed by the Institute of Tibetan Classics aimed at making key classical Tibetan texts part of the global literary and intellectual heritage. Eventually comprising thirty-two large volumes, the collection will contain over two hundred distinct texts by more than a hundred of the best-known authors. These texts have been selected in consultation with the preeminent lineage holders of all the schools and other senior Tibetan scholars to represent the Tibetan literary tradition as a whole. The works included in the series span more than a millennium and cover the vast expanse of classical Tibetan knowledge—from the core teachings of the specific schools to such diverse fields as ethics, philosophy, linguistics, medicine, astronomy and astrology, folklore, and historiography.

The Tibetan Book of Everdyay Wisdom: A Thousnad Years of Sage Advice includes texts from a genre of Tibetan writing known as "wise sayings" (*lekshé*) containing guidance on both worldly and spiritual virtue, but the texts may be generally characterized as secular. Drawing inspiration from classical Indian wisdom literature pertaining to secular ethics and governance (*nītiśastra*), including the folktales in *The Pañcatantra*, the goal of the authors of these Tibetan texts is to educate young minds in the intricate ways of the world, especially by distinguishing the conduct of the wise from that of the foolish. This anthology contains Sakya Paṇḍita's celebrated thirteenth-century classic *A Jewel Treasury of Wise Sayings*, Paṇchen Sönam Drakpa's *Ganden Wise Sayings*, Gungthang's *Treatise on Trees* and *Treatise on Water*, as well as commentaries on the first two works. The volume also features Dromtönpa's *Garland of Essential Advice*, the Fifth Dalai Lama's *Pearl Garland of Advice*, Kyilsur Lobsang Jinpa's *Treatise on Wind*, and Panchen Chökyi Nyima's *Treatise on Earth*. Historically these works have been used for educating the wider public, especially those outside the monastery. The final work in this volume is the intriguing *Khaché Phalu's Advice.* Though ostensibly written by a wise Tibetan Muslim, this last work is widely suspected to have been authored by a Buddhist monk. This versified text enjoys great popularity within the Tibetan-speaking communities, such that most people are able to recite at least a few verses from memory.

THE LIBRARY OF TIBETAN CLASSICS • VOLUME 27

Thupten Jinpa, General Editor

The Tibetan Book of Everyday Wisdom

A Thousand Years of Sage Advice

Translated by Beth Newman

Introduced by Thupten Jinpa

Wisdom

in association with the Institute of Tibetan Classics

Wisdom Publications
199 Elm Street
Somerville MA 02144 USA
www.wisdompubs.org

Library of Congress Cataloging-in-Publication Data
Names: Newman, Beth, translator. | Thupten Jinpa, writer of introduction.
Title: The Tibetan book of everyday wisdom: a thousand years of sage advice / translated by Beth Newman; introduced by Thupten Jinpa.
Other titles: Legs bshad lugs kyi bslab bya'i dpe tshogs. English.
Description: Somerville, MA: Wisdom Publications, 2017. | Series: The library of Tibetan classics; Volume 27 | Includes bibliographical references and index. |
Identifiers: LCCN 2017026925 (print) | LCCN 2017039139 (ebook) | ISBN 9781614295136 (ebook) | ISBN 1614295131 (ebook) | ISBN 9780861714667 (hard cover: alk. paper) | ISBN 0861714660 (hard cover: alk. paper)
Subjects: LCSH: Didactic poetry, Tibetan—Translations into Tibetan. | Spiritual life—Buddhism.
Classification: LCC PL3735 (ebook) | LCC PL3735 .L4613 2017 (print) | DDC 895/.410080382943—dc23
LC record available at https://lccn.loc.gov/2017026925

ISBN 978-0-86171-466-7 ebook ISBN 978-1-61429-513-6

23 22 21 20 19 18
5 4 3 2 1

Cover and interior design by Gopa&Ted2. Set in Adobe Garamond Premier Pro 10.5/13.5.

Wisdom Publications' books are printed on acid-free paper and meet the guidelines for permanence and durability of the Production Guidelines for Book Longevity of the Council on Library Resources.

♻ This book was produced with environmental mindfulness. For more information, please visit wisdompubs.org/wisdom-environment.

Printed in the United States of America.

MIX
Paper from responsible sources
FSC® C011935

Please visit fscus.org.

Message from the Dalai Lama

THE LAST TWO MILLENNIA witnessed a tremendous proliferation of cultural and literary development in Tibet, the Land of Snows. Moreover, owing to the inestimable contributions made by Tibet's early spiritual kings, numerous Tibetan translators, and many great Indian *paṇḍitas* over a period of so many centuries, the teachings of the Buddha and the scholastic tradition of ancient India's Nālandā monastic university became firmly rooted in Tibet. As evidenced from the historical writings, this flowering of Buddhist tradition in the country brought about the fulfillment of the deep spiritual aspirations of countless sentient beings. In particular, it contributed to the inner peace and tranquility of the peoples of Tibet, Outer Mongolia—a country historically suffused with Tibetan Buddhism and its culture—the Tuva and Kalmuk regions in present-day Russia, the outer regions of mainland China, and the entire trans-Himalayan areas on the southern side, including Bhutan, Sikkim, Ladakh, Kinnaur, and Spiti. Today this tradition of Buddhism has the potential to make significant contributions to the welfare of the entire human family. I have no doubt that, when combined with the methods and insights of modern science, the Tibetan Buddhist cultural heritage and knowledge will help foster a more enlightened and compassionate human society, a humanity that is at peace with itself, with fellow sentient beings, and with the natural world at large.

It is for this reason I am delighted that the Institute of Tibetan Classics in Montreal, Canada, is compiling a thirty-two-volume series containing the works of many great Tibetan teachers, philosophers, scholars, and practitioners representing all major Tibetan schools and traditions. These important writings will be critically edited and annotated and will then be published in modern book format in a reference collection called *The Library of Tibetan Classics*, the translations into other major languages to follow later. While expressing my heartfelt commendation for this noble project, I pray and hope that *The Library of Tibetan Classics* will not only make these important Tibetan treatises accessible to scholars of Tibetan studies but will also create a new opportunity for younger Tibetans to study and take interest in their own rich and profound culture. It is my sincere hope that through the series' translations into other languages, millions of fellow citizens of the wider human family will also be able to share in the joy of engaging with Tibet's classical literary heritage, textual riches that have been such a great source of joy and inspiration to me personally for so long.

The Dalai Lama
The Buddhist monk Tenzin Gyatso

Special Acknowledgments

The Institute of Tibetan Classics expresses its deep gratitude to the Ing Foundation for its generous support of the entire cost of translating this important volume. The Ing Foundation's long-standing patronage of the Institute of Tibetan Classics has enabled the institute to support the translation of multiple volumes from *The Library of Tibetan Classics*. We are deeply grateful to the foundation for offering us the opportunity to share many of the important texts of the Tibetan tradition with wider international readership, making these works truly part of the global literary, knowledge, and spiritual heritage.

We also thank the Scully Peretsman Foundation for its generous support of the work of the Institute's chief editor, Dr. Thupten Jinpa, enabling him to contribute a major essay as the introduction to this volume.

Publisher's Acknowledgment

The Publisher wishes to extend a heartfelt thanks to the following people who have contributed substantially to the publication of *The Library of Tibetan Classics*:

Pat Gruber and the Patricia and Peter Gruber Foundation
The Ing Foundation

We also extend deep appreciation to our other subscribing benefactors:

Anonymous, dedicated to Buddhas within
Anonymous, in honor of Dzongsar Khyentse Rinpoche
Anonymous, in honor of Geshe Tenzin Dorje
Anonymous, in memory of K. J. Manel De Silva—may she realize the truth
Dr. Patrick Bangert
Nilda Venegas Bernal
Serje Samlo Khentul Lhundub Choden and his Dharma friends
Kushok Lobsang Dhamchöe
Tenzin Dorjee
Richard Farris
Gaden Samten Ling, Canada
Evgeniy Gavrilov & Tatiana Fotina
Ginger Gregory
Rick Meeker Hayman
Steven D. Hearst
Heidi Kaiter
Paul, Trisha, Rachel, and Daniel Kane
Land of Medicine Buddha
the Nalanda Institute, Olympia, WA
Craig T. Neyman
Kristin A. Ohlson
Arnold Possick
Elizabeth Mettling
Russ Miyashiro
Quek Heng Bee, Ong Siok Ngow, and family
Randall-Gonzales Family Foundation
Andrew Rittenour
Jonathan and Diana Rose
the Sharchitsang family
Nirbhay N. Singh
Kestrel Slocombe
Tibetisches Zentrum e.V. Hamburg
Richard Toft
Timothy Trompeter
Tsadra Foundation
the Vahagn Setian Charitable Foundation
Ellyse Adele Vitiello
Nicholas C. Weeks II
Claudia Wellnitz
Bob White
Kevin Michael White, MD
Eve and Jeff Wild

and the other donors who wish to remain anonymous.

Contents

Introduction

by Thupten Jinpa

One of the things I still retain from my primary school years at the Central School for Tibetans, Shimla, is a deep fondness for a specific set of Tibetan verses I memorized as a child. These verses came from a genre of texts referred to as "wise sayings," or *lekshé* in Tibetan, a word that I later learned was a translation of the Sanskrit word *subhāṣita*. The names of three texts stood out for me then, Sakya Paṇḍita's famed *Treasury of Wise Sayings* and Gungthang's *Treatise on Trees* and *Treatise on Water*. Every time our Tibetan teacher would share a few verses from these texts, I would be pulled in by the freeness and immediacy of the language and the vividness of the imagery. Reading these lines, whose mind could fail to conjure the image of some crafty crow wiping off its dirty beak?

> The wicked usually attribute
> whatever faults they have to others.
> Crows diligently wipe on something clean
> their beaks dirtied by eating filth. (*Treasury*, 63)

What could rival these lines when chiding a kid for failing to do his chores?

> Those who rush to where they can eat and drink
> and sneak off when assigned important tasks
> may know how to tell stories and jokes,
> but they are simply old dogs without tails. (*Treasury*, 70)

How about this for reminding students to respect their teachers?

> A person who has no respect for his teachers
> may know a hundred texts, but they will be of no use.
> A dry branch may be put in water and left for a hundred years,
> but it can never sprout leaves. (*Trees*, 4)

So, decades later, when the opportunity arose to create a series representing the vast corpus of classical Tibetan literature within a manageable collection in *The Library of Tibetan Classics*, I made sure that this unique genre of Tibetan texts I loved so much as a child would be fully represented. The present work is a complete translation of the Tibetan volume I compiled on the Tibetan *lekshé*, or "wise sayings" literature. The volume contains nine original works and two prose commentaries on the lengthiest verse texts.

Our Anthology of Tibetan Wise Sayings

(1) The first text, *A Garland of Essential Advice on Societal Values*, contains an anthology of practical advice that Dromtönpa (1004–64) gave to his disciple and translator Naktso as the latter was embarking on a long journey to Nepal and India. Naktso tells Dromtönpa that he is quite familiar with the Dharma teachings but would like practical advice on how to deal with people and maintain his composure, as he is bound to encounter all sorts of unpredictable challenges when away from the familiarities of home. (2) The second work in our collection is *A Jewel Treasury of Wise Sayings* by the great Sakya Paṇḍita (1182–1251), which later came to be known affectionately as the *Sakya Lekshé* (*Sakya Wise Sayings*). This seminal text effectively established the tradition of Indian *subhāṣita* literature in the Tibetan language. (3) The third text is the earliest prose commentary on the *Jewel Treasury*, composed by Rinchen Pal and corrected and revised during Sakya Paṇḍita's lifetime by Martön Chögyal. (4) The fourth work is *Ganden Wise Sayings: A Bouquet of White Lotuses* by Paṇchen Sönam Drakpa (1478–1554), a famed scholar and noted historian as well a tutor of the Third Dalai Lama. (5) This is followed by a lengthy prose commentary on the same text by Yangchen Gawai Lodrö (1740–1827). (6) The next is a verse work by the Great Fifth Dalai Lama (1617–82) entitled *A Pearl Garland of Advice*, containing advice on both the religious norms of Buddhist practice and the worldly norms of human society. (7–8) The next two entries are original works by the great scholar and poet Gungthang Tenpai Drönmé (1762–1823) that use trees and water as metaphors and are thus titled *Treatise on Trees* and *Treatise on Water*.

(9–10) The ninth and tenth texts, inspired by and fashioned on Gungthang's two treatises, likewise use elements, in this case wind and earth, and were written by Kyilsur Losang Jinpa (b. 1821) and Paṇchen Chökyi Nyima (1883–1937), respectively. (11) The final text in our anthology is the popular *Khaché Phalu's Advice*, ostensibly written by a Tibetan Muslim named Phalu Ju (a pseudonym) for the benefit of his fellow Tibetans who are Buddhists.

Despite containing specific advice on Buddhist Dharma, the primary subject matter of all these texts are issues of everyday life and how these should be guided by basic human values, societal norms, and perhaps most importantly, commonsense wisdom. Furthermore, all these texts were written specifically for a lay audience, for whom questions of how to lead a good family life, how to relate to a ruler, how to treat servants, how to conduct such mundane tasks as commerce, and so on are pertinent. The beauty and power of the *lekshé* texts come from their unique literary style, which shuns the discursive approach and chooses the four-line verse, written in easy Tibetan and often structured so that the first two lines convey a point while the remaining two lines provide a striking analogy. The following from Gungthang's *Treatise on Trees* illustrates this style:

> For yogis to whom every perception appears as a metaphor,
> there is an abundance of spiritual instruction.
> In clearings within densely forested valleys,
> there is no end to the masses of leaves. (verse 2)

As we will see, the developed form of Tibetan *lekshé* reveals a strong Indian influence, particularly of the literary genre known as *subhāṣita*, which is in turn a subset of the *nitiśastras*, or treatises on ethics or morals. *Subhāṣita*, or "wise sayings," not only contained "beautiful thoughts but were also drawn and set down in beautiful language."[1] As for the Indian *nīti* treatises, the influential *Sanskrit-English Dictionary* by Monier Monier-Williams describes them as dealing with "right or wise or moral conduct or behavior, prudence, policy, political wisdom or science."[2] *Nīti* is a secular category of literature within which the classical Indian tradition organizes the important topics concerning everyday life in a society. They are *dharma* (law and duty), *artha* (statecraft, economic policy, and warfare), and *nīti* (common sense and wise judgment). The Sanskrit term *nīti* is, like the word *dharma*, impossible to translate into a single English word.[3] The early Tibetan translators chose the Tibetan word *lugs*, which can mean "norms," "system," "way," "tradition," and "custom." As shall be explored later, this Indian influence can be discerned in three important aspects of *lekshé* literature: its poetic form, its similes, and its embedded stories.

Despite the Indian influence, there are clearly indigenous sources for the later *lekshé* writings traceable to pre-Buddhist Tibetan oral tradition, with its rich repertoire of stories, proverbs, and pithy sayings. For example, when it comes to the morals or values themselves, even a later text like Gungthang's *Treatise on Water* displays extensive influence from indigenous Tibetan sensibilities and norms. We know from anthropological studies of ancient preliterate peoples that stories and pithy sayings play a crucial role in perpetuating the values and norms of a given society across generations, and Tibet is no exception. We have explicit acknowledgment of this in Tibet's early historical writings. For example, according to the *Deu History* (*Lde'u chos 'byung*), a text dateable to the twelfth or thirteenth century, the Tibetan polity was governed through narratives or stories (*sgrung*), symbolic languages (*lde'u*), and rituals (*bon*) during the rule of the first twenty-seven kings.[4] Here "symbolic languages" refers to a host of sayings whereby a key point is made through an oblique or metaphoric reference. For example, if you wish to emphasize the need to cultivate a resource before you need it, you could say, "A cow to be milked in summer should be fed from winter onward." And if you wish to tell someone that he is caught in a no-win fight, you could say, "If you hit a rock with butter, the butter loses; and if you hit butter with a rock, the butter loses as well."[5]

Societal Values and Dromtönpa's "Garland of Essential Advice"

Thus while today most classically educated Tibetans think of Tibetan *lekshé* as inspired by Indian *nītiśāstra*, Sakya Paṇḍita's *Treasury* being the archetypical example, the story is more complex, with Tibet's indigenous tradition of stories and pithy sayings finding their way into later *lekshé* works as well. We also have two known earlier texts that display hardly any awareness or influence of Indian wisdom literature. One is Dromtönpa's *Garland of Essential Advice*, featured in our volume, while the second is a remarkable secular work in prose, in the format of questions and answers between two brothers, found among the cache of Tibetan texts disovered in the Dunhuang caves at the turn of the last century.[6] A central concept in these two Tibetan texts is *mi chos* (pronounced *michö*, lit. "human dharma"), a term that can be translated as "human virtues" or "human values" or "societal values." In its original use, and as intended in these works, this term seems to be understood in contrast to *lha chos* (pronounced *lhachö*), which could be translated as "religious virtues" or "religious values." What is a societal value as opposed to a religious value, and how might one differentiate between the two? We find the following brief definition in Dromtönpa's text:

> Wherever you travel, in whatever direction,
> wherever you make camp or find a place to stay,
> whoever you seek to befriend or associate with,
> being considerate of others is the basis of societal values. (verse 2)

Here Dromtönpa identifies being considerate of others as the fundamental societal value. Thus any attitude and behavior that promotes mutual consideration could be understood as part of societal values.

The context of Dromtönpa's advice allows us to understand clearly what he meant by "societal values" (*mi chos*). As recorded in the text's preamble, the advice was ostensibly given by Dromtönpa at the behest of Naktso Lotsāwa, who asks specifically for advice on human norms. Naktso states that when it comes to things that need to be done on the Dharma front, for the sake of his future life, he knows what to do. What he would like instead is advice on how to deal with people in a way that is in accord with the norms of civil society, so as to get along with people while living in a foreign country. After identifying consideration of others as the root of societal values, Dromtönpa offers specific examples of what might promote mutual harmony. He lists the following: not boasting about one's accomplishments or what one has done for others, not belittling others, not showing off one's wealth, not coveting the wealth of others and having less greed, refraining from insulting both the learned and the untaught, having less pride and conceit, being humble and easy to engage with, being consonant with others whatever tasks one might be engaged in, respecting the collective laws of society, and maintaining confidence with respect to matters that need to be kept secret.

The text then spells out more specifically how these social norms and human values provide criteria by which one can differentiate between wise and foolish behavior. Drawing on these values, Dromtönpa offers a series of specific verses to Naktso Lotsāwa on how he might best navigate the challenges he will encounter during his time away from home. What is remarkable about Dromtönpa's text is that, despite his initimate familiarity with

Indian Buddhist literature, his close association with the Bengali master Atiśa, and his reading knowledge of Sanskrit, there is very little detectable Indic influence on his advice text with respect to content, literary style, or even the metaphors used. The text is as indigenously Tibetan as it can get, except for the concluding reference to having "inscribed these wise utterances in the *lañca* script," a form of Indian writing.[7]

The second early Tibetan work, the Dunhuang text *Advice from an Elder Brother to His Younger Brother*, is not included in this volume. It is at least a century or so older than Dromtönpa's text.[8] This notable work of prose is composed in old Tibetan. The preamble sets the specific context, which is strikingly similar to that of Dromtönpa's text. In the opening scene the younger brother has to go elsewhere to do important work and is concerned that missing his brother might be too painful. As he prepares to leave, he asks his older brother for advice from a wise, experienced man to an inexperienced brother. In a long exchange of questions and answers, the older brother offers his younger sibling advice on life, family, relationships, society, and leadership.

Although the first exchange has a strong Buddhist flavor—"What is the best form of happiness in a human life? Mental happiness is the highest form of happiness"[9]—the exhanges then move quickly to matters of life, family, relationships, society, and leadership. Speaking of society, the older brother defines a just kingdom as fair rule. He goes on to explain how fairness is essential for anyone who wishes to lead. One of the remarkable features of these exchanges is the clear differentiation drawn between key terms like "just" (*drang*) and "fair" (*snyoms*), and being "wise" (*mdzangs*), "intelligent" or "learned" (*mkhas*). Of all the qualities of a leader, fairness is said to be the most important, and a leader should be as fair as the sky that makes no discrimination against anyone.[10] In the course of these discussions, the crucial term *mi chos* is introduced with the following exchange:

Younger brother: What are human values and what are the opposites of human values?

Elder brother: Human values are being just and serving others, being honest and truthful, being compassionate and devoid of contempt for others, being conscientious and having a regard for your own legacy, and being kindhearted and diligent. If you possess these, everyone will find you appealing, and you will enjoy stability at home and in your community. What are the opposites of

> human values? Being unjust and aggressive, being unreliable, having no conscience or regard for your own legacy, not knowing compassion and delighting in belittling others, being conceited and indolent. These are the opposites of human values. Anyone who possesses these will be unappealing to others.[11]

Reacting to his older brother's explanation, the younger brother expresses skepticism: Love of service could be a form of flattery, and honesty a form of polite trickery. Even out of compassion, aren't there some things one should not tolerate? Could aggression be a form of heroism?[12]

The Concept of "Mi chos"

As we saw above, the term *mi chos* is composed of *mi*, "humans," and *chos*, the Tibetan equivalent of the Sanskrit word *dharma*. The meanings of *dharma* range from "duty" and "norm" to "law," "virtue," "attribute," "thing," and even "reality." The word *dharma* is derived from the root syllable *dhṛ*, which means to "hold or maintain," hence *dharma* means something that upholds its reality, whether it is a thing or law. Etymologically, the Tibetan *chos* connotes "transformation" or "change," and over time the term came to be used as referring to Buddhism in contrast to Bön, Tibet's pre-Buddhist native religion. Thus we read of the "dispute between Dharma and Bön" (*chos dang bon gyi rtsod pa*). This said, there is adequate textual evidence to suggest that around the eighth century, at least, the word *chos* (*dharma*) was being used more as a generic term referring to a system of beliefs and practices, wherein the "great religion" (*chos chen po*) of Buddhsim is contrasted against "small religions" (*chos chung ngu*) of ritual-based native beliefs.[13] Given the state of our current knowledge, however, it is difficult to determine whether this usage as a generic term predates the arrival of Buddhism. Understanding *chos* to mean a system of beliefs and practices, *mi chos* would then refer to a system of beliefs and practices associated with human society. Hence my translation as "societal" or "human values."[14]

Tibetan historians trace the terms *mi chos* (societal human values) and *lha chos* (divine religious values) all the way to the seventh century and the activities of the Tibetan emperor Songtsen Gampo. They recognize the formulations of common laws and societal values as one of the great civilizing achievements of this emperor, others being the invention of a writing system, standardization of a measurement system, and the building of the great Lhasa temple. Songtsen is also credited with promulgating the "ten virtues of divine religious values" (*lha chos dge ba bcu*) and the "sixteen pristine societal values" (*mi chos gtsang ma bcu drug*). The ten virtues are abstention from the ten negative actions of body, speech, and mind: killing, stealing, sexual misconduct; telling lies, engaging in divisive speech, harsh speech, and senseless gossip; and covetousness, harmful intent, and wrong views. Abstention from these deeds constitutes divine religious values since they pertain to one's fate in future lives.

In contrast, *mi chos* or societal values relate more specifically to the well-being and health of a person in this life within society. The sixteen societal or human values are (1) cultivating reverence for the Three Jewels, (2) seeking and following the sublime Dharma, (3) repaying the kindness of one's parents, (4) having respect for those who are learned, (5) honoring those who have higher staus and who are older, (6) helping one's neighbors and fellow natives, (7) speaking with fairness and being humble, (8) being loyal to one's family and friends, (9) emulating civilized people and maintaining a long-term view, (10) practicing moderation in food and wealth, (11) remembering those who have shown you kindness, (12) repaying debts on time and not tampering with measuring scales, (13) curtailing envy toward others, (14) ignoring bad suggestions and maintaining personal integrity, (15) using gentle speech and avoiding excessive talk, and (16) maintaining a resilient and courageous mind.[15]

Most of these sixteen values have to do with promoting greater societal well-being and living one's life with dignity, honesty, and respect for others. Even the first two, though ostensibly religious in nature, could be perceived as crucial to a society in which faith and loyalty to Buddhism are deemed essential for greater societal cohesion and meaning. As we will see below, this concept of a dual value system, of human society and religion—*mi chos* and *lha chos*—evolved into the concept of dual norms (*lugs gnyis*)—worldly secular norms (*'jig rten gyi lugs*) and Buddhist religious norms (*chos kyi lugs*)—in the Tibetan *lekshé* literature. Although the word *lugs* ("norms") is the Tibetan equivalent of the Sanskrit *nīti*, its usage framed in a dual system of secular and religious standards appears to be a Tibetan invention. This brings us to the question of the relationship between the Tibetan *lekshé* genre and the Indian wisdom literature the *nītiśāstras*.

Sakya Paṇḍita's Treasury and the Indian Wisdom Literature

There is no doubt that Sakya Paṇḍita's *Jewel Treasury of Wise Sayings* is the first Tibetan text to be composed in the style of Indian wisdom literature, and the explicit use of the word *lekshé* (*subhāṣita*, or "wise sayings") in the title indicates this close association.[16] By Sakya Paṇḍita's time several well-known works of Indian wisdom literature had already been translated into Tibetan. These include, among others, the famed *Cāṇakya Treatise on Kingship* (*Cāṇakyarājānītiśāstra*), *A Hundred Stanzas on Wisdom* (*Prajñāśataka*), *Staff of Wisdom* (*Prajñādaṇḍa*),[17] and *A Drop to Nourish a Person* (*Jantupoṣaṇabindu*)—the latter three attributed to Nāgārjuna—as well a *Nītiśāstra* (*Treatise on Norms*) by Masūrakṣa.[18] Of these, the first was translated in the eleventh century, the next three in the ninth century, and the final work sometime in the tenth century. There is no doubt that these Tibetan translations of Indian wisdom literature served as an important source for the composition of the *Jewel Treasury*. Contemporary scholars have identified some thirty-two stanzas in Sakya Paṇḍita's *Jewel Treasury* that have parallels in Indian wisdom literature.[19]

As noted above, I see three areas where a Tibetan *lekshé* work such as the *Jewel Treasury* displays a direct influence from the Indian wisdom literature. First and foremost is the unique poetic form that was adopted directly from Indian wisdom texts such as *A Hundred Stanzas on Wisdom*. Within a four-line, seven-syllable verse, an important piece of wisdom is shared followed by an analogy that often references a story. In Daṇḍin's *Mirror of Poetics* (*Kavyādarśa*) classification of the use of similes in Sanskrit poetry, a system introduced to Tibet first by Sakya Paṇḍita himself, this particular usage is called "simile in the form of a parallel" (*zla bo dgnos po'i dpe*).[20] The following two examples, the first from the *Jewel Treasury* and second from the Sanskrit *Hundred Stanzas on Wisdom*, illustrate this distinctive poetic form:

> A wicked man can destroy in an instant
> a treaty reached through the effort of great men.
> Hail can reduce to dust in an instant
> lands tended by farmers for months and years. (*Treasury*, 33)

And,

In whom the eyes of wisdom have opened,
for them misfortunes will come to cease;
just as in front of someone holding a lamp
there can be no darkness at all. (*Hundred Stanzas*, 9)

Although we do see seven-syllable verses in Tibetan prior to the *Jewel Treasury*, I know of no original Tibetan work composed in this unique *lekshé* poetic form prior to the *Treasury*. It is Sakya Paṇḍita's *Jewel Treasury* that gave birth to this particular genre of indigenous Tibetan literature. The poetic form was adopted as the standard format in which later Tibetan wise sayings were composed.

The second area of Indian influence on Tibetan wise sayings can be seen in the choice of metaphors or similes used in these texts. Whether it is the metaphor of "a hungry tiger's growl paralyzing and bringing down a monkey from a tree" (*Treasury*, 102) or "the scent of sandalwood trees blown by wind across the ten directions" (*Treasury*, 31), many of the analogies used in the Tibetan wise-sayings texts are clearly Indian in origin. Indic similes, so abundant in Indian wisdom texts such as *A Hundred Stanzas on Wisdom*, are appropriated by Tibetan authors and used in their own compositions. This is not to say that the Tibetan authors do not use analogies drawn from Tibet's own geographical, cultural, and historical resources.

The third area where we discern a powerful Indic influence is in the stories that are referenced in the second halves of many verses. Take the following example from the *Jewel Treasury*:

If you know how it's done, how can it be hard
to employ even the great as your servants?
Even though a garuḍa is very powerful,
the golden-clad one made him his mount. (*Treasury*, 17)

The story of how the Hindu god Viṣnu made the powerful garuḍa bird his mount is drawn from the ancient Indian Purāṇa (or origin myths) literature. There are two categories within these embedded stories. The first includes stories of such as myths of the Hindu gods, while the second are moral tales, often of animals, found in such well-known Indian works as the *Pañcatantra*, attributed to Viṣṇuśarma, and its popular later version known as *Hitopadeśa*.[21] Although none of the Hindu Purāṇas were translated into Tibetan, thanks to Tibetan translations of works such as Prajñāvarman's extensive commentaries on the two hymns to the Buddha, *Praise of the Exalted* (*Viśeṣastava*) and *Praise of the One More Perfect Than the Gods* (*Devātiśayastotra*), which both contain many of these Purāṇa stories, the Tibetan authors and readers were familiar with many of the well-known Purāṇa stories.

As for the animal stories found in the *Pañcatantra* and their use in Tibetan wisdom literature, the situation is little more complex. To begin with, not only was the *Pañcatantra* never translated into Tibetan, but nowhere does any classical Tibetan author of wisdom literature, including Sakya Paṇḍita himself, make any reference to this important Indian work. There is a passing mention of the *Pañcatantra* in Sakya Paṇḍita's biography, where this text is listed alongside other Indian wisdom literature he is supposed to have studied with his teacher and uncle Drakpa Gyaltsen.[22] However, given that most of the animal stories cited in the Tibetan wise sayings can be found in the *jātakas*, the birth stories of the Buddha's former lives, or in the canonical Vinaya texts, which are filled with stories (*avadāna*) illustrating karmic consequences, most likely it is the Buddhist sources that served as the resource for Sakya Paṇḍita rather than the *Pañcatantra*. One popular collection of *jātaka* and *avādana* literature in the Tibetan scriptures is the *Sutra on the Wise and the Foolish* (*Damamūkanidānasūtra*), translated from Chinese.[23] In addition, two important Indian works on the *jātakas*—Āryaśura's *Garland of Birth Stories* (*Jātakamālā*) and Kṣemendra's *Wish-Granting Tree* (*Avadānakalpalatā*)—are available in the Tibetan Tengyur, the collection of Indian Buddhist works translated into Tibetan.[24]

To return to the *Jewel Treasury* itself, Sakya Paṇḍita succinctly defines what he means by "wise sayings," the subject of his text, in the second opening stanza:

> This exposition is a jewel treasury of wise sayings
> pertaining to how respectable people behave,
> which, when examined with reason, does not contradict religion
> and helps accomplish all worldly activities.

Similarly, toward the end of the *Jewel Treasury*, the author returns to this same point about the synergy between secular worldly ethics and religious Buddhist practice:

> A person who thoroughly understands worldly activity
> is adept in the method of the holy Dharma.

> Thus the practice of the Dharma is indeed
> the way of life of the bodhisattvas. (457)

So, according to this definition, *lekshé* are wise sayings that, while not contradicting Buddhist teachings, help a person accomplish his or her worldly pursuits. This echoes a verse from the Indian text *Hundred Stanzas on Wisdom*, where we read:

> If you properly practice human ethics,
> the journey to the god realm will not be long.
> If you thus ascend the stairs of men and gods,
> even the liberation of nirvāṇa will be close by. (98)

With this understanding of *lekshé* as wise sayings that help a person to accomplish his or her pursuits, the *Jewel Treasury* can be seen as consisting of two main parts—the domain of secular worldly aims (chapters 1–8) and the domain of Buddhist religious practice (chapter 9). The overarching theme in the first part revolves around the characteristics and conduct of the wise, the learned, and the cultured, on the one hand, and the foolish, the ignoble, and the uncultured, on the other. The characteristics of an intelligent, wise person are given in chapter 1, followed in chapter 2 by the characteristics of a cultured, civilized, and honorable person. In chapter 3 we then find an analysis of the characteristics that make a person foolish, imprudent, and unwise. Having identified the differences between the wise and the foolish, the cultured and the uncultured, chapter 4 provides a series of comparisons between these two types of people. In chapter 5 the author elaborates on the theme of the preceding chapter and offers a separate treatment on the actions and deeds that are bad and dishonorable. Chapter 6, the second longest in the text, presents a series of what might be called commonsense wisdom drawn from tendencies that can be observed in people and the world. Some of the analogies cited in this chapter are the most memorable ones, my favorite being the statement that although we have eyes to look at others, we need a mirror to look at ourselves (193). Chapter 7 identifies conduct that is undesirable and unseemly from the point of view of societal values and norms of decency. Chapter 8, the longest in the text, contains the greatest quantity of explicit advice addressed to the reader, and many lines are phrased in the imperative "do this" and "don't do that" (*bya* and *mi bya* in Tibetan). The final chapter covers many key topics of Buddhist interest, such as taking refuge in the Buddha, the importance of generosity, appreciating the opportunities of birth as a human, awareness of death and impermanence, respecting the law of karma, dealing with anger, the value of studying the Dharma, the need for wisdom, and so on.

Drigung Rinchen Pal's commentary, featured in this volume, identifies three principal goals behind Sakya Paṇḍita's composition of the *Jewel Treasury*. One is to illustrate the use of metaphors or similes, so essential in poetry. Second is to teach Buddhist Dharma based on the approach of the Indian *nītiśāstras*. Third is to offer the Tibetans a gift of verses on wise sayings akin to the ones found in India, "in regions lying to the south" (*lho phyogs kyi rgyud*) of Tibet, where scholars utter wise sayings as a mark of learning when they meet each other and when they are in the presence of the king at the court.

Ever since its appearance the *Jewel Treasury* has enjoyed a widespread popularity among Tibetans. Unlike India and China, Tibet's two ancient neighbors with long civilizations, there is very little secular literature in Tibet's vast, written, language-based high culture. So a large part of the *Jewel Treasury*'s appeal and reputation probably came from the fact that the work is essentially secular in nature, and the rarity of that in Tibet made it a great gift to the educated lay elite.

Sakya Paṇḍita's close personal association with the Mongol court also meant that his *Jewel Treasury* attracted the attention of the Mongolians; the work was rendered into Mongolian quite early. Some of the aphorisms that are part of the *Treasury* are even said to have found their way into Mongolian folk songs.[25]

In Tibet it became a tradition for many people, especially those training to become lay officials, to memorize key parts of the *Treasury*. Writers would cite poignant verses to articulate particular points: "Until you beat a drum / what distinguishes it from other objects?" (verse 6), "Do not give up your former abode / before proper evaluation of another place. / Raising a foot without first planting the other / can cause you to fall" (verse 331), and so on. Most important, the *Treasury* ushered in an entirely new literary genre in Tibet, directly inspiring works such as Paṇchen Sönam Drakpa's *Ganden Wise Sayings* and Gungthang's *Treatise on Trees* and *Treatise on Water*.[26]

One footnote to Sakya Paṇḍita's *Jewel Treasury* is its relationship with his other lesser-known verse work *Necklace for the Youth: Differentiations of People*.[27] This shorter work in five chapters is also composed in four-line, seven-syllable verse but not using the poetic device of parallel analogies typical of the *Treasury*. The text is written in a straightforward style as a series of maxims or aphorisms that capture commonsense wisdom and traditional Tibetan cultural sensibilities and societal norms. Like the *Treasury*, its central theme is to differentiate the characteristics of the wise and the foolish. There is even a shorter text in prose by the author, titled *Wise Sayings: A Magical Net* (*Legs bshad 'phrul gyi dra ba*), which is essentially a compilation of select maxims and aphorisms drawn from various sources, especially the ancient folk tradition. Space prevents us from exploring these two texts here other than to observe that they could be viewed as a valuable link between earlier indigenous Tibetan works, such as Dromtönpa's *Garland of Advice* and the Dunhuang text, and the subsequent Indian-inspired wise-sayings genre so powerfully represented by the *Treasury*.

Later Tibetan Collections of Wise Sayings

Second to the *Jewel Treasury*, the most well-known Tibetan *lekshé* text is Paṇchen Sönam Drakpa's (1478–1554) *Ganden Wise Sayings: A Bouquet of White Lotuses*. This work explicitly acknowledges (in verses 121–22) its debt to the *Treasury* and is ostensibly written to help perpetuate the popularity and use of Sakya Paṇḍita's *Jewel Treasury*. The entire work, running to 125 stanzas, focuses on the single theme of differentiating between the wise and learned, on the one hand, and the foolish and the unintelligent, on the other. Thus the work can be seen, as intended by the author himself, as an important supplement to the *Treasury*, elaborating particularly its first four chapters. Panchen adopts the exact same poetic form as the *Treasury*: there are allusions to stories woven in the last two lines of the four-line stanzas that provide analogies to a wise point being made. Paṇchen follows the norms established by Sakya Paṇḍita of framing the wise sayings within the context of the dual norms of secular and religious Buddhist practice. This is evident beginning in the opening salutation verse, where the author pays homage to the Buddha as embodying "the knowledge of the two norms exactly as they are" (*lugs gnyis ji bzhin mkhyen pa*).

Just like the *Jewel Treasury*, Paṇchen's *Ganden Wise Sayings* draws on numerous sources, including the Hindu Purāṇa myths and on moral tales often involving animal stories from the *jātakas* and found in various Buddhist sources, including the *Sutra on the Wise and the Foolish*. Also featured in this volume is the extremely helpful commentary on the text by the nineteenth-century Mongol-Tibetan author Yangchen Gawai Lodrö. Though a much shorter text, Paṇchen's work contains proportionately far more references to stories than does the *Treasury*, a consequence perhaps of Panchen's love of history and tales. One unique feature of Paṇchen's text is its inclusion of important anecdotes from Tibetan history, including references to myths from the *Pillar Testament* (*Bka' 'chems ka khol ma*) and the *Cycle of Teachings on the Maṇi Mantra* (*Maṇi bka' 'bum*), both attributed to the seventh-century emperor Songtsen Gampo, as well as the birth stories of Dromtönpa's former lives as recorded in the Son Teachings of the *Book of Kadam*. All of these references have been sourced and can be identified in the endnotes to the commentary.

Next is the Great Fifth Dalai Lama's *Pearl Garland of Advice*, which also engages the dual domains of polity and religion. He laments that there has been a decline in the dual norms rooted in ancient tradition in lands such as India, China, Mongolia, and Tibet (verse 4). Interestingly, unlike Sakya Paṇḍita's *Jewel Treasury* and Paṇchen's *Ganden Wise Sayings*, the Fifth Dalai Lama's text explicitly invokes (in verse 6) the earlier Tibetan schema of the twofold system of *mi chos* (societal values) and *lha chos* (religious values). With respect to its poetic form too, the *Pearl Garland* deviates from the *Treasury*'s seven-syllable verse and parallel juxtaposition of a wise point and a poignant analogy and reverts more to the style of Dromtönpa's *Garland of Essential Advice*. In verses composed of nine syllables, the tone is more authoritative and prescriptive compared with a typical wise-saying work like the *Jewel Treasury*. After the opening salution and two verses stating the intention to compose the text, the main part of the *Pearl Garland* relates to the two domains of secular worldly matters (stanzas 4–41) and the spiritual Buddhist path (42–56). Toward the end of part 1, the author warns the reader to guard against conflating what might seem like similar attributes but are contrary: a coward and a prudent person, a simpleton and a charlatan, a courageous individual and a foolhardy one, a kind-natured person and one who does not care, an honest man and a fool, and so on (verse 39–40). The text ends with some interesting historical reflections on the flourishing of Buddhism in Tibet and its spread to Mongolia, especially of the Geluk teachings that came about thanks to the meeting of the Third Dalai Lama with the Mongol ruler Altan Khan. The colophon indicates that the work was composed at the behest of the Tüśiyetü Khan, a Mongolian ruler of Genghis's descent who was on a pilgrimage in Tibet.

The next two texts are Gungthang's *Treatise on Trees* and *Treatise on Water*. Partly because of their compact size, the first consisting of 106 verses and the second of 140 verses, and partly because of their incomparable poetry, the two treatises became hugely popular in Tibet and its cultural sphere. They display the exceptional poetic and literary skills of Gungthang as well as the expressive power and fluidity of Tibetan versification in the hands of a truly gifted writer. As someone trained in Tibetan poetics, I have no hesitation to add that, of all the Tibetan wise-sayings texts I have read, when it comes to sheer elegance and poetic beauty, nothing compares to Gungthang's two treatises. Each has one element, trees or water, that runs through all the metaphors in the text. In these two works Gungthang explicitly invokes the dual-norms framework established by Sakya Paṇḍita and followed by earlier Tibetan authors. In his *Treatise on Trees*, for example, Gungthang reverses the sequence of the two norms and deals with the religious Buddhist practice first (3–35) followed by secular wordly norms (36–104). The treatise ends with two concluding verses, one extolling the benefits of looking into the mirror of the two norms—that is, his own treatise—and one dedicating the merits of having composed the advice work.

In his *Treatise on Water* Gungthang reverts to the traditional approach of first presenting the secular worldly norms (6–80) followed by the religious Buddhist norms (81–137). The treatise ends with three concluding verses, the first two celebrating his treatise as "an ocean of magical wise sayings" and the third dedicating the merits from having composed the text. As stated in the colophon, Gungthang wrote this second text as a "meaning commentary" to his *Treatise on Trees*, which had come to enjoy such great popularity that readers requested that he write a commentary to it. Other than an explanatory glossary of key terms in the *Treatise on Trees* by Yangchen Gawai Lodrö, I am aware of no commentaries on either of these two treatises by earlier Tibetan authors. My own teacher, Kyabjé Zemey Rinpoché (1927–96), wrote a lucid word-by-word explanation of the *Treatise on Trees* aimed primarily at young Tibetan students.[28]

Inspired directly by Gungthang's two treatises, and modeling his use of only one element as the key metaphor, later Tibetan authors wrote other wise-sayings treatises using elements like wind, fire, and earth. In our volume we have included Kyilsur Lobsang Jinpa's *Treatise on Wind* and Paṇchen Chökyi Nyima's *Treatise on Earth*. I had heard of the existence of similar treatises on the remaining elements of fire and metal but had not succeeded in obtaining those texts at the time of compiling our Tibetan anthology.[29]

Although not included in the present anthology, two other Tibetan treatises belonging to the *lekshé* genre need special mention here. One is the famed *Ornament for Kingship: A Treatise on Norms* by Ju Mipham Gelek

Namgyal (1846–1912). Modeled on the *Cāṇakya Treatise on Kingship*, it is a long text running to 1,200 verses composed at the behest of, and as advice to, a prince who aspired to the throne of the Dergé kingdom of Kham in eastern Tibet.[30] The second is a treatise by Jampal Rolpai Lodrö (1888–1936), similarly written at the behest of a Tibetan ruler in the Amdo region by the name of Akyong Tenzin Drakpa. The treatise combines advice to his subjects and advice on rulership. Titled *The Wish-Fulfilling Tree: A Treatise on Norms*, it consists of approximately one thousand verses in thirteen chapters.[31] The scope is wide and ambitious, covering both secular and religious topics. At this point we have no adequate understanding of the context in which this later text emerged, although my conjecture is that it was written sometime around 1928. This author is more known, at least in central Tibet, for his work on grammar—an extensive critical commentary on Thönmi Sambhota's *Thirty Verses* (*Lung ston pa sum cu pa*), one of the founding works of the written Tibetan language. Judging by his rather lengthy verse text on Dzogchen, *Heart Essence of the Great Perfection of Mañjuśrī*,[32] this Geluk master seems to have been an active member in the Geluk-Nyingma ecumenist movement as well.

The Intriguing Advice of the Muslim Phalu Ju

The final work in our anthology is the intriguing and much-loved Tibetan text known as *Khaché Phalu's Advice*. The Tibetan word *khaché* can mean either Islam or Kashmir (the latter being the primary region that the Muslims in central Tibet traditionally hailed from). The verse text is written in vernacular style, making it easy for even less-educated lay Tibetans to understand and enjoy both the wit and wisdom of the verses. Almost every Tibetan would know what is meant when someone says, "If you do not guard your oblong tongue, / your round head might find itself in trouble" (76), or "Your eyes and stomach, the two can never be sated, / so it's best to set limits on your food and eating" (100), or "This world has many plateaus and valleys. / With countless differences in wealth, status, and strength, / clearly no two people are the same, / so it's best to find your own contentment" (66), or "I, Khaché Phalu, have offered my heartfelt advice. / Whether you listen or not, that is your own choice" (37).

Ostensibly penned by a Tibetan Muslim by the name of Phalu Ju and written as advice to Tibetan Buddhists from a Muslim, the text contains a remarkable series of observations about the attitudes, values, and habits of the Tibetan people and their religious sensibilities as well as explicit references to Islamic practices. The work appeared sometime in the eighteenth century and is rumored to have been written by Paṇchen Losang Palden Yeshé (1738–80) or by someone in his circle at Tashilhunpo Monastery.[33] We know from several sources that this Paṇchen was quite ecumenical in his interest and supported an eclectic group of scholars and religious practitioners at Tashilhunpo, including Muslims and Hindus. Thanks to his mother's background and links to Ladakh, Paṇchen spoke Hindi, the main Indian language, through which he maintained a lengthy communication with the British colonial officer George Bogle (1746–81).[34] So the conjecture that this Paṇchen was the author of this vernacular Tibetan work does not seem as preposterous as it appears at first glance.

Strictly speaking, *Khaché Phalu's Advice* does not belong to the *lekshé* genre. Nor could it be classified in the earlier, indegenous category of *mi chos*. However, given its huge popularity, especially among lay Tibetans,[35] the text has been included in this special anthology.

Acknowledgments

I would like to congratulate Beth Newman for her masterful translation of all the Tibetan texts featured in this volume. They cover a period of nearly a millennium, and being able to read, comprehend, and render into English such diverse works as Dromtönpa's eleventh-century advice to his student Naktso Lotsāwa, or Sakya Paṇḍita's *Treasury*, or the highly vernacular *Khaché Phalu's Advice* is truly a remarkable achievement. I would like to thank our editors at Wisdom Publications, David Kittelstrom and Mary Petrusewicz, for their incisive editing.

As the chief editor of the Tibetan volume on which this anthology is based, it is a real joy to see these much-loved Tibetan texts finally made available in a quality translation to the larger English-speaking readership. Now international readers can savor the wisdom and sharp wit of the Tibetan mind, refined with the poetic and literary sensibilities of Indian wisdom literature, and conveyed so powerfully and poignantly in these memorable Tibetan verses. I cannot imagine the development of either my poetic and literary sensibilities or my practical, commonsense approach to life had I not been shaped by many of these lines that had been part of my mindscape for all these years. With the publication of this volume, it is my hope that

Tibetan wisdom literature will become part of the world's shared literary heritage.

It has been an honor and a joy to compile and edit the original Tibetan volume, to offer this introductory essay to help English readers appreciate the larger context of these precious Tibetan texts, and to share my own enthusiasm for this genre with the reader. Foremost, I would like to express my deepest gratitude to the Ing Foundation for its generous patronage of the Institute of Tibetan Classics, which has helped support the entire cost of this translation project. Without this support no amount of good will and dedication on the part of the translator or myself would have led to the realization of this work. I would also like to offer my gratitude to the Scully Peretsman Foundation for its support of my own work on classical Tibetan texts and culture.

Translator's Note

I AM DEEPLY GRATEFUL to Geshé Thupten Jinpa, president of the Institute of Tibetan Classics, for giving me the opportunity to translate this anthology.

This work could not have been completed without the help of many others. In particular, I was privileged to work with Geshé Ngawang Chösang of Sera Jé Monastery. For four months Geshé Chösang patiently explained many of the verses, the stories used to exemplify them, and their moral and ethical implications. His explanations were so intriguing that some of his young students would gather outside the door to listen. This attention was proof of the method of these texts: good stories attract listeners, and it is hoped that those listeners will heed the advice implicit in the tales. Leonard Zwilling was tremendously helpful in numerous ways: critiquing and clarifying my translation of *Khache Phalu's Advice*, comparing my translation of that text to an Italian translation, doing bibliographic research, and solving grammatical puzzles in some of the other texts. John Davenport and Geshé Jinpa provided me with rough drafts of their translations of a number of texts. John Newman offered assistance in translating some difficult passages of the texts. Tashi Tsering at Central Tibetan University, Sarnath, checked to make sure I had employed the correct Sanskrit proper names and tracked down a number of those that I could not find on my own. I had the immense benefit of three editors: David Kittelstrom and Mary Petrusewicz of Wisdom Publications checked and improved the English, and Geshé Thupten Jinpa of the Institute of Tibetan Classics closely read my English translation along with the Tibetan and made important clarifications. Geshé Jinpa also added invaluable bibliographic and historical information in the notes. Despite all this assistance, if a reader finds any mistakes in the translations, they are mine alone.

I hope that these English translations provide readers with the instructive entertainment that the authors of these texts intended to impart.

Technical Notes

The full Tibetan title of the volume translated here is *Legs bshad lugs kyi bslab bya'i dpe tsogs*, which literally means "an anthology of advice texts of wise sayings that provide guidance on norms." This edition was prepared specifically for *The Library of Tibetan Classics* and is the English equivalent of the critical and annotated Tibetan edition published in New Delhi in modern book format by the Institute of Tibetan Classics (2006, ISBN 81-89165-27-5) as volume 27 of the *Bod kyi gtsug lag gces btus pod phreng* series. This Tibetan volume provides detailed notes on what editions of each of the constituent texts the Tibetan editors consulted when compiling their critical edition.

Most of the stories and examples found in the texts in this volume came originally from classical Sanskrit literature. In translating these stories I use the Sanskrit proper names found in the original texts. In cases where the original Sanskrit could not be found, I indicate a reconstruction by placing an asterisk (*) before the name at the first occurrence in each text. If a story is based on a Tibetan source, a phonetic transcription of the Tibetan appears in the text. The appendix of proper names lists the Sanskrit, Tibetan, and Chinese names as they appear in this translation, and a second column gives the spelling of the name in transliterated Tibetan.

Sanskrit diacritics are used throughout except for Sanskrit terms that have been naturalized into English, such as samsara, nirvana, sutra, stupa, Mahayana, and mandala.

The conventions for phonetic transcription of Tibetan words are those developed by the Institute of Tibetan Classics and Wisdom Publications. Transliterations of phoneticized Tibetan terms and names used in the text can be found in the table in the appendix.

All the references to canonical works have been reproduced from the Tibetan edition. When referring to works from the Tibetan canon, the Dergé edition was used as the primary source with all details such as genre, volume, and page numbers provided accordingly. *Toh* stands for the Tohoku catalog entry of the of the Dergé editions of the Kangyur and Tengyur.

Pronunciation of Tibetan Phonetics

ph and *th* are aspirated *p* and *t*, as in *pet* and *tip*.
ö is similar to the *eu* in the French *seul*.
ü is similar to the *ü* in the German *füllen*.

ai is similar to the *e* in *bet.*
é is similar to the *e* in *prey.*

Pronunciation of Sanskrit

Palatal *ś* and retroflex *ṣ* are similar to the English unvoiced *sh.*
c is an unaspirated *ch* similar to the *ch* in *chill.*
The vowel *ṛ* is similar to the American *r* in *pretty.*
ñ is somewhat similar to the nasalized *ny* in *canyon.*
ṅ is similar to the *ng* in *sing* or *anger.*

The Tibetan Book of Everyday Wisdom

A Thousand Years of Sage Advice

Translated by Beth Newman
Introduced by Thupten Jinpa

1. A Garland of Essential Advice on Societal Values[36]

Dromtön Gyalwai Jungné [1]

I PAY HOMAGE TO the exalted Lord Avalokiteśvara. This text is a garland of essential points regarding religious and secular ethics made by Atiśa and his two close disciples in question and answer format.

Dromtön Gyalwai Jungné imparted *A Garland of Essential Advice on Societal Values* as travel advice for the very kind translator Naktso Tsultrim Gyalwa, who was born in Gungthang in the region of Tö. To see him off, Drom escorted Naktso twenty-five leagues beyond the village of Or in Nyethang and offered him a meal. Holding hands with each other, unable to bear the impending separation for a moment, they discussed heartfelt matters.

The man from Gungthang said, "You are never apart from the very center of my heart. From the perspective of ordinary Tibetans, we have indeed been extremely close. Nevertheless, I have no regrets because our actions together in complete accord were good karma done well. Today as I set out on my travels to the distant valley of Nepal, please give me a bit of travel advice to benefit my mind. I understand something about actions to be done for future lives, but please drive into my heart societal values that will put me in harmony with the ordinary people I associate with in this life that can't be despised by critical people."

Drom Jé's face lit up with a smile, and throwing back his head to toss his braided hair behind him, he said:

1 I am a cherished child from the lands of the north;
I have met many people in my travel to distant places.
I've understood their many exchanges, so my explanations are apt.
I've discerned the way things are, so I'm known for perspicacity.

2 Wherever you travel, in whatever direction,
wherever you make camp or find a place to stay,
whoever you seek to befriend or associate with,
being considerate of others is the root of human values.

3 Based on that I'll explain ordinary goals for this life, so listen.
I'll differentiate the nature of everything, so listen.
I'll elucidate instructions about pacifying gods and nāgas, so
listen.
As for values, these are the most profound societal values. [2]

4 Know what you're doing when you take on helping someone;
minimize your frustration and exaggerating the credit due you.
Whatever you do and however you do it,
let everything you do conform to the people in question.

5 No matter how many good qualities you have,
minimize your contempt and disdain for others.
No matter how much you desire riches for yourself,
minimize covetousness for others' wealth.

6 You may be skilled in achieving your goals,
but minimize transgressing the common laws of the land.
You may have some wealth saved up,
but minimize flaunting it when among many others.

7 Even if everyone holds you up as an authority,
minimize your prideful egotistic thoughts.
Even if you are better than everyone else,
eliminate the slightest pride in your superiority.

8 Even if others beg you to be their spiritual teacher,
minimize looking down on anyone, be they learned or lowly.
Even if there is no one higher or more important than you,
be happy to mix with those beneath you.

9 No matter how bad another group's leader is,
greet him and respond to his salutations respectfully.

Although someone may be your equal,
respectfully honor him as your superior.

10 No matter who requests the Dharma, even lepers and beggars,
go among them and generously give instruction.
Even if someone looks to vie with what you say,
with the highest degree of perfection, expound even more.

11 Someone may be worthy of being offered feasts, reverence, and so on,
but disregard that and treat everyone equitably.
If something is definitely worth keeping secret,
stay silent in a quiet place as if you were a mute.

12 This is just a rough and general presentation.
I have still more essential advice, so listen!
Check whether your associates are hostile; that is being careful.
Be honest giving advice to children; that is being reliable.

13 Do your daily recitations quietly; that is being dignified.
Be honest when discussing faults; that is being skillful.
Dig out your faults yourself; that is being wise.
Be unconcerned about the faults of others; that is being virtuous.

14 Sincerely nurture your trust; that is most wonderful.
I have still more essential advice, so listen!
Sharing confidences with someone as soon as you meet is a mistake.
Trusting someone you haven't checked out is a mistake. [3]

15 If on checking you know he's dishonest, continuing to trust is a mistake.
Pursuing activities with careless people is a mistake.
Seeking a long-term relationship with someone unkind is a mistake.
Taking someone without faith as a disciple is a mistake.

16 Taking someone without compassion as a guru is a mistake.
Relying on someone with no conscience as a friend is a mistake.
Giving instructions to those who don't listen is a mistake.
Having important consultations with the ignorant is a mistake.

17 Now that you've recognized these to be errors,
if you don't give them up, you should know you are crazy.
I have still more essential advice, so listen!
When you eat and drink together, everything may seem fine,

18 but after associating for a few days, their many flaws are evident.
Things will go wrong quickly if you assign a task
to anyone, friend or stranger, whom you haven't known a year.
Talking about the faults of those who rely on you is bad.

19 If it draws the attention of one person, worry about it spreading.
If two people know the gossip, it becomes a source of trouble.
If three know it, your disrepute spreads on the wind.
If you can let it evaporate into thin air, you are skillful.[37]

20 If you recognize your own errors of speech, you can laugh at yourself.
If you attract mockery with your demands, it delights the demons.
If you befriend destructive people, it is a huge mistake.
I have still more essential advice, so listen!

21 Don't be too gluttonous; share your food with people.
Don't be too stingy; make religious offerings with your wealth.
Don't change your expression too much; meet everyone with a smile.
Don't be too biased; be evenhanded to friends and enemies.

22 Don't praise those around you too much; hold it in your mind.
Don't be too quick to criticize others; use skill to get them to stop.
Don't make too many promises to anyone; keep your agreements.
Don't assign blame indiscriminately; figure it out together.

23 If you err, don't feel guilty afterward but prevent it recurring.
I have still more essential advice, so listen!
Unpleasant speech beckons enemies; completely cut it out.
Undertaking too much leads to misfortune; completely cut it out.

24 Indecision mixes up important goals; completely cut it out.
A bad disposition is the way to accrue enemies; completely cut it out.
Fantasies are a host of evil ghosts; completely cut them out.
Bad servants are the basis for gossip; completely cut them out. [4]

25 Evil companions are a source of regret; completely cut them off.
Wicked places are encircled by misery; completely cut yourself free.
Worldly customs are ankle restraints; completely cut them off.
I have still more essential advice, so listen!

26 The five degenerations are rampant in this evil time:[38]
desire and hatred, the obstructive demons of all religious people, cause harm.
Wherever you go, minimize your attachment and hatred.
Whatever you do, please adopt a humble attitude.

27 The distant valley of Nepal is extremely hot;
please be careful about what you drink to slake your thirst.
There are very fearsome enemies south of the high pass;
please be careful of their animosity and evil spells.

28 To the north of Nyangshap there are many disputatious people;
please be careful of their vague and idle words.
In Purgyal, the land of Tibet, there are evil, shameless men;
please be careful of those with agitated angry minds.

29 Nowadays many people are very friendly when first met;
please be careful of these deceptive, seductive acquaintances.
I have still more essential advice, so listen!
Do not lose faith in your chosen deity.
Place little faith in men of this degenerate time.

30 Without diminishing your concern for how others perceive you,
minimize discussing the qualities and faults of others.
Do not plan to procrastinate positive activities;
be someone who applies himself to the holy Dharma.

31 Without exaggerating your desire for success in all your endeavors,
respect your guru with your body, speech, and mind.
In brief, bear all those superior to you above you like a crown;
protect yourself from inferiors as if they are sharp blade's edge.

32 Gladly befriend your equals as if you were yoked oxen.
Whatever you do, minimize your personal desires
and in all your endeavors make the general welfare paramount.
Thus this is the advice I'm offering to you.

33 Like a bird that doesn't lose her focus on her eggs,
I set the words of this advice in *lañca* script.[39]
In a hermitage look at these words as great entertainment;[40]
if you familiarize yourself with them for a long time, it will be
very helpful.

34 From now on, throughout all our lives
may we act together to guide living beings.
Just as it says in Samantabhadra's prayer,[41]
I single-pointedly set forth joyful wishes.

This is what was said by Dromtön Gyalwai Jungné. [5]

2. A Jewel Treasury of Wise Sayings[42]

Sakya Paṇḍita Kunga Gyaltsen

THE SANSKRIT TITLE: *Subhāṣitaratnanidhināmaśāstra.*

I respectfully prostrate to the youthful noble Mañjuśri.

I prostrate to the omniscient leader of transmigrating beings,
he whose feet are honored with the touch of the lovely crowns
of great gods, nāga lords, and major mystics,
such as the sages Vyāsa, Vālmīki, and Akṣapāda.[43]

This exposition is a jewel treasury of wise sayings
pertaining to how respectable people behave,
which, when examined with reason, does not contradict religion
and helps accomplish all worldly activities.

Chapter 1. An Examination of the Wise

1 The wise possess a trove of good qualities
because they amass precious wise sayings.
The great ocean is a treasury full of water
because all rivers flow into it.

2 Among those who have knowledge and those who do not,
it is the wise who know what to do and what to avoid.
Iron filings that are mixed with dust
are identified when extracted by a magnet.

3 A wise person understands good advice,
but a fool's mind is not like that.
Owls will go blind
when the sun's rays shine.

4 Those with wisdom can eliminate their faults,
but the foolish cannot do so.
A garuḍa can kill poisonous snakes,
but a crow cannot do so. [6]

5 When an intelligent person's situation worsens,
his intellect increases and becomes stronger.
When the king of beasts is hungry,
he swiftly attacks an elephant's head.

6 You cannot fathom a wise man's depth
until you question or debate him.
Until you beat a drum,
what distinguishes it from other objects?

7 Study, even knowing you could die tomorrow.
Although you may not become wise in this life,
in future lives you will claim that wisdom as yours
as if it was wealth that had been safely deposited.

8 If you have good qualities, everyone will be attracted
to you with no need of additional enticement.
Even if a fragrant flower is far away,
bees will be drawn to it like clusters of clouds.

9 A single wise man who has perfected his training
in every positive trait illumines the entire world.
There may be many shrewd, devious men,
but like stars they cannot shed light.

10 A wise man emulates the smallest good trait of others
even if he has innumerable good qualities of his own.

Through continual application of this technique
he will quickly proceed to the state of omniscience.

11 When the wise are protected by insight,
how can even multiple enemies harm them?
The brahman boy of Ujjayinī
conquered an entire host of enemies on his own.[44]

12 When the unintelligent are disturbed by problems
the intelligent skillfully restore them to happiness.
A stream muddied by turbulence
is cleansed by a water-purifying gem.

13 No matter how desperate a wise man may be,
he never follows the path of fools.
Although a thirsty bird craves a rain shower,
it will not drink water that has fallen to the ground. [7]

14 Even if the wise are misled,
they are not perplexed about what to do.
Ants may be sightless creatures,
but they are quicker than those with sight.[45]

15 When two intelligent people converse
it is possible that more good sense will emerge.
Mixing yellow turmeric with white borax
will produce another color.

16 An upright person who has accumulated merit
overcomes all others even if he stands alone.
Lions, the king of beasts, and universal monarchs
have no need for allies.

17 If you know how it's done, how can it be hard
to employ even the great as your servants?
Even though a garuḍa is very powerful,
the golden-clad one made him his mount.[46]

18 Wisdom is what produces happiness
in this life and future lives.
The wisdom of Prince Candra
saved Sudāsa in this and future lives.[47]

19 Even those who are strong and brave
will not achieve glory if they lack wisdom.
Even if someone obtains wealth,
how can it last if they have no merit?

20 Distinct good qualities and flaws are clear to everyone,
but a wise man can distinguish them when they are mixed.
Everyone can get milk from a cow,
but swans can extract milk when it is mixed with water.[48]

21 Comprehension arises even in animals
if they are continually lectured and exhorted.
A man is wise when he knows what to think
without urging and without instruction from others.

22 If you have intelligence, without being told
you can know the thoughts of others from their demeanor.
Even without eating a Nepalese apple
you can know its taste from its color alone. [8]

23 The wise receive more honor
in countries other than their own.
How can jewels sought after in other lands
be marketable on the island from whence they came?

24 The wise endure hardship while studying;
it is impossible for a hedonist to become learned.
It is impossible for those who crave small pleasures
to obtain the gratification of great joy.

25 An intelligent person may be physically weak,
but what can a powerful enemy possibly do?

Although the king of beasts was powerful,
an intelligent rabbit killed him.[49]

26 A wise person is someone who knows
how to congenially get along with others.
Even animals live in a herd
of their own kind, do they not?

27 Some events are certain to happen;
the time to evaluate them is before they occur.
Know that this is the difference between wise men and fools:
a fool's approach is to evaluate them after they occur.

28 Someone is counted to be among the wise
if he knows the subjects investigated by the wise.
A fool may be skilled in assessing the age of a cow,
but that is not good, quality education.

29 Water doesn't make the ocean overflow;
wealth doesn't glut the king's treasury;
indulgence never satisfies the senses;
good advice never satiates the wise.

30 Even if the wisdom comes from a child,
a wise person will fully embrace it.
Although musk comes from animal glands,
it is used to produce fragrant perfume. [9]

Chapter 2. An Examination of the Cultivated

31 Qualities that always remain excellent
are acclaimed especially by noble people.
The fragrance of Malaya sandalwood[50]
is spread in ten directions by the wind.

32 Goals are realized and happiness is obtained
when an excellent person is installed as a ruler.

The wise proclaim, "The realm will prosper"
when a jewel is honored atop a victory banner.

33 When people are oppressed by an evil ruler
they strongly yearn for a righteous king.
People who are afflicted by fever
think only of icy mountain streams.

34 Those tyrannized by sinful rulers
are carefully sheltered by religious kings.
Those who are afflicted by evil spirits
are meticulously cared for by tantric adepts.

35 The noble eliminate even minor peccadillos;
the ill-bred do not reject even grave wrongdoing.
Dust motes clinging to yogurt are wiped off;
yeast is deliberately added to make beer.

36 Even when a noble person's fortune is in decline,
his behavior remains ever more appealing.
Even if a torch is turned upside down
see how the tongues of flame blaze upward.

37 Even when a noble person lives far away
he helps his associates, supporting them from afar.
The buildup of large clouds in the sky
causes harvests on earth to really increase.

38 A good reputation causes you joy while you live;
merit brings joy when you go on to another life.
Mere wealth that lacks either of those
cannot bring joy to the wise.

39 Seeing far into the future,
a careful person is very patient.
Even a servant can become a leader
through perseverance and steadfastness. [10]

40 Those who always delight in generosity
have fame that rises like the wind.
While the poor gather to entreat alms
there will be more people who wish to give.

41 The signs of a superior person are:
not taking back what has been given,
accepting the disdain of the ill-bred, and
not forgetting even the smallest favor received.

42 A noble person hides his good qualities,
but they shine forth throughout the world.
Even if you totally cover a jasmine plant
its fragrance will spread everywhere.

43 A king is great only in his own realm,
but excellent people are honored wherever they go.
Flowers are ornaments usually for a day,
but crown jewels are always venerated.

44 Espaliered trees bear a lot of fruit.
Domesticated peacocks have beautiful tail feathers.
Trained good horses run swiftly.
A noble person's discipline is a sign of his wisdom.

45 A noble and an ordinary man may be treated the same,
but their gratitude will not be equivalent.
There may be no difference in seeds sown in various fields,
but the difference in the harvests is immeasurable.

46 If you assist an excellent person
even in a small way, it will bear fruit.
Look how the man who gave a single sour fruit[51]
became equal to the righteous king's son.

47 You preserve a good lineage with your conduct;
if your behavior worsens, ancestry is irrelevant. [11]

The good fragrance of sandalwood delights people,
but who wants the ashes after it is burned?

48 The great may experience a decline at some point,
but they need not feel miserable about that.
Although the moon is occasionally eclipsed,
it is immediately freed afterward.

49 When great men feel love for their enemies,
those very enemies come under their sway.
Because Mahāsaṃmata cared for everyone,
he was unanimously appointed king.[52]

50 No matter how destitute the honorable may be,
they will not eat food tainted by evil.
Although a lion may be starving,
he will not eat filthy vomit.

51 Even if a noble person is at the point of death,
how could he abandon his good character?
Even if you incise or smelt fine gold,
its color never fades.

52 Even if their inferiors are hostile toward them,
how could excellent people retaliate in anger?
Although the jackal howls haughtily,
the king of beasts protects him with kindness.

53 People seek for faults in excellent people,
not in those who are inferior.
People examine jewels for flaws;
who bothers to scrutinize a charred log?

54 Not being elated by praise,
not being downcast by derision, and
being secure in their own good qualities:
these are characteristics of noble people.

55 Wealth obtained through evil and coercion
is not real wealth.
Dogs and mice may have full bellies,
but they are paradigms of shamelessness.

56 When the population is prosperous
it is a sign of the greatness of the ruler.
Don't the decorations that adorn a horse
make its master look beautiful?

57 To the extent that a ruler governs
his people with kindness,
to precisely that extent
the citizenry do their ruler's bidding. [12]

58 Who would value other learned men
in a place where a great person lives?
When the sun rises in the sky
even a multitude of stars cannot be seen.

Chapter 3. An Examination of the Foolish

59 An evil person may become wealthy,
but his behavior will become even worse.
No matter how you try to reverse a waterfall,
you must accept that it flows only downward.

60 Good manners may appear among the coarse,
but that is an instance of artificiality.
You may color glass to make it look like a jewel,
but its true hue is revealed when it contacts water.

61 Although a fool may do something well,
it is an accident, not deliberately done.
The silk thread from a silkworm's saliva
does not come about because of the worm's skill.

62 A wicked man can destroy in an instant
a treaty reached through the effort of great men.
Hail can reduce to dust in an instant
lands tended by farmers for months and years.

63 The wicked usually attribute
whatever faults they have to others.
Crows diligently wipe on something clean
their beaks dirtied by eating filth.

64 If you delegate a job to a fool,
the work suffers and he is injured too.
It is said that when a fox was appointed king,
his subjects suffered and he was killed too.[53] [13]

65 While the ignorant wish for happiness,
their actions only bring about suffering.
Look how some people afflicted by demons
commit suicide to get rid of their pain.

66 Sincere unintelligent people destroy themselves,
and some cause harm to others.
Straight trees in the forest are sought and cut down,
and straight arrows are used to kill others.

67 Someone who never thinks of the welfare of others
conducts himself in the same manner as cattle.
As for only obtaining food and drink,
aren't even animals capable of this much?

68 People who do not evaluate what is helpful and what is not,
who do not engage in contemplation and study,
and who seek only to fill their bellies
are simply pigs without body hair.

69 People who are joyous and playful among fools
and are timid and shy in front of the wise

may not have a hump or a dewlap,
but they are simply bulls with upper teeth.

70 Those who rush to where they can eat and drink,
and sneak off when assigned important tasks,
may know how to tell stories and jokes,
but they are simply old dogs without tails.

71 It is easy to fill a hoof-print with water;
it is easy to fill a small treasure-box with jewels;
it is easy to plant a small field with seeds;
it is easy to please the dim-witted with knowledge.

72 Arrogant fools who make promises
come to ruin even if they are powerful.
Bāli, the mighty one, lost the three realms
by giving the land traversed by a single step.[54]

73 Unintelligent people who are vindictive
signal their intent before doing harm.
When a vicious dog sees his enemy,
it barks first and then comes out to bite. [14]

74 Fools undergo the suffering of amassing wealth
but do not experience the pleasure of using it.
Constantly roaming and searching,
they are like pack rats coveting wealth.

75 Among fools, a man with a monkey on a leash
is more valued than a wise man.
The man with the monkey is offered food and gifts;
the wise man goes away empty-handed.

76 People who are without good qualities
are exceptionally hostile to those who have them.
In a snowy land, plants growing in winter
are said to be a bad omen.

77 Some who are badly trained in the arts and sciences
have contempt for those who were properly educated.
On some islands, those lacking goiters
are considered to have a deformity of their limbs.

78 Those who defile ritual practices
disparage those who do them properly.
If you go to the land of one-legged folk,
those with two legs would not be considered human.

79 Those who undermine ritual practices
abuse those who do them perfectly.
Folk who have faces like dogs
belittle women who are beautiful.

80 Those who acquire food and wealth through corruption
despise a wise man who is poor.
Old monkeys catching sight of a man
ridicule him, saying, "He has no tail!"

81 Thus if afflicted by past karma,
a wise man may wander among fools.
A fragrant *mallika* flower carried off by the wind
is trodden into rubbish.

82 Zealously clinging to their faults
and never retaining any good qualities,
wicked people are like a sieve:
catching the flawed and letting the good slip through. [15]

83 Those without the sense to discern right from wrong
are ignored in the presence of the wise.
Those who pass time talking only of food and wealth
are referred to as two-legged cattle.

84 Many dim-witted people may get together,
but they cannot complete important projects.

Many thin twigs may be bound together,
but it is hard for them to support a house beam.

85 A goal may be reached without any analysis,
but who considers that to be shrewd?
The marks left by insects feeding
may look like letters, but bugs are not literate!

86 Wishes expressed by those of inferior intellect,
great horses that are not thoroughbreds,
and daggers that have been dropped in battle:
there is no surety whose friend they will be.

87 Even a multitude of ignorant fools
will fall under an enemy's sway.
An entire herd of powerful elephants
was subjugated by one clever rabbit.[55]

88 Those without wisdom may be rich,
but it usually is of little benefit to them.
A wish-granting cow may provide milk,
but it is rarely given to her calf to drink.

89 Although a person may be wise,
there is no certainty that fools will respect him.
Although the sun shines brightly,
don't demonic spirits run away?

90 What concern for their friends and family
have fools who hoard material goods?
They only do wrong, cause misery, and talk nastily;
like pack rats, they hoard and then they die.

91 How can someone with good qualities
be respected within a group of wicked people?
In a place where poisonous snakes dwell,
even a bright lamp will not provide light.[56] [16]

92 A person may be rich, but owing to bad karma
he may not be free to enjoy it.
During the season for eating ripe grapes
sores always erupt in a crow's mouth.

93 Those who always need help from others
will certainly come to ruin at some point.
There is a well-known proverb that goes,
"Carried by crows, the turtle fell to the ground."[57]

94 The signs of a fool are: ingratitude,
not knowing good from bad,
not holding inspiring narratives as wonderful,
continually questioning the obvious, and following meekly.

95 A coward talks about subjugating enemies;
he shouts threats when he sees them from afar.
Meeting with a fight, he pleads for mercy
and then boasts when he returns home.

96 A coward is brave when it's time for discussion;
when assigned duties he offers money instead;
when he must go illnesses appear;
far from the battlefield he shouts orders.

97 The dull-witted are satisfied with small victories,
they blame their friends if they are defeated,
they incite disputes in group discussions,
they tell secrets about confidential negotiations.

98 They polish their medals on the battlefield,
when faced with the enemy they hide behind allies,
when charging they scare allies more than the foe,
they fling their weapons into the enemies' hands.

99 When the army marches off, he takes the rear;
when it returns, he takes the lead.

Seeing food and drink, he partakes with zest;
seeing hard work, he artfully avoids it.

100 As to the signs of a wicked person:
although many things can be said,
who would draw water from a polluted well?
What wise person would taste vomit? [17]

101 Communicating by moving their lips,
winking when it is time to speak, and
groaning when hearing of superiors' lives:
these signify vulgarity whenever they occur.

Chapter 4. A Comparative Examination of the Wise and the Foolish

102 Ill-bred people may be very wealthy,
but they are outshone by destitute nobles.
A hungry tiger's roar is the cause
for a monkey to fall from the treetop.

103 Fools flaunt their knowledge;
the wise hide their knowledge within.
Straw floats on top of the water;
jewels sink when placed on the water's surface.

104 Those with little knowledge are arrogant.
When someone becomes wise they stay humble.
A small stream incessantly burbles;
what noise is produced in the ocean depths?

105 Low-class people disparage the worthy;
excellent people belittle no one.
The lion protects foxes well,
but the fox is hostile to its own kind.[58]

106 Even if he's angry, a noble person will be appeased if you defer.
If you defer to coarse people, they become more rigid.

Silver and gold are hard, but they can be melted;
if dog shit is melted, a stench is emitted.

107 The wise have every good quality;
fools have only shortcomings.
Wish-fulfilling jewels produce everything desired;
poisonous snakes cause every misfortune.

108 Evildoers degenerate even in a forest retreat;
the exalted are disciplined even when residing in town.
You see fierce carnivores in the jungle,
and the best horses are trained in towns. [18]

109 A superior person sees his own shortcomings;
an inferior person finds faults in others.
A peacock examines its own body;
an owl hoots to send bad omens to others.

110 Through discipline, the righteous nurture themselves and others;
through rigidity, the wicked torment themselves and others.
A fruit-laden tree shelters itself and others;
a dry and brittle tree will burn itself and others.

111 When you are prosperous everyone is your friend,
but if you are destitute they all become your foes.
Islands with jewels attract people from afar,
but everyone leaves when a lake goes dry.

112 A fool is happy when he acquires wealth;
a superior person is happy giving everything away.
A leper feels happy when he scratches himself;
a wise person views leprosy with fear.

113 The great turn those who harm them into friends.
The lowly make those who harm them enemies.
The wind fans a forest fire
but extinguishes a small lamp-flame.

114 Saying, "This is my friend, that is my enemy,"
the unintelligent categorize everyone.
The intelligent have affection for everyone,
for it is uncertain who might be helpful.

115 Those with knowledge delight in learning;
those without knowledge do not.
Honeybees take delight in flowers;
bluebottle flies are not like that.

116 The wise are valued among the wise.
How can a fool know who is wise?
Sandalwood is more precious than gold,
and look how a fool made it into charcoal.

117 The wise know to investigate for themselves,
but fools just follow what is popular.
When an old dog howls,
other dogs join in for no reason. [19]

118 Even when the wise fall into terrible decline,
they please others by giving good advice.
Even when fools become prosperous,
they only argue, burning themselves and others.

119 Some people count talking as getting things done;
others do not talk but put effort into the work.
Mean dogs bark aloud at their foes;
herons quietly ambush mice.

120 A superior person helps even those who attack him;
a bad person harms even those who befriend him.
Wrathful gods will protect living beings;
Yama, the lord of death, may smile but kills others.[59]

121 Noble people are like jewels;
they never change in any situation.

Bad people are like a scale's balance arm;
the slightest thing makes them go up or down.

122 Agreeable people are helpful even if they live far away.
A contentious person is extremely divisive if nearby.
Growing from mud, a lotus is unsullied by muck,
and it is always nurtured by the sun.

123 Good qualities are your finest ornaments
as long as you have a sense of modesty.
If you pass beyond modesty, those qualities
become subjective and opprobrium increases.

124 Worthy people instruct well without being asked;
ignoble people speak falsely even when asked.
A bodhisattva is compassionate even when insulted;
Yama, the lord of death, will kill even when propitiated.

125 An action may be helpful to one person
but could be harmful to others.
When the moon rises
night lilies open, but a lotus closes up.

126 A goal may be accomplished through corrupt actions,
but what wise person would admire that happening?
Although something done right may go wrong,
wise people are not ashamed of that. [20]

127 Some acquisitions are profitable;
some acquisitions are inimical.
A pregnant mare will increase your wealth;
when a mule becomes pregnant she dies.

128 Noble people are hard to alienate and easy to reconcile;
the ignoble are easy to alienate and difficult to reconcile.
Look at the difference between a living tree
and a charred log in regard to cutting and grafting.

129 You may be weak, but if you are cautious,
even the strong will find it hard to break you.
Someone may be strong, but if he is careless,
the weak often bring him to ruin.

130 When replete with wealth, your power increases too.
When you lack wealth, your power diminishes too.
Because the mouse's precious jewel was stolen,
we hear that his ability to steal declined.[60]

131 People who engage in virtuous actions
give things away, but goods fall on them like rain.
Those without virtue may accumulate assets,
but consider who is using them.

132 A noble person may decline for a while,
but like the moon he waxes full again.
If an ignoble person declines just once,
he is snuffed out like a butter lamp.

133 Intelligent people take a long view of their foes
and in the end they control their enemies.
Because those with little intelligence react to their foes,
they experience unending difficulties.

134 It is a sign of courage
when the wise change course to avoid danger.
When a lion is about to kill a superb bull,
is it cowardice to stay clear of its horns?

135 It is a sign of foolishness to attack an enemy
without analyzing the situation in full.
Does assaulting a butter lamp's flame
make a moth a hero? [21]

136 Evil people destroy their own supporters;
noble people protect those who depend on them.

A parasite eats until its host is no more;
the lion protects his domain and subjects.

137 Inferior people keep meaningless things secret
and talk for no reason about what should stay secret.
Noble people do not keep secrets without a reason
and protect what should be secret with their life.

138 If the ignoble get rich it makes them arrogant;
if the noble get rich it makes them refined.
When the fox is well fed it howls with conceit;
when the lion is well fed it sleeps peacefully.

139 The behavior of the noble and the ignoble
are different owing to the power of habituation.
Is it necessary to teach a bee to seek flowers
or show a goose how to dive into a lake?

140 When a wicked king encounters an enemy,
he punishes his own court.
Some fools who have not accomplished their aims
are obstacles to themselves and meet their death.

141 When a righteous king encounters an enemy,
he takes even more care of his subjects.
A mother becomes particularly anxious
for a child who is ill.

142 When the noble befriend the ignoble,
wickedness will leave its mark.
The delicious water of the Ganges River
becomes salty when it reaches the ocean.

143 When the coarse rely on superior people,
they assimilate the behavior of the noble.
See how a person daubed with musk
exudes the sweet fragrance of musk.

144 A great mountain is never shaken by anything;
a great person is similarly stable.
A coarse person's behavior vacillates greatly,
just like cotton fluff wafts about. [22]

Chapter 5. An Examination of Bad Behavior

145 The pleasant speech of cunning people
is for their own ends, not to be polite.
The laughter-like hooting of an owl
delivers a bad omen; it's not done out of joy.

146 Bad people first mislead others with words.
Later when others have relaxed, they deceive them.
See how fishermen disguise hooks with bait
in order to kill the fish.

147 As long as uncouth people are weak
they will display a pleasant disposition.
Until a poisonous bush grows to maturity
its thorns cannot prick other things.

148 Someone who keeps one thought in mind
while saying something else with his words
is known as a dissimulating person:
he is a fool masquerading as a wise man.

149 Excessive duplicity carried too far
may succeed for a while but ends in destruction.
The donkey covered with the leopard skin
ate the crops, but others killed him later.[61]

150 If someone is clever he can deceive others
by blatantly lying about something.
Because the thieves called it a dog,
the brahman lost the goat he was leading.[62]

151 Cunning people deceive others with words
while blatantly committing evil deeds.
When the monk Mahādeva lamented aloud,
some said that he proclaimed the truth of suffering.[63]

152 A cunning person's pretenses and sweet words
should not be trusted until you examine them.
A peacock has a beautiful form and melodic cry,
but its food is extremely poisonous. [23]

153 Cunning people lure you in with pleasant manners
and later deceive you to attain their objectives.
A brazen man sold donkey meat
by exhibiting the tail of a deer.

154 People with few scruples use the wealth of others
to prove their own importance.
They display a friend's clothes before a guest
and present them as a sign of their own status.

155 Those beyond shame whose depravity is deep
bear their ill repute as an accolade.
Some royal families in the land of Kañcī
beat royal drums when they commit patricide.[64]

156 The help offered by those with little intelligence
can sometimes be harmful to others.
A magpie chick plucks out its mother's feathers
thinking it is repaying her kindness.

157 Those with bad characters think that what comes
from the kindness of others is due to their own greatness.
The rain that falls because of a nāga's endeavors[65]
is thought by farmers to be for their own glory.

158 The evil-minded enjoy the results of past karma,
thinking, "I got this through my own effort."

An old dog gnaws a bone, thinking
blood from his punctured palate is the bone's marrow.

159 We see the unwise destroy their friends
and care for those unconnected to them.
Would anyone other than a lunatic
cut off a peacock's crest to ornament its tail?

160 Fools never give where there is need
but do too much where there is no need.
An inferior spring overflows in summer
but is dry when it is needed in springtime.

161 Evil people are especially hostile
toward honorable, peaceful people.
A log saturated with oil
catches fire, but others do not. [24]

162 The savage are subdued with harshness;
how can they be tamed by gentleness?
Burning and incisions remove boils;
mild treatment makes them toxic.

163 Kings rule their realms according to the law;
if they do not, it is a sign of the king's decline.
If the sun does not eliminate darkness,
it is a sign that there is an eclipse.

164 Those living under the following are always afraid:
under an evil man appointed as ruler,
under the damaged roof of a house,
under the collapsing peak of a mountain.

165 Even if a person is knowledgeable,
avoid him if his character is bad.
A poisonous snake may be crowned with a jewel,
but what wise person would take it into his lap?

166 Some kings are like a blazing fire:
too close, doing his bidding is hard;
turn away, they rarely hold you dear;
and stay in the middle, you live on a precipice.

167 Who would depend on a wicked spouse,
a depraved friend, or an evil ruler?
Would an intelligent person continue to live
amid the ferocious carnivores of the jungle?

168 Arrogance causes knowledge to decline.
Desire causes modesty to degenerate.
If his subjects are continually harassed,
the ruler will come to his downfall.

169 Those who speak helpfully are rare;
rarer still are those who listen.
It is difficult to find a skilled physician,
and few follow his prescriptions.

170 If you are extremely conceited,
suffering will continually befall you.
We hear that because of a lion's great pride
a fox was able to make him carry a load.[66] [25]

171 Assistance given to the bad-natured,
seeds planted in poor fields,
things hidden by crows:
all exemplify too much hope and little utility.

172 Do not consult with or have faith in
someone you have not checked out.
Mistakes arise from carelessness,
and enmity often comes from conversation.

173 There are many bad things in the world,
but nothing is as terrifying as a wicked man.

Although other bad things can be remedied,
destruction awaits those trying to reform an evil man.

174 Evil people can never be satisfied
even if assisted in hundreds of good ways.
Making enemies of those who support them
is a special characteristic of evil people.

175 No matter how much a wicked person reforms,
it is impossible for their nature to become good.
Even if you vigorously wash a lump of coal,
it is impossible to make it turn white.

176 Shun places dominated by wicked people
even if you see a holy person there.
Flee from a place with dangerous snakes
even if you see a golden necklace there.

177 You should honor noble people;
honoring the coarse is the source of faults.
Milk is nourishing nectar for humans;
if you give it to snakes their venom increases.

178 You may strive to care for them in every manner,
but how can evil people ever accord with your hopes?
No matter how often you feed a sparrow,
it is impossible for it to be at ease.

179 A person who constantly strives for disunity
will separate even the firmest of friends.
Won't cracks appear in rocks
when continually eroded by water? [26]

180 Some say, "I have duped others and done wrong."
They criticize preceptors, teachers, and friends.
If they are lying, such liars cannot be trusted;
if they're telling the truth, you should be even more afraid.

181 The wise should be cautious of someone
who talks in the presence of others
about matters that should remain secret,
regardless of whether they are true or false.

182 Those of bad character who cherish wealth
should not be trusted even if they are your friends.
Friends who have taken bribes
have ruined great people many times.

183 People who reveal their malevolence
are enemies who are easy to combat.
How can you combat enemies
who make false overtures of helpfulness?

184 With skill it is possible to heal various wounds,
but there is no mending the cuts from vile words.
Because the crow insulted the owl,
look how they have been enemies for eons.[67]

185 "Hold fast to malice in your heart
while speaking pleasant words."
This is the advice of pernicious sages;
it is contrary to noble behavior.

186 "Root out a contentious enemy
just like you uproot poisonous plants."
This appears in treatises of advice for rulers,[68]
but treat someone like your son and they will act like a son.

187 Who could befriend a person
who acts only in self-interest?
In an intensively cultivated field,
other plants rarely grow to maturity.

188 How could you ever befriend a person
who never remembers acts of kindness?

Who would continue to cultivate a field
where nothing grows despite much effort? [27]

189 People quickly get into trouble
because of rash behavior.
Doesn't a stubborn old bull
quickly break anything that can be broken?

190 No matter how much you give to coarse people,
what do they give when you need something in return?
Does an iron marble ever return the grip
of pincers that always hold it tight?

191 Scoundrels say, "I'm doing this for the sake of others."
With this false pretext they engage in misdeeds.
What wise person would destroy himself
with the pretense of working for the well-being of others?

192 Outstanding debts, remnants of enmity,
bad legal statutes, bad reputations,
bad ancestry, and bad behavior:
these tend to multiply without being propagated.[69]

Chapter 6. An Examination of Natural Tendencies

193 When appointed to a high position
people rarely know the job's duties.
Although you have eyes to look at others,
you need a mirror to look at yourself.

194 Even those knowledgeable about one subject
find it difficult to master everything.
You may have very sharp vision
but not the capacity to hear sound.

195 Someone who tells the truth may have faults;
someone who twists words may have good qualities.

Some straight roads may endanger your wealth;
the right-spiraling conch brings good luck.[70]

196 If someone has some learning but lacks merit,
they could be destroyed because of their learning.
Oysters that cling to pearls within
lose their lives because of those pearls. [28]

197 If you are too dependent on someone,
even if he is learned, regrets often arise.
Although sugarcane is extremely sweet,
if always served most people will refuse it.

198 Even those who have good natures
will become vicious if continually abused.
Although sandalwood sticks are cool by themselves,
if you rub them they will burst into flame.

199 Although there are many, many rulers,
those who rule righteously are rare.
Although there are many celestial palaces in the sky,
none emit clear light like the sun and moon.

200 Someone who is able to cause harm
is also someone who can help others.
A king with the power to behead his subjects
is a king with the power to give away his realm.

201 An honest and intelligent minister
accomplishes all his ruler's and subjects' goals.
When a skilled archer shoots a straight arrow,
whatever target he aims at is hit.

202 If a king pays no heed to others,
even if he is omniscient he will not be esteemed.
Although a corpse may look lovely,
who would embrace something with no life?

203 Even the weak can accomplish great things
when many think along the same lines.
It is well known that a swarm of ants
joined together and killed a lion cub.[71]

204 A discouraged person who gives up trying
weakens even if he is hearty and strong.
Although a bull is very powerful,
he is bound to servitude by a tiny cowherd.

205 If you generate great confidence and effort
you can outshine even the great.
Although a white conch is very small,
it is the executioner of huge sea monsters.[72] [29]

206 The great have no need to strut;
what use is a wicked man's strutting?
Precious jewels do not need to be advertised;
who buys trinkets even if they are promoted?

207 The wealth of great beings is everlasting;
evil men's prosperity is prone to decline.
The sun always gives off light;
The moon waxes and then wanes.

208 If a king lauds his high status too much,
he will cause his own eventual demise.
When you throw an egg up into the air,
what can happen except for it to break?

209 The people who cause us greater injury
are usually the most like us.
When the sun shines brightly
other sources of light lose their strength.

210 Rely on the helpful even if they are your enemies;
discard the harmful even if they are your friends.

Purchase ocean jewels for what they are worth.
Treat the pain inside you with medicine.

211 If internally you think, "I'm rather rich,"
you display haughtiness externally.
When clouds are fully laden with water
they swirl and make the sound of thunder.

212 Rarely does anyone have every good quality;
rare too is someone with no good qualities at all.
From this mix of good qualities and faults
the wise cultivate essential good qualities.

213 At the outset there is no certainty
whether someone will be your enemy or friend.
Food may be poison if it is not digested;
but poisons can be medicinal if you know how to use them.

214 Those with favorable karma are prosperous;
those lacking such accumulated karma are poor.
Geese will not stay if they are held in a coop,
but they circle back when driven from a lake. [30]

215 The wise will pay to study and gain knowledge;
fools forsake knowledge even though they've been taught.
Most people take medicine when they are ill,
but there are some who even commit suicide.

216 All those who are independent are happy;
all those controlled by others are miserable.
Things owned jointly are the basis for quarrels.
And promises are a source of constraints.

217 Even someone with every internal good quality
is disparaged by everyone if their appearance is bad.
It is well known that although the bat was wise
all the birds rejected him because he had no feathers.[73]

218 Unsuitable people, even when very honest,
are the downfall of themselves and others.
An arrow will kill someone else
or it will be shattered itself.

219 Rain and rivers fall to the sea.
Intelligence and knowledge permeate the wise.
Kings accumulate wealth and subjects.
Forests grow where it is damp and warm.

220 Springs that flow in summer, grass fires,
the sun or full moon hidden behind clouds,
friends with weak intelligence and meager knowledge:
there is no certainty these will appear when needed.

221 It is nicer when a fool speaks little.
It is nicer when a king stays hidden.
It is nicer to see magic show once in a while.
Goods fetch a high price when they are rare.

222 When love is lavished excessively
it becomes the cause of enmity.
Most of the disputes in the world
arise from such relationships quite often.

223 It is possible that even a very intense dispute
will become the cause for a strong friendship.
We have seen many times that arguments
often end in reconciliation. [31]

224 Miserly people may have possessions,
jealous people may have friends,
people with evil minds may have knowledge:
they may have these, but these cannot produce joy.

225 The greedy are pleased by possessions,
the haughty are pleased by praise,

fools enjoy those who agree with them,
excellent people are pleased by truthful words.

226 The knowledge of a wicked person,
the wisdom of a cowardly braggart,
the gratitude of an evil ruler:
there is little chance these benefit others.

227 Wealthy people's words are liked by everyone;
poor people's words are disregarded even when true.
Even ordinary logs fetch a high price
if they come from the Malaya mountains.[74]

228 Talking too much is the cause of trouble;
silence is the basis for avoiding trouble.
Because parrots speak they are put in cages;
mute birds fly happily away.

229 If someone with no thought of deception
always gives assistance to his enemies,
even his enemies will respond without deceit.
Such respect from enemies is real greatness.

230 What good is it for the powerless to get angry?
What need is there for the powerful to get angry?
Thus anger is useless for getting things done;
it only causes harm to oneself.

231 Generosity draws even your enemies to congregate;
without it, even your friends keep their distance.
When a cow's milk runs out,
her calf tries to flee even if it is restrained.

232 Being a master of some particular subject
does not ensure you know other things.
Swans know how to separate milk from water
but imagine that a reflection in water is edible. [32]

233 A master who always treats people kindly
finds it easy to obtain servants.
Swans naturally gather on a lotus lake
even though they have not been summoned.

234 The wealthy who use their resources well,
the self-disciplined who become learned,
the great who take good care of their inferiors:
these three make others happy and benefit themselves.

235 Things accomplished through powerful merit,
like the light of the sun, depend on nothing else.
Things accomplished through powerful effort,
like the light of a butter lamp, depend on everything else.

236 Even inferior people can achieve greatness
if they depend on those who are great.
By taking a tall tree as its support,
look how a vine can climb to the tree top.

237 Although a knowledgeable person may have faults,
those who enjoy knowledge should cultivate them.
Even though rain clouds mar the sky,
they bring joy to the common folk.

238 Even if those who lack knowledge look nice,
their appearance cannot delight the wise.
If a stunning horse does not have a good gait,
it has little value despite being impressive.

239 Among fools, there are many with wealth;
among carnivores, there are many who are brave;
but a righteous person who gives good advice—
such learned ones are rare in the world.

240 Whatever qualities someone possesses,
he or she will come to be known by them:

a learned man is known for his knowledge
just as a hero is recognized for heroism.

241 Things honored by the great people
are treated with contempt by the lowly.
The moon, which adorns Śiva's crown,
is treated as food by the demigod.[75] [33]

242 Knowledge that is just in books,
mantras of those who do not practice,
precepts of the forgetful:
they often fall short when most needed.

243 It is difficult for the lazy to attain high positions
even if they are intelligent and wealthy.
Although it is the ears that grow first on deer,
aren't antlers seen to have greater prominence?

244 Delicious-smelling food for dogs and pigs,
lamp light for those born blind,
food for those who cannot digest it,
and Dharma for fools: what use are any of these?

245 Knowledgeable people, fine gold,
heroic warriors, good horses,
skillful doctors, and lovely jewelry:
these will be in demand wherever they are.

246 Is there anything that cannot be accomplished
by those with intelligence and perseverance?
We hear it said that Pāṇḍu's sons destroyed
twelve battalions of the Kaurava army.[76]

247 Usually the conduct of descendants
follows that of their preceding generations.
It is hardly possible for a cuckoo chick
to mature into a sparrow hawk.

248 Mountains and rivers, elephants and horses,
wood and light, jewels and stones,
even men and women of the same class
have unique good and bad qualities.

249 The weak find it difficult to bear
even just the words of someone virtuous.
There is a well-known saying,
"Just the Gauḍa king's words chained the ocean king."[77]

250 Although you strive hard to complete tasks,
accomplishing them depends on strong merit.
Jewels that are not found by merchants at sea
are in use in the king's treasury. [34]

251 Signs of a fool's love and hatred are recognizable;
a shrewd man's love and hatred are misleading.
When old dogs bare their teeth it is a sign they will bite;
when the Death Lord smiles it is a sign he will kill.

252 The best asset is generosity.
The best happiness is a joyous mind.
The best ornament is learning.
The best friend is the one most reliable.

253 Who hasn't been worried about wealth?
Who has lived happily all the time?
Every sort of pleasure and suffering changes,
just as summer turns into winter.

254 The weak are protected from others
merely by taking the names of the mighty.
It is explained that taking the name Aṅgulimāla
will protect you from most false guides.[78]

255 Whatever relationships living creatures have
is a function of their previous actions.

Look how vultures carry off rodents
and otters make offerings to owls.[79]

256 For those who desire to amass possessions,
the best insurance is to give them away when they increase.
If you desire a lot of water in a pond,
draw it down and the pond replenishes.

Chapter 7. An Examination of Unseemly Tendencies

257 Servants who are very haughty,
ascetics who are too pretentious,
kings who do not act with righteousness:
these three engage in unseemly behavior.

258 Undertaking actions beyond your capacity,
resenting many people, quarreling with the powerful,
trusting women, befriending the bad:
these five are causes of quick ruination. [35]

259 Wanting fine clothes when you have no money,
begging from others while having excessive pride,
wanting to debate without understanding the treatises:
these three are objects of others' laughter.

260 Although there are good places to be,
bad people are poor and attached to bad places.
Who else but a jackal would expect
that a flame-tree flower is meat?

261 Important people are more often harmed
by their associates than by their enemies.
Apart from the parasitic worms on its body,
what other creatures make a meal of a lion?

262 What man can be kept safe
when a ruler is determined to harm him?

When a shadow is cast upon a figure,
there is no way at all to see it.

263 It is despicable to harm
a righteous person living in peace.
Who would say "He is a hero" about someone
who kills those who come seeking protection?

264 Wicked people cause others harm
even if they derive no benefit from it.
Even if a poisonous snake subsists on air,
if it sees something else, doesn't it kill it?

265 Although you think sex is pleasurable,
indulging in it is only a cause of pain.
Those who think drinking beer is pleasurable
imagine that being intoxicated is happiness.

266 The world respects those with knowledge.
Knowledge is found in those who strive hard for it.
What good does it do to blame anyone else
if you have not tried to become knowledgeable?

267 People wish to have a long life
but look at growing old with fear.
Fear of old age while desiring longevity
is the perverse thinking of a fool. [36]

268 Someone who does not learn anything
from the wise when they are present
is either possessed by a demon
or suffering the results of past karma.

269 Someone who has possessions
but neither uses them nor gives them away
either is afflicted by illness
or is obviously a hungry ghost.

270 What use is Dharma to someone
who knows the religious tradition but does not practice?
There may be an excellent harvest,
but how can that make carnivorous beasts happy?

271 Sentient beings suffering the results of bad karma
may have wealth but be unable to enjoy it.
Crows hide food even when they are hungry,
so how can they eat until they are full?

272 If you imagine yourself rich
with wealth that you can neither use nor give away,
then imagining a mountain is made of gold
would be a simple way to become rich.

273 Although there are many scholars discoursing
on what is righteous and what it is not righteous,
there are extremely few in the world
who know these and put them into practice.

274 You may have good ancestry, a fine figure, and youth,
but if you lack knowledge you are not attractive.
Although peacock feathers are considered beautiful,
how are they fitting ornaments for the great?

275 A fake nose, a purchased child,
borrowed jewelry, stolen goods,
and the knowledge of those with no teachers:
these may exist, but others do not esteem them.

276 Someone who does not repay the kindness of others
harms himself more than others do.
Those who create malevolent spells
suffer some bad consequences before their enemies do. [37]

277 Even if you see the prospect of obtaining wealth,
who would take it from an improper place?

We have heard that the fox's head was smashed
because he licked the blood of battling rams.[80]

278 For the sake of some relationships
do not cast off others casually.
For even if you are the god Indra himself,
your retinue will evaporate like the scent of camphor.

279 Do not abandon long-term friends
and put your faith in new acquaintances.
It is a well-known saying that the owl king
was destroyed by trusting the crow minister.[81]

280 You may endeavor to placate a bad person,
but he will never be on your side.
No matter how much you boil water,
it can never burst into flame.

281 Justifiable anger is somewhat understandable,
and how to quell it can be known.
Who knows how to dispel
anger that arises for no reason?

282 Do not harass your enemy, even if he seems weak,
without first assessing his capabilities.
The garuḍa triumphed over the ocean
because it mistreated the *taḍibha* bird.[82]

283 When merit is used up bad thoughts arise.
When a lineage declines bad sons are born.
When wealth runs out avarice arises.
When a lifespan is spent signs of death appear.

284 Even Indra cannot disparage you
if you did not commit any negative deeds.
If a spring does not run dry on its own,
could burying it with dirt stop its flow?

285 Some people start hundreds of tasks
but bring not a single one to conclusion.
Their agitated minds mostly wander
like old dogs roaming in towns. [38]

286 Even intelligent people go the wrong way
when driven by powerful karma.
Śiva, the supreme teacher of the tīrthikas,
upholds the conduct of a madman.[83]

287 Someone who transgresses the law in some way
may succeed for a while but will lose in the end.
Balāka may have acquired the entire world,
but the lion killed him because he violated the law.[84]

288 The extremely intelligent undermine themselves
if they undertake too many actions.
Kings who have excessive plans
have ruined kingdoms many times.

289 The wealth of those who have accumulated
way too many possessions will be what kills them.
The wealthy often experience devastating losses
while the poor go about quite happily.

290 Developing excessively strong martial skills
is like making preparation for suicide.
For the most part, death on the battlefield
is usually experienced by those with martial skill.

291 Wealth, intelligence, power, and so forth
are supports for those with merit.
For those without merit, all those things
can become the cause of ruin.

292 No matter what tasks the wise undertake
they investigate their stock of merit and then act.

In troubled times those with great merit
are even rarer than one in a hundred.

293 When a substandard reservoir is filled with water
one side or another will collapse.
Similarly, someone who possesses wealth
very rarely has an enduring family line.

294 Those with children are rarely very rich;
if they have wealth, their enemies destroy them.
When everything becomes perfect,
many times a person dies quite soon. [39]

295 Merit is the sole cause of prosperity;
therefore the wise accumulate merit.
Whenever someone is wealthy,
it is a sign that they have accumulated merit.

296 Thinking, "I'll deceive him by lying,"
is to deceive only yourself.
Someone who tells a lie just once
is doubted even when he tells the truth.

297 Getting angry and harming others
without checking what is right or wrong
is like the pigeon who killed his mate
and became miserable without her companionship.[85]

298 Without dwelling on the future,
work hard when the time comes.
You take off your boots when you reach a river;
why take them off before you even get there?

299 It is improper to begin even a worthy task
if you will not be able complete it in the future.
If a food is indigestible,
who would eat it even if it is tasty?

300 Those who give up striving and lay around
will not succeed in this or future lives.
If it is not worked on, even a good field
will not produce a harvest.

301 If you are too subdued in the wrong situation,
everyone will order you around.
Although cotton is used to fill a mattress,
who would fill one with cotton stalks?

302 Fools undertake bad deeds and impossible tasks,
and they even order others to do so.
Who trusts a person purchasing poisons?
Who can say, "I'm giving everything away!"?

303 Accumulating wealth but not using it well
is gathering firewood for your own cremation.
Although bees do not eat their honey,
they commence suicidal attacks when others take it. [40]

Chapter 8. An Examination of Actions

304 The wise always consult others
about a course of action even for minor tasks.
Even their unfinished work is something to admire,
so what needs to be said about things they complete?

305 Because living creatures' wishes are varied
it is hard for anyone to please them all.
If you have good qualities within yourself
you come close to making everyone happy.

306 Even when you get very old
you should pursue more education.
The benefits to future lives from just studying
are greater than those coming from generosity.

307 Either rely on someone with perfect wisdom
or enjoy friendship with someone ordinary.
It is easy to carry vessels filled with water
as well as those that are completely empty.

308 Who would dare to depend on a person
who had cultivated only a little knowledge?
Who could carry on their head
a vessel half filled with water?

309 Someone who has properly distinguished
the differences between noble and coarse people
and also knows how to accomplish his own tasks
is the solid foundation of everything that is good.

310 Even a coarse person can become excellent
if properly looked after by someone intelligent.
If trained by someone who knows how to teach,
a parrot will know how to do recitations.

311 Even the low and weak will succeed
if they rely on others who are great.
Although a water droplet is small and fragile,
it cannot be evaporated when mixed into the sea. [41]

312 If you are not very intelligent
you should consult those who are more intelligent.
If you cannot kill your enemy with your bare hands
wouldn't you pick up a weapon?

313 Even an enemy who causes you harm
will become your friend if you have the skill.
Although strong poisons will harm your body,
they are medicinal if you know how to prepare them.

314 Accept food and wealth that were acquired properly;
reject coveting inappropriately acquired things.

Pick fruit from high in a tree,
but reach beyond that and you will fall to the ground.

315 Wise people who are not paying attention,
to that extent they will have problems.
If intelligent people are really attentive,
it is rare for problems to arise.

316 Some other treatises advise you
to placate your foes only for the period of time
during which your strength is limited;
when your power is absolute, act accordingly.

317 Even if their enemies speak cordially,
intelligent people do not believe them.
Through stealth, herons and cats
always attempt to kill other creatures.

318 Even if your country's ruler is hostile,
serve him graciously and stay there.
Even if your foot slips on the ground,
it is that very ground that supports you.

319 Excessive craving for sensual objects
quickly brings people to ruin.
Because they desire the bait on a hook,
fish are killed straightaway.

320 Consistent generosity will attract around you
even men worthy of honor along with their retinues.
All beings, from gods to hungry ghosts,
will protect you when appeased with ritual cakes. [42]

321 The great abstain from desire
for frivolity, pleasure, and food.
It is said that Rāvaṇa of Laṅka was killed
as a result of his lustful craving.[86]

322 In matters of both love and dispute,
engage with the great, never the coarse.
Likewise, in matters of buying and selling,
deal with valuables not toxic concoctions.

323 To increase tax revenue, the king's treasury
is filled by small levies, not excessive ones.
Anthills, bee hives, and the waxing moon
all increase little by little.[87]

324 Kings should collect revenue appropriately
without injuring the populace.
If too much of its fragrant resin is tapped,
the sal tree itself will dry up.

325 A ruler especially must be good-natured;
it is wrong for him to be angered by trifles.
Even if a snake possesses a jewel,
what sensible person would stand before it?

326 Anyone who desires prosperity
should primarily safeguard the Dharma.
How can mere riches that debase the Dharma
endure even in this world?

327 Do not be overly affectionate even to friends;
do not excessively harm even your enemies.
Friends' expectations are the basis of resentment;
retaliating against harm is easy for everyone.

328 Gentleness subjugates the mild-mannered;
gentleness also conquers the brutal.
Because gentleness can accomplish everything,
the wise say, "Gentleness itself is sharp!"[88]

329 Even if there is enmity, do not publicize it.
Saying, "That person does not like me,"

even about someone who is your enemy,
is clearly divisive when said aloud. [43]

330 Do not stay in the homes of people
who do not care about modesty and shame,
who don't know the difference between respect and disdain,
and who crave food and wealth.

331 Do not give up your former abode
before proper evaluation of another place.
Raising a foot without first planting the other
can cause you to fall.

332 You should strive to mask your behavior;
many are ruined by revealing too much.
If a monkey did not dance,
why would a rope be tied around its neck?

333 Even if you see an obvious flaw,
do not speak of it in the wrong situation.
The common folk say that misfortune befalls
people who talk about seeing a bad omen.

334 What is the use of wealth and food
that is despised by others?
What wise person would admire
the filth eaten by dogs and pigs?

335 Words that painfully strike the hearts of others
should not be spoken even to enemies.
Like the resounding of an echo,
they instantly rebound on yourself.

336 If you desire to harm your enemy,
have good qualities of your own.
This will inflame your enemy's mind,
and your own merit will increase.

337 Develop compassion for difficult people,
but tame them with harsh measures.
People who wish to heal their bodies
remove diseased flesh with surgery.

338 Even if you harm someone just slightly,
clear it up quickly to make peace.
Haven't you seen that after water flows
through small gullies, they become large channels? [44]

339 The wise do not do what should not be done
even though they know how to do so.
Because elephants crush enemy armies,
see how kings always keep them chained.

340 Do not reject your allies even if they are hostile;
do not bow down before an enemy even if he is nice.
Even though crows harass other crows,
they are ruined if they rely on a day-blind owl.[89]

341 The wise always act with vigilance
whether doing something great or small.
A lion's attention never slackens
whether killing a rabbit or an elephant.

342 What wise person lives in a place
where the learned are not respected?
Are crystals ever sold at all
where they're used as flints to start fires?

343 A learned person either teaches others
or meditates in a peaceful forest.
Either a jewel is used in a crown
or remains on an island in the ocean.

344 You will accrue benefits for yourself
if you serve holy beings superior to you.

All birds on the slopes of Mount Meru
come to be as radiant as gold.

345 You will not achieve greatness
if you rely on someone jealous and mighty.
Look how the moon wanes
because it approaches the radiant sun.

346 Who would embrace as a friend
someone whose affection is unreliable?
Although a rainbow has pretty colors,
if you hope it will last, you are a deluded fool.

347 Whatever does not please you
should never be done to others.
Think about how you felt
when others harmed you a little. [45]

348 If you extend to others
whatever is pleasurable to you,
others will do what pleases you.
That is the way to become respected.

349 The wise avoid both disputes
and friendship with violent people.
Neither animosity nor intimacy
is the right way to charm them.

350 Relying on those who are holy,
asking questions of the wise,
befriending those of good character:
whoever does these is always happy.

351 Everyone despises someone
who tells tales at inappropriate times.
Don't we infer that someone is drunk
from the fact that he talks too much?

352 The modest think that everything
they have to say is erroneous.
Therefore such people do not speak
and are definitely respected by others.

353 Think carefully and say a few things
at the appropriate time and place.
Even good advice, if given too often,
is as unmarketable as leftover merchandise.

354 Even the wise find it difficult
to recognize their own faults as flaws.
If many people tell you this,
you should conclude that you have faults.

355 A person who is afflicted by a demon
recognizes his flaws but does not eliminate them.
If you do not apply the corrective right now,
Do not consider yourself to be human.

356 Those who think a little bit
should focus on a fault and get rid of it.
Those who engage in such remedies
will improve more and more. [46]

357 Whether you are intelligent or kindhearted,
whether you heed advice or are brave,
even if you do not know how to do other things,
you protect yourself by behaving in the above ways.

358 You will be happy if you give up relationships with crude people
even if you have been friends for a long time.
The elders say you will be happy if you extract
a constantly wobbly tooth, even if it is a nice one.

359 Constant complainers who hang around you
should be given a little something and sent away.

A wound from a snake's bite
will kill you if you cannot cut it away.

360 When you obtain a high position
stop being stingy with other insignificant things.
Why be stingy with just a few jewels
when you have gained control over a kingdom?

361 When the wise desire possessions and so forth
their best insurance is to give a bit away.
If you wish to increase the water in a well,
drawing off some water is good advice.

362 Anyone who desires worldly affluence
must engage in a lot of planning and activity.
If you think that hustle and bustle causes misery,
give up hoping for prosperity.

363 When you set out to do a particular action,
consider both its advantages and disadvantages.
If it should be avoided if the two are equal,
what needs to be said if the drawbacks are greater?

364 Respectfully rely on an honest, intelligent person.
Be careful if you know someone intelligent is dishonest!
Lovingly protect those who are ignorant but honest.
Quickly distance yourself from the ignorant who are dishonest.

365 Even if you do not have wealth or servants,
you can succeed if you have an intelligent friend.
If this is true even for animals,
what needs to be said about human beings? [47]

366 Assign tasks to those who know how to do them;
do not appoint someone who is incapable.
You cannot travel across water in a wagon.
How can a boat cruise on land?

367 A long-term malicious enemy may become friendly,
but do not associate with him.
Even if water is very hot,
won't it put out the fire it's poured on?

368 Someone with integrity and humility
can be trusted even if they are a foe.
We hear that some people's lives were spared
by going for refuge to an honorable enemy.[90]

369 You may say, "I have no ill will,"
but do not trust everyone else.
Deer are always sweet tempered,
but creatures with fangs think of them as food.

370 When fools go down the wrong path
it is sufficient to know they are fools.
When the wise go down the wrong path
you should investigate how they reasoned.

371 The wise make good use of their possessions;
even if they do not give, their things are not stolen.
Avoid places that have few resources;
even if there is no theft, deceptive loans will ruin you.

372 Even if you know something well,
every action should be done in consultation.
A person who does not like to take advice
is someone who pays the price of regret.

373 When involved in delicate negotiations
do not consult a third person, not even a friend.
If you get bad instructions for a zombie ritual,
the first to succeed will be devoured.

374 Someone skilled in acquisition and giving impartially,
who is disciplined and considerate of everyone's feelings,

who is fearless and does not act inefficiently,
can have the entire world if he or she so wishes. [48]

375 If an enemy comes to you for refuge,
honor him and then speak pleasantly.
A crow became happy by relying on a mouse;
so says an ancient tradition.[91]

376 Bad friends and bad scholarship,
bad thoughts and bad actions,
are things with which the wise do not get involved.
And if they do, they are nothing but fools.[92]

377 How could an action possibly be ineffective
if done after careful consideration?
How could a person walk off a cliff
if he has good sight and watches where he is going?

378 Cultivating good qualities that benefit
yourself and others is the sign of wisdom.
Simply knowing some fields of knowledge,
like archery, will destroy your lineage.

379 If you truly desire high status,
only do things beneficial to others.
People who wish to clean their faces
wipe off the mirror first, don't they?

380 If you truly desire to subdue others,
work hard to develop good qualities.
Look how those who wish to slay their foes
work hard to succeed by mastering weaponry.

381 Swindlers' words are duplicitous,
so the honest must examine them carefully.
After being duped what is the use
of self-promotion, of saying, "I'm honest!"

382 Deal with deceptive people in cunning ways,
deal with honest people in candid ways,
treat the unstable with firmness.
This is what is written in ancient records.

383 It is always right for the wise
to act kindly, even toward their enemies.
Even if it does not help with reconciliation
it is definitely the cure for malice. [49]

384 Because it is impossible to achieve your aims
if you say nasty things in public,
your words should be agreeable to everyone
even if you act with your own interest in mind.

385 To accomplish your own and others' goals,
both gentle and harsh means are appropriate.
However, the Buddha did not teach deception
as part of the practice of skillful means.

386 The wise rely on advice with long-term benefits
even if enacting it is painful at present.
When the wise are old and ill
they teach positive traits to their only child.

387 Your downfall is very near
if your possessions increase too much.
A reservoir that is too full of water
is emptied, otherwise its banks will fail.

388 Actions that are helpful for some people to do
are not appropriate for others to do.
Garlic cures nervous tension
but is poisonous for those with bile diseases.

389 Although the weak should always be protected,
the strong risk decline if they befriend them.

If you place clarified butter in a container,
don't mice come to gnaw on it?

390 If you rely on wicked people,
their bad influence will harm you.
Look how fish that live in the water
of irrigation canals are scattered over the fields!

391 When an ill-natured person comes to depend on you
give them a little something and send them away.
If a bad omen appears to a family
they must use some of their wealth to counteract it.

392 Even if a holy person goes somewhere else
pay him homage and maintain close relations.
If you always revere a wish-fulfilling jewel
good fortune increases and wishes come true. [50]

393 If inferior people are praised too much
they will despise those who did so later.
If filth is thrown up in the air
it comes down on the thrower's head.

394 When an intelligent person is maligned,
the criticism will rebound on the slanderer.
When a torch is held upside down
the hands of the person holding it are burned.

395 Everything has its own place;
leave things where they belong.
One does not wear a crown on the feet;
nor are foot ornaments for the head.

396 When it is time to do important tasks
make an effort to get help from good friends.
When a fire burns a huge forest
the wind helps it without question.

397 Speak words imbued with kindness;
it is easy to do and the best way to attract others.
Who can please others just with wealth?
Even if life and limb are sacrificed, half will be unsatisfied.

398 Do not be depressed even if you are destitute.
Do not be excessively happy even if you are rich.
Because the effects of actions last a long time,
varieties of happiness and sorrow are yet to come.

Chapter 9. An Examination of the Dharma

399 Being devoted to other teachers
while the Buddha, the refuge of beings, is present
is like digging a well to get brackish water
near a river whose water possesses eight good qualities.

400 Whatever there is that needs to be done
is not difficult if you are familiar with it.[93]
Just as you can learn technical crafts,
you can easily master the holy Dharma. [51]

401 Someone who can be satisfied with a little
will never know the depletion of wealth.
A continuous rain of misery falls on
those who insatiably look for more.

402 The Buddha taught that the wealth one obtains
should be given away when there are others in need.
If you stockpile wealth the way bees hoard honey,
it will be used by others at some point.

403 In the world there is no guarantee
that loans you have made will be repaid.
But even a small amount given to a beggar
effortlessly brings a hundredfold result.

404 It is impossible for misers to be wealthy;
it is impossible for the generous to be poor.
So it is as if misers have little interest in riches
and the generous ardently desire possessions.

405 Fearing generosity will impoverish them,
the miserly never engage in giving.
Knowing avarice will surely impoverish them,
the intelligent give even the little they get.

406 Assets do not increase if they sit unused,
so merchants spread their wares for sale.
Like traders, the wise give widely
since riches and power do not come from hoarding.

407 Those who have treasures worth billions
but do not give anything to anyone
are the poor of this world.
This is what the learned ones teach.

408 Fearing their descendants will be destitute,
those of little intelligence hoard the little they obtain.
So that their descendants will achieve greatness,
the wise give to others as if distributing bribes.

409 Thinking to make their heirs wealthy,
some sacrifice themselves to enrich their children.
But wicked children fight with their father;
squandering the wealth, they roam like dogs. [52]

410 To the extent parents love their children,
children do not love their parents in return.
Having cared for their children so long,
when old, parents are mistreated by children.

411 There are wealthy people who hoard their riches,
and there are wealthy people who give to those in need.

The people of the world can differentiate
these two types and their descendants.

412 Those who are slaves to worldly existence
pursue wealth even at the risk of their life.
But when those who are content obtain riches
they calmly give them to others.

413 By giving away your possessions you perfect generosity.
If that angers others, you can increase your patience.
If that satisfies others, you can cultivate joy.
Thus generosity is the supreme Dharma.

414 As a receptacle for an ocean of misery,
this body of ours may be like an enemy;[94]
if an intelligent person knows how to use it,
this body can be the basis for creating merit.

415 Your life can be destroyed in an instant,
but the imprints of virtue go on for a long time.
The scent of sandalwood carried by the wind
produces delight even though diffused from afar.

416 After enjoying something pleasurable for a long time,
the pain of losing it is even more acute.
Those who believe life is permanent are devastated,
for, not having any control, we all must die.

417 At death, surrounded by friends and relations,
your voice is weak with fear, your vision is failing,
and you have no idea where you are heading.
At that time anything other than virtue is ruinous.

418 The maladies of the three lower realms[95]
should be remedied before they arise.
It is like a lightning bolt striking your head;
what can you do after it has struck? [53]

419 There are people who go peacefully to sleep
while knowing they will certainly die
and be separated from everyone they love.
What can they possibly have in their minds?

420 Even if you cannot be diligent in everything,
at least strive to not fall into the lower realms.
A warrior may not slay his enemies,
but does he ever kill his allies?

421 Even if something causes a little discomfort now,
the wise stick with it to gain lasting happiness.
Removing diseases by moxibustion and bloodletting
are established practices of skilled physicians.

422 If your mind cannot bear
the prosperity of others,
that alone will destroy your affluence.
So this is just aiming jealousy at yourself.

423 If you destroy enemies because they cause harm,
you only need to obliterate your own hatred.
Because of hatred you have endured misery
beyond measure since beginningless time.

424 You may want to eradicate every foe,
but how can killing get rid of all of them?
You can slay all your foes at once
by destroying just your own anger.[96]

425 If you get angry at someone powerful and rash
they will harm you even more.
What reason is there for you to get angry
at holy people who are totally peaceful?

426 Leaves growing on a single branch
are scattered to the ten directions by the wind.

Similarly, people born as twins
have separate individual fates due to karma.

427 People embrace connections with those not seen before,
and then, once again, they die and migrate elsewhere.
If you have a relationship with this sort of person,
after they die it will cause you great suffering. [54]

428 If you strongly wish to accomplish your own goals
you should undertake the interests of others first.
Those who make only their own concerns primary
find it impossible to accomplish their own ends.

429 When people make the welfare of others primary
they are like tricksters seeking their own ends.
Those who make only their own welfare primary
are like honest people supporting others.

430 Even when the intelligent strive for this life,
they achieve happiness if they practice Dharma.
Look at the differences between the wealth and glory
possessed by holy men and thieves.

431 Half of a short human life
is spent sleeping like the dead.
Owing to the varied miseries of sickness and aging
there is no enjoyment in the other half.

432 When you actually see the Lord of Death
sitting in front of all living creatures
you will be unable to remember to eat,
to say nothing about doing anything else.

433 "Have you finished what you are doing?"
The Death Lord will not ask you and wait.
So if there are things that truly must be done
you must strive to do them this very day.

434 Even if, choked with tears, you plead,
"I have not finished what I'm doing,
so please wait for a while today,"
how can that sway the Lord of Death?

435 Abandoning distractions is happiness.
If that is impossible, befriend good people.
How can nurturing a poisonous snake be good?
If you do so, you had better work at saying mantras!

436 Someone whose mind is very distracted
never has the opportunity to practice the holy Dharma.
Someone whose mind is completely calm
is very close to having a serviceable mind. [55]

437 Someone who understands all appearances,
has tamed his mind with meditative stabilization,
and is well trained in the Dharma of the noble one
is a field of all good qualities.

438 Fools believe those who study are strange;
those who do not study astound the wise.
Thus even when the wise grow old
they continue learning for the sake of their future.

439 Because fools have no wisdom
they do not learn anything positive.
If they do contemplate, because of this lack of wisdom
fools must make extra effort to study.

440 Having seen that some are fools in this life
because they did not study in prior lives,
study hard in this life, even though it is difficult,
out of fear you will be born a fool in your next life.

441 "There is no need to study if you meditate,"
is said by fools with little intelligence.

Without study, mere meditation, even done assiduously,
is the way to be reborn as an animal.

442 The infallibility of the law of cause and effect
is the distinctive doctrine of the omniscient one.
If someone unlearned can become omniscient,
how could the law of cause and effect be true?

443 Meditation that is without learning
may bring temporary attainments, but they soon fade.
Even if you thoroughly melt silver and gold,
taken away from the heat they become hard.

444 The meditation that eliminates faults and their causes
is to examine the depth of reality with wisdom.
The results of concentration last for a while
but, like washing your body, dirt returns.

445 Even realizing selflessness will not result in Buddhahood
if the causes and effects of excellence are not complete.
If the way you see reality is not established by the supreme method,
then you will not even be an arhat. [56]

446 Therefore properly understand all phenomena,
and when you place your mind in equipoise
faults and their imprinted tendencies
will be eliminated and you will become fully enlightened.

447 Although the treatises are excellent,
can someone without intelligence appreciate them?
Although gold jewelry set with gems is lovely,
do cattle even look at it?

448 If the wise do not put into practice
the intent of all the good advice they have received,
even though they know it to be exactly right,
what good is their understanding of the treatises?

449 Every day take to heart some words
of advice that you need from the scriptures.
And just as anthills and honey are built up,
before long you will become wise.

450 If you wish to engage in proper behavior,
listen to whatever such a person says.
Always have the fortitude to do what is noble;
defend good conduct even at the risk of your life.

451 Thus if you can employ the antidotes with determination,
just as they are described in scriptures,
you will see the benefits of doing this in the future
for the wise do not speak what is false.

452 Those who acted like this in the past flourished.
We can see it is like this even for practitioners now.
This is a good way to infer that in the future
practitioners will enjoy perfect good fortune.

453 Intelligent people may understand on their own,
but they read the treatises of the wise with reverence.
Although a gemstone may be very fine,
it has little value until it is sold.

454 Although there are a lot of forests,
few are good for growing sandalwood.
Similarly, although there are many wise men,
it is hard to find a source of good advice. [57]

455 A good horse is identified when it is ridden.
Gold and silver are identified when melted down.
An elephant is identified in battle.
A wise man is identified when he composes good advice.

456 Someone who wishes to be considered
authoritative by everyone in the world

will succeed by examining this text well
and striving to cultivate the antidotes.

457 A person who thoroughly understands worldly activity
is adept in the method of the holy Dharma.
Thus the practice of the Dharma is indeed
the way of life of the bodhisattvas.

This concludes "An Examination of the Dharma," the ninth chapter of *A Jewel Treasury of Wise Sayings.*

Just as Kumāra Jīvaka cured the very ill
by convincing them that his medicines were food,
I have taught this holy Dharma
by following the customs of the world.

This marvelous *Jewel Treasury of Wise Sayings,*
which arose from an island amid an ocean of learning
and held by intelligent nāga kings, has been opened wide
by the Buddhist monk Kunga Gyaltsen Palsangpo
on the basis of examining things with a virtuous mind.
This is to help fill the treasurehouse minds of the intelligent ones
and to help the learned ones accomplish their wishes.

May the flawless virtues that arise from this composition
shine brightly like cooling rays of moonlight,
clearing away darkness from the hearts of living beings
and causing the flower of their intellect to blossom.

Through study of all that is to be known
the state of omniscience will be attained.
Therefore I composed this treatise
so that we may attain complete buddhahood.

This treatise entitled *A Jewel Treasury of Wise Sayings* was composed at the glorious temple at Sakya. It was written by the Buddhist monk and logician Kunga Gyaltsen Palsangpo, someone who resides at the splendid Sakya temple located in the Tö Drompa region of Tsang, in the northern land of snows, a hundred leagues from Bodhgaya, the crux of enlightenment. The author is one whose lotus of intelligence was opened a little by the rays of Mañjuśrī's wisdom, and as a result he studied, understood, and mastered grammar, logic, poetics, [58] rhetoric, expressive ornamentation, and the majority of the renowned scriptures of the Buddha. Through inquiry he attained an unmistaken understanding of the essence of the scriptures, logic, and quintessential instructions. It is this possessor of virtue, confident in the means of exposition, composition, and debate, who composed this treatise. [59]

3. A Commentary on "A Jewel Treasury of Wise Sayings"[97]

Rinchen Pal

I RESPECTFULLY BOW MY head to the feet of my revered teacher, who possesses great compassion.

> I always pray to the feet of the lama produced by the buddhas of the three times.
> He is free from conceptual elaborations and embodies every asset.
> He is a supreme Buddha, the light of the three realms, and our dearest friend.
> His omniscient eyes always benevolently gaze on transmigrating beings.
>
> I pay homage to the spiritual friend who is the axis mundi
> fashioned from precious things that are faultless objects of knowledge,
> unmoved by the winds of opponents' ideas,
> and who encompasses the ocean of stainless enlightened deeds.
>
> Your path comprehends the meaning, so it penetrates every existent and completely illustrates the nature of everything.
> From this joyful path came an exalted, festive teaching, a treasure of marvelous delight:
> It is a victory banner beyond compare, a victory banner of the teachings, a victory banner of wisdom and compassion,

well arrayed with splendor, immeasurable glory, and the stainless
perfection of all types of beings.
I will expand a bit on this lovely text that was beautifully conceived and elegantly written.[98]

The great being Sakya Paṇḍita Kunga Gyaltsen Palsangpo wrote many treatises that are essential for the well-educated: *Gateway for the Learned*, a treatise on poetics, rhetoric, figures of speech, and synonyms; *Bouquet of Various Flowers*, a treatise on composition; and *Treasury of Words*, a treatise of synonyms. Here in *A Jewel Treasury of Wise Sayings* his intent was to illustrate by way of examples the purpose of similes, such as the way they beautify the meaning, ornament by way of analogy, and clarify points by correlating analogies and their references. [60] Further, his intent was to explain the holy Dharma by relying on treatises of proper behavior for those who desire to become skilled in distinguishing correct from incorrect ordinary worldly actions.

Furthermore, in many places such as in the southern regions (India), when scholars meet with other scholars or rulers, those educated sophisticates are delighted by the gift of a new, previously unknown verse with superior connotative embellishments. Mere gifts of food and wealth are customary among women, merchants, and city dwellers, but that is not a custom particular to the learned. In that regard, Sakya Paṇḍita Kunga Gyaltsen Palsangpo thought it would be nice to have a gift of verses like this for the educated here in Tibet. That is why he wrote this text.

Invocation

The invocation has three topics: the words of invocation, the promise to explain, and the meaning of the title. The first topic, the words of invocation:

I prostrate to the omniscient leader of transmigrating beings,
he whose feet are honored with the touch of the lovely crowns
of great gods, nāga lords, and major mystics,
such as the sages Vyāsa, Vālmīki, Akṣapāda.[99]

The meaning of this verse is as follows: I too pay homage to our guide because all Buddhist texts say that the ascetics and supreme beings made offerings and paid homage to our leader—that is, the holy omniscient one descended from the solar dynasty. The great ones who offered their jeweled crowns to the dust below his feet include Brahmā, Indra, and all the other supreme gods who are lauded as honorable and praiseworthy by worldly beings; the many nāga lords including Nanda, Upananda, and Vāsuki; the universal monarchs Megavāhana and so forth; and the major mystics. This group also includes the great sages who taught the Vedas: Vyāsa, the father of Śuka; Vālmīki, the great sage who mastered asceticism by practicing on an ant hill; and the sage Akṣapāda, who cherished his religious observances and sponsored the composition of the text about how he became known as Nine-Headed Rudra. This occurred because when Śiva assigned him to guard the goddess Umā, [61] he looked at her and desired her lovely body. Therefore eyes descended from the heavens and remained on his throat, shoulders, palms, and soles of his feet.[100] Included among the "such as" are the many Parivarjikas, Vyāsa, and Supriya.

Now the second topic, the promise to explain, sets forth the meaning of the title of the text.

> This exposition is a jewel treasury of wise sayings
> pertaining to how respectable people behave,
> which, when examined with reason, does not contradict religion
> and helps accomplish all worldly activities.

The passage means that the author promises to teach this text in the way that gold is proved to be pure by three tests.[101]

The master Nāgārjuna said that faultless ordinary conduct is the means to attain liberation:

> If you properly practice ethical behavior,
> the journey to the god realm will not be long.
> If you thus ascend the stairs of men and gods,
> even the liberation of nirvāṇa will be close by.[102]

Master Āryadeva says:

> Various types of worldly behavior
> are said to be religious norms.
> Thus it seems as if worldly norms
> have more power than religious ones.[103]

The *Guide to the Bodhisattva's Way of Life* says:

> After observing and questioning all behavior
> distrusted by the world, you should abandon them.[104]

If you ask about the title of the text, the third topic, this was taught for those who wish to study every aspect of the conduct of upstanding people; as expressed in the above excerpts, it is called *A Jewel Treasury of Wise Sayings*. [62] This well-spoken advice is a heap or source of precious things. The *Uttaratantra* says:

> Because its arising is rare, because it is stainless,
> because it is powerful, because it is an ornament of the world,
> because it is supreme, and because it is immutable,
> it is truly a precious thing. [105]

This excerpt establishes the meaning of the title of the text.

The "meaning of the title" also refers to the purpose of the text, which is imparted in nine chapters. Many parts of the teaching are clearly found in the jātakas. An expansion on those can be seen in the bodhisattva corpus, the treatises of worldly behavior, and the teachings of the venerable lama Sakya Paṇchen Kunga Gyaltsen. Nevertheless I will write a bit about the scraps of instruction that I have obtained.

Chapter 1. An Examination of the Wise

1 The wise possess a trove of good qualities
because they amass precious wise sayings.
The great ocean is a treasury full of water
because all rivers flow into it.

This verse indicates that when you become wise you immediately achieve the best results and so on.

There is the ancient story of Sumāgadhā, the daughter of Anāthapiṇḍada, who lived in the pleasure garden of Śrāvastī.[106] A layman from the south wrote asking to marry her, but her father would not give her away. He received request after request. Then the father asked the Teacher. The Buddha said, "Give her away." So she was given in marriage. The girl was very unhappy after going to live in her married home. Her new relatives asked, "What is making you unhappy?"

She replied, "I am not unhappy."

"Well then, young woman, why do you look so blue?" they said.

She said to them, "There are no fields."

"There are fields! It takes a good part of a day just to walk to the middle of a single one!" they replied.

The young woman said, "That is not what I mean."

They inquired, "Well then, what kind of field?"

"There is no field for generosity."

They said, "We have that too. Look how many ascetics there are."

She said, "How can they be of use?"

Her relatives asked, "Well then, what is?"

She responded, "The Teacher, the Buddha." [63]

They all discussed that. In order to make the young woman happy, they called her in and said in acceptance, "We have conferred. Young woman, you may invite your teacher."

The young woman said, "Therefore prepare provisions worthy of inviting his sangha."

Her husband and the others said, "It is too soon to get ready. The road takes a month to travel." She said, "That doesn't matter, prepare!" As they got ready, the young woman went to the rooftop of the house. Holding an incense burner, she uttered clearly the words of her appeal to the Buddha to come.

The Teacher blessed her prayer so that it was heard by all the monks of Śrāvastī. The Teacher said to Ānanda, "Those of my monks with miraculous powers should take an inclusion stick and go there.[107] Those without miraculous power should remain here to beg for alms in town."

While everyone was doing that, a learned scholar without miraculous powers picked out a stick. "You don't have miraculous powers," said the others.

The scholar said, "I have abandoned what is to be abandoned. I have the wisdom that is able to comprehend. Thus I can achieve them right now. Just wait a bit." The scholar meditated and attained miraculous powers. Because he demonstrated them, the others developed faith. Thus the realizations of the learned come swiftly.

Then everyone traveled south on different vehicles: some sons of Śākya rode the elephant that is Indra's mount, some went on clouds, some rode on fragrant mountain incense, some rode on Mount Malayagiri, and some traveled on masses of snow. As each one arrived in the south, everyone there, with faith and humility, asked the young woman, "Is this your teacher?"

She replied, "No, he is not." She recounted the name of each one. For example, "This is Śāriputra, the best of my teacher's wise śrāvakas." At the end of the procession the Teacher himself arrived. The desire-realm gods were below him, the form-realm gods were above him, groups of bodhisattvas were to his right and left, and on his left many men and gods offered all sorts of inconceivable offerings.

At that point her father-in-law and the others asked, "Is this your teacher?"

"Yes," the young woman said, "this is my teacher." Once she so indicated, many people paid reverence with conviction. [64] They developed aspirational faith from being taught the Dharma. This development enables you to understand verse 219 of the root text:

> Rain and rivers fall to the sea.
> Intelligence and knowledge permeate the wise.
> Kings accumulate wealth and subjects.
> Forests grow where it is damp and warm.

This verse shows that a person who has become learned is a treasure trove of good qualities. Great beings delight in achieving the unexcelled results of good advice. Moreover, such a person does not give up endeavoring to do what is worth doing and what is proper to strive for.

There is a story regarding right behavior. Nāgārjuna created leaves for flying through the sky by using techniques that appear in the corpus of magical practices.[108] Holding two leaves he traveled to an island in the ocean to meet a sage who was a master alchemist. Nāgārjuna requested, "Please teach me alchemy."

The sage said, "For most people it is extremely difficult to get to this place. How did you manage to come here?"

The master Nāgārjuna hid one leaf and, showing him the other, said, "I came via the power of this leaf." The sage thought, "Using strategy I will separate him from this leaf. Then it will be OK to give him instruction in alchemy. Without the leaf he will not be able to go back to the land of men." With this deceptive thought, he said:

Knowledge is exchanged for knowledge,
or wealth can ransom knowledge;
sometimes knowledge is passed on to one's son,
but there is no way to get it if nothing is given in return.

Then he said, "First give me this leaf for sky travel. This is the price for instruction in alchemy." The master Nāgārjuna did as requested. He paid the price and received the special instructions. Then, holding the leaf that he had hidden, he flew off and returned to Jambudvīpa. Using alchemical processes, he helped all sentient beings.

In another story, the glorious Dharmakīrti had crossed to the far shore of the ocean of objects of knowledge. However, to set forth what is logical and what is not, and to refute the incorrect positions of other schools, he gave up the signs of being a Buddhist monk and grew a topknot so that he could study opponents' deceptive techniques, philosophical views, and so forth, with a teacher of Sāṃkhya.[109] For twelve years he pretended to be the Sāṃkhya teacher's disciple. [65] Although he acted as his servant, he did not obtain any special instructions. In order to get them, he got a youthful, attractive, and intelligent barmaid to do his bidding. The Sāṃkhya teacher with a topknot moved into her house. When the barmaid and the Sāṃkhya teacher lay together on the bed, the master Dharmakīrti hid underneath. Dharmakīrti had her ask about the Sāṃkhya teacher's philosophical positions that he had not understood previously. He listened from below. If he wasn't happy with the Sāṃkhya teacher's answer, from underneath the bed the master Dharmakīrti pulled a thin cord tied to the girl's leg. She would ask further questions so that the great ascetic's answers could be understood by Dharmakīrti.

And the scholar Vādisiṃha studied in order to master Dharmakīrti's seven expositions of epistemology and their commentaries. When he debated, however, he was confused about a few terms. Later, with his teacher, a paṇḍita, he studied a treatise called *Rājaśrī's Grammar.*[110] When he obtained the siddhi (powerful attainment) of speech so that no one could best him in debate, he voiced a verse of delight in his intellectual abilities:

O Vādisiṃha! When you set forth an argument
even Śiva is unable to understand the mere letters.

In such manner he proclaimed the power of his reasoning.

* * *

2 Among those who have knowledge and those who do not,
it is the wise who know what to do and what to avoid.
Iron filings that are mixed with dust
are identified when extracted by a magnet.

There once was a king called Bhojadeva in an Indian lineage. He was a magician skilled in the principles of mechanical devices. His palace had many sentries that were tall men carved from wood. When people came to the palace these guards would tie them to the spindle of a machine and beat them with cudgels and sticks. In addition, the king kept in his presence a monkey bodyguard who wielded a sword. Despite all this security, a local brahman went to rob the king's fortress in order to repay his gambling debts. There he saw a snake on top of the sleeping king. [66] The monkey bodyguard also saw the snake. He was about to strike it with his sword. The brahman thief could not tolerate that. He thought, "What does it matter if I die, but the death of this singular lord of men would be a great loss." So he grabbed the monkey's sword and shouted out. His shout woke the king from sleep. "What is the reason for this?" he asked. The brahman's good explanation delighted the king. He honored the brahman, saying:

> A wise man is good even if he is your enemy.
> A fool, even if he is your friend, is not.
> Look how the brahman thief prevented
> the king from being killed by the monkey.[111]

* * *

3 A wise person understands good advice,
but a fool's mind is not like that.
Owls will go blind
when the sun's rays shine.

Long ago there was an intelligent king called Brahmadatta.[112] He brought together many wise men, including the brahman scholar Vararuci, to debate. The king had great respect for the very learned Vararuci and gave him his daughter Suvarṇottamā in marriage. But the girl said, "I am more learned than he is. I will marry only a man who is a more learned master of the Dharma than I."

Vararuci was angered by that. He thought, "Since she has no respect for a scholar like me, that girl must be tricked." He searched throughout the city for a fool but did not find one. Then in a far-off place he saw a handsome cowherd with dull faculties. Vararuci could tell he was a fool. The youth was sitting at the very top of a tree and cutting the base below him. He said to himself, "I will teach him secretly and then I will say he is my greatly learned teacher. He will marry the girl and be the recipient of the king's gifts."

First he cleaned up the cowherd. He massaged his body with milk and prompted him to practice reciting "*Om svasti*." With the cowherd made up to look like a paṇdit, they entered the palace amid a crowd of people. Vararuci told the cowherd, "Say '*Om svasti*' while placing a flower on the king's head. Do not say anything to anyone else." When they were seated on their thrones, the cowherd placed a flower on the king's head [67] but forgot the phrase "*Om svasti*" that he had learned earlier. Instead he said "*Om sentur*." *Sentur* is an impolite word that means "big vaginal labia." Everyone was embarrassed and stared. When they began to reproach him, the scholar Vararuci said, "This very thing proves he is a wise man. You should say this word drawing out the sounds of each of the syllables—*om*, *sen*, *tur*. This way of saying it conquers pride."

The girl asked the cowherd disguised as a paṇḍita, "*Asti kaścitā vāga viśva*?" which can be rendered as "Do you possess some extraordinary speech?" But he made no reply at all.

Once again Vararuci spoke to rescue him: "How could my guru, a great wise man, give an answer to a woman?"

Then the young woman brought him to the palace. Once again she said the same words and again did not receive an answer. After that she took him to see the main temple. His eye was not drawn to any of the Buddha images. But when he saw the animal realm in the wheel of life behind the door, bad propensities connected to having previously lived with cattle awoke. Stretching his hand toward the image, he blurted out "buffalo" and so forth. She thought, "Now I'm sure that Vararuci has deceived us."

Upon deliberation, Suvarṇottamā thought, "If this man has any aptitude, I will teach him grammar, logic, and so forth. I will make him a greater master than Vararuci." She made him train his mind. His mind had no aptitude, so she made him do a Sarasvatī practice. But even after a long time at this he did not accomplish anything. So she made him practice saying a tongue-twister mantra in a Sarasvatī temple. Even that yielded no results. This depressed her. Now, to have him granted intelligence, she instructed her servant, a girl named Kāli, "You stand behind the clay statue of Sarasvatī in the old Sarasvatī temple. Just before dawn, make it seem that the statue is talking. Say, 'Do you want any attainments?' When he says, 'Please grant me attainments' and reaches out his hands, take a sweet out of the statue's mouth and put it into his mouth." She did as she was told. It seemed to the practitioner that Sarasvatī had given him a sweet. The instant he ate [68] it he became a great wise man. He composed three plays, including the *Kumārasambhava*, in answer to the young woman's earlier question as to whether some of those words were particularly special. From that time he was famed throughout the world as the scholar Kālidāsa—the slave of the servant girl Kāli.

A great scholar of that sort can intuit what someone's entire body is like merely by seeing the orb of their face. At one time an artist drew a portrait of the queen. He then asked Kālidāsa, "Is it a good likeness?" Examining it, Kālidāsa said, "It is very good likeness. However, she has a mole on her pudenda, so it is not complete in that regard." In consideration of that tidbit, the artist amended his work accordingly.

The king said, "Even I didn't know she had a mark like that! This man has definitely had intimate relations with her!" So he banished the scholar.

After a long time had passed the king assembled many poets and scholars in a hunt for a wise man who understood reality. He didn't find anyone. Finally, in order to test the scholars, the king, who was also a wise man, wrote a half verse asking a question:

> What is the cause that makes
> a lotus quiver in water?

He sent notices to every dwelling place—monasteries, royal palaces, humble homes, taverns, and so forth—saying, "If anyone knows the reason why, I will give him a great reward."

Because of this publicity, many people sent answers hoping for the reward. None of the responses pleased the king. At this time, Kālidāsa was staying in a tavern. Some men purchasing beer were talking about this noteworthy story. The other men did not know the answer, but Kālidāsa said, "I know why."

> It quivers because when the sun sets,
> a bee resting there wishes to fly away.

He offered this half verse as an answer to the question in the earlier half verse. The question and answer together form a complete verse.

The barmaid of that tavern coveted the king's reward. She killed the paṇḍita, buried his corpse, and went before the king. The king was impressed when shown the answer to the question. He asked her, "Who knew the reason?"

The barmaid said, "Me."

The king looked into it. He knew that it wasn't her. [69] When nothing came of questioning her, they went back to her house and found the corpse. Then the great lord Śiva brought him back to life. We have heard it said:

> Even the gods look after
> a man who is very wise.

* * *

4 Those with wisdom can eliminate their faults,
but the foolish cannot do so.
A garuḍa can kill poisonous snakes,
but a crow cannot do so.

A long time ago a king was investigating whether a man was worthy to be a minister.[113] So he made the young man, Mahauṣadhi Dāraka, care for a mule. Then after some time elapsed, he sent another man to steal it. The second man got the mule. When the king went to Mahauṣadhi Dāraka's place to take back his mule, the youth was riding on his father's back and beating him. The king said, "Why are you acting like that!"

"I am taming this father," he said.

The king said, "Oh my! In the world, spiritual teachers, the Three Jewels, and one's parents are to be venerated. You should give up behavior like this."

"O king, do not say that. As for veneration, it should go to the son. Why should it be for parents?" the young man said.

The king responded, "Because of parents' great kindness and so forth."

The young man said, "O king, if that is so, is it just my father who is to be held as good, or are other fathers good too?"

The king said, "In society, sons must hold as good all those who are parents." The young man gave the king a donkey and said, "If that is so, since this is the father of the mule, please take it, O lord of men!" The king admired the young man's intelligence and made him a minister.

* * *

5 When an intelligent person's situation worsens,
his intellect increases and becomes stronger.
When the king of beasts is hungry
he swiftly attacks an elephant's head.

As a reward for his service, the Indian king Dharmapāla made a man named *Jālika a minister.[114] When this bad man was granted power as a lord over many ordinary men, not heeding the king's kindness, [70] he murdered the king and exiled his two sons, Rāmapāla and Pāla, and seized the kingdom.

King Dharmapāla had had a minister named Paṇdit Vikṛti. Jālika said to him, "Because I did not kill you, you must be my minister."

He replied, "Indeed, you are the murderer of my lord. I will not serve as your minister." As a consequence, the king put him in a deep pit with very little for sustenance. Each day all he received to survive on was a three-finger pinch of parched flour and a similar ration of water. Just after three months, Jālika's minister went to see him. His entire body was completely covered in hair. He was pulled from the pit. Jālika said the same thing as before and received the same response. The evil king then said, "Because this man is very wise, I will refrain from killing him. But because he is an enemy, he is to be exiled." And so Vikṛti was exiled.

Then the minister Vikṛti went in search of his lord's two sons. After a while he found them amid a group of children. He drew the children around him. He pretended to be a brahman spiritual master. He sat cross-legged and put Rāmapāla on his lap as if it were a lion throne. Designating the other children to be ministers, army generals, and so on, he anointed Rāmapāla king. Later, when the children had grown up, he fixed a time to fight the murderer of the king. He assembled a few of every possible type of military troop and a herd of elephants to use as mounts.

The day before the battle, King Jālika had the faces of his elephants covered with nets of gold. This greatly angered the elephants, who did not understand why they were kept that way. Then when the opposing sides were set up for battle, the elephants' faces were uncovered. The elephants saw the enemy as their helpers. Extremely agitated, they turned around and crushed their own side's army. Thus Prince Rāmapāla was made king.

* * *

11 When the wise are protected by insight,
how can even multiple enemies harm them?
The brahman boy of Ujjayinī
conquered an entire host of enemies on his own.

It is said that in the environs of south India there was a great city called Ujjayinī.[115] [71] A dwarf named *Khapara lived there. He was a thief and had become very wealthy. Not very far away, a clever brahman youth named Śikhī lived with his old mother. They had no possessions other than a nanny goat. The youth thought about a means to find wealth, but he had no goods to trade and he wasn't able to do any sort of work. Then he saw the unworthy dwarf Khapara and decided to trick him. Śikhī borrowed some jewelry, good clothes, and so forth. He dressed up in them and prepared a small amount of special food. He set up a picnic and waited in the lane by the thief's house. When the thief came out Śikhī gave him portions of the food until he was satisfied. At that point the thief thought, "This man must be very wealthy."

When Khapara set out to rob him Śikhī instructed his mother to remain in the kitchen storeroom and not say anything. He left a chest, empty except for a dish made of bell metal, in front of a gap in the wall where the thief would come in during the darkest part of the night. Śikhī thought, "The thief is certain that I am very wealthy, so now he will think the box is filled with gold coins and come in." When the thief leaned into the chest Śikhī slammed it shut with the thief inside. "You did this and that to harm every group and individual, and now you are trying to steal a brahman boy's only possession, a single plate. Since you are like this, why shouldn't I hand you over to the king?"

The thief replied, "You are right. However, do not commit me to the king. I'll give you whatever riches you desire." In the end they agreed on a ransom of five hundred gold coins. The youth sent his mother with the ransom message. And she was to command that the coins be delivered very secretly. When this occurred he set the thief free.

Then the youth thought, "Since I did this to such a man, he will definitely come to kill us." So he prepared to go to a city called Pāṭaliputra in the south. He wrapped each of the five hundred gold coins in a leaf and fed them to their only possession—the goat. Then he and his mother set out. On the road he asked a householder, "May we stay the night?"

"Certainly," said the householder, and invited them in for the night. [72]

To pay the little owed, Śikhī struck the goat's stomach with his fist. The goat vomited up a gold coin and the youth gave it to the householder. "What is this?!" asked the householder.

"This nanny goat is called Source of Various Precious Things. She is a wish-fulfilling goat."

The householder said, "Sell her to me!"

He said, "I will not sell," even when the householder urged, "You must sell her to me, do not refuse!" In the end he sold the goat for ten thousand gold coins.

Then the youth instructed the householder: "Feed her grass and water and so forth. Ask her for a gold coin and punch your fist into her stomach, and you will get what you wish. At first do this gently. Then gradually ask with more and more force and you will get more." After he explained this method Śikhī left only around a hundred coins in the goat's stomach. He removed the rest of the coins and carried them off. In order to avoid robbers he sent his old mother along one road and he went on another. The two planned to meet in Vārāṇasī.

The rich householder did as he had been told. He was made very happy when he got something by punching only one or two times. Then when no more gold coins came out he kept punching and the goat died. At that point he knew he had been deceived.

Meanwhile the brahman youth traveled a long time. In the middle of a dense forest he came across a bear afflicted by hunger. In their struggle there was nothing else he could do other than twist the bear's ears in his hands. Because the two struggled for a long time, his chest jacket ripped apart and the cloth pouch holding the gold coins was torn. The coins scattered, covering the ground all around.

At that time a prince, the son of the king of the city of Mathurā, beautifully adorned himself and his horse and went out for a refreshing interlude. He saw this fearsome struggle. "Tell me who you are and why you are doing this!"

The only sound Śikhī made was "uhn uhn."

"I am the king's son, so you must speak!"

Śikhī said, "*Sva ha lo*" ("So be it!").

Again the prince asked his question.

Now Śikhī said, "You are doing me great harm. I am propitiating the god of wealth."

"What god is this?" asked the prince.

Śikhī said, "This is a demon who has taken the form of a bear. I want it to grant me supernormal power."

The prince asked, "What power will it get you?"

The brahman youth said, "Does the prince not see this rain of gold? This is it."

The prince said, "It is so." And in great amazement, he said, "Confer it to me."

Śikhī replied, "You wouldn't be able to do this practice. [73] There isn't another practice as special as this in the world. It is more precious than even life. Please do not ask me."

The prince said, "Take my horse, my jewelry, and so forth and in return reveal the instructions to me!" Śikhī replied, "Even if you put all these things of yours together, it wouldn't be worth a hundred thousand gold coins. I get that much every day from this demon. However, I agree, let's do it. You can propitiate this god of mine now. I'll propitiate another one." This made the prince happy. The brahman youth pressed the bear's ears into the prince's hands and taught him the method of practice. He gave him the oral transmission of this mantra: "*Om*! Seeking the opportunity to twist. Oh my, what a wonderful hope! Later it will be obvious. You will understand. *Hung hung hung sva ha*." He gave him this profound mantra recital along with its particular practice.

The prince's horse, jewelry, and so forth were now Śikhī's. He gathered up the scattered gold coins and went to Vārāṇasī. There some merchants from the estate of the householder who had bought the goat before recognized him. They reported Śikhī to their lord, who, in turn, presented the case to the king. The merchant appealed to the king, "Please entrust this evildoer to me, a man of substance." The king handed the brahman youth over to the rich householder who had been deceived.

The householder had the youth tied up in a gunny sack. Two coolies came to carry him off on their heads. When they neared the River Ganges, Śikhī urinated, and it dripped on the heads of the men carrying him. "Even now this guy is doing stuff!" they said. Delegating a young cowherd to watch him, the men went to wash. The cowherd then asked Śikhī what was going on. "I am the son of the king. He won't give me leave to go practice the Dharma. So they have tied me like this, and despite what I want I will be made king."

The cowherd said, "You shouldn't say that."

Śikhī responded, "Now since I recollect death I aspire to practice the Dharma. You should become king in my place!"

The cowherd said, "That is not possible."

The brahman youth replied, "It is possible. Get in the bag now, and do not come out until it is placed on the jeweled throne. The person seated on the throne is the king." The talk of riches made the child keen to become king. He got into the sack, and the brahman climbed to the top of a tree and hid there.

Then the men came back and lifted the bag on their heads. One said, "Why has the load become so light?"

His partner said, "It seems lighter, but it isn't. Everyone knows that a burden seems lighter after you take a rest and drink some water." Without checking further, they went to the bank of the Ganges. [74] Recounting in detail all of Śikhī's deceptions one by one, they threw the sack in the river.

Then Śikhī retrieved the horse, lovely ornaments, and so on that he had before. He went to the door of the rich householder who had meant to have him thrown in the Ganges. He called to the rich man, "Come on down!"

When he came out, the householder said, "How did you come here? Aren't you dead?"

The brahman said, "Hey! I'm alive and very happy. Look at my horse and ornaments! You have been very kind to me and I have come to repay your kindness. I will give you a gift of many precious things, gold and so forth."

The rich householder said, "How can this be?" Śikhī responded, "Because you had me thrown in the river, I was granted the domain of an underwater lord who died this year. He had possessions inconceivable even to the mystic vidhyādharas. These are his things."

The householder said, "Is it like this only for you, or can anyone go there? Can everyone have all this?"

The brahman said, "If other people go there, they can have a kingdom like I have. Nowadays there are lots of them."

The householder said, "I am going there too!"

"OK," said Śikhī, "then you should go the right way. The right way is exactly like before." He wrapped the rich householder in a coarse sack and threw him in the Ganges.

Then he went to Vārāṇasī. He wanted revenge on the king who had not protected him. To trick the king of Vārāṇasī, he went and asked for an audience with the father of the prince killed by the bear. He was granted that. Śikhī said to this king, "Where has your son gone?"

The king said, "He is seated on the jeweled throne of a kingdom."

Śikhī said, "Oh, that is certainly not the case. How do I know that?

Because I saw him murdered through the doings of your enemy, the king of Vārānasī."

The king said, "That is not true!"

Śikhī said, "It is true. It is as I say." And he showed him the prince's horse and jewelry.

The king said, "It is true." And he commanded, "Now you must kill the evil king of Vārāṇasī!"

Śikhī said, "It is easily done! May I make whatever arrangements are necessary?"

The king said, "Make it so!"

Then Śikhī went before the king of Vārāṇasī and said, "Do you want to kill your enemy, the king of the central land of Mathurā, or not? If you want to kill him, you should know that I am his favorite."

The king said, "What proof do you have?"

Śikhī said, "For proof I can get any of the king's best ornaments."

The king of Vārāṇasī said, "Well then, bring me his jeweled crown." In accord with that command, Śikhī took what was asked for and returned. By that and many other measures, he deceived and deluded the king of Vārāṇasī into trusting him. Then Śikhī led the king of Vārāṇasī and a small retinue to the castle of the king of the central land of Mathurā. When they entered, the outer door was shut behind them. Śikhī gave the sign that they were inside, saying, "We have arrived." The king of Mathurā's forces killed the king of Vārāṇasī. The Mathurā king took the defeated king's wealth and gave the kingdom of Vārāṇasī to Śikhī.

* * *

14 Even if the wise are misled,
they are not perplexed about what to do.
Ants may be sightless creatures,
but they are quicker than those with sight.

People with wisdom cannot be confused by others. In a country called Vārāṇasī there was an evil and avaricious king.[116] He cared only for his own enjoyment and paid no attention to anyone, not even to his entourage. At that time in that region there was a rich brahman. A wellspring appeared inside his house as a result of his former merit. Whatever material things he desired came from the well. When he became very wealthy, the brahman said, "I will invite the king to honor him."

His daughter said, "That would not be good. This king is very greedy. He will steal our well."

The brahman said, "Do not be so suspicious!" And so he hospitably honored the king.

The evil king thought, "I must separate this brahman from his wealth." When he returned to his palace, the king sent a messenger to say, "Oh! I have heard it said that you have a good well in your house. You must send it to me on loan for a few days. If you do not, I will punish you!" The meaning was obvious.

The brahman was terrified and regretful. He thought, "Alas! This king is someone who speaks contemptible words. It is indubitable. He certainly will steal my great wealth." Thinking this way about the good qualities of his house and so forth, he became very depressed and confused. [76]

At that point the brahman's daughter asked her father what was the matter. When he explained, she said to her father with a sad laugh, "Father, you have perfected the three types of knowledge, so why are you confused about how to respond to this little thing?"

Her father said, "True, but this has never been heard of before. His words surely indicate that we will be harmed!"

The girl said, "No, that will not happen. You should say, 'I promise to offer you the well. However, although I want to give it to you, the well will not go. It says it must have an entourage if it goes to the proud king's palace. Without one it won't go.' Send this verse in reply to the lord of men."

> Wealth attracts wealth,
> just as elephants do elephants.[117]
> O King, please send me a well;
> then my well will come to you.

They explained the meaning of the verse to the king's emissary and had him convey the verse to the king.

The king assembled his ministers. "Send an army to bring me the brahman's well!" he ordered. "If that doesn't happen, I will cut off your heads!"

The ministers went to confer. "This king says very imprudent things. If we don't kill him, there will be other unworthy commands like this present one. Let's kill him." They went back and killed the king.

Thus the king's evil intentions were not brought to completion and the brahman was saved from punishment. This is clearly the way to understand the meaning of verse 314 of the root text.

Accept food and wealth that were acquired properly;
reject coveting inappropriately gotten things.
Pick fruit from high in a tree,
but reach beyond that and you will fall to the ground.

* * *

17 If you know how it's done, how can it be hard
to employ even the great as your servants?
Even though a garuḍa is very powerful,
the golden-clad one made him his mount.

We have heard that Golden-Clad is one of the names of Viṣṇu, as is, for example, Wheel-Bearer, Wrathful-Expression, and Consort-of-the-Goddess.[118]

When Viṣṇu and the garuḍa were brawling, [77] Viṣṇu was not able to conquer him because of the garuḍa's special strengths. Viṣṇu called for a peace conference, intending to employ a strategy to trick him. When the fighting ceased and they were in their normal states, Viṣṇu said, "Oh my! I admire your ability to subdue opponents. So now ask me for a boon and I will grant it."

The garuḍa was very arrogant and said, "Oh my! How could it be possible for someone great to ask for a boon from an inferior? You ask me for a boon and I'll give it to you!"

Viṣṇu repeated himself and got the same response. After the third time, Viṣṇu said, "Let it be so. Since you are very fast and powerful you must be my mount!"

So it came to be. The garuḍa was subjugated. He was tricked by Viṣṇu's strategy and his own arrogant anger. From then until today the garuḍa has been Viṣṇu's mount.

* * *

18 Wisdom is what produces happiness
in this life and future lives.
The wisdom of Prince Candra
saved Sudāsa in this and future lives.

This is the jātaka of Prince Candra of the illustrious royal lineage of the Kuruvamśe.[119] He had great respect for spiritual teachers and the elderly. He loved the miserable and downtrodden. He was adorned with many good qualities by nature and education.

At one time Sudāsa, a king in the South whose name translates as "excellent servant," had gone into the forest to practice archery and so forth. There a libidinous lioness accosted him. She dragged the king away and forced him to copulate with her.

Eleven months later, the lioness gave birth to a son. He had a handsome form from his father's side. From his mother's side he had body hair, a liking for meat, physical strength, and ferocity. Although the prince was named Kalmāṣapāda, he became known by the name Lion Sudāsa. When he grew up he inherited his father's kingdom. As was customary for kings, he had many queens, and among these he had two favorites. He commanded these two: "Tomorrow I will go for a walk in the pleasure gardens. [78] I will always make love to the one who comes into my path first. I will not touch the one who arrives later."

The two great queens adorned themselves with clothing and jewelry and set out at the same time. On the road there was a temple. One of the queens got down from her mount to pray, so she fell a bit behind. The other one arrived first. She was made the foremost queen of the king. The queen who had fallen behind became furious because she was ignored. She said to the temple deity, "Because I, this woman, worshiped you for a while, I was left behind and did not become the king's favorite queen. If you had any power, you should have been my friend!"

Later she made a plea to the king: "Please let me do what I wish for one day." The king granted her request. Then she destroyed the temple.

The temple deity was angry so he decided to harm the king. He went to the door of the palace. At that very moment he saw the sage who was Prince Kalmāṣapāda's officiating priest going elsewhere to eat. This sage was served only the three pure foodstuffs and so forth. The deity seized this opportunity. He transformed himself into the shape of the sage and went inside. He said to the cook, "From now on serve me meat."

The cook said, "I must ask the king."

When asked, the king said, "Oh my! It is extremely strange for an ascetic to eat meat. But there is nothing else we can do. Serve him what he wants now." The cook served him meat. The imposter sage ate it and left.

The next morning when the real ascetic officiating priest came to eat he was served meat. He demanded of the serving woman, "Who said to serve meat to me?"

She replied, "The king said so."

That infuriated the sage and he hurled a curse: "King! You will eat human flesh for twelve years!" After saying this he went to another kingdom.

Soon thereafter a virtuous monk gave one-day precepts to the city dwellers. Because they forswore killing, the king's cook was not able to find any meat. Seeing no other alternative, she went to the charnel ground and found the corpse of a child who had just died and had been carried there. She cut off some of its flesh and secretly prepared it.

Finding it very tasty, the king said, "What kind of meat is this?" [79]

The terrified servant could not speak. The king ordered, "You will not be punished, speak!"

The servant explained why meat was difficult to find and said, "This is the flesh of a deceased child."

The king ordered, "From now on, prepare this kind of meat!"

Then the cook said, "It cannot be obtained."

The king ordered, "Steal it in secret!" She did as she was told. On many occasions one of the city's children was lost. The city folk conferred. They lay in wait at a narrow point of the road and seized the king's servant, who was carrying a child. They reported this to the king.

He said, "I gave the order for this. You keep quiet."

Then the ministers and city folk deliberated. They gathered up a large army and surrounded the palace. They were going to kill the king. The king could find no escape route from the palace, so he went to the roof. He prayed, "By the power of whatever seeds of virtue are in my consciousness, may I instantly become a cannibal demon who knows how to fly!" With that power, he flew into the sky and fled the palace. Thereafter he lived in a powerful fortress in a cemetery and continually engaged in many activities beyond the realm of ethical behavior. Killing and eating the city folk one at a time, he became known as the cannibal prince Kalmāṣapāda.

In particular, he made a vow to slaughter and offer as a sacrifice a thousand princes all at once. He held the princes in prison. When he was short by just one prince, the bodhisattva Prince Candra and his entourage came near Kalmāṣapāda's abode. A brahman from another area approached Prince Candra in search of a kind donation. He pleased the bodhisattva with four verses. Just then the bodhisattva prince saw all the assembled people flee. "What is going on?" he wondered. Then he saw the disturbance was caused by a king wearing filthy clothing, wielding a sword, a shield, and so forth. He went to him and said, "Oh! Please wait. I am the man called Prince Candra."

As soon as he said that, the wrathful and savage Kalmāṣapāda carried the bodhisattva off to his abode on his shoulders.

After arriving there Kalmāṣapāda was amazed by the bodhisattva's radiance. Placing the bodhisattva in front of him, [80] he sat down and examined him in detail. The bodhisattva was thinking, "Alas! I did not satisfy the wishes of that brahman who offered me the gift of good advice. How can I do that now?" As soon as he thought that, tears came to his eyes.

At this point King Kalmāṣapāda laughed, "Now that you are in my hands, it is right for you to feel fear like that!"

The bodhisattva said, "How could I be afraid of being in your hands? Nevertheless I feel like this." He explained the former situation with the brahman and said, "Therefore you should let me go for a short time. Once I satisfy the sage I will return to gratify you."

Kalmāṣapāda said, "Right, absolutely. How could your excuse deceive me? Is it possible to be freed when caught in the jaws of death?"

The bodhisattva said, "Do not equate an evil-natured person like yourself with me. I am Prince Candra. I am foremost among those who speak only the truth."

Kalmāṣapāda could not withstand that speech, and he thought, "When I examine what he said, I believe he might return. Even if he doesn't come back, since I already have nearly one thousand princes, getting just this one is of no matter." So he said, "If that is so, go and come back quickly. I will prepare a fire to cook you."

Then the bodhisattva prince left the evil king's abode. He gave the brahman a thousand grams of gold for each verse. At that point his father, the king, said, "The kingdom too depends on wealth. If you protect its wealth, the kingdom will succeed. It is appropriate to give brahmans only clothing, mounts, and so forth."

In response the prince said, "Father, what are you saying? If you could put a price on this advice, wouldn't giving the entire kingdom for one verse be too little?" He said this and more.

Because the prince was going to return to Kalmāṣapāda, his father used many specific reasons and methods to stop him. He said, "It is not right for you to cultivate the teaching's method practices like this. That is not any great kindness to me. Please do not make me suffer with worry." The king, the assembly of ministers, ordinary people, and so forth all made urgent requests to dissuade him from returning. Nevertheless the bodhisattva set forth alone on the road to the great cemetery. [81]

Seeing the prince coming, Lion Sudāsa was amazed and disbelieving. He prepared a huge fire and waited. When the bodhisattva arrived, Lion Sudāsa said, "Tell me what was the particular benefit of that offering you said that you went to make? Tell me the meaning of the instructions you received from the brahman."

In response the bodhisattva said, "What use is good advice to someone with an evil nature like you? Now just go ahead and eat me!"

Lion Sudāsa said, "I can wait a bit before I eat. And anyway, the roasting pit is still smoking. Meat roasted on a smokeless fire is tastier. Explain that good advice to me for a while."

The prince responded as before. Although the prince objected a second time, Lion Sudāsa persisted in asking a third time.

Then the bodhisattva saw that it was the right time to tame him, so he said, "If that is to be so, you must listen with the right behavior for listening to Dharma. As to that behavior":

> Sit on a very low seat.
> Fully develop marvelous self-control.
> Observe with joyful eyes,
> as if drinking the nectar of the words.
> Practice the preliminaries and focus only on this.
> Have faith and do not look for faults.
> Like a sick person, listen to the physician's words.
> With these preliminaries listen to the Dharma.[120]

Then Lion Sudāsa took off his filthy shirt and spread it on a large, flat rock. He placed the bodhisattva on top of it. Placing himself in the bodhisattva's sight, he said, "Noble one, now please speak." The bodhisattva made this profound and melodious speech:

> Whether you encounter holy beings
> for just a moment or for as long as you wish,
> without the need of your request
> there will be excellent instruction.[121]

Lion Sudāsa was pleased and said, "Great sage, please say more." The bodhisattva said to him:

Never be away from holy beings;
always rely on them in a virtuous manner.
If you are near them, all their good qualities
will rub off on you and you will understand.[122]

"What I am hearing is true. Please say more now." The prince nodded his head and, snapping his fingers, said this:

You should honor in every way
the virtuous who give good advice. [82]
Give them gifts of wealth and lands.
Exert yourself and what you seek will befall you.[123]

"Please say more," Lion Sudāsa said.

Royal carriages ornamented with jewels and gold,
and even our bodies, age and become ugly.
The holy ones' religious practices never get old;
they exhibit passion for the good qualities of virtue.[124]

"You have let fall a stream of nectar. Because of that I feel great inspiration. Now please speak," said Lion Sudāsa. So again the prince spoke:

Greater than the distance between the earth and the sky,
greater than the distance between the ocean's near and far
 shores,
greater than the distance between the mountains where the sun
 rises and sets,
is the distance between the ethics of ordinary and holy men.

This discourse made Lion Sudāsa become faithful and astonished. Once again he spoke: "O Sage, in return for your advice, please accept four promises from me."

The bodhisattva said, "Who would ask for a great favor from someone without any shame like you?"

Lion Sudāsa hung his head and said, "Do not doubt me like that." The bodhisattva said, "In that case":

Engage in honest behavior. Cease killing living beings.
Let go every one of those you have imprisoned.
You, powerful one, give up eating human flesh.
These are the best promises. Give up these four.[125]

Lion Sudāsa said:

I grant you the first three promises.
Please ask something else for the fourth vow.
I cannot eat that which is not human flesh.
Didn't you know this before?[126]

In response Prince Candra utterly reproved him with many reasons. He said the following and more:

Eating human flesh is the source
of the ruin of your spiritual and temporal
happiness and repute.
O how could it not be right to give it up?[127]

Lion Sudāsa freed all the princes he held in prison and established each of them in their own kingdom. The lion prince went back to his father's realm and the conditions of his rule were happy. By always upholding his layman's vows he established everlasting happiness. Thus it is said that Sudāsa was saved in this and future lives. If someone says, "It is better to say, 'Lion was saved in this and future lives,'" I say that Sudāsa is how he is primarily known in the world. [83]

* * *

25 An intelligent person may be physically weak,
but what can a powerful enemy possibly do?
Although the king of beasts was powerful,
an intelligent rabbit killed him.

A rabbit and a lion lived together for a long time in one place.[128] The lion had a very haughty nature. Because the other creature was less powerful, the lion bullied and injured him many times. Finally the rabbit became irritated and angry. He thought up a plan and said, "O lord, please bear with the regrettable thing I have come to say. Another creature, who looks just like you, my lord, said, 'If there is someone able to challenge me, let us compete. If he cannot do that, then he will be my servant.'"

The lion became even more arrogant and said, "Where is he? I shall challenge him just as he said." They went with the rabbit leading the way.

The rabbit showed him a very deep well and explained, "He is in there."

The lion went to the mouth of the well. He saw his reflection and thought it was his enemy. When he growled, the other one seemed to growl. When he put on a show of ferocity, the reflection also acted ferocious. When he bared his fangs, the other one appeared to bare his fangs, and so forth. No matter how he postured, the other did the same. Then the lion jumped on his opponent. He fell into the well and died. The clever rabbit won the battle.

This concludes "An Examination of the Wise," the first chapter of *A Jewel Treasury of Wise Sayings*.

Chapter 2. An Examination of the Cultivated

46 If you assist an excellent person
even in a small way, it will bear fruit.
Look how the man who gave a single sour fruit
became equal to the righteous king's son. [84]

This verse reveals the difference between the happiness and suffering that come from associating with companions who have good or bad characters, respectively.

Once there was a father and son.[129] When the father was on the brink of death he gave his son this advice: "Now I am going to die. You should not rely on or befriend those who have a bad character and little wisdom. Stay with those who are their opposites."

Then to test the truth of his father's words, the son went to serve an evil king as a courtier. He found a girlfriend with a wicked nature and settled down with her. After a while he and the king went into the forest. A man-eating tiger came at the king. It was about to kill him when the young man slashed the tiger's throat with his sword. The king was pleased and said, "You have been very kind. You have saved my life."

Then, sometime later, the young man stole the king's dear pet, a dancing peacock. He entrusted it to a friend to hide. Then he brought a peacock that he caught in the forest to his wife and said, "I saved the king from a tiger. Although I helped him that way, I got nothing for my kindness in return. Now I will kill the king's peacock." The couple dined on its meat.

Then the king realized his peacock was lost. He sent out envoys to search for it. He announced, "I will give a reward of whatever he desires to the person who finds my peacock."

Desiring to obtain the reward for herself, the young courtier's spouse went and told. The king said, "It was my beloved, why did he kill it?" She explained the earlier matter.

The king ordered, "Summon him now!" When the young man came, the king said, "Did you kill my peacock?"

The courtier said, "I killed it."

The king said, "Why?" and the young man explained the reason as before.

The king said, "Servants are supposed to serve. Why should their kindness be considered? Execute this man now!"

At that point the young man knew that the king had a bad character. He gave back the king's dancing peacock, abandoned his spouse, and departed.

To test the truth of his father's words further, the young man found a good king and an ill-bred friend and settled down.[130] On one occasion he and the king went into the dense forest together. The summer heat was extremely oppressive and the king became very thirsty. The young man said, "Lord, please have my three tiny sour fruits that are suitable for consumption." The king was pleased and said, "You have saved my life."

At that time the king had a single son. The young man kidnapped the boy. [85] He entrusted the prince's clothes and ornaments to his friend and instructed him: "Conceal these."

Then the king promised: "I will give a huge reward to the person who finds my son."

When this resolve was widely proclaimed, the friend, desiring the reward, went and informed. The king said, "This cannot be true."

The bad man said, "It is true," and showing him the prince's things, said, "These are his ornaments."

The king believed him. "It is true." He ordered: "Bring him here now!"

Because the young man was summoned, he came. The king asked, "Is it true? Did you kill my son?" The courtier said, "It is true." The king ordered: "Execute him now!"

The courtier said, "O King, have you forgotten the kindness I extended toward you?"

The king said, "What kindness?"

When he recounted the history of the earlier incident, the king remembered. He said, "It is true. You did me a kindness. But now you are also the person who has caused me the great loss of my son. So to repay the kindness of the first small, sour fruit, I release you from the death penalty. To repay the kindness of the second one, I give you my daughter in marriage. To repay the kindness of the third, I give you half of my kingdom."

The young man now knew the king's character. With respect he said, "How can I accept these rewards from the king? How could I have dared to kill your noble son?" Then he brought forth the prince and promised, "I will obey your commands."

This story makes clear the wisdom of his father's advice and the couplet from verse 45 of *A Jewel Treasury of Wise Sayings.*

> A noble and an ordinary man may be treated the same,
> but their gratitude will be not equivalent.

* * *

48 The great may experience a decline at some point,
but they need not feel miserable about that.
Although the moon is occasionally eclipsed,
it is immediately freed afterward.

If you ask, "How can that be?" Patience, the verse is like the story about the Prince of Vārāṇasī and will be explained.[131]

As to that story, a man with very good qualities, known as the mahārāja prince of Vārāṇasī, had no sons from his twenty thousand queens. After propitiating the gods for a long time, the foremost queen and a queen from the middle ranks became pregnant. The foremost queen had an amicable nature; she was a religious woman and so had become peaceful and composed. [86] The middle-ranked queen was the opposite. For this reason, the brahmans named their sons *Śubhārtha, Virtuous, and *Papārtha, Sinful. By the time the two were twelve there were indications of what their future behavior would be like. Papārtha was jealous of his elder brother. Their parents understood this.

Sometime later Śubhārtha saw the distress of farmers, laborers, and women spinning thread. He saw the harm done to sheep, buffalo, and so forth. His compassion arose. So he said to his father, "Please grant me a request."

His father said, "I grant it."

"Then give our wealth to the poor."

"Let it be so," said his father. Then they summoned the poor from the four directions and gave everything away.

At that point the ministers convened. They said, "The kingdom depends on wealth. Since there is nothing left now, we must find some way to generate income." To that end, one suggested trade, another suggested agriculture, yet another suggested animal husbandry, and one said, "Let us get jewels from the far ocean."[132]

The prince said, "That is right. Please let me be the one to go to sea." His parents would not give him permission. The prince said, "Then I will die right here."

His mother said, "O King, please give him permission. It is quite possible that he will come back from the journey. Even if he does not return, most likely he will not die. However, if he does not get permission he will die right now."

Because of her words, the king summoned everyone and announced, "You may go with five hundred merchants."

In addition, the king entreated a maritime expert who lived in Vārāṇasī to go along. The maritime expert was worried and said, "Only one or two of those who go to the sea live to return. O King, why did you give him permission?"

The king said, "I could not oppose my son's request. Please be his captain."

"Well then, I will go."

Papārtha was very disturbed. He thought, "He will acquire jewels. How can it be fair if I do not get any too?" So he went too.

When they all arrived at the boats, the captain said, "Anyone who is not at ease should go back now." He said the same thing every day. Then when a favorable wind arose they departed. Because of Śubhārtha's merit and compassion they quickly crossed the ocean. Then the maritime expert gave these instructions, "Take only what the boat will handle. If you take too much, it will sink and the journey will have been pointless."

Śubhārtha said to the others, "Now you may return home to be happy. I am going to search for a wish-fulfilling jewel." He and the maritime expert traveled across waters only knee-deep for seven days. [87] Finally they reached a place where the sand was silver and gold. The maritime expert said, "I am exhausted and will die here. Go east for seven days and you will reach a mountain of gold. Then go on for seven more days to find ruby lotuses. After seven more days, there will be jewel poppies. Beyond that there is a stronghold of seven treasures. Inside it there lives a nāga king. You must ask for the precious gem in his left ear." Then Śubhārtha lifted the captain onto his lap. After weeping he surrounded the captain's body with golden sand and departed for the nāga's realm.

On the way, under a lotus there was a snake that was poisonous to the touch and even to sight. The prince meditated on love and the snake went to the top of the lotus.

He arrived at the gate of the nāga king's castle. He knocked to go inside. In front of the door he saw two crystal girls spinning thread of crystal. "Who are you?" he asked. "We are servants who guard the nāga king's outer door. You must pass through four middle doors made of silver and eight inner doors of gold."

When the Prince of Vārāṇasī came before the nāga king, the king thought, "This is not an ordinary person. Who is he?" The nāga king asked, "Why did you come here?"

The prince said, "The people of the world are destitute. I came to ask for the precious jewel that will relieve the suffering of poverty."

The nāga said, "This jewel is very difficult to obtain. But since you are working hard for others, I will give it to you." And he gave it to him. Śubhārtha departed carrying the jewel wrapped up in a piece of ordinary cloth. Because of the jewel's power he could fly, and in an instant reached the shore of the ocean. There he met his younger brother.

Śubhārtha asked, "What are you doing here? Where have your companions gone?"

He replied, "The boat sank and everyone died. I held on to a corpse and came up here."

Śubhārtha said, "It will be all right. The most precious thing in the world is your body."

The corpses in the charnel grounds are said to utter the epigram, "It is fine to die rich. What point is there in being poor and alive?"

Śubhārtha said to him, "As for that, I have the jewel."

The younger brother said, "Show it to me! Where did you put it?"

"In this bundle," he said. And then he said to his younger brother, "When you are tired, I'll guard it. When I'm tired, you guard it. You guard it now. I need to sleep."

The younger brother was hostile toward his brother because of his parents' earlier favoritism. [88] He said, "I'll take care of it, you go to sleep." Then when Śubhārtha was sleeping, his younger brother stabbed his eyes with bamboo slivers.

Śubhārtha shouted, "Thieves have come! Take the jewel and run!" Then he heard nothing at all. Śubhārtha thought, "My younger brother has been killed and the jewel carried off." Although his eyes were very painful, the thought of his younger brother's death was more painful still.

Then a tree spirit said, "It was your younger brother who stabbed you with bamboo splinters. The enemy who did this is your younger brother." Śubhārtha was downcast.

Papārtha took the jewel and went to his parents. He said, "I acquired this!" When asked about his elder brother, he said, "He drowned." Both his parents fainted dead away. Cold water was thrown over them to revive them. Papārtha became angry because they loved his elder brother, so he hid the jewel.

Meanwhile Śubhārtha had no way to remove the bamboo slivers from his eyes. He writhed on the ground in pain. Eventually he made his way to the domain of King Liśī in the empire of Vārāṇasī. The daughter of this king and Śubhārtha, the prince of Vārāṇasī, had been betrothed as children. At that place there was a cowherd who had charge of five hundred cows. He let the cows out of their pen. Śubhārtha was right in the path of the herd that was keen to reach grass and water. He was about to be trampled when the best cow of the herd sheltered him. She licked Śubhārtha's eyes and the bamboo slivers came out.

The cowherd asked him who he was. Because Śubhārtha still loved his younger brother and doubted that his brother had harmed him, when asked to explain his background, he said, "I am a destitute blind man."

The cowherd examined him and saw he had many good features. He said, "We are near my house, I'll provide for you." And he led him to his home. Thereafter the cowherd gave him his own rations. When barely a month passed, he said to himself, "I cannot survive like this now."

Hearing this Śubhārtha was saddened and said, "I must go."

The cowherd said, "What will you do if I throw you out?"

Śubhārtha said, "Please take me to a place where there are many people." The cowherd escorted him to the city of Śubhārtha's intended father-in-law.

The prince recited many stories, legends, and so forth in melodious poetry. The city folk gave him a lot of food, beverages, and gifts, so he was able to help five hundred destitute people. Then because there were so many fruit trees within an enclosure, one of the stewards said, "Can you help us protect them?" [89]

He said, "Because I lack eyesight, what could I do?"

They responded: "You can do it. We'll tie a bell on each tree and you pull the cord."

"Well then, let's do it that way." He pulled the cords again and again. In addition he played a type of finger cymbal called a *jiu* (*byi'u*). When that no longer frightened off the birds, he added what are known in Tibetan as *cha lang chung ngu* (little hand cymbals). The music he made drew many people. Even the king's daughter came to hear him. She asked, "Who are you?"

"I am a blind man," he said. The girl was attracted to the blind man and sat next to him.

The girl was summoned to her father, but she said, "Have my food brought here. I will eat with this blind man." Further, the girl said to her father, the king, "Please give me in marriage to this blind man."

The king said, "Daughter! Have some sweet words corrupted your mind? You were given in marriage to Prince Śubhārtha. Why are you pursuing this destitute man?" They discussed this.

The girl said, "I have promised to be this poor man's wife." The king listened. He established the two, his daughter and the penniless man, in the palace.

After three months had passed the destitute man said to the girl, "In the past you have committed the sin of being with another man." These piercing words made the girl depressed.

"As the measure of my purity, I swear on one of my prince's eyes, 'This girl is without the sin of having been with another man!' Since these words are true, may vision come back to one of your eyes!"

As soon as she said this, one of his eyes could see. To repay the girl's kindness to him, the blind man said, "Do you know who I am?"

She said, "You are a destitute man."

"I am not penniless. I am the son of the king of Vārāṇasī."

"No," she said, "He went off to the sea."

Śubhārtha swore on his other eye that this was the truth, "It is absolutely true that I am Prince Śubhārtha! Since these words are true, may my other eye come to see!" Instantly his vision returned.

The girl related to her father the king the story of how the former destitute man was Śubhārtha.

He said, "It is not true."

"It is true, look!"

The king observed and understood. He said, "Please forgive me."

Śubhārtha said, "I need nothing. Please reward the cowherd." So the king gave him the seven sorts of precious things.

Meanwhile in the palace of Śubhārtha's former kingdom there was a white goose that had been his dear playmate. [90] His parents tied a letter to the goose's neck and sent it out to seek the prince. After flying a long time it finally landed right in front of the prince. Śubhārtha took the letter from the goose's neck. In response he wrote a straightforward account of what had occurred and tied it to the goose's neck. His parents were very happy to see this. Moreover, they had Papārtha's limbs chained and he was put into the dungeon.

Then King Liśī gave his daughter in marriage to the prince of Vārāṇasī. Śubhārtha, accompanied by his wife, was escorted to his former realm. They were met by a welcoming party. They prostrated to his parents. His father explained that he and the prince's mother had now gone blind.

Then Śubhārtha asked, "Where is my younger brother?"

His father responded, "Because he was so sinful, we acted so."

"Please father, I would like to see him." So the younger brother was taken out of the dungeon pit and freed from his chains. Then the younger brother dug up the jewel from where he had buried it and gave it to his elder brother. That offering restored his parents' sight.

On the fifteenth of the month they bathed, put on clean clothes, and made offerings in thanks for receiving the gift of the jewel. That day a rain of rice fell, rising almost to peoples' knees. Similarly, vast amounts of clothes and many other things made all the poor people in the world happy. The joy of his parents and the court increased.

From this story we can clearly understand the meaning of the following couplets from *A Jewel Treasury of Wise Sayings*. From verse 118:

> Even when the wise fall into terrible decline,
> they please others by giving good advice.

From verse 209:

The people who cause us greater injury
are usually the most like us.

* * *

49 When great men feel love for their enemies,
those very enemies come under their sway.
Because Mahāsaṃmata cared for everyone,
he was unanimously appointed king.

The narrative that goes along with this verse is well known to nearly everyone, so I do not need to write about it.[133]

This concludes "An Examination of the Cultivated," the second chapter of *A Jewel Treasury of Wise Sayings*. [91]

Chapter 3. An Examination of the Foolish

64 If you delegate a job to a fool,
the work suffers and he is injured too.
It is said that when a fox was appointed king,
his subjects suffered and he was killed too.

You ask, "How can that be?" Listen, the verse is made clear in this story.

It is said that a fox was wandering everywhere in search of food.[134] One day he fell into a dye master's dye cauldron. After rolling around inside, he got free. The tips of his fur had become the purple color of sesame flowers.

At that time all the animals had gathered together in search of a leader. One said to the fox, "Who are you?"

He replied, "I am called the jewel of living beings. I am also called the king of carnivores."

They all agreed that because of his lovely color and behavior he was suitable to be the king. They made him their king. The lion was made his minister. When they traveled, the fox rode on the lion. Even though every creature paid homage to him, he was hateful to his followers in general and was particularly nasty to his own race of foxes.

All the foxes gathered together to confer. "This leader seems like one of us. But even if he is of our kind, he has only harmed us. To see if he is or isn't one of us, let's all get together on the night of the fifteenth of the month and howl. If he is one of us, he'll howl no matter the color of his fur." At the appointed time they did that. The ruler went off to the side, but when he howled too all the animals got together and cursed him. Finally they explained what happened to the lion. The lion killed the fox king.

* * *

72 Arrogant fools who make promises
come to ruin even if they are powerful.
Bāli, the mighty one, lost the three realms
by giving the land traversed by a single step.

The individual called Bāli was lord of the asuras.[135] He held sway over the three realms: [92] below earth, on earth, and the heavens above. He made all living creatures suffer. Because his hatefulness tyrannized all beings, Viṣṇu formed a plan to deceive him. He turned himself into a dwarf, went before his uncle Bāli, and made a request: "Please grant me a secluded spot, just the amount of land that I can cover in a step, in order to make a great offering."

Without investigating, Bāli said, "In that case I will give you the amount of land you can traverse in three steps."

Viṣṇu placed one foot on the golden base of the universe. He put his other foot on the peak of Mount Meru. "This is my first step," he said. "What can you give me for the second?"

Bāli was mortified. He slunk under the earth and remained there.

Moreover, it says in the *Viśeṣastava*:[136]

> Viṣṇu took the form of a dwarf;
> with that illusion he tricked his uncle.

Bāli's brutal actions were a waste. He was trapped by his gift of three steps. With this story we are able to understand verse 381 in *A Jewel Treasury of Wise Sayings*:

> Swindlers' words are duplicitous,
> so the honest must examine them carefully.
> After being duped what is the use
> of self-promotion, of saying, "I'm honest!"

* * *

87 Even a multitude of ignorant fools
will fall under an enemy's sway.
An entire herd of powerful elephants
was subjugated by one clever rabbit.

So it is said.[137] There were many rabbits who lived in a dense forest. There was a pond not far from there to which the rabbits went to drink and so forth. At one time, a large herd of elephants were suffering from the summer heat and came to the pond. They trampled the pond and forced the clever rabbits to leave. The rabbits got together and discussed what to do. One said, "I have a plan."

The others said, "What is it?"

"Toss me up to the top of a high tree," he said. All the rabbits carried him up.

When the herd of elephants gathered under the tall tree, in a mysterious, exalted voice the rabbit said, "Hey there! Sit down!"

All the elephants looked up and said, "Who are you?"

The rabbit replied, "I am the messenger of the auspicious moon."

The elephants said, "Why were you sent here?" [93]

The rabbit said, "If you banish those rabbits who reside in my center, I will emit heat rays on you." And he continued, "Until the fourteenth day of the month, the moon will remain behind a bank of clouds. Then the moon will show itself and chastise you twice as much as before. Therefore if you want to be happy, even though my words are unpleasant to hear, listen to them! Also, do not harm me."

The herd conferred. "Blessed moon, please do not hurt us. We will listen to your speech. How could we harm your messenger?"

The rabbit said, "Well then, I will descend on your heads."

They said, "Go ahead."

So he jumped down and the moon came out from behind the clouds. "I, the auspicious moon, have done away with any punishment for you. Now in order to be happy go away."

Everyone lived where they belonged and had cause to be happy.

This concludes "An Examination of the Foolish," the third chapter of *A Jewel Treasury of Wise Sayings*.

Chapter 4. A Comparative Examination of the Wise and the Foolish

113 The great turn those who harm them into friends.
The lowly make those who harm them enemies.
The wind fans a forest fire
but extinguishes a small lamp-flame.

These two examples, of a forest fire and the flame of a lamp, illustrate the power of countermeasures and former merit.

A long time ago in the land of Vārāṇasī there was a king called Candraprabha.[138] He examined the causes that he had created earlier in order to become the ruler of the world in the present. He brought together his family and ministers and promised to make all the living beings in his kingdom equally fortunate. All the destitute people in the kingdom assembled. He provided them with whatever they desired.

When he heard of the king's good qualities, another king, named Bhīmasena, was completely unsettled by jealousy. He summoned a brahman who for a long time had pleased him because he did whatever the king desired. After making offerings to the brahman, Bhīmasena said, "I am oppressed by misery and cannot even sleep. Please think of a means to ease my misfortune."

The brahman questioned him about the cause of his troubles.

"King Candraprabha has destroyed even my name!" [94]

The brahman said, "He has become like a mother to everyone. You should not bear him ill will." Without concern for his own livelihood the brahman departed.

Bhīmasena was even more disturbed. He vowed, "I will give half my kingdom to anyone who can cut off King Candraprabha's head."

When he heard that, a brahman named *Lehuducha came before the king and said, "I promise to do it."

The king lauded him. Lehuducha prepared for seven days. During that time there were epidemics and so forth. The earth cracked open and the sky was filled with lightning, meteors, and birds crying, "Have pity! Have pity!" Eighty-four thousand minor kings had dreams in which golden victory banners shattered and the skins of kettle drums split open. The king's minister, Mahācandra, dreamed that a huge preta stole the king's crown. Everyone was oppressed by misery.

The sentries of King Candraprabha's realm recognized the bad omens. They criticized the brahman Lehuducha and would not let him inside the palace for a long time. A pure-land god knew that King Candraprabha was about to complete the perfection of generosity. So he came to the king in a dream and said, "You have given gifts that accord with the sentiments of every recipient. Now to complete your vow there is someone at the gates who is not able to pass through." When the king awoke he requested his minister Mahācandra to intervene. The minister went and explained to the gate sentries what the god had said.

They said, "All right. Even though there are so many bad omens, we cannot disregard what the god said."

They called the brahman in. They set out piles of the seven sorts of precious jewels that were five hundred times the size of the king's head as ransom for the king's life. Nevertheless the brahman made his request to the king. The king replied, "Because it will please you, I will do it."

The brahman asked, "When will you give your head to me?"

"In seven days," was the answer.

The ministers clutched at the brahman to dissuade him. The brahman wouldn't listen. He said, "The only thing I want is the king's head."

The king rode an elephant out from his palace for a thousand leagues. Then he summoned all the gods and men of the land. All his subjects, his ten thousand ministers, his twenty thousand queens, his five hundred sons, and so forth pleaded with him, but the king paid no heed. Then the king told them to make prayers and after that he would give his head to the brahman.

The brahman said, "Only you, no others. If you are truly going to bestow this sacrifice, come to a secluded garden empty of people."

The brahman and the king went off together in just that way. The brahman said, "King, fasten your hair to that tree."

The king said, "No. My hair must pass from my hand to yours. I wish to attain enlightenment." [95] When the female tree spirit there objected, he looked at her and said, "At the foot of this tree I have given my head just one short of a thousand times. Today will be the thousandth time. Please do not create an obstacle to my attainment of enlightenment." Then with his own hand he cleft his head from his shoulders. The earth shook violently.

Bhīmasena had a heart attack and died when he heard the news that

Candraprabha had completed the perfection of generosity. Then when the brahman arrived carrying the king's rotting head and heard the news that Bhīmasena had died, he threw the head away. He immediately vomited blood and died. The two of them went to hell.

According to the sutras King Candraprabha was a former life in the continuum of our teacher, the Buddha. Bhīmasena was the demon Māra. The brahman Lehuducha was Devadatta. The tree spirit was Maudgalyāyana. And the minister Mahācandra was Śāriputra.

This makes clear the meaning of verse 336 of *A Jewel Treasury of Wise Sayings*:

> If you desire to harm your enemy,
> have good qualities of your own.
> This will inflame your enemy's mind
> and your own merit will increase.

And verse 422:

> If your mind cannot bear
> the prosperity of others,
> that alone will destroy your affluence.
> So this is just aiming jealousy at yourself.

* * *

116 The wise are valued among the wise.
How can a fool know who is wise?
Sandalwood is more precious than gold,
and look how a fool made it into charcoal.

In regard to this verse, once there was a man who had some marvelous, top-quality sandalwood.[139] He went everywhere trying to sell it, but he was not able to find a buyer. When he went to a vacant house to sleep, a seller of charcoal was also there. The two chatted.

The owner of the sandalwood said, "In this region there is never a buyer for goods."

The next morning the two went out to sell their separate wares. That night they met again at the vacant house. The sandalwood seller saw that the other man's sack of charcoal was empty. He thought, "Oh yes! Now I have found the special method I need!" He made his sandalwood into charcoal and sold it.

Just as that fool thought he had made a profit, foolish people do not recognize the good qualities of the wise. Even if they understand them a little, they do not hold these good qualities to be especially good and throw them away. [96] It is said:

> There are two kinds of excellent people:
> either they are honored by everyone
> or they live alone in the forest.[140]

* * *

117 The wise know to investigate for themselves,
but fools just follow what is popular.
When an old dog howls,
other dogs join in for no reason.

Starting things without investigating them first is how most people with little intelligence do things.

A long time ago a rabbit was on a river bank and a tree branch fell into the river near him.[141] The rabbit was terrified and fled.

His friend said, "What happened?"

The rabbit answered, "There's a chal!" They both ran off. As they went, they answered the same question asked by a fox, a wolf, and others who wanted to know what had happened. They all fled. The same question was asked by jackals, tigers, brown bears, grizzly bears, elephants, and so on. Finally they met a lion who asked them what was going on. They gave the same short response as they were running off.

The lion said, "Wait a moment! Who said there is a chal?" Then the clear-thinking lion said, "Show it to me." They all went to the place where the commotion had started. In the water they could see a piece of the tree. The lion said, "This was it!"

Thus we should use logic and analysis like the king of beasts and cease being like those creatures who live on dry land and are stricken helpless by a tree branch falling into the water.

* * *

130 When replete with wealth, your power increases too.
When you lack wealth, your power diminishes too.
Because the mouse's precious jewel was stolen,
we hear that his ability to steal declined.

In the hinterlands there lived a mouse who had a precious thing: a jewel beyond price. Its power was very strong. It made the mouse a skilled thief.

At one time the mouse robbed a brahman who lived in the area. The brahman said, "Whoever did this cannot be caught. His power cannot be counteracted. I therefore infer that he definitely has a special jewel." [97]

A local thief named Parivarjika overheard him. He went to the brahman and asked him about this special jewel. The brahman replied, "He surely has one. It is explained like this in the Vedic texts."

> The first of the first is adorned with fire.
> The fifth vowel is made for that purpose.
> The fifth has three parts
> and so obtains the appellation *great*.

The thief carefully analyzed this response. He waited a long time to find an opportunity, but then got hold of the jewel. When the mouse went back to his home and saw what had happened he became very unhappy and stayed there in despair. Others asked him what was the matter. He explained what had happened. Because of his loss he could not protect his own possessions, not to mention his inability to steal from others. Then he abandoned his home and went to the forest. As to what happened to him, it is revealed in this verse from the *Treatise on Norms:*

> Wealth is worldly human affluence.
> When you obtain that high status,
> anyone who had ever seen you before—
> teachers, friends, and so forth—gathers around.
> When your wealth is gone and position reduced,
> not even your family will respect you.[142]

Regarding this fall from greatness, verse 227 of *A Jewel Treasury of Wise Sayings* says this followed by an analogy:

Wealthy people's words are liked by everyone;
poor people's words are disregarded even when true.

Does this mean that one should just seek wealth? The answer is "no," and this is explained in verse 239:

Among fools, there are many with wealth;
among carnivores, there are many who are brave;
but a righteous person who gives good advice—
such learned ones are rare in the world.

This concludes "A Comparative Examination of the Wise and the Foolish," the fourth chapter of *A Jewel Treasury of Wise Sayings*. [98]

Chapter 5. An Examination of Bad Behavior

145 The pleasant speech of cunning people
is for their own ends, not to be polite.
The laughter-like hooting of an owl
delivers a bad omen; it's not done out of joy.

A screech owl perched on a turret of Indra's mansion in the Heaven of the Thirty-Three.[143] The younger gods heard its cry and said, "It's a bad omen, we should kill it."

The owl deceived them by saying, "Let me live a while because I possess the skill of imparting profound, good advice."

The six sweetest sounds in the world are
that of mine, that of the friend of gems,
that of the melodious voice, that of the stone picker,
that of joyful tune, and that of the raised throat.[144]

So said the owl and flew off. Similarly, regarding such a person, it says in this very chapter in verse 187:

Who could befriend a person
who acts only in self-interest?

You should examine what people say in accord with this verse.

* * *

146 Bad people first mislead others with words.
Later when others have relaxed, they deceive them.
See how fishermen disguise hooks with bait
in order to kill the fish.

There is no need to explain this. The meaning is obvious.

In another story, there was once an old heron afflicted by hunger on the shore of a pond. A fish with little judgment came up.

"What's wrong?" the fish asked. "Did your helpful friends go away?"

The heron said, "You are all going to die."

The fish said, "Why?"

The heron said, "This pond is going to dry up and I will have nothing to eat."

All the fish got together and begged the heron to help them. He said, "On the far side of this pass there is a nice lake. I know the route. Let's all go there."

The fish said, "We can't fly like you do. However, you are wise, tell us how we can go."

The heron said, "I'll carry you one by one and convey you there."

All the fish agreed. The heron carried the fish one by one to a distant, flat rock where he ate them. [99]

After a while a frog named Kulīraka came up. He and the heron conversed as before. The heron carried the frog off and placed him on top of the flat rock. The frog understood what had happened. He seized the heron's neck. By clutching it tightly he killed the heron. Then all the creatures who lived there said, "Kulīraka killed the greedy heron!"

* * *

149 Excessive duplicity carried too far
may succeed for a while but ends in destruction.
The donkey covered with the leopard skin
ate the crops, but others killed him later.

Once there was a devious householder who owned a donkey.[145] Rather than feeding the donkey fodder, he covered the donkey in a tiger skin he had found and sent it out to find something to eat. All the people said, "A tiger has come into the fields!" After it had done a lot of damage in a number of fields, everyone finally got together and killed the tiger. Then they knew it was the conniving man's donkey.

Once a fool was wandering about and found a radiant treasure chest that had been hidden by King Vikramāditya. He picked it up, took a little gold from it, and brought it to his clever friend. He put the gold in front of his friend and asked, "What is this?"

His clever man said, "This is gold."

The fool said, "Oh good. I have lots more."

His friend said, "In that case, it would be good to share it equally with me!"

The two went and hid the treasure chest at the base of a tree. Whenever they needed some gold they went together to get it. Then a deceitful thought arose in the clever one's mind. He hid the treasure chest in another place. Then he called on his friend to go and get some gold. The treasure chest was not there. The clever one said, "You stole you the chest!"

The simpleton said, "If I were a thief, why would I have voluntarily shared it with you in the beginning? Therefore I didn't steal it."

The clever one wouldn't listen. "It wasn't me. It couldn't be anyone other than you."

The clever one took the simpleton before the king and explained what had happened. He said, "Please punish him!"

The king said, "First I must investigate."

The clever one said, [100] "In that case, let's go ask the forest god of the place where we had stashed the gold."

The king said, "Let it be so," and gave an order for that to be done. Then they set a time to go.

The clever man instructed his elderly father to say that the simpleton had stolen the chest of gold. Then when the time came, his father hid in the hollow of the rotten tree. Many people, with the king at their center, came to propitiate the local god. "Please be our faultless witness. Speak truly and relate in detail what happened earlier."

Then the old man, pretending to be the god, decided the matter of contention. The clever man said, "See, what did I say!"

The king said, "It is true. Absolutely."

The fool said, "If all of you are right, and since I too am right, if someone is not truthful it must be this god who is untruthful. So first let me burn down this tree god and then you can kill me."

The clever man said, "This is a god! To set it on fire wouldn't be right. If you burn it undesirable things will happen to you."

The fool said, "I am about to die this very moment, there isn't anything worse than that!" Not listening, he piled many sticks against the tree and set them on fire.

The swirling smoke made the old man move, and he fell out of the tree. Seeing him, they recognized he was the clever man's father. "What are you doing?" asked the king. The old man said:

> The extremely clever one isn't so wise.
> The extremely simple one isn't such an idiot.
> If the extremely clever one were wise,
> would he be killing his father with smoke?

After hearing that allegory, the king had the clever man put to death. The father was found guiltless and let go. The chest of gold was given to the fool.

Thus two stories elucidate this verse.

* * *

150 If someone is clever he can deceive others
by blatantly lying about something.
Because the thieves called it a dog,
the brahman lost the goat he was leading.

A young brahman procured a goat in order to make an offering to the gods.[146] As he led it along, five thieves saw him. They thought, "We should get this goat from him." Having decided that, they went to a place on the road that would provide them their opportunity. Then the first thief came up to the brahman and said, [101] "Oh my! What in the world is this? A brahman leading a dog!"

The brahman was merely puzzled about this statement. Now the second thief came up to him and uttered the same words. After a bit he came on the third thief, who said the same thing. The brahman became a bit uncertain, looked behind him, and went on. Then when the fourth thief said the same thing, the brahman really checked to make sure it was not a dog. He examined the goat in order to make sure it had horns, a beard, hooves, and so forth. Having made certain, he went on. Then at last the fifth thief came up and said the same thing.

The brahman thought, "This is definitely an evil spirit taking the form of a goat. It has come to consume my offerings. That is why to everyone else it appears to be a dog." Immediately he abandoned it and went off. At that point the thieves grabbed the goat and left.

Therefore even if many people collaborate assiduously, do not have confidence that what they say is right.

* * *

151 Cunning people deceive others with words
while blatantly committing evil deeds.
When the monk Mahādeva lamented aloud,
some said that he proclaimed the truth of suffering.

This is the story of a rich man with little learning and very unruly senses. He called himself Venerable Mahādeva and claimed to be an ordained disciple of the Buddha.[147]

A long time ago in the great south Indian city of Varuṇa there was a rich layman. Because he had no sons he propitiated the gods. After ten months he was granted a newborn son. They named him Mahādeva. In order to pay for the extensive birth feast, his father went to the sea to acquire jewels. He was on that journey for twelve years. During that time his son matured into a youth with very strong desires. He lived with his mother and committed incest with her.

At that time the mother said to her son, "Son, I enjoy being with you and desire our union, but your father is about to return from the sea." She ordered, "Go wait on the road and kill your father." The son did as he was told. He killed his father secretly on the road. After a while his old mother took another man as her lover. Mahādeva got angry and killed his mother too. [102]

After that Mahādeva listened to various religious teachings from an arhat who was his officiating priest. Fearing that the clairvoyant arhat would know about his earlier evil deeds and tell others, Mahādeva murdered him too. Then his mind was sickened by his former bad deeds. He no longer wanted to live in his family home. He gave his possessions away to anyone who wanted them. Then he went to another country not far from his own. At that time there was a famine in the land. He saw that laymen could not find sustenance, but people had faith in the sangha so the monks had food to eat. Mahādeva found saffron robes in cemeteries and other places. Without relying on an abbot and preceptor for ordination, he gave himself the right to wear the essential signs of a monk.

Having foisted this sham, he went and took up residence in a border region of the country. When he begged for alms in the villages his heart was not at ease because of what he had done previously. Disquiet showed on his face. Over time the buffalo, goat, and sheep herders saw him. They came before him. Mahādeva explained the Dharma to the herders and others. He gave profound instructions that were pleasant to hear. He displayed the appearance of being disgusted with cyclic existence. They said, "This great meditator has meditated on the defects of this world. He is a holy being who has practiced Dharma from the heart." They began to have faith and belief in him.

The phony's good reputation spread to the people of the city. At first women, children, and so forth venerated him. Then over time most of the men gathered around too. They gave large amounts of alms to him.

At that time Mahādeva received goods from those who had wealth. He stockpiled it and gave to those who had nothing. Those who received things from him and those on whom he practiced his social skills of flattery, artifice, and so forth were impressed by his great religiosity. They said, "This very compassionate person has both spiritual and societal mastery. He is even more holy than a noble arhat." Motivated by admiration, everyone offered him whatever wealth they had. The wealthy even opened the treasure stores accumulated by their ancestors. Because of these offerings Mahādeva gave away food, cooking implements, clothes, and whatever else accorded with peoples' desires.

Mahādeva said, "I am an arhat. [103] I have extinguished all defilements. I have done what is to be done!" Even though he had not really attained that state, his lies about being a spiritual teacher rather than a master of worldly matters bamboozled and deceived everyone. Everyone thought, "He is truly excellent." Some people requested ordination out of the arising of faith, but most of them requested it for material sustenance. He gave material goods, and many people took ordination and gathered around him. Monks from elsewhere also joined for the livelihood he provided. Many hundreds of thousands of monks joined the assembly around him.

During that time he gave Dharma teachings to his disciples. One day before dawn Mahādeva engaged in self-reflection. He recollected that first he committed incest with his mother and because of that he killed his father. Later he killed his mother. He killed an arhat, he took his vows from himself, he exploited people's faith and offerings, he lied about being a teacher of societal ethics, he misled many living beings, and so forth. Remembering that the nature and bad consequences of these actions would be to suffer in hell, he suddenly said, "Oh! Misery! Misery!" three times.

Some disciples in nearby huts heard those words. In the morning when they went to pay their respects they asked, "O abbot, since you are an arhat you have exhausted all suffering, so why before dawn did you cry out in a loud miserable voice?"

The abbot said, "What are you talking about?"

They repeated what he had said. The abbot said, "Didn't you hear anything else?"

They said. "No, we didn't hear anything else."

The abbot said, "I was naming all the noble truths. I also proclaimed, 'Oh! The source of suffering. Oh! The cessation. Oh! The path.' Didn't you hear the other exclamations?"

Although he had misled those disciples, because his facial expression was different than usual all the others began to have doubts. One said, "O abbot! If you are an arhat, how could you not know the answer to our Dharma questions?"

He answered, "In addition to myself, many others among the Buddha's disciples who spread his message—for example, Śāriputra—are like this. The only one who has totally gone beyond uncertainty is the Buddha."

The entire assembly gathered. Someone asked, "Abbot, please demonstrate your magical powers for us."

He replied, "My arhatship was destroyed early this morning. I don't have any magical powers now." [104]

"Can arhatship cease to exist?" they asked.

Mahādeva replied, "Very much so. I have said that arhats have the characteristic of complete deterioration. Similarly, previously I said that arhats have the characteristic of not knowing some things. Moreover, arhats have the characteristic of maintaining their vows, of slaying the ego, of possessing the good fortune of full conviction, and of being unwavering." Although he spoke such self-flattery, his entourage felt something wasn't right.

Nevertheless, because of his powers of illusion some of his mistakes slipped into the sutras of the Bhagavān. After his lifetime was over he fell into hell. This is well known.

* * *

153 Cunning people lure you in with pleasant manners
and later deceive you to attain their objectives.
A brazen man sold donkey meat
by exhibiting the tail of a deer.

A cunning man was not able to get anyone to purchase his meat.[148] Then he found the tail of a deer. Holding that in his hand while leading his donkey, he cried out, "Will you buy meat?" When people asked what type of meat he was selling, he showed them the tail and said, "It is the meat of this." Through this performance he was able to find buyers. He thought, "This ruse is the essential sales technique." He continued to attribute good qualities to his meat.

* * *

155 Those beyond shame whose depravity is deep
bear their ill repute as an accolade.
Some royal families in the land of Kañcī
beat royal drums when they commit patricide.

In a royal lineage of south India there was a king who was called Lord of *Naramatima.[149] The law of that land was that once a prince reached twenty years of age, he was not allowed into the presence of his father. He was put in an iron prison cell and made to study texts about temporal affairs and so forth. Whichever prince was oldest would be made ruler when the father died.

At that time the ruler had a son who was eight years old. The boy had a set of clothes he particularly liked. He said to his mother, "Dear mother, please put away these garments of mine. I will wear them when I obtain the kingdom."

His mother said, "You will not acquire it. You have an elder brother."

The boy said, "What can I do?"

His mother replied, "You will obtain the kingdom if you kill your father now and have the royal drums beaten."

The boy said, "I will do precisely that." Holding a sharp dagger given to him by his mother, he went before the king, who was sitting on the throne. He beguiled his father with a little joyfulness and playfulness. Then he climbed into his father's lap and killed him by stabbing him in the stomach with the dagger.

"From today I am the king," he said.

Because the royal drums were beaten, [105] all his subjects said: "Since this boy was able to do this, we know he should be called a great hero." He was granted the kingdom.

* * *

159 We see the unwise destroy their friends
and care for those unconnected to them.
Would anyone other than a lunatic
cut off a peacock's crest to ornament its tail?

It is said that an insane man had a dancing peacock. He could not bear it when one of its tail feathers fell out. He cut off the peacock's crest feathers and attached them to its rump. This is impractical in every case.

* * *

161 Evil people are especially hostile
toward honorable peaceful people.
A log saturated with oil
catches fire, but others do not.

As to this verse, the buffalo Mahiṣavarda lived in a dense forest.[150] Every aspect of his body and mind, the way he moved, and so forth were all magnificent. He was someone who was protected by his completely controlled behavior. A vulgar monkey lived in his presence. The monkey was contentious and insulting to the superior buffalo.

> This vulgar being acted arrogantly and haughtily
> toward the very compassionate and loving one.
> Knowing that the monkey was not dangerous to him
> the buffalo remained perfectly content.

Sometimes the monkey rode on the buffalo. Sometimes he sat on his head and covered his eyes. Sometimes he lay down on the path to block the buffalo. The bodhisattva buffalo always practiced patience even though he sometimes was discouraged.

Then a troublesome spirit who lived there called out this verse and more:

> The force of the adamantine tips of your horns
> like thunderbolts can shatter stone mountains.
> If you stamp your feet in anger
> it's as if high rocky peaks sink into mud.

The bodhisattva said:

> The use of force is not suitable.
> What would employing it do?
> What else is needed other than the practice
> of patience and virtuous controlled behavior?

The troublesome spirit saw that harming was not right. He dropped the monkey behind the buffalo. Thereafter the monkey lived without harming him.

* * *

169 Those who speak helpfully are rare;
rarer still are those who listen.
It is difficult to find a skilled physician,
and few follow his prescriptions.

Long ago, even though he saw the validity of the Buddha's teachings, a naked teacher of an outsider system practiced incorrectly and so came to grief. And likewise, the monk Devadatta fell ill from medication.[151]

Long ago when the Bhagavān was staying in Śrāvasti, he and the monks of the sangha caught a severe cold. They called for the king of physicians, Jīvaka. He came and taught Ānanda how to prepare a butter-based medicine of sixty-four ingredients. He instructed, "Because the Bhagavān has an adamantine body that is strong, firm, and incorruptible, serve him twelve measures of the medication. Give each of the other monks no more than a single measure each." Ānanda did as he was told.

Devadatta said, "Give me two measures! What is the difference between Gautama and I in terms of caste and so forth?" Therefore Ānanda gave him two measures. Devadatta could not digest the medicine and was near death. Ānanda summoned the physician Jīvaka. He said, "There is no cure for undigested medication that has become poison."

Then they asked the Bhagavān. He said, "There is a cure." He placed his right hand on Devadatta's head and said, "I felt the same toward Rāhula, the son born from my body, and Devadatta, who thinks of me as an enemy. Because my words are true may Devadatta's illness subside." Devadatta became free of sickness. [107]

As thanks, Devadatta said, "This monk Gautama is known to be skilled in medical practice, so he won't die of starvation in his old age." Insulting and disparaging the Bhagavān's words of truth, Devadatta turned and left.

Coming two verses after the above-cited stanza comes the following:

* * *

172 Do not consult with or have faith in
someone you have not checked out.
Mistakes arise from carelessness,
and enmity often comes from conversation.

Those who are insensitive and careless about another person's kindness will experience suffering and fear, as in this story about the bodhisattva monkey.[152]

When the bodhisattva monkey was residing in a deep forest, a man wandered in searching for his lost cow. He went further and further and lost his way. He was confused and meandered all over. He was afflicted by the misery of hunger and thirst and was hot and physically tired. His thoughts were gloomy and his mind tormented. He sat down at the base of a tree. He saw a tinduka tree with a few fruits that were becoming yellow in color; they were nearly ripe. The man thought that if he ate them, the pain of his hunger would be eased. So he looked around in search for more of them. He saw a tinduka tree growing from the face of a cliff, its branches bent because they were heavy with ripe fruit. Desiring the fruit, the man climbed down a fissure in the mountain cliff. He inched out on the fruit-laden branches of the tinduka tree hanging over the abyss. He climbed, plucking the fruit as he went, until he reached the summit of the tree. Then, burdened by his heavy weight, the thin branches of the fruit tree broke as if deliberately cut by an ax. He fell. The man and the branch fell into a cirque, like a well, surrounded by rock cliff walls.

However, because he fell on top of the branches and bunches of leaves on the surface of the water, he was only slightly injured. He got out of the water and looked at the walls all around. He could not see any way out, [108] nor find any means to do so. He was pessimistic. Thinking he was definitely going to die and not having any hope of survival, tears flowed from his eyes and he made whimpering sounds:

> The forest wilderness is difficult to penetrate;
> there are no travelers passing through.
> I have fallen into a place like this;
> wherever I look I see nothing but death.

He continued emitting other pitiful moans. The bodhisattva monkey was scampering around in the forest looking for something to eat. Eventually he came to the mouth of the crevasse. He saw the man with an emaciated body, bad skin tone, and red eyes groaning with misery. The monkey said:

> There is no escape from this crevasse
> for a man. Who are you?
> Why have you come here?
> Please be forthright.

The man prostrated to the monkey and said:

> Glorious god! I am a man.
> I wandered, straying into the forest.
> Trying to get the fruit of this tree,
> I fell into this predicament.

And he told the whole story. The bodhisattva felt unbearable compassion for him. To give him relief he searched for the fruit of a tinduka tree and gave it to him. To become accustomed to the only way to get him out, the monkey practiced carrying a rock the weight of the man. Then, feeling grounded in experience, the bodhisattva went into the crevasse and said to the man:

Come here. Get on my back.
I will carry you up to the top.
Hold on to me with all your heart
until we get out.

He said this and more. The man said, "Let's do it like that!" and bowed to him. He got on the monkey. They almost didn't get out because the monkey had limited strength and the man's body was heavy. But thanks to the monkey's courage and tenacity, they got out. The bodhisattva rejoiced in having helped the man. Then the bodhisattva relaxed and said:

In every part of the forest around here
large carnivores come at will.
I am weary and must sleep a bit.
I might awake, but please keep an eye out
to guard the two of us, you and I.

Then the evil hypocrite promised to stand guard. [109] The bodhisattva went to sleep on a flat blue boulder. The evil man thought, "Forget about his earlier kindness. If I kill him and eat his flesh, I can take care of my physical needs. Later in my own country I can purify the evil deed." Thinking this way, he corrupted the very notion of the Dharma and abandoned compassion. He picked up a large rock and threw it at the monkey's head. The rock glanced off the edge of the boulder, not touching its target. The noise woke the monkey from sleep. He jumped up to see what had happened. There were no ferocious beasts. He saw only the evil man hanging his head in embarrassment and hiding his perspiring face.

The monkey couldn't endure the evil man's abandonment of gratitude. He said:

Friend, although you are a man,
you have done a deed like this.
I hauled you from this crevasse.
As if pulling you out of the jaws of death,
I saved you from going to your next life.
But now you will fall into another hell.

He spoke many other verses as well. Sorrowing for the man, the monkey counseled him and escorted him to a village nearby. He showed him the path and instructed, "Now go to be happy in your own country. Turn away from evil deeds. Make an effort to repent your earlier faulty actions." The monkey turned and went back into the forest.

Then the man's mind was tormented by the fire of regret for his unlimited evil actions. He was immediately afflicted by a terrible case of leprosy. His body was like a burning abscess. He was frightening to see. He could not go into town and stayed where he was.

At a later time a great king passed by hunting for deer. He saw the tormented man. Although he seemed to have the shape of man, the king wasn't sure, and said:

> Who are you? Are you a preta? Or a spirit?
> The embodiment of evil? Or a rotting corpse?
> Are you a collection of many illnesses?
> How did you come to be so diseased?

The man prostrated to him and said, "O great king! I am a man. I am a man. I am a man!" The king asked, "Well then, tell me how you came to be like this." The man who had committed evil deeds said:

> Right now I am experiencing
> the flowering of callous heartlessness.
> In future I will experience results
> even more unbearable than this.

Having now shown the results that could be seen and heard in this life, in order to reveal the results that would be experienced in the future, a huge crack appeared in the ground and the man fell in head first. [110] So even before he had discarded the present bodily existence, he took rebirth as a great hell being.

Moreover, as to tales of how enmity often comes from unnecessary conversation, there is the similar story of the monkey and the little bird in Nāgārjuna's *Drop to Nourish a Person*.

* * *

170 If you are extremely conceited,
suffering will continually befall you.
We hear that because of a lion's great pride
a fox was able to make him carry a load.

A fox had become habituated to eating the meat of animals that had been killed by a lion.[153] One time the lion killed an elephant and said to the fox, "Carry this. If you do not, you'll never eat meat again."

The fox thought, "There is no way I can carry this elephant. How can I possibly continue to eat meat?" So he said, "O lord! I cannot do two jobs. I'll do one. Please do the other one, my Lord."

The lion said, "What are the two jobs?"

The fox replied, "The proper way to do things in the world is that when a great being is endeavoring to carry a load, someone must follow him grunting. One of us must carry the elephant and the other must grunt."

The lion thought, "I am the king of the beasts. How can I follow behind someone grunting like that?" Therefore he went first, carrying the elephant. The fox followed behind grunting a happy song as he ambled along.

* * *

182 Those of bad character who cherish wealth
should not be trusted even if they are your friends.
Friends who have taken bribes
have ruined great people many times.

To exemplify this verse there is the story of a deer called Ruru who lived near Vārāṇasī in a forest so dense most people could not pass through it.[154] Although he had the body of an animal, he was marvelous. He appeared like a moving mass of jewels and had a pure mind. Moreover:

> Is there anyone who would not honor
> someone with a superlative body and mind,
> adorned with skillful mastery of actions,
> and who is helpful to you?

A man who lived in a nearby village was swept away by a strong river current. He cried out: [111]

> Swept away by a powerful, turbulent river,
> I have no savior; nor is there anything to float on.
> In order to save a bereft and tormented person like me,
> come quickly and help me out of pity for my distress!

Ruru was nearby. Seeing what happened, he went directly to the river. He rescued the man and made him happy. The man was overjoyed. He said to Ruru, "Since you saved my life, I must make some small offering to you. So please come to my town."

Ruru said, "The things that please people differ from what pleases me, a deer. Since they are different, the honor you can pay me is to not tell anyone what I am like." Then he went back into the forest.

The king of Vārāṇasī had a favorite queen. She had a dream in which she saw a deer with an especially marvelous, radiant, and splendid form sitting on a lion throne teaching the Dharma. She told the king. He promised a reward to anyone who found the deer. They all strove to find him.

For a long time the rescued man had vacillating thoughts. "Oh my! Should that deer's former kindness be most important or should my own needs take precedence? Should I maintain the principles of noble people or should I undertake the means to fulfill my greatest desire? Should I act in the interest of the entire world or should I obtain happiness now?" After he had these and other thoughts, yearning for a way to achieve his own great ambition, the man went before the king and said, "I have seen it, so tell me who I should show it to."

The king said, "Show me!"

They went forth with an army. The troops spread all over. Hearing the great noise made by the people, the deer thought, "Alas, some very greedy people are coming here." About to go elsewhere, he saw that an army had completely surrounded him. Just then the evil man saw him and shouted, "Hey!" to the king. "What you want is over there!" He pointed with his finger. The hand with which he had signaled broke at the wrist and fell off.

The king put an arrow to his bow and was about to shoot Ruru. [112] The bodhisattva asked in a mysterious human voice, "O lord of men, please wait a moment. From whom did you hear that I would be here?"

The king indicated with his arrow tip at the rescued man and declared, "This one said it."

Ruru recognized him and said, "Oh my!"

It is said that it is easier to retrieve
a log carried off by a raging river
than to rescue a shameless man.
Is this the repayment I get?

The king was amazed to hear this and moved to pity. He said, "Oh! If it would please you, tell me more to clarify what happened so that I can understand what you said."

In response, Ruru explained what had happened.

In rejoinder, the king looked at the man and said, "What! Is what he said true?"

The man couldn't say anything. The king was displeased. Reprimanding the man, he was about to shoot him with his arrow. Ruru went right before him and entreated, "O lord of men! Do not act like that! I beseech you not to respond by murdering a man who held you in the highest regard. Moreover, O lord of men, didn't he accomplish what you wanted? Do not punish this bad man and grant him what you said you would. To do that is right."

The king promised to do what the bodhisattva asked. Filled with gratitude for the teaching Ruru had given him, he undertook to reward the man. Then he invited Ruru to the palace. Ruru sat on a lion throne. His clear expositions were melodious and attractive. They delighted vast numbers of people and made them happy.

* * *

183 People who reveal their malevolence
are enemies who are easy to combat.
How can you overcome enemies
who make false overtures of helpfulness?

In the past there was a group of six elders belonging to a lineage that was somewhat undisciplined. One elder, named Udayī, stayed home to protect their house; the other five went to Nepal. They returned in the company of a merchant. On their return home the axle of their wagon broke and the six men carried the merchant's baggage through an isolated mountain region. All the people of that isolated place were afraid. They wondered if an army or a herd of elephants was coming. Because the five holy elders were carrying loads, the fearful people inquired if they had temporary or permanent enemies. [113] The elders responded, "Do holy men have enemies? We are just helping out by carrying a load."

* * *

184 With skill it is possible to heal various wounds,
but there is no mending the cuts from vile words.
Because the crow insulted the owl,
look how they have been enemies for eons.

All the birds gathered together in search of a king.[155] One said, "Look at the owl. He is the most splendid among us. He can see when he goes out at night. He has feather horns on his head. So he should be our king."

The crow said, "What are you saying? Because his legs have cracks, they are the feet of a servant. His eyes are yellow because he ate meat he stole from mother Yarmo, and she poured the meat broth into his eyes. His cry is repellent. He is called *owl* because he always makes the noise *oo*. It is a bad omen when horns appear on a bird's head. So count me out!" And he flew away.

All the other birds said, "It's true. His reasons are comprehensive." And the birds scattered and left the owl there all alone.

> "Hold fast to malice in your heart
> while speaking pleasant words."
> This advice of the pernicious sage the owl
> is contrary to noble behavior.[156]

> The ancient non-Buddhist sages
> *Latrotala, *Masūrakṣa, and so forth said:
> For so long as the time is not right,
> genuflect your shoulders before your enemy.
> When the right time for battle comes
> crush him like a rock smashes a clay pot.

And:

> Do not give quarter to your enemy
> even if he is down and cries for mercy.

Do not have compassion for him;
vanquish those violent doers of harm.

And:

Those who crave affluence
act like trustworthy defectors.
They bow their heads with respect
and weep with mortification.

And:

Residual enemies are just like
outstanding debts and remaining embers.
They will escalate over time;
therefore do not leave any behind.

In contrast to these verses and other such sayings, we have:

Act to please righteous people.
Do not serve uncouth people.
Do not put your faith in improper people. [114]
Rely on those who are superior.[157]

To say the following is contrary to the ways of the righteous:

Confuse all who are not perplexed;
always confound those who are mixed up.

In connection with this couplet, bear also in mind verse 316 of *A Jewel Treasury of Wise Sayings*:

Some other treatises advise you
to placate your foes only for the period of time
during which your strength is limited;
when your power is absolute, act accordingly.

This concludes "An Examination of Bad Behavior," the fifth chapter of *A Jewel Treasury of Wise Sayings.*

Chapter 6. An Examination of Natural Tendencies

198 Even those who have good natures
will become vicious if continually abused.
Although sandalwood sticks are cool by themselves,
if you rub them they will burst into flame.

This advice is similar to the maxims found in texts such as the *Legend of Kumbhakarṇa*, or the Śākya minister of Vaiśālī.

> Even if you have good qualities internally,
> if your comportment is poor, everyone will belittle you.
> It is well known that even though the bat was clever,
> the birds all rejected him because he had no feathers.

When the birds began to search for a king, they said, "Whoever sees the sun rise first will be made king." A bat and a dove usually saw it simultaneously. However, the bat put some crumbs in a box and tricked the dove. He prevailed in seeing it first. Although the bat won, they didn't make him king.

Then they said, "Whoever can fly highest in the sky will be appointed king." The bat rode in the vulture's feathers. Eventually all the other birds broke off and fell away. The vulture said, "I am in contact with the heavens," and stretched out his wings. The bat emerged from his feathers, said, "I am touching the heavens higher than that!" and flew off.

However, all the birds said, "What good is this ugly, featherless, horned one? Forget about being king!"

Just as a bat isn't included among ordinary birds, noble people should ignore testimony about the reformed actions of those who are despised and belittled by others.[158] [115]

* * *

246 Is there anything that cannot be accomplished
by those with intelligence and perseverance?
We hear it said that Pāṇḍu's sons destroyed
twelve battalions of the Kaurava army.

The story of these two lords elucidates the meaning of the word *kaliyuga*, the age of strife.

The age of strife began when the human lifespan was twenty thousand years. At that time two householders each sold his house to the other. Each seller sold his house along with its contents. Each buyer believed he had purchased only the house. Whereas the two householders had corresponded politely in the past, their attitudes reversed after the births of the brothers Duryodhana and Yudhiṣṭhira.[159] Once in an ancient time when the human lifespan was eighty thousand years there was a great king called the Sage Vyāsa.[160] He took a kshatriya wife and she bore his first son, Prince Pāṇḍu. After taking a brahman wife, a younger son, Prince Dhṛtarāṣṭra, was born. Sometime later the kingdom was ruled by Prince Pāṇḍu. Later, because Prince Dhṛtarāṣṭra had no sons, he went to the Sage Vyāsa to pay his respects and ask for assistance. His father offered the prayer, "May your holy queen Gandhārī have one hundred sons."

When ten months had passed the queen gave birth to a round ball of flesh like a stomach. Dhṛtarāṣṭra explained what happened to his father: "Not even one son was born, much less a hundred."

His father said, "There are a hundred sons inside that ball of flesh. Chop it into a hundred pieces, wrap it in cloth, and hide it. When seven days have passed, the one on top will be the eldest son. You must examine the signs for his virtuous or evil qualities."

Dhṛtarāṣṭra and his consort did so. After seven days they investigated and found a hundred tiny infants there. The sage grandfather examined the eldest and declared, "If we do not quickly kill him, this lineage will ultimately die out even though there are a hundred sons. So kill him."

The mother of the hundred tiny infants said, "Even though this is a bad omen, because this child is cut from my flesh, I cannot bear to have him killed." So they ignored the prediction.

Then she picked up the next infant, who was younger than the first, [116] to see what was portended. His grandfather, the sage, said, "He has birthmarks on both soles of his feet, both his palms, and on his throat and the top of his head. When there are six birthmarks in pairs, a person is born under the sign of the Pleiades. He is blessed, for he cannot die even if his head were to be cut off, unless all six birthmarks are punctured simultaneously." They gave him the name Duryodhana, "difficult to combat," because others could not stab him and he would be unafraid of others. The names of the remaining sons are too many to recount.

At that time Prince Pāṇḍu had no sons. He renounced the kingdom and gave it to his younger brother Dhṛtarāṣṭra, since he was a father. Pāṇḍu went to the forest with his two wives, Devī Kṛṣṇā and Kuntī, for relaxation and in quest for the truth.

In the forest two sages, a man and a woman, had transformed themselves into deer and were copulating. Prince Pāṇḍu saw the two deer and shot the male with his arrow. The mortally wounded sage was furious. He said, "Because you did this while I was in congress with my wife, may your life come to an end the moment you have intercourse with your queen!" After cursing the prince, the sage died. His body burst into magical flames. The female sage said, "You jealous prince! When you die, may your queen commit suicide like this!" She jumped into the fire and died too.

Prince Pāṇḍu was frightened by these curses. He turned his back on the pleasures of intimacy. So that the royal lineage wouldn't be cut off, his wife princess Kuntī asked the king for permission to enact a plan. Then the princess Kṛṣṇā went and filled with milk the begging bowl of a forest ascetic who was engaged in a meditation of inexhaustible concentration while sitting in the middle of a ring of fire. By making this offering, the flesh on her hands was so burned that the white of her bones was exposed. The sage awoke from his meditation and looked around. He saw that Kṛṣṇā was making an offering and was pleased. He said, "Do not offer alms with your scorched hands. What do you seek?"

Kṛṣṇā requested a mantra for giving birth to children sired by gods. He gave her mantras for five pregnancies, one of which, the mantra of request to the medicine gods, the Āśvina, would yield twin brothers.

Then Devī Kuntī propitiated the sun god. From lying with him a son was born. [117] His name was Karṇa. Feeling that this would shame the king, she put the baby in a brass chest and ordered that it be carried to the ocean and thrown in.

A demoness named Aśvarūpa picked up the chest, opened it, and looked inside. She found the baby boy. She said, "I'll make you my son," and carried him off. She paid homage to a sage with extrasensory powers and pleaded, "Please make my son's skin as strong as diamonds!"

The sage said, "Let it be so."

He put the baby in his lap, and just as he was starting to bless him, Viṣṇu manifested as a brahman and said, "Do you know what you are doing? It is not right to pick up a naked infant just emerged from an unclean womb and put him in your lap without tying some clean cotton thread around him."

The sage said, "That is true," and he tied a thread around the baby's waist. As a result, Karṇa's skin became as hard as a diamond everywhere except for where the thread touched his waist. Over that they tied a belt of diamonds.

Then Devī Kṛṣṇā propitiated Yama, the lord of death. A son named Yudhiṣṭhira came from lying with him. This son inherited some of the good physical qualities of his father's lineage. His body was radiant—that was the benefit of never telling a lie even at the risk of losing his life. He had many other good qualities too. After that, Devī Kṛṣṇā propitiated Indra. From that union a son named Arjuna was born. Among his father's good qualities, he inherited the attribute that made him famous as the most skillful archer in the world. This superiority that excludes all other archers is used as an example by glorious Dharmakīrti as well.[161] Next she propitiated Brahmadeva of the desire realm. Their son was called Bhīma. He became renowned as the strongest man in the world.

Then the princess Kuntī propitiated the twin medical gods, the Āśvina. This resulted in the twins Nakula and Sahadeva. As to the good qualities of their father that they inherited: the former had stable visual clairvoyance and the latter had an alluringly beautiful form.

Because Kuntī's first son, Karṇa, had been cast into the ocean, five sons remained in the human realm: three sons of Devī Kṛṣṇā and two of Devī Kuntī. Although these five were actually sons of gods, throughout the world they were known as Pāṇḍu's five sons. [118] Therefore, because there were five male children, everyone was free from worry that the lineage would come to an end.

Then Prince Pāṇḍu said, "To not experience the joy of intimacy while having a wife like Devī Kṛṣṇā is like death." Having said this, he went to lie with Kṛṣṇā. When his sperm fell into her womb, the curse of the former sage fell on him. A huge magic arrow fell from the sky and hit the king. The instant that happened, his body burst into flames. Then Kṛṣṇā said to Kuntī, "Please watch over my three sons as your own, so that you have five children." Saying these last words, she jumped into the fire and died.

Then mother Kuntī along with the children went to their former palace. While they lived there, the city's populace was unified in their love for them.

This caused her brother-in-law, King Dhṛtarāṣṭra of the Kauravas, to feel animosity toward the children.[162] He advised, "When these boys grow up, they will come to steal my kingdom. Thus we should kill them with trickery now while they have little power." They built a lacquer house with only one pillar. They put the mother and children inside and shut the door. After that, they set the house on fire. Tongues of scorching flame came up. Nakula saw with his clairvoyance that their maternal uncle, Viṣṇu, had made a secret escape tunnel under the pillar with his adamantine scepter. Nakula beckoned the others. Bhīma lifted the pillar, and the children with their mother escaped through the tunnel. They reached the land of the demons, the country Sri Lanka.

At that time the demons did astrological calculations. They predicted, "When the goddess Caṇḍālikā manifests as a girl in the year of the horse, and King Yudhiṣṭhira with his brothers come from the land of men, the demon kingdom will be destroyed because these two events are in astrological conflict." In response to that prophecy, all the demon girls born in the year of the horse were cast into the water. At that time a demon carrying his newborn daughter came by, and Yudhiṣṭhira asked him what he was doing. The demon explained what had happened. Yudhiṣṭhira recited a melodious praise of Caṇḍālikā in **dhandhaka* meter that began, "Give me a piece of cloth." This praise pleased the goddess. The baby transformed into Caṇḍālikā and flew off into the sky.

Then Yudhiṣṭhira and his brothers killed all the male demons and appropriated the country. [119] At that point Yudhiṣṭhira and his five brothers took a single demoness as their joint wife. To indicate which one was going to sleep with their wife, they would hang their sandals on the door and then go in. One time Bhīma hung his sandals on the door and went in to sleep with their wife. A mouse chewed through the sandal lace and the shoe fell to the floor. A dog found the sandal and ate it. Then Arjuna checked and saw that there was no sandal on the door and went into the room. Bhīma was embarrassed at being seen sleeping with their wife. "Why did you come in while I'm here?" he asked.

Arjuna said, "There were no sandals."

Bhīma didn't believe him. They looked into the matter and understood what had occurred. The woman cast a curse: "Because mice were harmful to us while we were sleeping in conjugal embrace, may the tip of a male's penis be cut off in the female's womb whenever they have sex!" Because of this curse, this is what happens to mice even to this day. She also said, "Because a greedy dog ate the sandal while we were sleeping together, dogs will be stuck together when they have sex." We hear that this is the reason for dogs getting stuck together nowadays.

Then after ten months the demoness gave birth to Bhīma's son. From his father's side he got a lovely physique, but from his mother's side he inherited stiff red hair that stood up like a horse's mane. His name was Kumbhakarṇa. Thus there were eight in all: six men (the five brothers and their nephew) and two women (the brothers' mother and their joint wife). They lived happily. When the story became known throughout the world, the Kaurava brothers became jealous. They sent a message, "You cannot stay on that island. If you remain there, we will send an army."

In this dispute between the father kings, the two brothers, Viṣṇu emanated as a brahman, went before Duryodhana, and said, "You may choose. Will you choose twelve divisions of an army of this world or just one warrior, the son of the god of wealth?" Duryodhana said, "I choose the former." This angered Viṣṇu, and he joined the side of the Pāṇḍavas.

They all prepared to do battle on the ocean shore. Just when they were ready to enter into battle, Arjuna looked all around and saw that every combatant was his kinsman. Among them was Karṇa, [120] Kuntī's firstborn son, who had been brought up as the son of a demoness because he had been put into a chest and tossed into the ocean. Later the Kaurava king had supported him, sending him so much gold it took sixty men to carry it. Arjuna thought about those gathered there and said:

> I, this son of Kuntī,
> see all my relatives here.
> O Viṣṇu! To fight against family
> makes my body tremble.

"I do not want to harm those near to me." Saying this, he turned away.

In the *Tattvakaumudī*, Viṣṇu exhorts him as follows:

> Look! A lack of fortitude is the sole cause
> that defeats those engaged in numerous austerities
> or anything else that is commenced,
> such as your battle against the opposition.
> If you do not address that,
> what action could be equally harmful?

Would any able man's wishes be satisfied?
O hero! Pay attention. Harmful enemies
are hateful and must be entirely annihilated.[163]

Arjuna was confused about this advice. Viṣṇu said:

What! Are you a fool?
It is incorrect to think either
that a man is killed
or that there is a killer;
killed and *killer* are incorrect.

Caste and doing your duty is perfection.
Brahmans, cattle, elephants,
dogs, and outcaste butchers
are equal. See them as the same.[164]

He said this and more. After teaching Arjuna in accord with the view of those who hold that this life is desirable, he bewildered the youth. With Viṣṇu acting as his charioteer, Arjuna went into battle.

Previously Viṣṇu had known that in the future Arjuna would have to destroy Karṇa. Karṇa, Kuntī's son, had been adopted by demons. When a sage was asked to bless the child so his skin would be as hard as diamonds, Viṣṇu had employed the strategy of tying a thread around Karṇa's waist to leave a gap in that armor. Cutting this narrow strip of skin could kill him.

Arjuna was the son of Indra, and Indra had compassion for his child. So at this time Indra magically took the form of a brahman and went to pay his respects to Karṇa. Karṇa said, "What do you want by coming to pay homage to me?"

Indra said, "I don't want anything."

Karṇa said, "The cunning show respect because they want something. It isn't really respect. There is something you want, so tell me." [121]

Indra said, "Well then, I want your skin—please give it to me."

Karṇa loosened his belt of diamonds. He peeled his upper skin off his upper body and peeled his lower skin off his lower body and gave it to him. A god of the sky said, "There is no one so lacking love as Indra. There is no one as generous as Karṇa."

Indra draped Karṇa's skin over his son Arjuna so it fit perfectly. Weapons could not pierce it.

Then the hundred sons of the Kaurava king with a worldly host of twelve battalions fought against the seven: Arjuna and his brothers made five, with his nephew they were six, and with Kṛṣṇa they were seven. Most of the twelve battalions of that army were slain. When they were about to be defeated, a sky god spoke the following verse:

> No matter how many archers there are
> in the twelve battalions of the Kaurava army,
> when they face the best archer,
> you will see they are like women.

However, Duryodhana had been given the paranormal power by his grandfather that he could not die in combat unless all six of his birthmarks were pierced simultaneously. Viṣṇu conceived of a means to kill him. It involved Duryodhana's officiating priest, the sage Aśvathāma, who had magical powers, clairvoyance, and supernatural sight. Now because Yudhiṣṭhira never told a lie—whatever he said, to either friend or foe, was always the truth—Viṣṇu went and instructed Yudhiṣṭhira, "Today, when we are engaged in battle, shout, "The sage Aśvathāma is dead!" When you make that speech, we will triumph in battle."

Yudhiṣṭhira asked his teacher Viṣṇu, "Is Aśvathāma dead or not?"

Viṣṇu said, "He is not dead."

Yudhiṣṭhira said, "Even if I were to lose my life, I will not tell a lie."

At that time Viṣṇu found in the hinterlands a horse that had just died. The horse had had the same name as the sage, Aśvathāma. Viṣṇu said, "You should think, 'The horse Aśvathāma' but say 'Aśvathāma is dead.' "

Yudhiṣṭhira said, "Since that ends up being a lie, I will not say it."

Viṣṇu said, "Well then, do it this way. In a loud voice shout, 'Aśvathāma is dead!' [122] and in a soft voice say, 'As to that, I mean the horse Aśvathāma.' If you do it that way, it will not be a lie and it will work." This is how Viṣṇu urged him to distort things and speak.

Since Yudhiṣṭhira said it that way, Duryodhana heard what was said loudly and didn't hear what was said softly. Duryodhana was disconsolate. He put the sole of his left foot on top of the arch of his right foot. He also stacked his hands. And between his feet and hands he placed his bow, lining up and stacking his birthmarks on the upper and lower points. Atop his hands he rested his throat and brooded. At that point Viṣṇu pushed Duryodhana's head down with his hand and it pierced all six of Duryodhana's birthmarks simultaneously. Duryodhana died.

His elder brother, the king of the Kauravas, said to Arjuna, "My younger brother is dead. Since the peoples of the world will be miserable while the both of us live, one of the two should hide and the other seek. If the seeker finds the hider, the one found will be killed. If he doesn't find him, the seeker shall be killed."

Arjuna promised, "Let us do it like that." The Kaurava hid. Arjuna searched from sunrise to sunset. During the search, the Kaurava hid in the hollow trunk of a large tree, so although Arjuna searched until sunset, he didn't find him.

The Kaurava was very happy and laughed aloud. At that point light radiated from his mouth. It came through a crack in the tree trunk. Arjuna saw it and went to kill him. However, the Kaurava's officiating priest, an ascetic who was born blind, was a master of cursing. He had cast this curse: "The first one who throws my Kaurava benefactor's head on the ground, may his head too fall dead on the ground."

The way to not be harmed by that curse was to shoot arrows in the manner explained in the Vedas. The moment before an arrow would cut off the Kaurava's head, a thousand arrows would connect in the sky—one arrowhead would connect with base of the fletched shaft of the next—so that they would hit the target as one. In this way the Kaurava's head was hurled into the lap of that officiating priest sage. Not scrutinizing it, the blind man said, "What is this ball that has ended up in my lap?" And he threw it onto the ground. Because of the curse he had cast, his head too fell down dead on the ground. [123]

Thus almost all of King Dhṛtarāṣṭra's sons, the hundred Kaurava brothers, and their armies were killed. Yudhiṣṭhira was made king of the world by his brothers. However, the so-called five sons of Pāṇḍava were actually children born of the power of the gods.

One of the Kaurava soldiers said, "It would be better to die than be a subject of the murderer of my lord. Let us two, you and I, leave for the high mountains." They fled to Tibet. They are the ancestors of the Tibetans. It is said that this is why Tibetans have had good moral fiber.

* * *

249 The weak find it difficult to bear
even just the words of someone virtuous.
There is a well-known saying,
"Just the Gauḍa king's words chained the ocean king."

In a place called Gauḍa in the south there was a virtuous king named Rāmapāla.[165] In order to control all the surrounding countries and islands, he ordered, "Wage war to constrain the ocean king."

A long time later a young woman with superb ornaments appeared and said, "Set free my king that you have enchained."

Rāmapāla said, "I have not chained anyone up. Who is shackled?"

She said, "You said, 'Wage war to constrain the ocean king.' "

The king said, "In that case, now let him be free!" These very words liberated him. Verse 252 of *A Jewel Treasury of Wise Sayings* says:

> The best asset is generosity.
> The best happiness is a joyous mind.
> The best ornament is learning.
> The best friend is the one most reliable.

These four superlatives should be obtained equally by everyone. Generosity increases your worldly goods in the present, and you will not have to struggle for them in the next life. Thus it is an inexhaustible treasure house of assets. It is the means of satisfying the wishes of others, and it is the perfection of generosity. As to the second quality, those who wish to make their mind manageable turn away from selfish desires. It is said that "Among the types of happiness, the extinction of craving is the lord of happiness. There is nothing better." And, "You must tame your mind!" The Bhagavān said, "The mind is the foundation of the Dharma." As to the third quality, the good qualities that are achieved come from learning. Bhagavān Maitreya said in the *Ornament of Mahayana Sutras*: [124]

> Although immature people may wear lovely garments,
> they are stained with impropriety because they lack modesty.
> Bodhisattvas are garbed in knowledge of humility,
> so even if they are not of mature age they are very lovely.[166]

And the self-same great master Sakya Paṇḍita similarly said in verse 123 of *A Jewel Treasury of Wise Sayings*:

> Good qualities are your finest ornaments
> as long as you have a sense of modesty.

The fourth supreme thing is the unsurpassable Teacher. I quote:

> The bodhisattva has much learning,
> sees the truth, speaks masterfully, is loving,
> and is a superior person who will not be reborn:
> as such, he is known to be a great being.[167]

And I quote:

> He is the best of companions
> because he is satisfied with merely a little,
> has entirely woken from sleep,
> and is a friend through thick and thin.[168]

This concludes "An Examination of Natural Tendencies," the sixth chapter of *A Jewel Treasury of Wise Sayings*.

Chapter 7. An Examination of Unseemly Tendencies

277 Even if you see the prospect of obtaining wealth,
who would take it from an improper place?
We have heard that the fox's head was smashed
because he licked the blood of battling rams.

There were two people like this example of a fox: a proper brahman called *Aśthabhuti and a barber's wife who worked as a procuress.

But first, a fox went near a village in search of food.[169] There he saw two boisterous rams who had been battling for a long while. A lot of blood was dripping from their horns. He thought, "This is great." In order to get the blood, the fox stuck his head in between the two clashing rams. When they charged again, his head was split open like a cotton seed-pod. In order to understand this story, we make an analogy: a bear that sees honey is seduced only by its good qualities, disregarding the danger from the bees.

When the Bhaga brahman Aśthabhuti was wandering, he came upon another brahman of a similar caste [125] and accompanied him. However, that companion was not to be trusted, for after a while, the companion said as they approached a town, "Please wait here for a while. I will go visit a householder in town." When asked why, he said, "An atom of dust from that householder's home is stuck to my garment. If I do not take it back, I will have taken something that was not given to me."

The brahman Aśthabhuti believed that speech. To watch over all their possessions, he walked around them. After a while he went to the Ganges River to bathe. When he returned he found that the dusty brahman had taken all their possessions and left. Aśthabhuti cursed himself and went to the village.

At that time in the village there lived a whore who was the wife of a weaver. Her procuress was the barber's wife. She solicited a man. While all three were together, the husband of the whore came home. So the client ran off and the procuress hid in the kitchen. The husband looked into what was going on. He tied his wife to a pillar and left her there. Then he got drunk and fell asleep. The woman called to her procuress, "You didn't do anything wrong, so nothing will happen to you. Please take my place here for a bit."

Her friend the procuress agreed. She stayed there tied to the pillar. Around midnight, the man woke up. Contending that she had slept with many other men, he cut off her nose and fell back to sleep.

In terror, the procuress called out softly to the weaver's wife, "Please free me from these bonds since my nose has been cut off!"

Once free, she ran off. The weaver's wife, the one who had begun the misconduct, tied herself to the pillar and engaged in deception. When her husband woke up, the two argued for a long while. The woman said, "I have never committed the sin of being with another man. In accusing me of this you are the one at fault! If the words, 'I am without fault' are true, may my nose grow back!" From her swearing on her nose that her speech was true, her husband was completely fooled.

When the procuress got back to her own house, her husband was drunk and they too had a long argument just like the previous couple. He was so angry that he threw a razor at her. [126] She said, "You've cut off my nose!" and fell rolling onto the ground.

That is how these stories are told. In another version that I have heard, the barber says, "You deserve to have your nose cut off!" and his wife says, "You don't need to do it, I cut it off myself!" Just by those words she deceived her husband.

No matter how the deceptions were conducted, on seeing them the brahman understood and said:

> In these three cases: the hypocrite and I,
> the fox between two battling rams,
> and the procuress who was the barber's wife
> all brought about their own destruction.[170]

He told these stories to explain similar experiences to others.

* * *

279 Do not abandon long-term friends
and put your faith in new acquaintances.
It is a well-known saying that the owl king
was destroyed by trusting the crow minister.

If you ask how that came to be, it is as follows. Suparṇa, the king of the owls, and Rāṣṭrapāla, the king of crows, were very antagonistic toward each other. Each of them had a superb minister: the owl minister was called Suvarṇākṣa and the crow minister was called Balahāka. At one time the crow minister gathered all of his kind together and said, "We have not been able to defeat our enemy in combat. Even though we have a treaty, they are an awful enemy and so we must now deceive them. Pull out my feathers, break my legs, and go elsewhere." Then they did exactly that. They threw his nest, with him in it, to the foot of a ficus tree and left.

Then all the owls who lived in the craggy mountains gathered together and drew up for war. But they found no one there except for the minister pitifully crying. "What happened to you?" they asked.

"It's like this." he said, "I wanted to reconcile and they didn't agree. They love contention so much they threw me to the enemy."

Hearing that, the owl king said, "That's right. We should take him to our home."

In response, the owl minister Suvarṇākṣa said, "This minister is very clever. It would be better to leave him here and give him food and necessities." His king didn't listen and carried the crow minister back to their home. [127] He rejected his own minister, and Suvarṇākṣa departed.

Time went on and the crow minister behaved well for a while. They said to him, "You are very wise, so tell us how to build a nest that is better than this one."

"Do it like this," he said, "Assemble ten thousand dried sticks and fill it with powdered guano. It will be nice and warm." They did precisely that. They were all happy there. During the day the crow went out in search of food. He stayed in the nest to protect it at night. Then one day he went and joined his relatives and said, "Tomorrow at noon each of you bring a torch there." And then he returned to the owl nest.

The next day at noon the crows went to the owl nest. During the day all the owls were asleep in their nest. Each of the crows set a torch to the nest, and the owls were completely consumed by fire. We have heard that the owls who exist nowadays are descendants of the minister Suvarṇākṣa.

* * *

282 Do not harass your enemy, even if he seems weak,
without first assessing his capabilities.
The garuḍa triumphed over the ocean
because it mistreated the taḍibha bird.

A taḍibha is type of small bird.[171] It nests along the ocean shore. An ocean wave came in and swept away the little bird's nest along with its eggs. Then the little bird summoned all the other birds and told them what happened. One said, "What can we alone possibly do to the ocean? Therefore all of us together should summon the garuḍa in our distress."

They all agreed and said to the garuḍa, "You are of the same genus as us. Didn't you know the ocean had tormented us like this?" And they beseeched him for help.

The garuḍa seized the nāgas who lived in the ocean. Because he captured all of them, the ocean was forced to return the nest and eggs to the shore.

This is similar to the story about King Udayana Kañcī. Since his extensive fame and wealth are well known, there is no need to write about it.[172] [128]

* * *

286 Even intelligent people go the wrong way
when driven by powerful karma.

> Śiva, the supreme teacher of the tīrthikas,
> upholds the conduct of a madman.[173]

As to that verse, at one time Śiva was acclaimed as the greatest among the gods in the world. He was a teacher of some outsiders and he claimed that he was worthy of respect. All the gods gathered together. It was announced that there would be a feast and a council. Everyone was there except Śiva. After a long while he arrived with his body wrapped up head to toe. Because Indra and others laughed, their teeth fell out. Because some gods smiled, their eyes popped out.

The god Brahmā said to them, "I can explain the former life that set the groundwork for this." Because Śiva's lifespan was extended, he had a thousand heads and was a mighty lord. Because he was a zombie, a brahman was afraid of the pollution of being around him. So Śiva cut off his head at the neck with his fingernails. Then, unhappy and distressed that he had killed a brahman, Śiva wandered around wearing bone ornaments, an elephant skin, and pieces of skull on his body. He held a skull and a club in his hands. He danced and ran feverishly in front of many people. He behaved in a manner reviled by others. The followers of Viṣṇu proclaimed:

> He lives in a cemetery
> enjoying the company of evil spirits.
> If someone like this is a god,
> what is a cannibal like?

* * *

287 Someone who transgresses the law in some way
may succeed for a while, but will lose in the end.
Balāka may have acquired the entire world,
but the lion killed him because he violated the law.

The asura leader, the golden-clad protector of beings called Hiraṇyakāśyapa Balāka, propitiated the great god Śiva for one hundred thousand years.[174] After a long time Śiva said, "I will give you the best. Ask for whatever you want, such as wrathful powers."

Balāka said, "The magic power I want is that I cannot be killed outside my house, I cannot be killed inside my house, I cannot be killed on earth,

I cannot be killed in the sky, I cannot be killed during the day, I cannot be killed at night, I cannot be killed by a human, I cannot be killed by a nonhuman, I cannot be killed by weapons, I cannot be killed by something that is not a weapon, and I cannot be killed by a hand." [129] Śiva gave him exactly that.

Many of Balāka's sons grew old and died before him. At one point he said to one of his sons who was still young, "Praise me if you know how. If you don't know how, I will kill you. A son may be necessary to perform rituals when one dies. However, I am never going to die, so what do I need a son for?" The youth heard that. He did not have the courage to praise him, so he went to another place.

At that time Viṣṇu had taken the form of an ordinary person. The youth went before him and Viṣṇu asked him what had happened. The youth related the former events in detail. Viṣṇu said, "I will teach you to make praises in that regard." The youth was delighted and made a request for instruction. Viṣṇu taught, "Return home and right on the threshold set up a large throne. Invite your father to sit on it. Then make this speech:"

> Sages live throughout all mountains.
> Water sprites live throughout all waters.
> There are four choices at every crossroad.
> Viṣṇu is the one who is omnipresent.

Then the youth returned home and went before his father. He did precisely what he had been instructed to do. When his father was on the throne he praised him with that verse. The verse infuriated Balāka because it was not a praise of him but was about the greatness of Viṣṇu. He slammed his fist into the door lintel, cracking it. And he said, "If Viṣṇu is everywhere, is he right here or not?"

Viṣṇu emerged from the crack as the man-lion. He had the body of a man to counter the father's prior magic power of "cannot be killed by a nonhuman." He had the head of a lion to counter "cannot be killed by a man" He had hands to counter "cannot be killed by a weapon." Each hand had an iron claw to counter "cannot be killed by that which is not a weapon." They were on the threshold of the exterior door to counter "cannot be killed outside the house" and "cannot be killed inside." To counter "cannot be killed in the sky or on the earth," Viṣṇu put him on his lap. To counter "cannot be killed during the day or at night," Viṣṇu killed him by lifting him with his fingernails just as the sun was setting. This is how the properties of the magic powers that had been granted earlier were overcome. [130]

* * *

297 Getting angry and harming others
without checking what is right or wrong
is like the pigeon who killed his mate
and became miserable without her companionship.

Two pigeons, a particular type of dove, lived together in a meadow.[175] In the spring the female pigeon stayed behind to guard the seeds they had found. Meanwhile the male went to find more seeds elsewhere. Later, when he returned home, the pile of seeds had become smaller because the seeds had dried. Seeing that, he said, "You ate all the seeds!"

The female said, "I didn't eat any of them!"

But he didn't listen. Becoming angry, he beat his wife until she died. The next year, he examined all the seeds and just as before the pile shrank. Upon reflection, he realized, "Alas! My wife was not at fault at all." His mind was oppressed by sorrow. Some of the young meadow gods proclaimed:

> The pigeon who lived in the meadow,
> the one with piebald feathers and red eyes,
> didn't investigate what was right or wrong,
> so he killed his wife and lives in misery.

This concludes "An Examination of Unseemly Tendencies," the seventh chapter of *A Jewel Treasury of Wise Sayings*.

Chapter 8. An Examination of Actions

306 Even when you get very old
you should pursue more education.
The benefits to future lives from just studying
are greater than those coming from generosity.

In view of the above verse, think about acquiring the great result of education in the very life you have right now.

Once there was an old abbot of a major temple.[176] He thought, "I am old and so ignorant. What can I do? I must seek an education now."

When he made an effort to do that, the king of that region, named Dharmapāla, showed him a dry stick and said, "When you become a master scholar, even this dry stick will bear fruit!"

Hearing that speech was like beating him with a whip to make him go faster. He prayed to the conqueror Mañjuśrī. In seven days his wish to become a great master was fulfilled. [131] He went before the king and said, "Take the fruit of your dried-up stick!" The king was amazed. He and everyone else treated the old abbot as someone worthy of respect. This great scholar was known as *Bhakanbha. (This is a teaching of the stainless savior of Mar, me.)[177]

* * *

321 The great abstain from desire
for frivolity, pleasure, and food.
It is said that Rāvaṇa of Laṅka was killed
as a result of his lustful craving.

Rāvaṇa was the king of Laṅka.[178] Although he propitiated Śiva for a long time, he did not get any results. That tormented him, so he cut off each of his ten heads and made them a burnt offering. The all-seeing one heard him and said to Umā, "Go and give him a supranormal power."

She went and said, "I will grant you whatever you desire."

He said, "I propitiated Śiva!"

"Indeed, he sent me," she said.

He said, "I do not want a power from a woman."

Umā got angry and said, "Your kingdom will be destroyed by a woman in the future!" And she left.

Then Śiva sent his son, who went and explained why he had come. The conversation went just as before. Śiva's son got angry and said, "In the future your kingdom will be brought to ruin by one having the form of a monkey!" Then he left.

Then the stern one, Śiva himself, went before him and said, "What do you want?"

Rāvaṇa was angry and continued with his fire offering, saying, "You have little compassion."

Śiva said, "I'm here now, aren't I! What do you want from me?" According to what appeared in the mind of the teacher Mar based on what he had heard from the great venerable,[179] the king then said this:

> I want an iron enclosure that cannot be destroyed by anything:
> triple protection from oceans, fire pits,
> the divine physician Aśvinī shaped like a dog,
> an army of cannibal demons, and the king of the gods of wealth.

Because he said this and more, Śiva could see that he wanted the attainment of immortality. Śiva's tongue spoke melodically and deceptively. "Definitely. This statement is a desire for the power of immortality. [132] I give you the attainment of the immortality that you desire for so long as your horse's head is not cut off. Take it!"

Later, a girl was born while the king was living in his kingdom. She was shown to the brahmans, who evaluated her and said, "Because she is an evil omen, it is not suitable to keep her here." The king listened. He put the girl in a brass box and set it in the water. It came to the human world. In spring when some farmers drew water into an irrigation ditch, the box was there. The farmers opened it and found the girl inside. So they gave her the name Found in a Furrow. The baby girl grew into an enchanting young woman. The famers consulted among themselves. The king of their land was Rāma, so they offered her to him and said, "Her name is Sītā."

The king's mind was gladdened. He exhorted his younger brother Lakṣmaṇa, whose name when translated into Tibetan means "collected mind," "I am giving the kingdom to you—someone with a bit of an interest in worldly matters."

In reply the younger brother said, "O king! If someone like you has no desire for the kingdom, how could someone like me want it? I want to practice religion with you." So Rāma gave the kingdom to Bharata, the youngest of the three brothers. And the two brothers with Sītā went to a place for the practice of austerities.

At that time, the demon king Rāvaṇa was entranced by his own wife's youthful beauty. He asked someone whether there was anyone more lovely than her in existence. The person said, "It is said that there is someone in the human world." The demon king coveted her and so went to the place for the practice of austerities in the human world, transforming his appearance into a beautiful deer. The queen genuflected and requested King Rāma, "Please catch it!"

He replied, "The creature will bring misfortune. It is likely that it is a deceptive illusion."

Sītā said, "You are only saying that because you cannot catch it!"

Stung by this criticism the king went out but did not catch the deer. Then after a while, disguising his voice, Rāvaṇa cried out, "O Sītā!"

The woman said to the king's brother Lakṣmaṇa, "Go! It is the king. He must be in danger."

He said, "My king is so powerful, who could challenge him? He told me to stay here, and I am."

Again she said to Lakṣmaṇa, "Is it that if the king dies you want to take me as a wife? I could not bear that impure sexual conduct!"

He said, "How can you say this! I did not even want the kingdom. Do not go beyond this line until I return." He drew a magic circle and departed. [133]

At that point the demon king took the form of a brahman and begged for alms. Sītā said, "I cannot go beyond this line to give you alms." He transformed into an unbearable great light in order to seize her and the ground she stood on.

Then the two brothers met and questioned each other. The king now knew it was a trick. They returned and saw that the ground, and everything on it, had been carried off. They searched everywhere.

At one point they went near the brink of a large waterfall. There, on the upper part, they saw two monkeys about to fight. Seeing them there, one of the monkeys came up to them and, when questioned, said, "We are fighting over our kingdom. We have been battling for three days now. It seems he is about to win." The king agreed to become his ally.

The next morning, the king watched the vast spectacle of their battle until the sun set. The monkey came and said, "You lied."

Rāma said, "I did not. However, I was confused about who was who between the two combatants. Since that is the truth, you wear this mirror." The monkey tied it to his forehead and again went to fight. The king shot the other one, who said:

> In the battle between Vālī and Sugrīva,
> why was Vālī cast so far away?
> Why did Sugrīva receive help therein?

Then he died.

Then Vālī's wife said, "I am a virtuous monkey wife. If a dog is to carry his corpse, I will do it like that. His body should be conveyed to the snow peaks."

Sugrīva was pleased and said, "Whatever you want will be done." The monkey king communicated that objective to the monkeys.

When they had done as he commanded, he said to Rāma, "I will be your assistant. Let us go right away." The two departed. They went through every valley and mountain amid of a host of monkeys. In a distant place they encountered an emaciated monkey with three eyes. They each told him their histories. That monkey understood and departed. In one leap he reached the realm of the wind gods. Asking where he was, he was told, "It is the realm of the wind gods."

He avowed, "My maternal uncle is a wind god. So I will not depart until I go in and meet him."

They said, "Well then, please wait here." He was offered food prepared in a guest house. There he seized a skull that had been made into a plow. He was unhappy about not being able to entreat his uncle. His uncle appeared and he explained.

His uncle said, "Because of your strength, the nāgas below will protect you when they see that you will be harmed." [134]

Then the monkey returned. With a single leap he reached the primordial island of Laṅka. He looked about and saw that Sītā was imprisoned in an orchard's enclosure. He asked why, and the guards said, "She has no reverence for our king. She said, 'You are a demon king and I am the noble wife of a human king.' So she was put here."

The monkey, Hanumān, went into her presence. "I have been sent by the king, I will do your bidding."

She said, "I do not believe you."

Hanumān said, "It is true," and showed her the king's ring.

She said, "I have been kidnapped by demons. If you have the ability, steal me away. I cannot escape on my own."

The monkey said, "Now please give me something to eat."

She said, "I have nothing to eat. This fruit all belongs to the king. Although I have avoided taking what was not given, pick a small one." She pointed and said, "Eat that little one, you greedy monkey!"

He ate a little and then uprooted all the fruit trees and stuck them upside down into the ground. The demons gathered and said, "There is an unruly monkey inside the orchard fence!" They surrounded him, but he jumped far away. That happened many times. Finally they caught him.

As they prepared to kill him, he said, "You obey your kingdom's laws. I do too. There are two modes of execution, please choose one of them." Upon being asked, he said, "The two are the paternal method and the maternal method. By the maternal method, you put me in the storeroom and give me all sorts of delicious food until it sticks in my throat and I die. By the paternal method, you wrap my tail in cloth saturated with butter and set it alight."

They agreed on the latter. They started wrapping his tail in cloth. But though they used up all the cloth in the kingdom, they couldn't cover his tail. They dipped it in oil and set it on fire. Since it was like a wick, the fire on his tail swept the entire sky and melted all the demon king's palaces. Finally, just as he was about to put his tail into the ocean, all the nāgas held him back and extinguished it with their spit.

Then that monkey leapt back to go before Rāma. He related Sītā's story. The king said, "I must lead the army." When they arrived on the shore of the ocean, he ordered Hanumān to muster the host of monkeys. While building a bridge across the ocean, they asked the great sage Vālmīki [135] what sort of living beings lived in the great ocean. The sage said, "There is a very large fish called a *ti* that is a hundred fathoms long. In its gullet is another large fish. And in that one's gullet is another large fish."

Then they completed the bridge to the other side. King Rāma and his army went across and encountered Rāvaṇa's followers. In the battle, Rāma cut off the head of Rāvaṇa's horse. Then the king returned to his camp. The ten-headed Rāvaṇa's younger brother, Kumbhakarṇa, which means "pitcher nose," was absorbed in a trance. To wake him a demon poured molten metal into his ear. He woke up and asked, "What is going on?"

The demon told the story of the killing of his elder brother. He comprehended and inhaled the entire atmosphere through his nostrils. This reduced everyone except Rāma and the monkey Hanumān to skeletons. This satisfied Kumbhakarṇa, and he resumed his meditation.

King Rāma called the monkey to him. He sent him to get medicine from the high snow mountain Kailash in Tibet. He brought back the wrong herbal medicine. When sent back a second time, he brought back the entire snow peak. This revived the entire army. "Now take the mountain that bears the medicine back," Rāma ordered.

The monkey said, "You said to gather a lot." He hurled the snow peak

Kailash a long distance. It is well known that this is why the mountain's peak is a little crooked.

Then the king came to be happy. He and the goddess Sītā were reunited and were overjoyed. This is how the two curses placed on Rāvaṇa came to be fulfilled.

* * *

368 Someone with integrity and humility
can be trusted even if they are a foe.
We hear that some people's lives were spared
by going for refuge to an honorable enemy.

Kārtika and the asura *Karmadeva were at war for a thousand years.[180] Finally Umā gave her son Kārtika a radiant spear, and he killed Karma. Karma's followers went to live with the youthful Kārtika's maternal uncle. Kārtika went to his uncle and said, "Royal custom does not specify whether remaining enemies are to be left alive. Release them to me!"

His uncle thought, "All of those people depend on me," and to communicate his intent he said: [136]

> As soon as threshers take hold of the grass,
> they cut every last stalk in the bunch;
> to be seized instantly leads to falling down.
> What needs be said about these living beings?

His nephew said, "Well then, I'll take them by force." And he sent forth his army. His uncle killed him by piercing him with a spear, and his entire army was captured. This is well known.

* * *

363 When you set out to do a particular action,
consider both its advantages and disadvantages.
If it should be avoided if the two are equal,
what needs to be said if the drawbacks are greater?

This matter of advantage or disadvantage is similar to the dilemma of monkeys who focus only on potential problems and are afraid to eat the honey they have in their hands; or the boldness of bears who think only about honey's tastiness and stuff it right into their mouths.

* * *

375 If an enemy comes to you for refuge,
honor him and then speak pleasantly.
A crow became happy by relying on a mouse;
so says an ancient tradition.

There were two friends living in a forest: a mouse named Jewel Possessor and a pigeon named Painted Neck.[181] A flock of pigeons was caught in a fowler's net. They tried desperately to fly away. Their leader, Painted Neck, said, "Don't do that! Do what I do." So they all stayed enveloped in the net.

The old fowler thought they were all captured and let go of the net. At that moment, the leader took flight and the others flew off with him, all still covered by the net. They came to rest in front of Painted Neck's friend, the mouse. "Hey! Dear Jewel Possessor, please come here!"

The mouse came over and said, "What awful thing has happened?"

"All the birds and I were trapped in this net! Please, will you chew through it?"

"I can do that. Shall I cut you free first or not?"

Pigeon said, "No. First release my flock. After that do me." That is what he did and all the birds were freed from the net.

A crow was lurking nearby and saw what had occurred. He was pleased with it and thought, "I want to be his friend too." [137] So he went over and called to the mouse.

The mouse said, "What's up?"

Crow said, "Be my friend."

The mouse said, "I won't. I'm afraid that you will eat me."

Crow said, "I won't. I have faith in you." Then the two took an oath of friendship.

A deer, Decorated Body, saw that and asked for that bond too. Also a tortoise, Slow Going, saw them and requested the tie of friendship. They all made a similar oath.

After a while, when the tortoise was going to his friend's house a hunter encountered him. The hunter tied him around the middle with his bow string and carried him off. The tortoise cried out. The pigeon realized what happened. He and the deer went to the mouse Jewel Possessor to ask for help.

He said to the deer, "You go onto his path and play dead. He will put down the tortoise to come over. At that moment Crow should pick up the string. As soon as he does, the deer should flee."

By doing that they escaped to freedom. Working cooperatively is the right way to do things. Verse 304 in the same treatise says:

> The wise always consult others
> about a course of action even for minor tasks.
> Even their unfinished work is something to admire,
> so what needs to be said about things they complete?

And in another work too one reads:

> If consultation is the way to get things done,
> you should always ask wise people.
> What needs to be said if it goes well,
> and even if it comes to ruin it will be all right.[182]

This concludes "An Examination of Actions," the eighth chapter of *A Jewel Treasury of Wise Actions.*

Chapter 9. An Examination of the Dharma

399 Being devoted to other teachers
while the Buddha, the refuge of beings, is present
is like digging a well to get brackish water
near a river whose water possesses eight good qualities.

There once was a householder named Śrīgupta and a naked ascetic called *Assana.[183] Since the householder had faith in the ascetic, the ascetic said, "O householder, all those young Buddhist monks are [138] unjustifiably proud and should not have been ordained. You should deprive them of their livelihood. You will become famous for this."

The householder said, "I cannot do it."

"You can do it. Have a deep pit dug by your outer door. Inside it have placed a very hot but smokeless fire. Cover the pit with broom straw. Then invite the Buddha inside for poisoned food. We will see if he is omniscient or not! If he is not, he will fall into the pit and die with his faults. If he escapes, give him the food."

Then the householder bowed to the ascetic and went and ordered his servants to do precisely that. He himself went to Vulture Peak and made the invitation. The Teacher, fully understanding the matter, accepted. The householder acknowledged that reply, circumambulated three times, and left.

Meanwhile his wife, who was Anāthapiṇḍada's daughter, was watching. "My lord, who is your enemy?"

The householder said, "The monk Gautama."

The woman replied, "He is the Teacher. You cannot harm him. He is the unsurpassed, completely perfect Buddha."

He thought, "She is the daughter of a Śākya. She'll go and reveal this secret." So he confined her inside the house.

The time of the invitation came. The Teacher said to Ānanda, "Go and tell the other venerable monks not to go into the householder's presence before me." That morning, Brahmā with all the great gods and a crowd of those who take joy in the teachings assembled around him. There were many miracles as the Buddha went to the householder's place. There was an earthquake at that time.

When the Teacher placed his right foot on the threshold of the outer door, the blind gained sight, the deaf obtained hearing, the insane found their wits, and so forth. A holder of layman vows requested, "Please tell us the history behind these events."

The Buddha said, "O layman, even when I was an animal, fire could not harm me. Now that I am actually a fully accomplished Buddha what can it do?"

The layman requested that he elaborate.

The Teacher said, "Previously, when I was born as a fire bird in the forest of Kaliṅga, this layman was a rabbit, and Indra invited a brahman, and so forth." Then he went further and placed his foot on the edge of the fire pit. The fire died and became a patch of lotuses. He and his entourage walked across it. [139] Everyone was amazed. A great clamor arose.

The householder's chief wife, Anāthapiṇḍada's daughter, who was hidden inside, heard that. She thought, "Alas! The Teacher has passed away!" She came running. When she saw what had happened, she praised the good qualities of the magnificent one.

Śrīgupta and Assana were on the roof watching. They were frightened. Then they bowed and came outside. The householder entreated, "O Teacher, I was possessed by a nonvirtuous spiritual friend and made to do improper deeds."

Buddha responded, "Did you know what you were doing or not?"

He begged forgiveness. "Yes. I am ashamed." Then he bowed and said, "O Lord, please wait a little while. Because all the food is poisoned, now I must prepare some anew."

The Buddha responded, "This food is fine. Even when I was an animal, poison couldn't harm me. In a former life I was the queen of the peacocks, Golden Light, to whom King Brahmadatta's daughter Anupamā gave poison. Householder, you should recite this verse three times, with the appropriate substitutions, and serve the food."

> The three—greed, hatred, and ignorance—
> are the three worldly poisons.
> The Buddha is not overpowered by poison;
> the Buddha's truth conquers these poisons.[184]

For the next two recitations substitute "the Dharma" and "the Sangha" for "the Buddha."

> Every creature is poisonous
> in a vast land imbued with poison.
> They all come from the poison of desire;
> desire is the strongest poison.

Then say the above verse twice more substituting "hatred" and "ignorance" for "desire."

Then while the householder sat on a comfortable seat, he came to understand that all phenomena are free from passion and are separate from stains.

* * *

418 The maladies of the three lower realms[185]
should be remedied before they arise.
It is like a lightning bolt striking your head;
what can you do after it has struck?

I have not written more here because this story is clearly similar to the tale of the daughter of Sārthavāha.[186]

* * *

450 If you wish to engage in proper behavior,
listen to whatever such a person says.
Always have the fortitude to do what is noble;
defend good conduct even at the risk of your life.

To briefly explain the way to protect your conduct:

> The buddhas and bodhisattvas
> have omniscient sight. [140]
> Everything is in their presence,
> and I stand before them.
>
> Contemplating in this way, I shall remain
> possessed of shame, respect, and fear.[187]

And so forth.

* * *

451 Thus if you can employ the antidotes with determination,
just as they are described in scriptures,
you will see the benefits of doing this in the future
for the wise do not speak what is false.

How do you know that they do not tell lies?

> The words in the scriptures are trustworthy:
> the wise will never say words that are untrue
> because they have no reason for falsehood.
> You can be sure their instructions eliminate faults.[188]

And regarding the actual benefits of practice:

> If you had performed
> these practices earlier,

a situation like this, one that is not a buddha's
perfect bliss, could never have arisen.[189]

And:

There is nothing that doesn't
become easier through practice.[190]

And so forth. In the *Thorough Exposition of Valid Cognition* it says:

Accustom your mind to love and so forth;
they will become natural to you.[191]

And so forth. It is through the antidotes that this can be accomplished. To expand on what is accomplished:

Sugata (Gone to Bliss) is the elimination with three excellent qualities:
it's complete elimination; and because it's not a basis of suffering,
it is excellent; and it arises from
the method of seeing absence of selfhood.[192]

This concludes "An Examination of the Dharma," the ninth chapter of *A Jewel Treasury of Wise Sayings.*

Just as Kumāra Jīvaka cured the very ill
by convincing them that his medicines were food,
I have taught this holy Dharma
by following the customs of the world.

This is a story about Jīvaka, the king of all physicians in ancient times.[193]

There was a king named Pradyota who was terrified of butter because he was the son of a scorpion. He became disturbed if someone merely said the word "butter."

The king could not sleep at all, so they summoned the doctor. The doctor ordered the ministers: "Saddle up the fastest of the king's camels. Feed the partially trained elephant Naḍaparvata parched rice but give him no water. [141] And fill a skin bag with female elephant urine."

The physician mixed refined ghee into some good wine and poured it for the king. The king drank it and fell asleep. Meanwhile Jīvaka mounted the camel and fled in the direction of Śrāvastī carrying the skin bag of female elephant urine. Then the king woke up. He belched and there was the scent of butter. The king said, "That physician gave me butter! Kill him! No one should eat food offered to them by that trickster."

A minister mounted the elephant Naḍaparvata and chased after the physician. But just when he got close to catching him, the elephant stopped for quite a while in order to drink water from a nearby pond. Later, when the minister came close to catching him once again, the physician Jīvaka threw down the bag full of urine. The elephant became aroused, and while he was sniffing it Jīvaka reached the pleasure grove of Śrāvastī. When the minister arrived there, Jīvaka spread a diarrhea-causing drug on the fingernails of his left hand. With the fingernails on his right hand, he broke a myrobalan fruit in half. He said to the minister, "It is good that you are here. Please have some fruit." Jīvaka offered him the half in his left hand and ate the other half that was in his right. The minister thought, "Since he too is eating this, it is all right." So he ate it. Then the minister became sick with diarrhea and the physician cured him just as he had washed away the king's illness.

The minister went to the king and explained why Jīvaka should be honored. After consideration the king agreed. The king offered the physician a bolt of excellent cloth. In turn the physician offered the cloth to the Teacher. It is said that the Teacher made this cloth into his three robes and gave the remainder of the cloth to Ānanda for an upper robe. This is a clearly condensed account about what the scriptures say is the source of Buddhist monastic robes.

Just as the physician truly helped the king by employing a complete range of actions, including using butter, it is said that the great being Sakya Paṇḍita quoted from the texts of worldly norms and manners to explain the Dharma that should be studied by religious people. How is this so? For he writes:

> This marvelous *Jewel Treasury of Wise Sayings*
> arose from an island amid an ocean of learning,
> and is held by an intelligent nāga king.

Because the extent of the wisdom of the great being Sakya Paṇḍita cannot be comprehended by those who examine it, it is likened to the great depth of the ocean. [142] A *Jewel Treasury of Wise Sayings* is precisely what comes from an island amid an ocean of great depth. If you ask, "What indicates this?" this advice is comparable to jewels in that they share five qualities: both are rare, faultless, strong, serve as the best ornaments in the world, and are distinctively powerful.

If you ask, "Who possesses wealth like that?" Just as the king of nāgas has rubies, emeralds, and other jewels, it is said that this treasure trove of good advice is held tight by the nāga-like lord of intelligence. The particular nature of this wisdom is that it is the absolute best in the entire world. Every student who internalizes it becomes accomplished. Sakya Paṇḍita's wisdom is likened to rare gems because nāga lords are said to possess a treasure of incomparable jewels. Therefore this text is called the glorious *Jewel Treasury of Wise Sayings.*

Just as the ocean is the foundation and all jewels come from the nāga lord who lives in the ocean, our spiritual teacher Sakya Paṇḍita is a vast ocean of Dharma. He is a great being who gives every student everything he or she needs and so he is a boundless treasure. The flawless jewels of his good advice are inexhaustible and pertinent to every time and every circumstance. Therefore the analogy to a treasure trove is made. There are other examples of likening wisdom to a treasure, as in the first verse of the first chapter:

> The great ocean is a treasury full of water
> because all rivers flow into it.

If you ask, "What was the need for teaching such a text?" Sakya Paṇḍita said that he revealed this text to fill the mental treasuries of the intelligent, so that wise masters could accomplish their wishes, and in order to clear away ignorance everywhere.[194]

Jewels that come from the ocean fill the treasuries of kings and so forth. These jewels fulfill the needs and desires of those who possess them and these jewels can dispel darkness no matter where they are. Similarly, this good advice is a jewel from the shores of the ocean of wisdom. The words are free from hidden animus that does not accord with their actual meaning. It abjures trifles that serve to satisfy only a part of what is needed and it fills the treasury of intellect of all those people who aspire to clear understanding and enthusiastic perseverance. [143]

Sakya Paṇḍita revealed this treasure trove of good advice in order to create a pleasant way of speaking, writing, and teaching others that is appealing even to scholars in its use of examples already familiar to them and an impeccable variety of poetic ornamentation that demonstrate their various individual meanings. In addition to presenting a detailed classification of what should and should not be done, he wrote in order to shed light from every side on every aspect of a body of knowledge that had not been previously seen, so that the specific details could be distinguished and clearly ascertained.

A subsequent verse in the root text says:

> Through study of all that is to be known
> the state of omniscience will be attained.
> Therefore I composed this treatise
> so that others can attain complete buddhahood.[195]

Those who desire to obtain complete omniscience must practice and become familiar with everything to be known that is included in the three trainings. Similarly, Sakya Paṇḍita wrote this treatise called *A Jewel Treasury* so that disciples could attain complete buddhahood by untying the knots that bind them to samsara. It says in the *Ornament of Mahayana Sutras*:

> Even supreme āryas will not become omniscient
> if they do not apply themselves to study of the five sciences.
> Therefore they make an effort in those in order to care for
> others,
> to annihilate others' wrong views, and to completely understand
> reality.[196]

The *Guide to the Bodhisattva's Way of Life* says:

> There is nothing whatsoever
> that is not studied by bodhisattvas.
> For those skilled in living that way,
> there is nothing that is nonvirtuous.[197]

In addition, this saying appears in the great being Sakya Paṇḍita's own written discourses:

> If you do not study everything that can be known,
> omniscience is as far away as the end of space.
> It is said that buddhas and bodhisattvas understand that,
> so they intensely study the nature of everything that can be
> known.[198]

Therefore if you ask, "Who is the actual author of this?" The one who bestowed this teaching is identified in this line from of the root text:

> The Buddhist monk Kunga Gyaltsen Palsangpo
> examined things well with a virtuous mind.

Our guide who is beyond compare in the three realms has stainless splendor that cannot be encompassed by a name that identifies him in a single limited way. [144] And if you were to apply symbols and specify the many meaningful names for that object of marvelous activity whose holy mind extends completely over the sphere of everything that can be known, his epithets would be beyond count and measure. Because the grace of his name that is known to everyone comprehends this, he says "the Buddhist monk Kunga Gyaltsen."[199]

As to the author's particular intention, he said that he "examined things well with a virtuous mind." This is like gold that has been ascertained to be pure through the three types of analysis. Thus he wrote this text in order to make things clear in all respects.

As to dedicating merits of writing this text to benefit of others, the root text says:

> May the flawless virtues that arise from this composition
> shine brightly like of cooling rays of moonlight,
> clearing away darkness from the hearts of living beings
> and causing the flower of their intellect to blossom.
>
> Through study of all that is to be known . . .

This verse demonstrates that the dedication is in common with the purpose of the composition.

This treatise entitled *A Jewel Treasury of Wise Sayings* was composed at the glorious temple at Sakya. It was written by the Buddhist monk and logician Kunga Gyaltsen Palsangpo, someone who resides at the splendid Sakya temple located in the Tö Drompa region of Tsang, in the northern land of snows, a hundred leagues from Bodhgaya, which is the epicenter of enlightenment. The author is someone whose lotus of intelligence had been opened a little by the rays of Mañjuśrī's wisdom and, as a result, had studied, understood, and mastered grammar, logic, poetics, rhetoric, expressive ornamentation, and the majority of the renowned scriptures of the Buddha. Through inquiry he attained an unmistaken understanding of the essence of the scriptures, logic, and quintessential instructions. It is this possessor of virtue, confident in the means of exposition, composition, and debate, who composed this treatise. Thus narration of the stories mentioned in this text, by way of rough expositions, is completed.

> This commentary sheds light on a few of the edifying stories
> referred to in *A Jewel Treasury of Wise Sayings*
> to provide certainty about everything that should be practiced
> or avoided
> according to the dispositions of the lowest, middling, and best
> students. [145]

This commentary makes things clear by summarizing some of the ancient instructive stories that are referred to in *A Jewel Treasury of Wise Sayings.* Because the principal disciple of the Victor, the holy sage Kunga Gyaltsen Palsangpo, was an unmistaken master of the scriptures and the sciences, I—a person enmeshed in the web of doubts of those with intelligence—wrote and described only a bit about his treatise. I, Rinchen Pal, a hermit monk from the Dri region, produced this from the valley of Kyishö.

This commentary had seemed unclear, contained errors in the stories, and also had many gaps. To clean it up and make it free of mistakes, I prepared it at a later date in the presence of Sakya Paṇchen. Thus it was carefully rewritten with greater clarity by Martön Chögyal from central Tibet in accordance with the Dharma master's teaching.

4. Ganden Wise Sayings: A Bouquet of White Lotuses[200]

Paṇchen Sönam Drakpa

[147] Homage to the Bhagavān, master of the two systems of norms.

1 After respectfully bowing to the feet of Lord of Sages
who knows the two systems of norms exactly as they are,
I will briefly set forth some wise sayings
differentiating the wise and the foolish.[201]

2 Those said to be wise are those who know
the ways of the world or of Dharma.
Just as there are said to be two types of the wise,[202]
the foolish are also explained to be of two types.

3 The first type of wise person will be meritorious in this life;
the second will be meritorious in this and future lives.
The two types of fools are explained as
ruining this and their future lives, respectively.

4 Thus the difference between the wise and the foolish
is like the difference between Mount Meru and a dust mote,
like the difference between the ocean and a puddle,
and between the sky and the palm of your hand.

5 In front of the wise a wise person is attractive,
because his good qualities are seen as they are.
Look how a priceless jewel is held to be beautiful
when a top merchant holds it in his hands.

6 In front of the foolish a wise person is not attractive;
fools err because they do not see his good qualities.
Look at how a fool made into charcoal
sandalwood that is more precious than gold.[203]

7 The wise listen to what wise people say;
from that they obtain the relevant good qualities.
By listening to Captain Supāraga's words,
the merchants found treasure, as is well known. [148]

8 The foolish do not listen to the words of the wise;
from that they end up with the relevant problems.
It is well known that the turtle fell from the sky
because he did not listen to the geese's words.

9 The wise speak well of other wise people;
through that they inspire other people.
Look at what was said by the god Indra
about the renown of the bodhisattva hare.

10 Fools speak ill of the wise,
thereby forestalling other people's faith.
Look at the result of the ill-natured things
*Suhṛt said about the bhikṣu *Mallaputra.

11 When the wise see an indigent wise person,
they admire his superior mind.
Look how the ascetic's pure austerities
caused Indra to become delighted.

12 When fools see an indigent wise person,
with arrogant thoughts they treat him with scorn.
Look how old monkeys encountering a man
laugh, saying, "He doesn't have a tail!"

13 The wise care for their superiors like a crown,
through that they ascend higher themselves.

Look at the amazing superlative respect
Sumukha had for Dhṛtarāṣṭra.

14 Fools disparage their superiors;
through that they cast themselves down.
Look at the grave consequences for Śikhī
because he killed his father, an arhat.

15 Because the wise tell the truth,
others find their words convincing.
Look how the son of Sudāsa listened
to the prince because he told the truth.

16 Because fools tell lies,
others disregard their words.
Look how the layman *Eḍaka deserted
the non-Buddhist ascetics because they lied. [149]

17 Between the present and the future,
the wise hold future happiness to be superior.
Look how through the practice of austerities
Viśvantara obtained the bliss of the dharmakāya.

18 Between the present and the future,
the foolish believe present happiness is superior.
Look at the behavior of the evil man
who was helped by the Ruru deer.

19 The wise are friendly at first and thereafter;
they never abandon their friends.
Look at the way the chief of the monkeys
truly protected his troop of monkeys.

20 Although fools are amicable at first,
they turn on you for the slightest reason.
Look at the behavior of the evil lion
who was friends with the woodpecker.

21 A wise person may have little physical strength,
but with powerful discernment he overcomes his foes.
It is well known that because the rabbit was intelligent,
he slew the king of beasts.

22 Although fools may be physically strong,
because of their weak intelligence their enemies prevail.
The elephant had a huge, massive body,
but look how he was killed by the mongooses.

23 Because the wise have every good quality,
they are sought after wherever they go.
It is well known that good stallions
and lovely jewels are in demand in marketplaces.

24 Because fools have every kind of fault,
they are turned away wherever they go.
Look how no one will buy meat
if they know it comes from a donkey.

25 A wise man will obtain more honor
in places other than his homeland.
A jewel is only marketable in other places;
how could it be valued in its ocean home? [150]

26 No matter where a fool lives
everyone there will shun him.
Look how everyone rejected
the householder's son called Durāgata.

27 A wise man accomplishes his desired high goals
through the power of his pure vow.
Look how the partridge chick's altruistic motivation
diverted the incredibly huge conflagration.

28 Because the foolish make impure commitments
there are bad indications immediately,
and no matter what they do they come to ruin.

Look how Virūḍhaka, who was afraid of fire,
was burned up in a pleasure garden.[204]

29 The moment a wise person is defeated,
he gains courage to retaliate against his enemy.
Look how a northern yak took a hunter's life
because it was struck by the hunter's arrow.

30 If a fool is defeated just once,
he antagonizes his friends and loses the will to fight.
Look at the resentful, submissive behavior
of a bad dog when it is struck by a stone.

31 When a wise man confronts an important matter,
he has no fear, no matter who opposes him.
Look how Indra, all by himself,
brought about the defeat of the demigod army.

32 When a fool confronts an important matter,
he becomes frightened of the slightest thing.
Look how the tiger had a heart attack
because he mistook a man to be a *zak*!

33 When wise people assemble in a group,
they unite to do what is right by comparing ideas.
Look how the four creatures, the elephant and so on,
convened and created rules of ethical discipline.

34 When foolish people assemble in a group,
they unite to do evil by exchanging bad ideas.
Look how many non-Buddhist ascetics convened
and then killed the arhat Maudgalyāyana. [151]

35 The virtuous qualities of just one wise man
bring happiness to an entire country.
Look at the marvelous way the righteous king
nicknamed Flesh-Giver ruled his realm.

36 The actions of just one fool
bring misery to an entire country.
Look how Dukhamātṛka's actions
were the ruin of the Śākya clan.

37 Because the wise have subdued attachment and hatred
even their enemies become dear friends.
Look at the king's affectionate attitude
after he was rescued by the *śarabha* beast.

38 Fools naturally end up quarreling with everyone
because they are habituated to attachment and hatred.
Look how everyone runs away
when they see a vicious, poisonous snake.

39 The wise acquire possessions properly;
their things come from a worthy source.
Look at the amazing way the first king arose
because he was honored by many people.

40 A fool's property comes from wrong livelihood;
their possessions come from an unworthy source.
Because the fox was honored as a king,
look how the king of beasts killed him.

41 The wise complete whatever they undertake
no matter what difficulties they encounter.
Look at the courageous offering made to the sage
by the merchant who crossed a pit of fire.

42 No matter what actions a fool undertakes,
not a single one brings satisfaction later.
Look how the father of the child Jyotiṣka
kneaded his wife's belly.

43 No matter what others say, a wise man
pursues or rejects a goal after examining it himself.

Look how the brahman's student rejected
his teacher's command that he steal.

44 Without considering matters themselves,
the foolish are swayed by others' inducement.
Look how all the traders came to ruin
because they listened to what the ogress said. [152]

45 Even if they are in severe decline for a while,
the wise will rise again like the waxing moon.
It is well known that the minister Gar
was imprisoned but later got the better of everyone.

46 When fools experience a single problem
they are extinguished like a butter lamp.
Look at the king who attacked the sage Kṣāntivādi;
his state of mind was instantly wrecked.

47 A wise person's helpful attitude
restores harmony when others quarrel.
Because Prince *Śraddhā caused two nāga kings
to become friends, look at the auspicious signs!

48 A foolish person's warped mind
takes pleasure in others' quarrels.
Look how the mouse came to ruin
by ignoring the elephant and the mongoose.

49 The wise give away their accumulated wealth,
so it increases like water welling up in a spring.
Look how the youth *Kṣipratuṅga—"quickly exalted"—
created merit by making an offering to the Buddha.

50 Being stingy, fools do not use their possessions,
so they waste away like the waning moon.
Look how the honey hoarded by bees
is enjoyed and consumed by others.

51 The wise shun disputes at first,
but in battle they show their power to the foe.
Look how the king named Arjuna
overwhelmed the opposition's forces.

52 Fools are the first to incite disputes,
but in a fight they give victory to their foes.
It is well known that by wearing a mirror,
the king ceded victory to his minister. [153]

53 At the outset, the wise impose an agreement
on enemies who are able to harm them.
It is well known that when going to sea
a captain kills the sea monster at the outset.

54 Even though something will definitely harm them,
fools are carefree because they desire trifles.
Look at the problems that arose for Bimbisāra
because he made Vaidehī his queen.

55 Whenever a wise person is praised
he shares the credit with others.
Look how Gö obtained acclaim
for the king's establishment of the doctrine.

56 Fools insistently attribute
their own shortcomings to others.
Look how the deceitful one left
a bloody sword in front of Gautama.

57 Through the power of their skillful means
the wise bind even the mighty to servitude.
Even though the garuḍa was extremely strong,
look how the golden-clad one rode on him.

58 Because they are not skilled in strategy
fools become the servants even of the weak.

Look at the behavior of the haughty lion
who was made to carry a load by a fox.

59 The wise use the power of their astute intelligence
to skillfully clear away nasty rumors about themselves.
Look how a sage used skillful means
to purify the mind of the king.

60 Because fools do not have sharp minds,
they admire their own disrepute.
In a petty kingdom of Cūta, they beat drums
for those who become king through patricide.

61 Avoiding extremely dangerous situations
is a sign of a wise person's courage.
It is known that when killing a prime bull
a lion will avoid its horns. [154]

62 Thoughtlessly fighting with an enemy
is a sign of a foolish man's stupidity.
Look at the nature of moths
that battle with the light of a flame.

63 Because the wise do what is admirable
it is easy for anyone to grasp their worth.
Look how the desperate people knew
that the elephant had sacrificed his body.

64 Because foolish people act wantonly
it is difficult for anyone to grasp their worth.
Look how in some barbarian countries
men take their own mothers as their brides.

65 The wise promote the good traditions of the past,
so they achieve irrevocable happiness.
Look how Emperor Yongle, like his ancestors,
honored the teachings of the Conqueror.

66 Fools abolish good customs from the past
and as a result they obtain intense suffering.
Look at the negative consequences for King Langdarma
because he suppressed the doctrine.

67 Even if wise men blanket the great earth
we feel pained that there are too few.
Look how merchants are never satisfied
even though the ocean is filled with jewels.

68 There may be no more than a single fool,
but it is as disastrous as if there were many.
Because one frog had an infectious sore,
look how he brought ruin to his friends.

69 Even if a wise person is mistaken,
the degree of error is very slight.
If a builder who understands measurement errs,
it is well known that it will be just a smidgen.

70 When a foolish person makes a mistake
its magnitude is beyond measure.
Look how when a deer walks into a trap
there is the terrible consequence of losing its life. [155]

71 The wise bring together their own realm
and have success over odious enemies.
Look how the cannibal ogres kept their vows
and then ate the flesh of their human opponents.

72 Fools are craven before their enemies
but cause various disputes among themselves.
Look how a cur wags its tail for people
but chases away other dogs.

73 The wise take a long view regarding their enemies,
so in the end they have control over their foes.

See how the ascetic's patience
gained him control over the king.

74 Because fools retaliate against their enemies
they have difficulties continuously, without cease.
Look at the constant antagonistic behavior
between the two creatures—the crow and the owl.

75 Through power that comes from quelling pride
the wise serve the holy and get good advice.
Look at the story of how Kumāra Sudhana
sought for a spiritual teacher.

76 Owing to the force of the great arrogance of fools,
they have no opportunity to serve the holy.
It is well known that someone pompous
put on insignia without a preceptor or teacher.

77 It is difficult to initiate disunity among the wise,
but if they are estranged reconciliation is easy.
It is difficult to cut a fruit tree,
but look how it knits together when grafted.

78 It is simple to initiate disunity among fools,
and after an estrangement reconciliation is difficult.
Look how when a lump of charcoal shatters,
there is no chance of pasting it back together.

79 A wise person may become very angry,
but in the end his actions are only helpful.
Deities and protectors may be wrathful,
but look how they protect you from all obstacles. [156]

80 A fool may smile broadly,
but his actions are only harmful in the end.
Look how the lord of death displays a smile
and then slays the living creatures.

81 As soon as a wise person becomes affluent,
he lives happily without harming others.
When the king of beasts' hunger is sated,
look how he reclines on his right side to sleep.

82 When a fool becomes a bit rich,
all he does is injure others.
Look how when a fox is full of food
it yaps, proclaiming bad omens.

83 When the wise work to develop good qualities,
they have fortitude even when it is difficult.
Although it is difficult to cross the ocean,
look how gratifying it is to obtain treasure.

84 Fools addicted to pleasure indolently pass their time,
but without training how can good qualities arise?
If laymen are unable to trade or farm,
look how most of them are poor.

85 The wise see their own shortcomings,
so they are careful and obtain excellence.
King Ajātaśatru saw his own faults,
so look how he saw the truth.

86 Fools see other people's shortcomings,
so they are careless and become miserable.
Tiṣya saw the Buddha as having faults;
look at the inevitable consequences of that!

87 The wise acknowledge and repay the kindness
of those who have acted to help them.
Look how the wandering sage
made the king become free from sin.

88 Fools do not repay kindness;
in return for help they do harm.

Look at the behavior of the evil man
whom the monkey rescued from the abyss. [157]

89 When a wise person becomes prosperous
a wealth of enjoyment naturally arises.
Look how the lords of the gods are honored
with heavenly silk garments and ambrosia.

90 Even if a fool is rich and wealthy,
as if starving, he does not use or enjoy it.
Look how the fox who found some meat
came to ruin by eating a bowstring.

91 Disdaining ordinary amenities,
the wise esteem good advice.
A hero does not focus on anything else;
look how he emerges from battle as the victor.

92 Scorning a good reputation,
fools prize the littlest bit of wealth.
Look how even people who are thieves
adorn themselves to look attractive.

93 Because the wise are always careful
others can never destroy them.
Look how King Pradyota the Ferocious
found no opportunity to harm *Bhūdhara.

94 Because fools always are incautious,
others will definitely destroy them.
Look how Mashang Drompa Kyé
was put into a deep pit.

95 Even though others may harm them,
the wise respond with helpfulness.
Look at the story about the monk named Panthaka:
he helped the twelve even though they harmed him.

96 Although others try to assist them,
fools just respond harmfully.
Look at the negative consequences
when Ajātaśatru honored Devadatta.

97 Those who are close to the wise
are granted a carefree, cheerful mind.
Look how the lion brought relief
to all of the wild animals. [158]

98 Those who are close to fools
are naturally granted undesired misery.
Look how the rabbit who heard the sound
"*chal*" agitated all his animal friends.

99 The wise hide their knowledge inside,
so masses of people gather around them.
Look how many sea traders gather
to get the gems that are in the ocean.

100 Fools blab about their good qualities,
so people do not gather around them.
Look how no one ever picks up
chaff that is floating on water.

101 The wise have vast intelligence and do not chatter:
this indicates their trait of profundity.
Look how very difficult it is to fathom
the depths of a gently moving ocean.

102 Fools are full of themselves and talk a lot:
this indicates their limited intelligence.
Look how very easy it is to fathom
the depth of a babbling brook.

103 Even if a wise man is deeply offended,
he will be appeased if you pay proper respect.

Silver and gold are very strong,
but look how they can be melted.

104 Whether or not a fool is offended,
he is rigid when you pay proper respect.
When you melt a pile of dog shit,
look how it emits only a foul odor.

105 Because the wise are honest,
whatever they do is done sincerely.
Look how Kumāra Jīvaka's medical treatments
all came out satisfactorily.

106 Because fools have devious minds,
most of their actions backfire on themselves.
Look how, because of a woman's deviousness,
Udayana was slain after he escaped. [159]

107 The wise trust only people they know;
they are wary of random acquaintances.
Wild animals are not used to humans,
so look how they flee as soon as they see them.

108 Fools immediately trust random associates
even though they had no prior relationship.
Look at what happened to the king of Bhaṅgala,
who was deceived by a demoness.

109 A wise man doesn't let harmful words out of his mouth,
so his real enemies are unable to suppress him.
Look how even when a lion is asleep
the other animals are terrified.

110 A fool lets harmful words out of his mouth,
so his real enemies are able to suppress him.
Even though dogs constantly bark,
look how they are terrified of wolves.

111 Because of the force of their vast intelligence,
the wise act independently without relying on others.
Look how the king of those making ritual sacrifices
made them into religious offerings of the Dharma.

112 Because a fool's intellectual strength wavers,
he follows others' suggestions without control.
Look how Śrīgupta was convinced
to prepare poisoned food for the Buddha.

113 Because the wise do positive actions
they immediately experience good results.
Look how the man named Siṅghala
immediately obtained the kingdom.

114 Because fools engage in negative actions
they immediately experience unpleasant results.
Mākandika incinerated Śyāmāvatī and her retinue,
and look at what happened to him.

115 It is difficult to please the wise;
they take no pleasure in those lacking good qualities.
Look how Mālikā never took the time
to venerate non-Buddhist tīrthikas. [160]

116 It is easy to please fools;
a mere semblance of good qualities pleases them.
Look how most Tibetan lamas and officials
paid homage to the Chinese abbot.

117 The wise have every good quality.
A fool is someone with only faults.
Look how a gem yields everything desired
and a poisonous snake causes harm everywhere.

118 Therefore you must properly differentiate
the distinguishing features of wise men and fools.

It is right to hold the wise as an ornament
and throw away the foolish like straw chaff.

119 The wise stand out in the world
like a trumpeting elephant in a herd.
The charm of someone skillful and valorous
is the greatest of ornaments in this world.

120 Just like a wish-fulfilling jewel among gems,
among those learned in the Dharma,
someone who possesses all three—learning, virtue, and
goodness—
is a great ornament of the Buddha's teaching indeed.

121 Although Sakya Paṇḍita, lord among the learned,
gave us *A Jewel Treasury of Wise Sayings*,
which differentiates the wise and the foolish,
to be used as eyes to view the world . . .

122 Nowadays the beaming sun of the wise
has set over the western peaks and gone elsewhere.
The rise of ignorant fools in the form of the moon
has made the flowers of wise sayings mostly close.

123 Once again in the garden of my mind
the white lotuses of wise sayings blossom
because the sunlight of discernment shines
and they are moistened with rain of perseverance.

124 By having beautiful bodies of modesty
and far-seeing eyes of wisdom,
may the bee-like fortunate ones
enjoy and frolic here from now on. [161]

125 Therefore, owing to the merit of these wise sayings,
may every living creature now and in the future
have the wisdom to differentiate wise men from fools
and thus have unerring faith in the wise.

I, Sönam Drakpa Namchö Chokgi Dé, an eloquent speaker from central Tibet, composed this treatise examining the wise and the foolish entitled *Ganden Wise Sayings: A Bouquet of White Lotuses* at the request of some of my learned students who had interest in wise sayings. It was written at the victorious place of Ganden Monastery and was scribed by the expounder of wise sayings Ngawang Chökyi Drakpa.

5. Rays of Sunlight: A Commentary on "Ganden Wise Sayings"

Yangchen Gawai Lodrö

This work is titled *Rays of Sunlight: A Commentary on "Ganden Wise Sayings,"* a treatise examining the wise and the foolish.[205]

To the one who has crossed the ocean of the two collections,
has seen the nature of the two truths precisely as they are,
and has elucidated two systems of what to do and avoid,
to that best of humans—beings with two feet—I bow down.

I respectfully pay homage with my three doors
to Mañjuśrī, teacher of the three states of existence,
the spiritual guide of the three times, father of us all,
who has dispelled obstacles to the aims of the three realms.

I place atop my head as an ornament
the feet of the glorious spiritual teachers, father and son,
whose perfect wisdom knows every phenomena
and whose fame has spread throughout the three worlds.

It is right for those with intelligence and good fortune
who aspire to engage in honorable and holy behavior
to make use of this *Bouquet of White Lotuses*
that has the fragrant honey of good advice.

The Dharma lord Paṇchen Sönam Drakpa, who is unrivaled as a holder of the tradition of Jé Tsongkhapa, the spiritual teacher who was a manifestation of Mañjuśrī, bestowed on us, his followers, this excellent gift of wisdom entitled *Ganden Wise Sayings: A Bouquet of White Lotuses.* To explain this text there are three sections:

1. The meaning of the title
2. The meaning of the text itself
3. The concluding points

To present the first, the text reads, "This text examining the wise and the foolish entitled *Ganden Wise Sayings: A Bouquet of White Lotuses.*" The meaning of the title is as follows. The text has the two good qualities of correction and protection that come from investigating the differences between the wise—those who properly engage in and shun actions after correctly differentiating what should be done and what should be avoided both spiritually and secularly—and fools who are the opposite of that. It is called a "bouquet" because it arranges in one text the many white lotuses of wise sayings that arise from the power of the wisdom of the master who holds the Ganden tradition. [164] The subject, wise sayings, is compared to a bouquet of white lotuses. The metaphor of a white lotus is used because although lotuses grow in muck, they are not sullied with muddy stains, and white lotuses are the best sort of lotus. A bouquet ties together many individual flowers. Similarly, these wise sayings are not sullied by any imperfections, they are the best kind of wise sayings, and it is a compilation of precious, meaningful topics.

Although *A Bouquet of White Lotuses* analyzes the wise and the foolish, it is not for the purpose of pointing out the faults of others. Rather, it is for showing what should be done and what should be avoided after correctly differentiating those two courses of action. As for the wise, because they have every good quality, if you rely on them your own good qualities will effortlessly arise and increase like the waxing moon. As for fools, because their nature is faulty, if you rely on them your good qualities will decline and inevitably become tarnished. The *Cāṇakya Treatise on Kingship* says:

> Those with good qualities are to be relied on.
> Those without good qualities are to be avoided.
> The wise have every good quality.
> Fools are those persons having only faults.[206]

In the *Staff of Wisdom* it says:

The pure and those lacking purity are shown
to be just like the moon waxing and waning.
Those with good qualities may be low but they will improve;
those without purity may be exalted but they will decline.[207]

In *A Bouquet of White Lotuses*, the section on the meaning of the text has a prelude that precedes the exposition and the exposition itself. The prelude contains the homage and the pledge to compose the text. The homage is similar to a translator's homage in that it precedes the text, and there is a second homage in the body of the text.

The homage that precedes the text offers:

Homage to the Bhagavān, master of the two systems of norms.

He is called *Bhagavān* (Tibetan: *bcom ldan 'das*), the transcendent perfect victor, because he is victorious (*bcom*) over the four maras and in perfect in possession (*ldan*) of the six aspects of good fortune, and he is transcendent (*'das*) because he is superior to the worldly gods and is the pinnacle of all good things. Therefore, it says, we pay homage with body, speech, and mind to the Bhagavān Buddha, the sovereign who has seen the religious and worldly systems of norms without conflating them and has explained them to disciples exactly as he has seen them. [165]

The homage in the body of the root text then continues:

1ab After respectfully bowing to the feet of the Lord of Sages,
who knows the two systems of norms exactly as they are,

This means throughout all time I respectfully bow to the feet of the one who is foremost, the lord of all sages who knows the systems of both religious and worldly ethics precisely as they are. Sages are able to control every adverse aspect of the three doors of body, speech, and mind. There are non-Buddhist ascetics and Buddhist śrāvakas and pratyekabuddhas who are sages. The Buddha is the foremost sage of them all.

If you wonder why the root text says "after," a word that links former and later actions, it is to connect the homage to the pledge to compose: after bowing in homage I will compose this text of good advice. There are many reasons why an invocation is necessary at the start: paying homage by expressing the good qualities of holy objects blesses the mental continuum, clears away any obstacles to composition, and enables disciples to study, contemplate, and meditate on the text.

The second section of the prelude is the pledge to compose:

1cd I will briefly set forth some wise sayings
differentiating the wise and the foolish.

To "set forth" is to explain. This is a "brief" synopsis. It avoids the faults of having too many or too few words of advice on how to precisely differentiate between a wise person, upon whom holy, respectable people can rely, and a fool, who cannot be relied on.

A pledge to compose is needed because in order to bring a composition to completion, the author's virtuous intention must be firm. The glorious protector Nāgārjuna said: [166]

> Holy people do not make many promises.
> If they say they will do something difficult,
> it is as if engraved in stone,
> even death will not deter them.[208]

The second major section, the meaning of the text, refers to the exposition of the text itself. The exposition has three parts:

1. A brief presentation of the wise and the foolish
2. A detailed explanation of each one in particular
3. Summation and conclusion

First, the brief presentation of the wise and the foolish, has three parts: (1) differentiating between the wise and the foolish, (2) the detriments of being foolish and the benefits of being wise, and (3) an explanation of the important ways the wise and the foolish are different. As for the first, the root text says:

2 Those said to be wise are those who know
the ways of the world or of Dharma.
Just as there are said to be two types of the wise,
the foolish are also explained to be of two types.

There are two types of people who are called wise. There are the wise who precisely differentiate what should be done from what should be avoided in a worldly context. And there are the wise who precisely differentiate what should be done from what should be avoided in the practice of the holy Dharma. This is what it means to say there are two types of the wise. Similarly, there are two types of fools. Those who are confused about what should be done and what should be avoided in the world, and those who are confused about what should be done and what should be avoided in the practice of the holy Dharma.

As for the second, explanation of the benefits of being wise and the detriments of being foolish, the text reads:

3 The first type of wise person will be meritorious in this life;
the second will be meritorious in this and future lives.
The two types of fools are explained as
ruining this and their future lives respectively.

The holy beings explain that the first type of wise person does what should be done and avoids what should be avoided for this life, so he or she is meritorious during the present life. In other words, they will be increasingly happy, joyful, fortunate, wealthy, and so forth. The second type of wise person does what should be done and avoids what should be avoided for both this life and future lives, so in this life and in future lives he will be meritorious and will obtain happiness, joy, and so forth. [167] As for the two types of fools, they act improperly under the sway of ignorance about what to do and what to avoid for this and future lives, respectively. The first type of fool comes to ruin even during this life. The second will ruin his or her future lives and be reborn in a miserable state.

As for the third, the very significant ways that the wise and fools are different, the text says:

4 Thus the difference between the wise and the foolish
is like the difference between Mount Meru and a dust mote,
like the difference between the ocean and a puddle,
and between the sky and the palm of your hand.

These examples demonstrate the difference between the wise and fools. The difference in the volume of their learning is like the difference between Mount Meru and a mote of dust. The difference in the depth of their intelligence is like the difference between the ocean and a puddle. (The word "puddle" means a small pool of accumulated rainwater.) The difference in the range of their discernment is like the difference between the sky and the palm of one's hand. One should recognize that these are consequential differences.

* * *

The second part of the exposition is a detailed explanation of the wise and of fools in particular. Within that topic, the text explains how the wise are found to be attractive or not depending on context:

5 In front of the wise a wise person is attractive,
because his good qualities are seen as they are.
Look how a priceless jewel is held to be beautiful
when a top merchant holds it in his hands.

6 In front of the foolish a wise person is not attractive;
fools err because they do not see his good qualities.
Look at how a fool made into charcoal
sandalwood that is more precious than gold.

These verses say that a wise person who has good qualities is found to be attractive and beautiful when among other wise people. Wise peoples' minds perceive the superb ornament of good qualities just as they are, and with deferential language and [168] respect they please each other with the gift of fine discourse. For example, even though an incalculably priceless jewel may look like a worthless lump of rock, observe that when one gets into the hands of a leading merchant who knows its good qualities, he values its beauty, cherishes it as supreme, and so forth because he perceives its rarity and the difficulty of acquiring it.

The term "top merchant" can be used to mean bodhisattva or a leading merchant. Here it means a leading merchant. Moreover, it is similar to a passage in the Sutra Requested by Dhāraṇiśvarāja that explains how to treat a gemstone.[209] When a valuable and superb gemstone is unrefined and covered with dirt, its color and so forth are not good, so no one other than a knowledgeable, skilled merchant will recognize it. When novice traders go to the land of jewels, they throw away superb jewels, saying, "This is lightweight and its color and so forth are poor." And they grab a rock or glass bauble, saying, "This one is heavy and has a good color so it is the best."

When the wise are among fools who lack good qualities, they are not considered to be beautiful. Fools err because they lack the intelligence to perceive the superb ornaments of good qualities to be good qualities. That is to say, their intelligence is obscured by imperfections. For instance, special gośīrṣa sandalwood is even more valuable than gold. Look at the example of a fool who burned it in a fire to make charcoal.[210]

The terms "amid" (*gam*),[211] "among" (*gan*), and "in front" (*drung*) have the same meaning in this context. The word *gośīrṣa* literally means "cow head." It is the name of the white sandalwood that grows in the Malaya mountains that have the shape of a cow's head. Here the term *gośīrṣa* refers to something that is extremely expensive and special.

As the story goes, in the past a man had some very good gośīrṣa sandalwood. He went a neighboring country to sell it, but no purchasers came forth right away. That night he stayed in the same inn as a charcoal seller. Chatting with him, he said, "There aren't any buyers of merchandise in this area."

The next day, they went their separate ways to sell their wares. In the evening they met again at the inn. Seeing that the charcoal had been sold but there had been no buyers for his sandalwood, the fool thought, "Oh yes! Here's a good way. I'll definitely sell the sandalwood after turning it into charcoal."

He burned the gośīrṣa sandalwood in a fire, turning it into charcoal. [169] After selling it the fool thought he had made a profit. Thus when fools see other fools they are happy because they behave alike. A wise person among a group of fools is not sought after and is not considered attractive because his or her behavior and thoughts are dissimilar to those of a fool. Moreover, the *Staff of Wisdom* says:

> When a fool sees another fool,
> he makes charcoal even from sandalwood![212]

And:

> A flock of crows does not think the swan in their midst is lovely.
> A herd of donkeys does not think the well-bred horse in their
> midst is lovely.

A pack of foxes does not think the lion in their midst is lovely.
A crowd of fools does not think the wise person in their midst
is lovely.

Someone to whom the great bow their heads,
inferior people think is equivalent to straw.
The wise make obeisance to a stupa,
but crows use it as a roost.[213]

* * *

Benefits arise from listening to the speech of wise people and detriments arise from not listening:

7 The wise listen to what wise people say;
from that they obtain the relevant good qualities.
By listening to Captain Supāraga's words,
the merchants found treasure, as is well known.

A wise person is not confused about what should be done and what should be avoided. The verse reveals that one will obtain the good qualities that are relevant to the situation by listening to the meaning of a wise person's instructions. For example, by relying on the words they heard from Supāraga, the captain of the sea routes, the merchant passengers were freed from the terror of great misfortune and afterward came across treasure—that is, superb jewels.

Long ago in a region of the noble land of India called Surapāraka there lived a captain called the bodhisattva Supāraga.[214] His mind was very sharp and he was very skilled in the arts, reading omens, and so forth. When that great man had grown old, many merchants in pursuit of jewels implored him, "You must come and be our guide!" [170] Because of his affection for those merchants, he boarded their large boat and they set off on the ocean.

Then a fierce, ill-fated wind arose. Unable to withstand it, the boat was carried far away and came near to sinking in the ocean. As the sun neared the west, the tempest seemed to turn even the sea upside down and there was a terrifying cracking sound. The merchants despaired upon hearing it. Some wept, some lamented and cried for help, some lost their minds from terror, a few prayed for refuge to worldly gods.

When some of these despairing merchants came to the bodhisattva emitting cries of misery, he quickly took action. He said, "Merchants, have no fear now. I have a plan." He freed his shoulder from its garment, bowed on the deck, and prayed to the buddhas of the ten directions. "O gods of the ocean and sky, listen! Not even in my thoughts have I ever killed a living creature. From the power of recalling these words of truth and of my merits, may this great ship not sink in the sea and may these people be restored to happiness!" As soon as he spoke, the ship righted.

Then the great man instructed the merchants, "Fill the boat with as much sand and rock from the sea down to the strands of reeds as it can handle. Then the boat will not overturn." The merchants loaded the great ship to capacity with what they thought was sand and rock but was actually gold, silver, lapis, and so on. The night they reached shore, the boat glittered with its load of gold, silver, sapphires, lapis, and so on. In this way, by relying on the great man and doing as he said, the great ship was filled with treasure and the merchants achieved their goals just as they had wished. It says in *A Hundred Stanzas on Wisdom*:

> A wise person all by himself
> will achieve the superb goal he desires.
> A single lion, the king of beasts,
> destroys the most arrogant elephant.[215] [171]

8 The foolish do not listen to the words of the wise;
from that they end up with the relevant problems.
It is well known that the turtle fell from the sky
because he did not listen to the geese's words.

A fool is ignorant of what should be done and what should be avoided. This verse means that fools do not do what the wise say. Not listening, they behave improperly and do the opposite. Because of that they will obtain the related undesirable faulty consequences that are not good and will also acquire flaws that are not good. For example, in a well-known story a turtle fell from the sky and suffered greatly as a result of not listening to the helpful advice of two geese.[216]

Long ago a turtle and a pair of geese lived in a pond. After twelve years of drought, the pond dried up. Shortly after the world came into existence even the animals knew how to talk, so the two geese said, "We are going to another pond."

The turtle said, "O friends, please don't abandon me. We can all go if you two lift the ends of a stick and I'll hold on to the stick with my mouth."

The geese counseled, "If we do that, you must not speak, not even a word." The two geese picked him up like that and flew into the sky. Seeing that, some children in the mountains said, "Look! Geese are carrying off a turtle!" As they passed through another area, other children exclaimed the same.

The turtle wasn't able to keep himself from speaking. "The geese aren't carrying me off! I wanted to go!" The stick quickly slipped from his mouth and he fell to the earth. The children grabbed him and he suffered greatly. The gods said:

> Paying no heed to what he was told
> by dear friends who wished to help him,
> the turtle let go of the stick.
> Thus he fell and was lost.[217]

Thus fools who do not listen to the words of the wise and do whatever they want will be ruined like the turtle who fell from the sky. [172]

* * *

Explaining the advantages of speaking well of the wise and the disadvantages not speaking well of them:

> 9 The wise speak well of other wise people;
> through that they inspire other people.
> Look at what was said by the god Indra
> about the renown of the bodhisattva hare.

The wise see faults and good qualities exactly as they are. They only speak well of and proclaim the fame of others. Look at the amazing way all men and gods developed faith because Indra, the king of the gods, spoke about the glorious renown of the bodhisattva who took a life as a hare.[218]

Long ago when our teacher was on the path of training, through the force of his compassion and prayers he took birth as a hare in a pleasant, isolated place. He lived there with his dear friends otter, jackal, and monkey.

Contrary to their animal nature, these four were magnanimous, extremely compassionate, survived by living according to the Dharma, and so forth. Even the gods were astonished by their special good qualities. The bodhisattva hare wondered, "If a guest were to come here, what could I offer him?" Seeing that his body was the best thing to give, he vowed to give it.

The god king Indra was amazed. In order to test the bodhisattva, he transformed into a brahman. He went to the isolated place acting and lamenting as if he were suffering from hunger and thirst. The otter came and gave him seven fish. The jackal came and gave him a round loaf of bread and a pot of yogurt. The monkey came and gave him some mangoes. The hare had decided to give his own body. In preparation, Indra conjured up a heap of hot, smokeless coals. When the bodhisattva hare joyfully jumped into the fire without any hesitation, Indra was astounded and became very faithful.

Showing his true form, Indra lifted the bodhisattva hare from the fire and carried him to the god realm. He presented him to the gods, venerated, and lauded him. Having displayed an astonishing deed by an extremely difficult action, the bodhisattva hare made generations of gods throughout posterity, and even those living now on Jambudvīpa, have faith. In consideration of the beneficent deed that inspired faith, [173] Indra inscribed "the dwelling of the pious god" on the palace of the king of gods of the Heaven of the Thirty-Three, and drew an image of the hare on the orb of the moon.

10 Fools speak ill of the wise,
thereby forestalling other people's faith.
Look at the result of the ill-natured things
*Suhṛt said about the bhikṣu *Mallaputra.

Because fools mistake faults and good qualities, they do not see the good qualities of the wise. Therefore they say ill-natured and unseemly things about them, thereby forestalling the faith of embodied beings. For example, look what happened long ago because Suhṛt and *Bhūmija spoke ill of the bhikṣu Mallaputra again and again.[219]

Mallaputra, a very wealthy son of a general, lived in the land of *Pāpaja. He gave up his home and became a renunciate. Ārya Aśvajit gave him religious instruction. Because Mallaputra worked hard reciting, listening, contemplating, renouncing, and meditating, before too long he obtained arhatship. In other words, he was a realized and liberated teacher.

When even the Teacher, the Buddha, predicted that Mallaputra would be the best of the disciples living with Ārya Aśvajit, two monks, Suhṛt and Bhūmija, baselessly slandered him because of enmity from former lives. They said, "Mallaputra committed a downfall because he had sex with a beautiful bhikṣuṇī."

Further, on another occasion they saw the bhikṣuṇī Utpalavarṇā in the presence of Ārya Mallaputra in order to listen to the Dharma. They also saw a stag and doe copulating. So they said, "We saw Mallaputra and Utpalavarṇā. We also saw a sex act." On this unfounded implication, they spoke ill of him and so forth, slandering him repeatedly as being impure. The Teacher reproached both Suhṛt and Bhūmija many times, saying, "Ignorant people utter falsehoods," and so forth. Then the Buddha made a rule forbidding slander by implication.

Thus speaking well of the wise increases your own and everyone else's faith, [174] will bring forth pleasant results in this and all future lives, and is the basis for every good quality. Speaking ill of wise, holy people is to injure yourself and is the cause for experiencing intolerably unpleasant results in this and all future lives.

It says in a sutra that long ago a king ordered five hundred women to dance and play music for seven days in order to honor a bodhisattva Dharma teacher. Ten people disparaged the Dharma teacher because of these women. As a consequence of that action they experienced inconceivable misery: ninety thousand years in hell, five hundred lifetimes as eunuchs and savages with wrong views, and six hundred lives as blind mutes. Intelligent people should take heed.

* * *

Explaining the difference between the propriety of not ridiculing wise people who are indigent and the impropriety of doing so:

11 When the wise see an indigent wise person,
they admire his superior mind.
Look how the ascetic's pure austerities
caused Indra to become delighted.

Because wise people know the disadvantages of sensory pleasure, when they see another wise person who is impoverished they perceive his or her superior, good qualities and feel admiration. For example, look at how, long ago, the god king Indra was greatly pleased by an ascetic adhering to the pure practice of austerities for the sake of the Dharma. Because of that Indra respectfully worshiped him and highly praised him.[220]

Long ago seven brahman brothers gave up all their family's possessions and became renunciates. In a solitary place, on the bank of a pretty lake adorned by many lotus flowers, each brother made himself a thatched hut and settled down. Every five days the six younger brothers went before the eldest brother, a bodhisattva, to listen to the Dharma. Other than that they didn't go to see one another. The great man [175] gave advice to his entourage about the disadvantages of desire, the benefits of pacification, the quintessential instructions for meditation, and so forth.

They also had a female servant who served them respectfully. Each day she took lotus roots from the lake and put equal portions onto leaves. When she hit a gong indicating it was time to eat, the brothers came out in order of seniority. Each one took his own portion and in his own hut consumed it as if it were a ritual.

Their fame became great because of their incredible conduct. Indra heard of it and went to the bank of that pretty lake to test them. For five days he made the first portion of lotus roots for the bodhisattva disappear. The bodhisattva went out for his meal of lotus roots each day, but because his portion wasn't there he returned to his hut and lived without eating anything. On the afternoon of the fifth day, when the younger brothers went to him to hear the Dharma, they saw that their eldest brother's complexion had deteriorated and his body had become very withered. When they asked, "What's wrong?" he told them what had happened.

Then the entourage hung their heads in surprise and shame. In order to demonstrate their purity, each of the six younger brothers in succession swore an oath of denial in verse:

> O brahman, may those who took your roots
> become laymen adorned with signs of wealth.
> May they also find attractive wives.
> May they have sons and grandsons.

And:

> O brahman, may those who took your roots
> enjoy unceasing pleasure
> from holding ornaments touched by their sons—
> garlands, necklaces, sandalwood, and lovely clothes.

And:

> May those who took your roots
> find servants and wealth from plowing their fields.
> May they greatly enjoy conversation with their sons.
> May they see no faults in enjoying a householder's life.

And:

> May those who took your roots because of craving
> be revered by kings who bow down their heads
> as if they were disciplined servants and,
> in the manner of kings, become emperor of all the earth.

And:

> May those who took roots from a bodhisattva like you
> be pleased by praise and so forth
> when they come into the presence of the king.
> Likewise, may kings treat them with honor.

And:

> May those wanting roots and not wanting good qualities
> become teachers from studying the Vedas.
> May they be worshiped by everyone in the area [176]
> for their impressive, continuous practice of asceticism.

When each one had made his oath, the brahman elder brother showed he had no misgiving that anyone in his entourage had taken the roots, saying:

> As to whether someone will come to ruin or not,
> I have misgivings about whoever took the roots like that.
> At the time of death, what will become of someone
> who indulges every desire while living at home?

Then Indra showed his own form and asked why they deprecated desire. In response the bodhisattva explained the disadvantages of desire. Indra begged for his forgiveness and made the hidden lotus roots magically reappear. Indra joyfully and respectfully made obeisance, lauded the brothers, and disappeared.

Thus, since desire is the root of disaster, renunciates and those who aspire to the Dharma should not pray to become like the person in the oaths of the seven brahman brothers.

The words of the oaths were recorded here.

12 When fools see an indigent wise person,
with arrogant thoughts they treat him with scorn.
Look how old monkeys encountering a man
laugh, saying, "He doesn't have a tail!"

This verse teaches that fools are caught in the death-grip of material things. Infatuated with wealth, and swayed by their own arrogant thoughts, they act disrespectfully, discourteously, and so forth when they see an indigent wise person. Consider the well-known story about some old monkeys who encountered a human and reacted with ridicule and jokes: "He is one of our kind but has no tail!" A fool behaves like those old monkeys.

As the story goes, there were a number of monkeys in a great forest in a region to the south. A man went there looking for a site to farm. He encountered—that is, met—many monkeys. The monkeys surrounded him and said, "This is very strange. He is similar to our kind, but he doesn't have a tail!" All of them laughed and ridiculed the man. This story is well known.[221]

Thus a wise person may be destitute because, recognizing the disadvantages of sensory pleasure, [177] he does not work hard to gain wealth. Material poverty is an admirable situation, not something to be scorned. Because fools hold material wealth dear to their hearts, they view poverty and indigence very differently.

Moreover, in one of his past lives the future pratyekabuddha Svāgata called a pratyekabuddha a "low-caste beggar." As a result, he experienced a lot of harm and misery in all his lives. He took birth in the hells for a long time. Then in his last life in samsara he was a pauper and all the other beggars beat him, trampled him into dust, and so forth. Since it is said to be the cause of experiencing manifold misery, the disadvantages of disparaging a holy object are huge.[222]

* * *

The next verses relate the benefits of acting respectfully toward a holy superior person and the detriments of acting disrespectfully:

13 The wise care for their superiors like a crown,
through that they ascend higher themselves.
Look at the amazing superlative respect
Sumukha had for Dhṛtarāṣṭra.

Because the wise know the difference between someone who should be respected and someone who should not, they care for those who are superior to themselves in lineage, good qualities, and so forth as if those persons were a crown for their head. As an example, look at the superlative respect the minister of the swans, Sumukha, had for the king of the swans, Dhṛtarāṣṭra, even when he saw that the king was about to lose his life.[223]

Long ago in a large wish-fulfilling lake, the bodhisattva, a great man, was a king of the swans named Dhṛtarāṣṭra. His minister, named Sumukha, had the character of a wise man. Because the special, good qualities of both the king and his minister were astoundingly great, their fame spread all around. [178]

Brahmadatta, the king of Vārāṇasī, heard of them. As a means to draw the swans in, he ordered that a pleasure garden with a special lake ornamented with various flowers be built in a short time. A pair of swans saw it. They went to the wish-fulfilling lake and told the king of the swans about the new lake's splendid aspect. Because they repeatedly urged him to go there, the king could not refuse. The king of the swans, his minister, and his entourage went to the Vārāṇasī lake.

Snares had been set in the lake. When the swan king's feet got caught in a snare, all the other swans in the entourage flew off and scattered. However, even though Sumukha wasn't caught, he could not withstand his love for the king, so he set down nearby.

In pleasant human voices they said many delightful things to the bird catcher who came there. The man was extremely astonished. He brought both the swan king and the minister before King Brahmadatta and entreated him to listen to their pleasant speech. The king too was amazed and developed faith. He placed both the swan king and his minister on top of jeweled thrones and was immensely respectful and reverent. Both the swan king and his minister taught the Dharma extensively to the king and his court.

And after they returned to their former home they worked for the benefit of many living beings as if they were their own flock of swans.

Thus if you act respectfully toward holy beings, merit and pleasant results will be bestowed on you in the present and future. Therefore, even at the risk of losing your life, do not let go of your respect and deference for holy beings.

14 Fools disparage their superiors;
through that they cast themselves down.
Look at the grave consequences for Śikhī
because he killed his father, an arhat.

Because fools are ignorant about who is and who is not worthy of respect, they disparage—that is, do not respect—their superiors. The maturation of that action casts the fools down and ruins them. For example, Śikhi, the ruler of Rauruka, killed his own father, who had renounced the kingdom to become a mendicant and had attained the state of an arhat. [179] Consider the unending negative consequences Śikhi experienced even during his lifetime.[224]

Once Udayana, the ruler of Rauruka, and Bimbisāra, the king of Rājagṛha, were good friends and sent each other gifts. One time Udayana sent Bimbisāra a priceless suit of jeweled armor. As a return gift, Bimbisāra sent a portrait of the Buddha, below which you could see an illustration of the twelve links of dependent origination.

By analyzing how dependent origination arises and ceases, Udayana saw the truth. Then he bestowed the realm on his only son, Śikhi, and went before the Teacher, the Buddha. By the words "Come forth," he was made a fully ordained monk. Now after hearing that Śikhi was governing sacrilegiously, he went to Rauruka to reverse that trend. Two evil ministers urgently counseled Śikhi: "Your father the king is coming here to seize the kingdom. You must kill him!"

Śikhi agreed and sent forth executioners. In the interim, Udayana had attained arhatship as a result of his vigorous efforts. He said to the executioners, "You must explain to Śikhi that by committing two deeds of immediate retribution—killing his father and murdering an arhat—he will necessarily be reborn in the Avīci Hell, but he should confess." After he said that, the two executioners killed him.

Later by various deceitful means the two evil ministers implanted perverted views in Śikhi's mind. They urged him to throw dirt on Ārya Kātyāyana, and from that atrocious action a rain of dirt fell for seven days, covering the city of Rauruka. And the king, his evil ministers, and his entourage all went to the Avīci Hell.

Thus inflicting injury by disparaging holy objects and being in the grip of evil companions causes fearsome results that can be experienced even in this life. It would be better to lose one's life than do such things. You should recite prayers again and again that you do not act like that in this and all future lives. [180]

* * *

To relate the benefits of the truth and the disadvantages of lies, the text reads:

15 Because the wise tell the truth,
others find their words convincing.
Look how the son of Sudāsa listened
to the prince because he told the truth.

A wise person is cognizant of the beneficial qualities of the truth and the disadvantages of lies, so he tells only the truth. Therefore everyone else considers whatever words he utters to be valid. Consider the example mentioned in the above verse: because Prince Candra told only the truth, the cannibal son of Sudāsa, also known as the demon Kalmāṣapāda, trusted his word and listened to what he said.[225]

As the jātaka goes, a king named Sudāsa went into the forest. As a result of consorting with a lioness, a child was born. They named him Kalmāṣapāda and made him a prince. (*Su* means good, right, and so forth, and *dāsa* means servant or attendant, therefore *Sudāsa* means good servant or respectable retainer.)

Furthermore, in this distant time our Teacher took birth as a prince named Candra in the lineage of Kuru. The prince grew up like a lotus on a lake: he was a master of arts and sciences, very kind to his servants, gentle, generous, compassionate, and so forth. Because he was adorned with good qualities, he was appointed the regent of his father, the king.

A bit later when spring had just arrived, surrounded by a numerous entourage, he went for amusement to a lovely pleasure garden. A brahman bearing a gift of verses of good advice came before him. Suddenly the entourage became frightened and frantic. "O Lord! The son of Sudāsa, Kalmāṣapāda, who should be feared as much as the actual Lord of Death, is coming here!"

Now Kalmāṣapāda was a king whose actions had angered a brahman court priest. Because the priest cursed him, "May you eat human flesh for twelve years!" he was a cannibal. His servants turned on him. They resolved to murder him [181] and surrounded him in his pleasure garden. But by chanting perverted prayers, he instantly became an extremely powerful cannibal demon and flew off into the sky. After that he lived in a fortress from which no man could escape. He ate only human flesh. The blood, fat, and bones of the people he had abducted and killed were spread out, covering the floor.

Kalmāṣapāda came up to the completely defenseless Prince Candra, threw him over his shoulder, and carried him to his fortress. The prince thought, "I did not get to hear the brahman's good advice. He is waiting there in hope of my return." This compassionate thought made him cry.

Kalmāṣapāda laughed scornfully, saying, "Even if you were filled to the brim with tears, how could you escape from the death lord's jaws!" The bodhisattva prince replied, "I am not crying out of fear of my death, but because I did not get to hear beneficial instruction nor honor the brahman. Please grant me a little time. I will come back."

Kalmāṣapāda thought, "This man is known to be religious and to not utter falsehoods. He might come back. Let's see if this is the truth or a lie." So he let him go. The prince went to his own castle. He listened to four religious verses from the brahman and gave him four thousand pieces of gold as a religious offering. Not listening to any of the objections of his father, the king, and his court, he went straight back to the demon.

The son of Sudāsa was astonished and demanded, "Explain to me this good advice you heard from the brahman." Seeing that it was the time to train him, the bodhisattva prince taught him four verses of Dharma. The son of Sudāsa felt great regret for his former actions. His eyes filled with tears of devotion. He clutched the bodhisattva's feet and promised to undertake four vows: to behave righteously, to cease killing, to give up eating human flesh, and to set free from imprisonment the ninety-nine princes that he, the son of Sudāsa, held captive and restore them to their former kingdoms.

Therefore if you stick to telling the truth you can tame even wild savages, your words will be convincing, you will meet with holy beings, and when you listen to the holy Dharma your mind will become disciplined. [182]

16 Because fools tell lies,
others disregard their words.
Look how the layman *Eḍaka deserted
the non-Buddhist ascetics because they lied.

This verse means that fools utter falsehoods that lack veracity because they do not see the disadvantages of lies. Therefore other people disregard and do not accept anything they say. Consider this example: because the non-Buddhist ascetics were deceptive and lied, the layman Eḍaka ignored their words as if they were gobs of spit.[226]

Long ago in the city of *Bhadrāchara a layman named Eḍaka lived with his wife, his son, his son's bride, a manservant, and maidservant. These six people were very virtuous. The Teacher, the Buddha, saw it was the right time to train them and went to the city of Bhadrāchara. Some non-Buddhist ascetics who lived there heard that the Teacher had come and were displeased. They said, "That monk Gautama—who causes a hail of razors to fall, who destroys many people, and makes their sons and homes vanish—has come here. So we must go elsewhere."

To prevent them leaving, the householders said, "Please remain here." The non-Buddhist ascetics said, "In that case, in the countryside surrounding the city, mow down all the grass, destroy the dwellings, chop down the flowers and fruit trees, and put poison in all the water sources. Then all of you should gather together in the city and no one should go to see the monk Gautama. Anyone who does go shall be fined sixty silver coins for breaking this rule." They all did as they were told.

Then the Teacher gave a girl a message to take to the layman Eḍaka. It said, "I came here in order to help you. Just by my taking a glance at your empty storehouse, it became full of wealth. So there is no reason for you not to come here after paying sixty silver coins." The layman Eḍaka ignored the words of the non-Buddhist ascetics, paid the sixty silver coins, and went before the Teacher. Because he listened to the Dharma, he saw the truth. Later he went home and shouted, "I will pay the fine of silver coins for anyone who wants to meet with the Teacher!" [183] The people broke the non-Buddhist ascetics' rule. When they assembled before the Teacher he taught them the Dharma. Through his teaching he established a foundation for them in everything from refuge and the basis of the training to the four results.

Thus you should understand that telling lies is the cause of bringing yourself and everyone else to ruin. And if you listen to the commands of evil friends you degenerate from the great purpose. In the sutras it says that because a layman was blind, compelled by his former wife, and lacking volition, he said, "I have no notion of who carried off the material goods," even though he knew.[227] Condemned for telling a lie, he was reborn in a great hell and experienced all sorts of misery. Then, for five hundred lives, even though he was reborn as a human, he was just a ball of flesh with a penis, lacking eyes, nose, tongue, and limbs. Therefore you are advised not to tell lies even at the cost of your life.

* * *

On how one should act in relation to immediate happiness versus long-term happiness, the text reads:

17 Between the present and the future,
the wise hold future happiness to be superior.
Look how through the practice of austerities
Viśvantara obtained the bliss of the dharmakāya.

Because the wise do not crave merely the happiness of the moment, when choosing between happiness in the present life or future life, they see that the happiness to come is best and endeavor to create the causes for that future happiness. For example, as a result of the bodhisattva Viśvantara's difficult actions during his life—he gave his valuable wealth, his son, his wife, and so forth as gifts and practiced austerities in a forest—in the end he obtained the pure bliss of the dharmakāya, becoming the Buddha *Indraketu.[228]

As the jātaka goes, in the past, our Teacher, this being of great compassion, took birth as Viśvantara, the son of Sañjaya, king of the Śibi people. [184] The sweet fame of the prince spread in every direction. In general the prince was famous for his knowledge, self-control, and great compassion. In particular he was famous for his actions, which were executed without attachment to his wealth, his body, or his life, and which satisfied all beggars.

That great man had almshouses built around the city and every day gratified every poor person who came there with whatever goods he or she desired. A bit later a neighboring king became jealous and sent some of his brahmans to beg for the prince's superb elephant, which was very rare and the most valuable in the realm. The brahmans saw the prince ride his elephant out to inspect the almshouses and begged for it. The prince thought,

"It is difficult to find someone who dares to beg for a precious possession like this," so joyfully and respectfully he gave them the superb elephant.

Hearing about that, the Śibis became angry and went to the king. Impatiently, and forsaking the use of honorific language, they said, "O Lord! Why was that superb elephant, a creature of power that conquered our enemies and is the mount of the prince, disposed of as a gift to our adversary? It isn't right that we should endure this!"

The king said, "Don't be angry. From now on, I will make Viśvantara know the right amount to give. Something like this will not happen again."

The Śibis said, "This prince cares not for the kingdom. Since he enjoys the Dharma send him to Mount Vaṇka, which is a suitable location for practicing austerities." Although the king greatly loved his son, he couldn't overturn his subjects' certainty, so he acceded and granted their request.

When Viśvantara came to know this, he said, "It doesn't matter whether I am killed or sent into exile, being uncharitable is something I cannot do. If I can give away my body and even my life, what needs to be said about external wealth?" Then he gave gifts of whatever they desired to the poor. He prostrated at the feet of his suffering parents. Then as he left the city there was a loud sound of sobbing in the palace and many people lamented.

Along with his wife and children, the prince got into a wagon and took the reins himself. They went in the direction of Mount Vaṇka. Along the way, some brahman wanderers asked for the horses that were pulling the wagon, so he gave the horses to them. [185] When the great man was about to pull the wagon himself, through the force of his merit four spirits transformed into red deer and pulled the wagon.

After some time, a brahman came and asked for the wagon. The prince with his wife and child got down from the wagon and he gave it away. They proceeded on foot to Mount Vaṇka, the prince carrying his adorable son, Jālin, in his arms and his wife Mādrī carrying in her arms their daughter, Kṛṣṇā. There, in an attractive forest filled with the lovely sounds of many birds, many varieties of animals, near a pure, clear lake fragrant with the scent of many flowers, they lived comfortably and happily in a pleasant leaf hut.

On one occasion the queen went into the forest to search for roots and fruit. While she was gone, a brahman came to the hut in search of a servant for his wife. The brahman was covered in dust, had a wan complexion and bloodshot eyes, and was carrying on his shoulder a staff to which he had tied a round water pot. He asked for the two children. The great man said, "The mother of these two children has gone into the forest. Please wait a bit. After they see their mother, you may lead them away."

The brahman thought, "I suspect that if they rejoin their mother the children will not be given to me. I should take them away now." He immediately prepared to lead them away. Tears filled the eyes of the two dear youngsters while they bowed to their father. Because they let forth piteous cries, the brahman tied their hands with willow switches, threatened them with harsh words, and led them away.

> Then, the prince, the great man,
> could hardly breathe for sorrow.
> That heartless brahman has led away
> those children whom I call my dear ones.[229]
>
> They are young and were happy.
> How will they bear the misery
> of hunger, thirst, and exhausting travel on foot?
> How will they manage being the brahman's servants?
>
> Alas! The great fire of suffering separation
> from my two dear children
> scorches my mind excruciatingly.
> What will happen when their mother sees this?

After a while Mādrī came back. When she asked, "Where are the children?" [186] the great man's mind was so tormented with distress he was unable to speak. Mādrī, choked with tears, said:

> Gloomy misery envelops my mind!
> Alas! My children have disappeared.
> My body feels disjointed.
> Will this not break my heart?

After saying this, she fainted to the floor in sorrow. The bodhisattva revived her by sprinkling her with cool water and said:

> A brahman hard pressed
> by the misery of old age and poverty

came here; I gave him my two children.
Do not grieve; think of me.

Mādrī said:

Incredible! Wonder beyond wonders!
Your mind has not a moment of greed.
Henceforth too, may your heart never tire.
May you fulfill the hopes of beggars.

Then the earth moved. Because even Mount Meru shook, Indra wondered, "What is this?" He looked into it and came to know it was the power of the great man's swell of generosity. He transformed himself into the shape of a brahman beggar, went before Viśvantara, and asked for the queen. The bodhisattva happily made the gift of his wife. Indra was very surprised at that and said in his praise:

The ethics of those refined and those debased
are indeed vastly different.
Who among those who have not purified themselves
could possibly believe what has happened?

Because they are not free from attachment,
who among them could have such an upsurge
of generosity to give without attachment
his dearly beloved wife like that?

Your deed is beyond those of men.
It will be admired by spirits,
gandharvas, the gods of the Heaven
of the Thirty-Three along with Indra.

The moon sends forth moonbeams;
it is not right that they go elsewhere.
This woman, your queen Mātrī,
I present her back to you.

After he returned the queen, Indra immediately disappeared. Then the merit of the great bodhisattva and Indra's power led the two children to the realm of the Śibis and caused them to be ransomed. Having heard of the great man's deeds, the attitudes of his father, the king, and the Śibi people softened. They begged forgiveness of the princely couple. After welcoming them home they made them the rulers of the realm.

Therefore, with faith and esteem for these incredibly amazing and wonderful deeds of the bodhisattva, [187] you should thoughtfully pray, "Someday may I be able to act like that."

* * *

18 Between the present and the future,
the foolish believe present happiness is superior.
Look at the behavior of the evil man
who was helped by the Ruru deer.

This verse means that fools are careless about what will happen in the future. When deciding between happiness in the present or in the future, they are attracted to the mere pleasures of the moment and think they are best. For example, the Ruru deer rescued a man who was being swept away in a river. In return for saving his life, the evil man led the king and his army to capture the Ruru. Look at what happened after that.[230]

As to the meaning of *ruru,* the word refers to a deer that makes that sound. Some people explain that it refers to a snow deer.

Long ago in a thick forest that was adorned with various types of vegetation, the bodhisattva deliberately took birth as a Ruru deer. His body was the color of refined gold, his sharp intelligence knew which places were dangerous and which were not, and he was a sovereign who loved the creatures who followed him and protected their happiness.

On one occasion he heard someone piteously crying and wailing. He quickly ran toward that sound. Seeing that a man had just fallen into a waterfall near the forest and was being swept away, he felt strong compassion. Not considering his own life, he jumped into the raging torrent. Blocking the water current, the Ruru lifted the man onto his back. He was heavily burdened because of the man's weight. The raging water made progress very difficult, but his bravery and fortitude arose and they reached the bank of the river without harm.

The Ruru was happy. He warmed the man with his own body heat. The man was astonished. He bowed with faith and respect. He said, "Because you saved my life, please tell me what you want in return for that great kindness."

In a human voice, the heroic Ruru said, "If you would remember this wish to be helpful to me, please do not tell anyone that 'in this place a creature like this rescued me from the river.' [188] Because most people have strong desires and consider the flesh of my body good to eat, it would be good if you could safeguard my good qualities and me too."

The man paid heed, and after saying, "I will do as you request," he respectfully circumambulated the Ruru and set off for his home.

At that time the queen of the kingdom had a dream that a deer like gold sat on a glorious lion throne and explained the Dharma to the king and his court. She told this dream to the king. Because the queen's dreams were keenly prophetic, he believed her and had this proclamation made day after day: "I will give a great reward to anyone who has seen a golden deer like that."

That man forgot that he had given his word to safeguard the Ruru and said to the king, "Lord! I know that superlative deer." He led the king and a great army to the place. The army surrounded the forest. The king, wielding a bow and arrows, was led by the man along the path into the forest. The man said, "Lord! Here is that wonderful deer!" He extended his arm to point and his arm broke at the elbow and fell off. After seeing that, the king drew an arrow and prepared to shoot. The Ruru said:

> O great king, please wait a moment.
> Please tell me who told you
> "In a dense forest without humans,
> there lives a deer like this."

The king was astonished by that speech in a human voice. His mind was completely calmed. "That man," he said, and pointed with his arrow. The Ruru said:

> Alas! Wouldn't saving a log from being swept away
> be better than rescuing such a vulgar man!
> Through the force of compassion I saved his life;
> repayment like this will bring fearsome results.

The king asked the man, "Is this true?"

"Yes sir, it is." he said.

The king said, "Why should bad person like you continue to live!" When the king put an arrow to his bow and was about to kill him, the deer stood between them. From the force of his compassion he said:

> O great king! Desist! Desist!
> What use is murder? View him with compassion.
> Grant him whatever reward you promised.
> As for me, with bowed head I await your orders.

The king was astonished and a high degree of faith arose. He placed the bodhisattva deer in a splendid carriage and with great honor brought him to the palace. He entreated him to sit on a lion throne. With a pleasant, melodious voice, the Ruru taught the king and his ministers, queen, and court the vast Dharma of the Great Vehicle beginning with great compassion. [189] The king and his court were established in the Dharma. The king gave the gift of freedom from fear to all the birds and animals.

Thus if you desire the mere happiness of the present, you will lose sight of everlasting concerns and create the basis for accumulating extremely bad karma. Therefore enjoyment and desire for the mere happiness of the present moment are like poison. You should give them up.

* * *

The next verse concerns the difference between those who will be suitable friends and those who will not:

> 19 The wise are friendly at first and thereafter;
> they never abandon their friends.
> Look at the way the chief of the monkeys
> truly protected his troop of monkeys.

The verse reveals that because a wise person is like quality gold, he or she is agreeable in the beginning and never forsakes his or her friendly attitude later. The jātaka relates the behavior of the bodhisattva chief of monkeys toward his monkey followers. When the monkeys were in terrible danger, at the risk of his own life the monkey chief made his own body a bridge to save them.[231]

Long ago the bodhisattva was the chief of a troop of monkeys in a thick forest filled with trees bearing marvelous flowers and fruit in a region of snow peaks. The monkeys made their home in that forest near a fig tree whose lofty and expansive branches were weighed down with marvelously sweet and fragrant fruit. It happened that a ripe fig of a marvelous color and scent fell from a branch of the tree that was hanging over a waterfall. The water carried it downstream to a spot where a king, his queen, and court had gone for amusement. The king picked up the fig. Once he tasted it, he had a craving for its marvelous taste and scent. In order to find the tree that bore that fruit, the king and many of his troops traveled around the area. After going upstream, on the riverbank of the waterfall they came on a tree around which there was an aromatic scent. [190] They thought, "This is definitely the tree bearing that fruit."

When they were in front of the tree they saw that many hundreds of monkeys covered the branches and were eating the fruit. Thinking, "Those bad creatures are using up all the fruit that I want," the king became angry. So he ordered, "Beat them! Strike them! Subdue them! Kill them!" With a great clamor, the king's men approached the tree brandishing arrows, rocks, and weapons of various sorts. It was like a hailstorm of weapons when they threw them. The host of monkeys were frightened and panicked. They were desperate and had no idea what to do.

The bodhisattva monkey felt great compassion for them. He climbed to the top of the tree and jumped to the mountain side. He tightly tied his legs with a long, strong rope of twisted reeds, and making a very difficult jump just managed to reach back to the top of the tree. Then firmly seizing a branch of the tree, he positioned his body as a bridge so that the troop of monkeys could easily escape. The pounding feet and hands of the troop of terrified monkeys trampled his body, grievously injuring him.

Seeing that, the king and his court were greatly astonished. Shooting two arrows, they simultaneously cut the reed rope and the tree branch. When the bodhisattva monkey king fell down onto a cloth they had stretched out to catch him, he fainted. They spread medicine on his wounded body. When he revived a bit from his faint, with wonder and respect the king inquired about his condition. In response to inquiries about the reason he cast aside care for himself and let the monkeys use his body as a bridge to get across, the bodhisattva monkey king explained, "I accomplished what the others desired by cherishing them more than myself. In consequence, my mind is very happy and content." He also encouraged the king to rule his kingdom according to the Dharma. Then, because his condition was so painful and grueling, he gave up his body and went to a higher rebirth in order to benefit others.

Thus when you rely on a wise holy being, he or she will act to protect you from all fear and trouble in this and all future lives. So with the right intention we should rely on a holy refuge. [191]

* * *

20 Although fools are amicable at first,
they turn on you for the slightest reason.
Look at the behavior of the evil lion
who was friends with the woodpecker.

This verse teaches that fools are like a balance scale. Even though they may be friendly and amicable at first, they will act in the opposite way owing to the slightest change in circumstances. For example, when a lion's throat was pierced by a bone, a woodpecker relieved him from that miserable and pathetic condition. For a while they lived as amicable friends. But later, when that vulgar evil lion felt a slight craving for meat, look at his belligerent and despicable behavior that lacked any gratitude.[232]

To expand on this summary, long ago the bodhisattva took birth as a beautiful and attractive woodpecker and lived in a forest. His lifestyle was genial. Because of the force of his habitual compassion he subsisted on only fruit, never harming a living creature. He did whatever was suitable to help other living creatures by using skilled methodologies.

At one time a lion struck down with an ailment was writhing in wretchedness. The bird went to him and saw that the trouble was a piece of bone piercing the lion's throat. He made the lion open his mouth, wedged a stick between his teeth, gently seized the bone that was in his throat, and pulled it out. He also removed the stick that jammed the lion's jaws. Relieved of his misery, the lion was very happy and grateful.

At a later time the woodpecker could not find anything suitable to eat and suffered pangs of hunger. Then he saw the lion eating the flesh of a deer he had killed. He flew down before him and asked for a little bit. Moved by the force of anger and greed, the lion forgot the bird's earlier kindness. He scornfully and insultingly spoke harsh words:

Hey you! I let you live for a while.
This request lacks propriety and scruples.

Are you weary of living this life?
Do you wish to see what life comes next?

The bodhisattva bird was ashamed and flew away. Unable to endure this, a god of the forest said to the bird, "In addition to lacking gratitude, that evil lion acts in an insulting manner. [192] Your beak could poke out his eyes. You could steal meat from his mouth, so why do you put up with this?" In response, the bodhisattva bird said the following and more:

Please do not speak thus.
The virtuous do not act compassionately
toward the indigent in hope for a return.
Whether or not the other person understands this,
who could get angry at that other person?

By helping others you accumulate merit;
there will be results of that even in future lives.
In this life too, good repute and glory
will definitely be obtained.

The god became reverent and noticeably delighted. He praised the bodhisattva again and again, worshiped him, and then disappeared into suchness.

Thus holy beings do not get angry even when they are treated disrespectfully and insultingly like that. They never undertake sinful actions even if they are urged to do so. Therefore we really should train under holy beings.

* * *

Regarding the benefits of strong intelligence and the faults of minimal intelligence, the text reads:

21 A wise person may have little physical strength,
but with powerful discernment he overcomes his foes.
It is well known that because the rabbit was intelligent,
he slew the king of beasts.

The wise have the power of intelligence. No matter how little physical strength they may have, through relying on powerful wisdom that discerns right from wrong, they will be victorious over all their enemies. For example, it is well known that a rabbit who had little physical strength but whose powerful intelligence was not deficient killed the very powerful and physically strong lion, the king of beasts.[233]

Long ago a lion and a rabbit lived together amicably. The lion was proud and strong by nature. Because the rabbit was weak, the lion belittled and mistreated him again and again. Although the rabbit couldn't stand it, for a while there was nothing he could do.

The rabbit thought about a way to pay the lion back for that maltreatment. He found a way, and then said, "Hey lord! There is a creature just like your lordship over there! He is someone whose boastful speech lacks propriety. The creature said, 'If you are able to contend with me and my strength, let us compete! [193] If you are not able to do that, you are my servant.' "

The lion was very arrogant, and said, "So be it. Wherever he is, I am going to challenge his strength."

The rabbit led the lion along and showed him a very deep well. "He's in there," he said. The lion went to the edge of the well and looked. He saw his own reflection in the water but thought it was the enemy. Agitated with anger, he drew himself up ferociously, shook his mane, bared his fangs, and so forth. Whatever gestures the lion made, the other one did the same thing. The lion was totally engulfed in arrogance and fury. He jumped into the well, thus killing himself.

22 Although fools may be physically strong,
because of their weak intelligence their enemies prevail.
The elephant had a huge, massive body,
but look how he was killed by the mongooses.

Fools do not have the eye of wisdom that discerns right from wrong. So no matter how strong they are physically, because the strength of their intelligence is weak, others often trick and delude them, and they fall under their enemies' sway. For example, the size and power of an elephant is much greater than the bodies of other animals. But look how the mongooses, much smaller and weaker creatures, were able to kill an elephant. As for this story as well as the one that is embeded in the verse that appears later in the text, further search needs to be made:

> Look how because the mouse ignored them,
> both the elephant and the mongoose were destroyed.[234]

* * *

Showing how a wise person is sought after everywhere:

23 Because the wise have every good quality,
they are sought after wherever they go.
It is well known that good stallions
and lovely jewels are in demand in marketplaces.

This verse says that because wise people possess every precious and superb good quality, they will obtain popularity, honor, and esteem in whatever country in whatever direction they go to live. For example, there is a well-known saying that excellent stallions with a good gait and lovely ornaments that beautify their wearer are [194] in demand in marketplaces. Further, the *Staff of Wisdom* says:

> Kings and people who have good qualities:
> those two are not alike.
> A king is esteemed in his own realm;
> a person with good qualities is esteemed by all.[235]

A fool is not sought after no matter where he goes:

24 Because fools have every kind of fault,
they are turned away wherever they go.
Look how no one will buy meat
if they know it comes from a donkey.

This verse reveals that fools have no good qualities that benefit themselves or others, and they have every sort of fault and shortcoming that is harmful. So wherever they go in any direction, everyone avoids honoring them and shun them. For example, a man beyond shame showed a deer's tail as a sign in order to sell donkey meat. When other people recognized it to be donkey meat, look how no one, not a single buyer, appeared.

Long ago a shameless man who made his living through trickery took a tail from a deer carcass. When selling donkey meat, he tricked others by showing it to people and saying, "This is meat from this deer." On one occasion people investigated and realized that it was donkey meat. After that not a single buyer came forth. In addition, later no matter what kind of meat he had to sell, people didn't trust him. The story is well known.[236]

* * *

To state that the wise obtain honor in other places the text reads:

25 A wise man will obtain more honor
in places other than his homeland.
A jewel is only marketable in other places;
how could it be valued in its ocean home?

This verse teaches that a wise person who accords with the meaning of that term will obtain more honor and respect in realms other than his birthplace. [195] For example, how could a precious jewel be rare and marketable on the ocean island where it is from? It isn't. It is only marketable and rare in other places.

No matter where a fool lives, everyone avoids him:

26 No matter where a fool lives
everyone there will shun him.
Look how everyone rejected
the householder's son called Durāgata.

In whatever country a fool comes to live, he is shunned by all creatures because not only does he not help others but he also brings them harm. For example, there was a son of a householder who came to be called Durāgata, which means "misfortune bringer." Even though it was his final lifetime in samsara, a residual karmic condition caused everyone who came near him to experience problems. So look how everyone rejected him and chased him away.[237]

To expand, in the past there was a layman named Bodha who was so rich his wealth rivaled that of Vaiśravaṇa. From the moment his wife became pregnant, a hundred problems arose for that householder daily. As the fetus grew, the number of problems got greater and greater too. On the day of its birth, the householder experienced a thousand problems. Nevertheless, saying, "It is good I now have a son," he gave him the name Svāgata, which means "fortune bringer."

Then, in succession, all their wealth was all used up, the householder and his wife died, the house and its contents were burned in a fire, and passersby destroyed anything else that could be sold. All his relatives and servants abandoned Svāgata except for one elderly maidservant. She served him and taught him the alphabet. Then the old woman thought, "I wonder if this karmic retribution that is the exhaustion of merit will also destroy me?" Taking anything there was of value, she fled. After a dog ate the remaining food, the dregs were carried off by human thieves. [196]

After that Svagata went to the home of his relatives. When strife arose there, they said, "You aren't Svāgata, Fortune Bringer, you are Durāgata, Misfortune Bringer," and they threw him out. When he joined a group of beggars they did not get anything. After a while they divided into twos to go to get alms. Those who went along with Svāgata ended up with empty hands and begging bowls. Finally the beggars said, "This bad luck is his fault!" They beat him severely and drove him away.

Then because he followed behind traders who were going to Śrāvastī, the merchants and their cattle were quarrelsome. The merchants said, "We have always gotten along so well, so why are strife and problems occurring now that never did before?" Having considered it, they understood and said, "This is Svāgata who is actually Durāgata," and they chased him away.

Having become totally destitute, he went to Śrāvastī. Because the daughter-in-law of Anāthapiṇḍada was Svāgata's elder sister, she felt sorry for him and sent a servant girl with some clothes and silver coins to give to him. So he went to a bar, drank alcohol until he was drunk, and went to sleep in a pleasure garden. Then he was robbed by thieves. His elder sister thought, "It is not right for this one's karmic retribution to destroy my in-laws' house," so she cast him off never to see him again.

Once again he went to live among beggars and the same thing happened as before. Finally all the beggars beat him up. After smashing his head with their begging bowls they drove him away.

At that point the Buddha with his sangha came by because Anāthapiṇḍada had invited them for the noon meal. The beggars were stopped by the gatekeeper, who said, "Check whether Durāgata is among you." They looked and saw him there. So the beggars beat him severely, smashed his head with their begging bowls, seized his arms and legs, and threw him onto a rubbish heap. He sat there weeping.

The Teacher gazed on him with great compassion. He called Svāgata, gave him what remained in his alms bowl, and dedicated the merit. When the

Buddha departed, Svāgata followed closely behind him. A former childhood friend of his father had given Svāgata two silver coins that he had sewn into his clothes. They were still there, but because of his karma he had forgotten about them. In order to purify Svāgata's karmic stains, the Teacher caused them to fall out. He had Svāgata purchase blue *utpala* flowers to distribute to the sangha. [197] The blue meditative concentration that finishes off karmic stains arose in Svāgata. After being ordained by the Teacher, he practiced and obtained the state of an arhat.

Thus even though his real name was Svāgata, Fortune Bringer, he became known as Durāgata, Misfortune Bringer, because unfortunate things happened to others wherever he went owing to the results of his remaining karma.

* * *

To state that when a vow is pure, the desired goal is accomplished, the text reads:

27 A wise man accomplishes his desired high goals
through the power of his pure vow.
Look how the partridge chick's altruistic motivation
diverted the incredibly huge conflagration.

This verse teaches that a wise person perfectly protects and keeps pure whatever vows he has taken. Through the power of that, whatever great goal he desires will be achieved without difficulty exactly as he wishes. For example, when the bodhisattva took birth as a partridge chick, a fire erupted in the forest and many animals were about to be harmed. Look how the bodhisattva's altruistic motivation of great compassion and his words of truth instantly diverted the terrifying and exceedingly huge fire.[238]

Long ago through the force of his will, the bodhisattva took birth as a partridge chick in an isolated forest. Not many days had elapsed since he emerged from the egg, so he was very scrawny and downy feathers were just starting to grow on his body and wings. He lived in a nest of thick grasses and reeds with his many siblings. Because even at that time his religious sensibility was unfailing, he did not consume living creatures for food. Because he ate only grass seed and fruit from a fig tree, his diet was coarse and lacked nutrition. Therefore his body did not develop well and even his wings were not fully mature. Because the other chicks ate whatever worms and so forth their parents brought to them, their bodies and wings grew large.

A being unconscious of any shame lives well. This is said in the sutras:

> Those who are greedy and audacious as crows
> lack any sense of shame and live well.
> A person who is focused on a faultless livelihood [198]
> and has a sense of shame has an uncomfortable life.[239]

At that time a fire erupted in the forest. Stirred by the wind, it made a great roar, smoke swirled, sparks flew, and it became terrifying. All the animals who roamed the forest fled. All the birds flew away. Driven by the fierce wind, the fire spread through the thick grasses and came near the partridge nest. In terror and fear the other partridge chicks swiftly flew away. Only the bodhisattva was unable to fly off because of his weakness and immature wings. Then the great bodhisattva generated the altruistic thought of great compassion for countless living creatures. And in order to save their lives he spoke gentle words to the fire:

> My feet don't deserve that name and I have no wings.
> Both my parents have fled in fear of you.
> There is nothing here suitable for you as a guest.
> Therefore, O fire, you should retreat; turn away from here.[240]

As soon as he spoke these words of truth the fire went out.

When vows are not pure, undesired things occur. This is stated in the following in the text:

> 28 Because the foolish make impure commitments
> there are bad indications immediately,
> and no matter what they do they come to ruin.
> Look how Virūḍhaka, who was afraid of fire,
> was burned up in a pleasure garden.

This verse means that because whatever fools vow to undertake is imperfect and impure, bad omens of undesirable events immediately arise. And fools will destroy themselves no matter what methods they employ and no matter what they do. For example, both King Virūḍhaka and his minister Dukhamātṛka were afraid of the harm fire could cause. So they went to a pleasure grove and lived there to avoid fires. However, look how they were burned by a fire.[241]

Long ago both Mālikā, the queen of King Prasenajit, and the wife of one of his ministers [199] became pregnant on the same day. From that day forward the wife of the minister was afflicted with suffering. After nine months passed, both women gave birth to a child on the same day. The king's son was named Virūḍhaka and the minister's son was given the name Dukhamātṛka.

After they had grown up they went to hunt deer. Riding on horses, they went to the pleasure groves of Kapilavastu. The Śākyas could not tolerate their incursion into their forest and said, "Cut off the arms and legs of that child of a slave! He should be killed!"

Virūḍhaka fled. He said to his household, "One day when I become king the first thing I will do is kill the Śākyas."

Dukhamātṛka said, "Right. As for good people, their promises are firm."

Later, a short while after Virūḍhaka became king, Dukhamātṛka said, "Now the time has come to do what you promised to do to the Śākyas."

The king said, "One should always do exactly what one has said one would do. But because the reason for revenge is passed, let it go. It will corrupt royal affairs."

However, Dukhamātṛka urged him and Virūḍhaka was beguiled by his evil friend. He and his troops put on their armor and went to Kapilavastu to kill the Śākyas.

Because the Buddha had taught them the Dharma, the Śākyas had seen the truth. "We should not harm Virūḍhaka's troops. Whoever among us hurts them is not one of us." Having made a law to not inflict harm on others, they closed the city gate and waited.

Then Virūḍhaka sent word to them: "I will not harm you, so open the gates." Tricked by that evil demon, the Śākyas opened the gate. Virūḍhaka and his troops went in. The Śākyas who had not accumulated the karma to be killed escaped. The majority of the Śākyas, who had accumulated that karma, stayed, and Virūḍhaka killed seventy-seven thousand of them. After that he returned to Śrāvastī.

Then the Teacher, the Buddha, prophesized, "Seven days from now, Virūḍhaka of the Kauśala lineage along with Dukhamātṛka will be burned in a fire. Then while wailing lamentations they will be born in the Avīci Hell."

After hearing that prophesy Virūḍhaka became worried. Dukhamātṛka said, [200] "This is certainly just talk because you killed so many of the renunciate Gautama's relatives. Let us go to the pleasure gardens. Have a residence with four pillars built, and live there for seven days not using any fire." They did exactly that. Along with the queens and court they went and stayed in the pleasure gardens.

On the seventh day one of the queens left a mirror on top of some pillow stuffing. The sun hit the mirror and started a fire. The fire on the pillow stuffing spread and the queens fled. Both Virūḍhaka and Dukhamātṛka tried to flee while they were on fire, but nonhumans shut the door. Both cried out in despair. Dukhamātṛka wailed, "I'm burning!" and his lord cried, "I'm cooked!" And then they were born into the Avīci Hell.

* * *

When a wise person is defeated he retaliates against his enemy:

29 The moment a wise person is defeated,
he gains courage to retaliate against his enemy.
Look how a northern yak took a hunter's life
because it was struck by the hunter's arrow.

As soon as a courageous, wise person experiences defeat, the courage to retaliate against the enemy who bested him arises. For example, look how a northern wild yak that was struck by the arrow of a hunter took the life of the hunter before he died himself.

The term "northern yak" in the verse means a wild ox. In Camara dialect, the words "yak" and "wild ox" are used interchangeably.

Moreover, it is said that when pursuing a wild ox, a hunter should shoot only when he has concealed himself well. Because if the wild ox sees him, it will surely turn to charge and kill the hunter.

When a fool is defeated he is hostile to his friends:

30 If a fool is defeated just once,
he antagonizes his friends and loses the will to fight.
Look at the resentful, submissive behavior
of a bad dog when it is struck by a stone. [201]

This verse means that a fool lacks courage. If he is defeated just once, he is hostile to his friends and loses the will to retaliate against the enemy who contested and harmed him. For example, look at the behavior of a bad dog. It gets very antagonistic for no reason and barks. But if the person it is chasing throws a stone that hits him, the dog becomes timid. It lies down in its own spot and stays there. A fool in that situation senselessly harms others when he is defeated himself.

Long ago there was an elephant who dearly loved his wife, a wooly female elephant.[242] The female wooly elephant lusted strongly for another youthful elephant. So she said to her husband, "If that elephant comes back here, the two of us need a way to escape and go somewhere else."

Her husband said to her, "If we submerge ourselves under the surface of the pond where we go to bathe, who could see us?" They went to the pond and the elephant hid in the water and stayed there. The female elephant ran off, taking the young elephant with her.

After some time had passed the elephant came out of the water and looked around, but didn't see anyone. He thought, "Will I be defeated?" And once again he submerged himself under the water and stayed for as long as he could endure. Holding his breath until he couldn't any longer, he lifted his head and looked around. Not seeing his wife, he became infuriated. He churned up the pond, going back and forth, and killed many fish and turtles. The gods said:

> Alas! This huge heap of flesh
> has not a bit of intelligence.
> When his wife was stolen by another
> he brought misery to different beings.

* * *

The wise do not fear important matters:

> 31 When a wise man confronts an important matter,
> he has no fear, no matter who opposes him.
> Look how Indra, all by himself,
> brought about the defeat of the demigod army.

This verse teaches that a wise person's knowledge comes from reflection. [202] When a wise man confronts an important matter he has courage that does not fear any enemy who tries to harm him. For example, it is said that long ago in a battle between the gods and demigods, the gods were defeated and their army scattered. Indra, the lord of the gods, remained alone on the battlefield. Look how the power of his courage and glory defeated all the demigod's forces.[243]

Long ago the bodhisattva intentionally took birth in the form of Indra, lord of the gods of the Heaven of the Thirty-Three. His glory and courage were marvelous. Owing to the power of his merit, he fittingly ruled the realms of the gods and men with heavenly sublime magnificence.

The demigods could not bear the glory of his outstanding reputation. They prepared an army that had a great number of terrifying demonic divisions of elephants, chariots, cavalry, and infantry, all wielding weapons. They came to do battle. At that point the bodhisattva Indra, surrounded by a huge army of gods, went to meet the army of the demigods on the ocean shore in order to do battle. When the two armies clashed many gods and countless demigods were wounded and brought to ruin. At one point the great strength of the demigod army scattered the forces of the gods. The bodhisattva Indra alone remained on the battle field.

Then Mātali, Indra's charioteer, seeing the retreat of the army of the gods, turned Indra's chariot around. In the path of the chariot the bodhisattva saw a nest of garuḍa chicks on a silk-cotton tree. Feeling great compassion for them, he ordered his charioteer, "Turn the chariot around to face the demigods!"

Mātali said, "If I turn the chariot around, the demigod hosts will overpower Indra himself."

Nevertheless, the great being was willing to give up his own life in order to save the lives of the chicks. He said, "Even if I die, it is better to turn the chariot."

As ordered, Mātali turned the thousand-horse chariot once again [203] to face the demigod army. The power of the bodhisattva's courage and merit made the demigod hosts scatter and flee in fear and terror. Then the army of the gods reformed. Together with the great bodhisattva they conquered the demigods and then returned to the Heaven of the Thirty-Three.

Fools are afraid when something important happens:

32 When a fool confronts an important matter,
he becomes frightened of the slightest thing.

Look how the tiger had a heart attack
because he mistook a man to be a *zak*!

When cowardly fools confront an important activity, they become confused and are terrified of the slightest thing. Consider, for example, the well-known story that long ago a tiger heard that a *zak* (a "leak") is something to be feared. Wondering, "What is this *zak* like?" his mind was trapped by his fantasies. When he saw a human he thought, "This must be it." In his confusion the tiger panicked and from terror had a heart attack.[244] Although some versions of this story have *zap* ("deep") instead of *zak*, the word is *zak*, which literally means "drops of water dripping down."

To elaborate, long ago an old couple had a bull. A thief came, and to steal the bull he hid in the barn rafters and waited. After that a tiger came too and waited below the rafters. Then clouds covered the sky and it became dark.

The old lady said, "Do you think a thief will come tonight?"

The old man said, "Even if a sky spirit showed up, I wouldn't be scared. Even if an earth spirit showed up, I wouldn't be scared. But if a *zak* comes, I'll be scared."

Overhearing this, both the thief and the tiger thought, "If what the old man says is correct, this so-called *zak* is something that should be feared by everyone. I wonder if it will come tonight?" And they were scared.

After a little while, when the darkness of the twilight clouds had lifted a bit, the thief saw the tiger and thought it was the *zak*. [204] In terror he pissed himself, and it dripped on the tiger. On looking up and seeing the man, the tiger thought the fearsome *zak* had shown up. Because the tiger fled in terror, it is said he had a heart attack.

* * *

When the wise exchange ideas, they unite to do what is right:

33 When wise people assemble in a group,
they unite to do what is right by comparing ideas.
Look how the four creatures, the elephant and so on,
convened and created rules of ethical discipline.

This verse means that when many perceptive, wise people gather together they exchange judicious insights. They unite to do only what is good for themselves and others. Consider, for example, how after the four animals, the elephant and so forth, convened in the forest they created the rules of the five precepts of ethical discipline—that is, the auspicious safeguards.[245]

Long ago in the deep forests of Kāśī, a pheasant, a hare, a monkey, and an elephant were mutual friends. The four lived together in harmonious happiness. They decided to respect each other by order of age. The pheasant pointed to a banyan tree, and the elephant said, "When I first walked on this path, I saw that this tree was the same height as my body."

The monkey said, "When I first came here, I saw that this tree was just the same height as my body."

The hare said, "When this tree had sprouted only two leaves, I licked dewdrops from them."

The pheasant said, "After I ate a seed of this sort, I defecated it here and this tree grew from that."

They said, "Well then, we should honor one another in the order of our respective ages." When they traveled, they went with the pheasant riding atop the hare, the hare rode on the monkey, and the monkey rode on the elephant.

Then thinking in a similar way, the pheasant said, "Now we shall give up killing." Then they said in sequence, "We shall give up stealing, sexual misconduct, lying, and intoxicants." [205] Having successively given these up, they lived according to the five precepts of ethical discipline.

At that time the pheasant said, "Now we should help others too." They presented the precepts of ethical discipline to their own species, and to others too. Then all the animals in the area of Kāśī took up the five basic precepts and lived happily in the thick forest without harming one another. From the power of that benevolence the gods made it rain when it should, and the crops and cattle flourished. The land was filled with good fortune and auspiciousness.

The king, his ministers, and all the people of the realm each said this good fortune was due to the force of their own individual merit. Since they could not agree, they asked a sage who possessed the five supernormal powers. The sage said, "This is not due to the power of any of your merits; it is due to the power of the merit of the four creatures who live in this realm. So you too should take up the five basic precepts of ethical discipline."

So the king, his court, and in turn the vassal states and most of the people in the world kept the five precepts of ethical discipline. When they died, they were reborn in the Heaven of the Thirty-Three and increased the court of the gods. Then Indra said:

With respect and with deference
the pheasant living in a hermitage grove
taught pure conduct well
to everyone living in the world.

Thus when you respect, honor, and are deferential to your elders your merit will increase, the entire country will be prosperous, and auspicious omens will occur. Therefore you definitely should act in this way.

After fools exchange bad ideas, they unite to do evil:

34 When foolish people assemble in a group,
they unite to do evil by exchanging bad ideas.
Look how many non-Buddhist ascetics convened
and then killed the arhat Maudgalyāyana.

This verse means that when many fools come together in a group they exchange ignorant bad ideas. Therefore they unite to do sinful deeds that bring themselves and others to ruin. For example, look how when many non-Buddhist ascetic followers of Pūraṇa Kāśyapa came together, [206] they killed the arhat Maudgalyāyana.[246]

Long ago when the Teacher was dwelling in the bamboo grove, the supreme pair of disciples, Maudgalyāyana and Śāriputra, traveled to the hell realms and back. They then went to the Avīci Hell in order to relieve the hell-beings of their misery. Maudgalyāyana flew up into the sky and made rain fall as deep as a chariot's axle, thus dousing the hell fires that went up into the atmosphere. Then Śāriputra entered the meditative absorption called the "concentration with a wish" and cooled the Avīci Hell and broke the continuance of that suffering.

As a result of his heretical teachings, the non-Buddhist ascetic Pūraṇa Kāśyapa had been born in hell with a huge body and a tongue that was tilled with five hundred plows. Pūraṇa Kāśyapa said to Maudgalyāyana and Śāriputra, "Please give a message to my followers. Tell them that every little bit of worship they offer to my reliquary monument increases my unbearable suffering in hell. So do not make offerings from here on out."

Then the supreme pair returned to the human realm. Some wandering ascetics carrying staffs saw them on the road to the capitol and said, "Let's pick a fight with those mendicants and beat them up." They went in front of Śāriputra and said, "Are you Ājīvaka mendicants?" Śāriputra responded:

> There are no monks among the Ājīvakas;
> among the Śākyas there are.
> There are none with desire among arhats;
> and there are no ordinary childish folk either.

Because they did not understand what he said, they thought, "He is praising us," and let him go.

Then they asked Maudgalyāyana, "What sort of religious practice do you have?"

He said, "I visited your teacher who was reborn in hell and he asked me to bring you this message." He relayed Pūraṇa Kāśyapa's message.

They became incensed and said, "This shaven-head brute is saying unpleasant things about our teacher!" Then they beat him severely, crushing his torso and limbs as if they were swamp grass. Śāriputra looked back and saw Maudgalyāyana. He wrapped Maudgalyāyana up in a shawl and carried him like a child to the main temple.

The monks were furious: "How could something like this happen to you who were prophesized by the Teacher as the best of those with miraculous powers?"

Maudgalyāyana said, "Because of my karma I did not even remember to dissemble, what need be said about remembering to use my miraculous powers?"

Hearing of this, King Ajātaśatru became enraged. [207] All the ascetic wanderers fled. The eyes of the king and court filled with tears. Many physicians were summoned.

"Cure Maudgalyāyana in seven days. If you do not, you'll be out of luck!" the king declared. The physicians were frightened and beseeched Maudgalyāyana himself. So after seven days his injuries were miraculously gone. Because Maudgalyāyana came for alms the king was overjoyed. Knowing that Maudgalyāyana was entering nirvana, because of karmic imprints of friendship, Śāriputra went to the city of Nālada and there, together with eighty thousand arhats, entered nirvana. That afternoon Maudgalyāyana went to the village of Kāṣṭhavāṭa and, with seventy-seven thousand monks, entered to nirvana.

* * *

The wise bring happiness to the realm:

35 The virtuous qualities of just one wise man
bring happiness to an entire country.
Look at the marvelous way the righteous king
nicknamed Flesh-Giver ruled his realm.

This verse means that wherever there are truly wise men, the virtuous qualities of each one will bring good fortune and happiness to an entire country. For example, because the Dharma king Maitribala, nicknamed the Flesh Giver, religiously ruled his realm, look at the wonderful way he pacified the yakṣas, whose mode of sustenance had brought harm to other realms.

Long ago in Vārāṇasī there was a king named Maitribala who protected all living creatures with love in accord with the meaning of his name, Power of Love.[247] Because the king's mind was imbued with great compassion, through the strength of his cultivation of love he protected all his subjects from harm and placed them in a state of perfect happiness.

At another time the ruler of the yakṣas, Vaiśravaṇa, banished five vitality-sapping yakṣas from his realm, Aḍakavatī, because they had committed a crime. After a while they came to Vārāṇasī. [208] They wanted to steal the vitality of the people who lived in that realm, but because of the powerful protection of the king's love they were not able to steal the vitality of anyone.

They puzzled over that. "How could our power be broken?" Magically assuming the form of brahmans, they asked a cowherd taking his ease in a remote spot, "Aren't you afraid of demons and vicious carnivores?"

The cowherd laughed and said, "Because of the power of the virtuous qualities of our king, even Indra, the ruler of gods, cannot torment the living creatures of this land, so what needs to be said about anyone else!"

The yakṣas thought, "This is the reason we can't do anything," and became annoyed with the king. They went to the palace environs to beg for food from the king. When the king ordered lovely victuals placed before them as an offering, they showed their fearsome and ugly forms and said, "Warm human flesh and blood are what we eat and drink. So please give us that."

Then the great being, the king, felt great compassion for these yakṣas, having seen that hunger and thirst had weakened their vitality and that they were pleading expectantly. He thought, "How can I get warm flesh and blood for them without killing another living person? Killing one to nourish another is pointless. So the time has now come for me to give my own flesh and blood." The king summoned doctors and had them open his veins. Then he directed the yakṣas to drink his blood until they were satisfied. Then, using a sharp sword, he cut off pieces of his own flesh and gave it to them.

Satisfied by the flesh and blood, the savagery of the yakṣas was pacified. Out of faith and respect, they promised to do what the great man said from then on. The king gave them the five basic laymen's precepts. At that time the earth quaked. For that reason Indra, lord of the gods, came before the king and in astonishment praised him with faith and respect. Then Indra applied special human and heavenly medicines to the king's physical wounds so he was restored to what he had been before. After that Indra returned to his own realm. [209]

Fools bring countries to ruin:

36 The actions of just one fool
bring misery to an entire country.
Look how Dukhamātṛka's actions
were the ruin of the Śākya clan.

This verse teaches that not only do large groups of fools cause the ruin of themselves and others, but also that on the basis of just a single fool's bad actions, all the people of a realm can be made to suffer and experience calamity. Consider, for example, that because the foolish and ignorant man called Dukhamātṛka committed the negative action of urging King Virūḍhaka to do something inappropriate, approximately seventy-seven thousand of the Śākya clan who had seen the truth were killed and the clan was destroyed. This is the story of Virūḍhaka that was told earlier.[248]

* * *

Because the wise have subdued love and hatred everyone loves them:

37 Because the wise have subdued attachment and hatred
even their enemies become dear friends.
Look at the king's affectionate attitude
after he was rescued by the *śarabha* beast.

This verse means that the wise are unbiased. They have pacified both the attachment that is affection for those on their side and the hatred that disregards those on the other side. Therefore not just their friends but their enemies too come to have a positive attitude of friendship toward them. For example, the bodhisattva in a rebirth as a śarabha felt great compassion when an antagonistic king who wanted to kill him fell into a deep ravine. Because the bodhisattva rescued the king from the ravine, the king's attitude became faithful and joyful.[249]

A *śarabha* is a deer that is said to have eight legs. Because four legs are on the upper part of its body, it is also called "one with high legs" and "one with upward eyes." It is explained in the *Bhārata*[250] that a śarabha's great skill and strength can even overpower lions.

Long ago many sorts of animals roamed in a wild, remote area that was difficult to traverse because there were waterfalls, anthills, rocky cliffs, ravines, and the ground was covered in thick trees, shrubs, grasses, and so forth. [210] The bodhisattva intentionally took birth as a śarabha there. He had splendid skill and strength as well as a compassionate mind. He was like an ornament of that wild forest.

At one time a king came to that region to hunt deer. The king saw the śarabha off in the distance. In order to kill the deer, the king chased after him on a horse so swift he soon outpaced all his companions and was all alone. The bodhisattva deer, using the momentum of his speed, was able to jump over a huge ravine that was in his path of flight. The king's horse balked because its momentum in pursuit would not enable it to jump the ravine. The king fell off his horse and tumbled down into the ravine.

No longer hearing the sound of the horse's hoof beats, the bodhisattva deer wondered if the king had turned back. He looked behind him and saw the riderless horse at the mouth of the chasm. He thought, "The king has certainly fallen into the ravine. Are his limbs broken? Could he have passed out? In any case, he will not be able to get out of that deep ravine by himself." He felt great pity. He went to the edge of the ravine and saw the king down in the chasm. His body was covered with dirt, he had lost his turban, and he was writhing on the ground from the pain of his injuries.

Swayed by compassion, the bodhisattva deer forgot the very concept *enemy*. His eyes filled with tears, and he said, "O great king! Are you hurt? Is anything broken? I am a deer who lives in your realm, so please be at ease for I will get you out of this ravine."

The king was ashamed. "What sort of being has compassion that can extend even to his enemy?" he wondered in astonishment. With a respectful attitude he said, "I am not greatly injured, thanks to my thick robes. Please do not keep in mind my prior attack on you."

The bodhisattva śarabha practiced carrying a stone the weight of a man until he knew he could carry the king out of the ravine. Then he jumped into the chasm. He instructed the king how to sit on his back and hold on properly. Impelled by force of his courage, he leapt upward and reached the top. He took the king back to his horse and gave it to him.

The king was overjoyed. [211] With faith and respect he invited the bodhisattva deer to the palace. Although he did not accept the invitation, the śarabha taught the king the Dharma of abandoning nonvirtue, creating virtue, and so forth. Then he went back to live in the forest.

Because fools are habituated to craving and hatred, they come to quarrel with everyone:

38 Fools naturally end up quarreling with everyone
because they are habituated to attachment and hatred.
Look how everyone runs away
when they see a vicious, poisonous snake.

This verse means that fools are biased. Through the force of their habitual desire and hatred, all the people they counted as friends naturally come to feel hostility and mutual enmity. For example, because poisonous snakes are vicious and irate, look how everyone turns and runs away merely on seeing one.

* * *

Showing that a wise person's use of property is right:

39 The wise acquire possessions properly;
their things come from a worthy source.
Look at the amazing way the first king arose
because he was honored by many people.

This verse means that a wise person's possessions and honors are appropriate things to enjoy because they come about in an ethical manner from a worthy source. For example, in the beginning of the world many people agreed to appoint and honor a wise and learned man as their ruler and give him a sixth of their harvest. Look at the wonderful way the first king, called Mahāsaṃmata, "the one honored by the masses," appropriately governed his subjects.[251]

Long ago at the start of this eon most humans were miraculously born when gods transmigrated at death. They had many excellent qualities: they were radiant, they ate happiness as food, they could live infinitely long, and so forth. [212] There was no sun or moon, no year, and no differentiation of the sexes.

From the power of their desire to eat material food, gradually the earth became fertile and moistened, there were sprouts, and humans enjoyed the fruit of uncultivated crops. Owing to fruit consumption they lost most of the good qualities they had inherited from the gods. After their radiance diminished, when it became dark, the sun was differentiated from the moon, day was differentiated from night, and the cycle of years and so forth arose. Then the dregs of the fruit they had consumed became excrement and urine, and male and female sexual organs became the passages for their elimination. Although the uncultivated crops could be taken whenever needed, lazy people divided it into individual portions based on their desire to set aside some reserves. Some people took others' portions, and so stealing, robbery, and so forth were created. There was strife among people.

At that point all the beings came together. "From now on, in order to adjudicate right from wrong, we shall appoint as ruler a man with a good character. We shall give him a sixth of the harvest." Because that person was appointed by many and they were in unison, he was called King Mahāsaṃmata—"honored by the masses." The first king of the world arose this way.

At that time they wanted names to delineate the four castes. Those who had little desire and turned away from home to live in hermitages and in the forests were called the *brahman* caste. Those who did not steal and so forth became the *kshatriya* caste. Those who stole and so forth were given the names of *shudra* caste and outcastes.

The son of Mahāsaṃmata was Roca. His son was Kalyāṇa. His son was Varakalyāṇa. And his son was Upoṣadha. These were the first five kings. Māndhātā was born from scar tissue on Upoṣadha's head that burst open. Cāru came from his right thigh; Upacāru came from his left. Cārumanta came from his right foot. Upacārumanta came from a scar on his left foot. These five were called the five cakravartin kings. The latter four were in succession the gold, silver, brass, and iron cakravartin kings. It is known that

King Śuddhodana was the 1,211,514th descendant of this lineage. The *Basis of Discipline* says that the Bhagavān's son, Rāhula, was the last of Mahāsaṃmata's line. [213]

Showing that a fool's possessions come from wrong livelihood:

40 A fool's property comes from wrong livelihood;
their possessions come from an unworthy source.
Because the fox was honored as a king,
look how the king of beasts killed him.

This verse says that for the most part, a fool's possessions and reputation are the result of their own wrong livelihood. In other words, most arise from a dishonorable source and inappropriate practices. For example, long ago a fox had some good luck. For a while all the animals honored him as their king. He rode on an elephant and was accompanied by a court of lions, tigers, and so forth. Later when they realized he was a fox, the king of beasts killed him.[252]

Long ago when a greedy fox wandered in isolated places and towns in search of food, he fell into a laundryman's dye vat. After he got out he slept on a pile of salt. Because he felt uncomfortable he went into some water. When he emerged and was struck by sunlight, his fur turned the color of shiny onyx.

When the other foxes saw him they were astonished. "Who are you?" they asked.

He said, "I am called Indra's Envoy. Indra anointed me king of the four-footed beasts." In that way he confused all the foxes.

Amazed because they had never seen a creature that color before, many four-legged animals honored him as their king. He rode about on an elephant with lions as an entourage. Surrounding the elephants were tigers and all the other quadrupeds. The foxes were consigned to the edges farthest away.

He sent a fox with a message to his mother, who lived in a mountain cave. "Come to where your son enjoys royal authority."

His mother asked, "What sort of retinue does he have?"

The fox messenger replied, "In his court there are lions, tigers, and elephants. We foxes are the last."

His mother said, "I will not go to be treated so improperly."

The fox returned to the others and said, "This king of quadrupeds is a fox! I saw his mother."

To test whether this was the case, the foxes howled. It is the nature of foxes that when they hear another fox howl, [214] if they do not howl too, their fur will fall out. Because he let out a fox howl while riding on the elephant, the elephant knew, "A fox is riding on me!" He threw him off, trampled him with his feet, and killed him. A god spoke this verse:

> Just as the elephant did in the fox,
> Buddhists pretending to be heretics
> and heretics pretending to be Buddhists
> will be destroyed by acting like this.[253]

This is how the story goes in the *Basis of Discipline*. Some versions of the tale say the fox was riding on a lion and it was a lion who killed him.

Thus predominantly ill-gotten gains and honors will destroy you. The same scriptural source says:

> Plantain, bamboo, and rattan plants
> wither and die after they bear fruit.
> Just as bearing a colt will kill a mule,
> honors will destroy inferior creatures.[254]

* * *

The wise complete whatever they start:

> 41 The wise complete whatever they undertake
> no matter what difficulties they encounter.
> Look at courageous offering made to the sage
> by the merchant who crossed a pit of fire.

This verse means that a righteous, wise person will carry through to the end whatever task he begins, no matter what difficulties he encounters along the way, even at the risk of his life. For example, look at this courageous almsgiving of Dānaśūra. In order to make offerings to a pratyekabuddha sage, he crossed a flaming pit of terrifying hell fire that was by the entry to his courtyard. This fire had been magically created by a demon trying to block his generosity.[255]

As the story goes, long ago when our compassionate Teacher was training himself in the bodhisattva practices, he deliberately took birth as a merchant named Dānaśūra. He was wise, had mastered many disciplines, and was lord of the good qualities of compassion and perfect magnanimity. [215] Everyone in the world paid their respects to him.

One day when it was time to eat, he bathed, and a spread of marvelous food and drink was set out. Just then a pratyekabuddha came for alms and sat down by the entry to his courtyard. In order to block the merchant's groundswell of generosity, between the outer gate and inner door an evil-doing demon transformed himself into a roaring, terrifying, deep, and wide pit of the fire of the great hell of living beings.

The merchant had sent his wife to offer alms to the holy man. When his wife saw the hell fire, she was frightened. Terrified out of her senses, she went back inside. Then the merchant himself came out carrying excellent food and drink. Seeing the fearsome great hell between his outer gate and door, he wondered, "What is this?"

The evil demon manifested in the amazing form of a god and hovered in space. As if he were affectionate, he said kind words:

> This is the great hell Mahāraurava.
> By enjoying generosity you waste your possessions
> and are born here. Those who keep things are reborn in heaven.
> Thus you should turn away from this attitude of generosity.

The great being, the merchant, realized this was a demon and answered:

> You say that generosity leads to rebirth in hell
> and retention of wealth leads to rebirth in god realms.
> You are trying to turn me away from generosity,
> but despite that I will endeavor to give.

He had no hesitation about going into the hell. The power of the great being's merit caused a bridge of lotuses to appear. He went over it and made offerings to the pratyekabuddha.

> Thus through the power of his merit
> lotuses not of a swamp appeared there.

Flower petals like rows of white teeth
shook vigorously, as if rebuking the demon.

His attitude greatly pleased the pratyekabuddha;
that religious practitioner flew up into the air.
He beautified the sky like a magnificent cloud
glittering with rain drops and lightning.

Having not accomplished his intention,
the demon despaired and his radiance dimmed.
Unable to bear even looking at that sight,
he vanished along with the hell. [216]

Thus, no matter how he is threatened by others, a courageous, wise person is never deterred and carries through to its conclusion any virtuous action that he undertakes.

Whatever fools do will not be worth it:

42 No matter what actions a fool undertakes,
not a single one brings satisfaction later.
Look how the father of the child Jyotiṣka
kneaded his wife's belly.

This verse means that fools do not have the eye of intelligence. Whatever they undertake will be unsatisfying and will not be worth it later. For example, look how the layman Subhadra, the father of the child Jyotiṣka, rubbed his wife's belly in order to induce her to deliver the baby and so killed her. His action destroyed both himself and another.[256]

In a kingdom long ago, a layman named Subhadra had a pregnant wife. When the Buddha went there for alms, the prospective parents requested a prophecy. The Buddha foretold, "You will give birth to a boy. He will have dazzling intelligence and experience the splendors of gods and men. Having entered my teachings, he will attain the state of an arhat."

A naked ascetic knew that the Buddha had been there. He thought, "Because Gautama went into my sponsor's house, I can see that he will take away my benefactor!" So he went there and said, "What did Gautama prophesize?" The layman told him what he had said. The naked ascetic did a divination by picking up a white stone and knew that it was all true.

He thought, "If I tell them this is accurate, their faith in Gautama will increase even more." His face changed and he said, "As for *dazzling*, it is a word for fire. So as soon as the child is born your house will be consumed by fire. What human has ever experienced the splendor of the gods? So that is not true. Having nothing to eat he will become a renunciate. That is true. If Gautama himself is not an arhat, what needs be said about those who listen to him?"

The layman became despondent and said, "Well what should I do?" [217]

The naked ascetic said, "By following my instructions you will understand."

The householder thought, "That means I should make her abort the fetus." But even though he gave her drugs, he couldn't harm the fetus because this was to be that being's last samsaric rebirth. As he kneaded his wife's abdomen, the fetus dodged from side to side. His wife cried, so he took her to an isolated place and pressed her abdomen very hard. His wife died.

Then he took his wife's corpse to the charnel ground for cremation. The king and his court were there too because they heard that the Buddha, along with a hundred thousand gods and men, had gone there. As the woman's corpse burned on the heaped-up logs of the cremation fire, every part of it burned, but the placenta was unscorched. It burst open and from the heart of that lotus a beautiful baby emerged.

The Teacher said to the layman Subhadra, "Go pick up the infant."

The layman looked at the face of the naked ascetic and said, "I will not go get it."

So the Buddha said to Jīvaka, "Get it." Without any hesitation Jīvaka went into the fire. As he picked up the infant, it was as if he were cooled by the best-quality sandalwood. Then he presented the infant to King Bimbisāra, who gave him the name Jyotiṣka, "fire born."

A while after he was born his maternal uncle, who had been traveling in another realm, returned. Having heard what happened, the uncle said to the layman Subhadra, "You killed my sister and abandoned her infant too. I am going to tell the king." Out of fear, the layman Subhadra took in the child Jyotiṣka. Some time after that the layman died. Jyotiṣka became the owner of his property and enjoyed the splendors of the gods and men.

Then at a later time, after Ajātaśatru murdered his father and became king, he wanted Jyotiṣka's heavenly possessions. Seven times that heavenly wealth went back and forth between them: whenever Jyotiṣka sent it to the king, it came back. Jyotiṣka thought, "Ajātaśatru killed his own father. He will surely kill me to in order to get these heavenly possessions."

So after giving his possessions away, he went before the Teacher, who made him a monk by virtue of saying, "Come forth." Then he attained arhatship. [218]

* * *

The wise examine a goal and then either pursue or turn away from it:

43 No matter what others say, a wise man
pursues or rejects a goal after examining it himself.
Look how the brahman's student rejected
his teacher's command that he steal.

This verse means that someone skilled in discriminating what to do and what to avoid does not follow other people's exhortations, no matter what they say. They look at a goal and, after examination, they pursue or reject it. For example, look at the story of the bodhisattva who, as a brahman student, refused to follow his teacher's command to steal when the teacher said, "The Vedas explain that when a brahman is poor and destitute, stealing someone else's wealth is morally acceptable."[257]

Long ago, the bodhisattva took birth as a brahman of a high caste and perfect conduct. As he grew up, demonstrating proper service in both thought and deed, he pleased a learned teacher of a pure caste and good conduct enough to study the Vedas with him. Even the spiritual teacher admired, liked, and was pleased by the great being's good qualities.

At that time in order to test his students the brahman master constantly claimed to be suffering from destitution and poverty. His students couldn't bear that and gathered a lot of alms and gave them to him. In response their spiritual teacher said, "Mere alms cannot alleviate my privations. If you care for me, you should know how to strive to become rich."

The students asked about the means to become wealthy, and so the master said: "The way to become rich is set out in the scriptures. They explain that all the wealth in the world is brahmans' wealth. So when a brahman is in a state of decline it is morally acceptable to him to filch others' possessions, no matter who sees. Nevertheless, in order to guard against notoriety, do not take, snatch, or rob while others are looking." The other students agreed to act in the manner he instructed. The bodhisattva hung his head in embarrassment and said nothing at all. [219]

The master asked him, "When these brahmans are unable to bear my suffering from privations, why do you sit with a bowed head?" The great being, the brahman youth, genuflected and said, "It isn't that I do not love my teacher or that I am unpained by my spiritual teacher's suffering because of a hard heart. But,"

> When committing misconduct in the world
> it is impossible for anyone to not be seen
> because of the ever-present vision of the gods
> and the awareness of nonhuman spirits and sages.
>
> Knowing an action is wrong, who would lay waste
> to their good qualities in order to gain wealth?
> I cannot conceive in my mind that you would
> command us to do a blameworthy action.
>
> It would be better to wear rags and carry a begging bowl
> to my enemy's house and see their wealth
> than to abandon shame and act contrary to religion
> even if it meant I could be lord of the gods.

The master was very pleased. In amazement he got up from his seat. He embraced him in his arms and said, "Son. This is good. This is good. You are truly a great brahman. You are finely adorned with wisdom. Your learning has borne fruit. You have accomplished the goal for which you have striven." With heartfelt respect the brahman master extensively praised the great being, the bodhisattva.

Thus no matter how very kind your preceptors, teachers, and so forth may be, if they urge you to do an unseemly action, make an appropriate excuse and be someone who does not engage in sinful activity. Do not become distrustful because you may not understand their intention.

Fools rush to do what others dictate:

44 Without considering matters themselves,
the foolish are swayed by others' inducement.

Look how all the traders came to ruin
because they listened to what the ogress said.

This verse reveals that fools lack discernment. Not examining the potential danger and veracity of a matter, they rush to listen to others, fall under the influence of their encouragement, and act as directed. For example, consider how all the traders were shipwrecked [220] and eaten—that is, destroyed—by ogresses as a result of listening to the enticing words of the stork-maiden ogress of the subcontinent Tāmradvīpa. This tale is same as the one that will be told below in connection with verse 113.

* * *

Even if they wane for a while, the wise succeed in the end:

45 Even if they are in severe decline for a while,
the wise will rise again like the waxing moon.
It is well known that the minister Gar
was imprisoned but later got the better of everyone.

This verse says that the wise are those who know the ways of skillful means. Even if they temporarily happen to be in some sort of severe decline, their prosperity and well-being immediately reappear, just as the waxing moon's white face increases by degrees. For example, there is the well-known story that when the Tibetan minister Gar went to China to escort the Chinese princess Wencheng to Tibet, the Chinese monarch did not want to let him return to Tibet and made him live in China as if he were in prison. Although for a short while there was nothing Gar could do, later he confused the Chinese emperor and all his ministers and was successful. He caught up with Wencheng and her entourage on the journey to Tibet.[258]

To expand on this summary, long ago when it came time for the Buddha's teachings to spread in Tibet, the land of snow mountains, the noble Avalokiteśvara took birth as the son of King Namri Songtsen. He was known by the name Songtsen Gampo. When he reached the age of thirteen, he ascended the throne of the kingdom. Because Amitābha's head was on top of Songtsen Gampo's head, all the kings of surrounding countries heard, "Now the two-headed Tibetan king has magic powers that can send forth an unstoppable enchanted army." So out of respectful homage, they sent fine gifts and submissive messages.

Thönmi Sambhota was dispatched to India. From his study of various writing systems he devised a thirty-four-letter alphabet and eight treatises of important points for Tibet. He translated many Dharma texts, the sutras and tantras of Avalokiteśvara, and so forth. He spread the systems of reading, writing, and sixteen pure laws of secular ethics based on the religious ethics of the ten virtues. [221]

Then the king commissioned the monk Akaramatiśīla, who was a magical emanation, to bring from the ocean shore of South India a statue of the extremely compassionate eleven-faced Avalokiteśvara that had spontaneously arisen from a snake-heart sandalwood tree. He was also to bring sand from the eight great sacred sites and many relics of the Buddha. The minister Gar and his entourage were ordered to make a request to the Nepalese king Aṇśuvarma; he was to give his daughter, a princess who was an emanation of Bhṛkuṭī, to marry the Tibetan king and become queen. Indra was the patron of her dowry. It included a statue of Śākyamuni at the age of eight, called Lord Akṣobhyavajra, fashioned by Viśvakarmā from various precious substances of the gods and men and consecrated by the Buddha himself.

Then the minister Lord Gar, along with one hundred attendants, was ordered to the Chinese imperial palace to invite the Chinese princess Wencheng to Tibet.[259] She was an emanation of Tārā and the daughter of the Chinese emperor Taizong. At that time ministers of the kings of India, Persia, Golok, and Uighur had also been commissioned to request the hand of princess Wencheng. All four ministers arrived at the Chinese imperial palace.

At that point all the Chinese disliked the Tibetans. Not wanting to give the Tibetans his daughter, the emperor decided he would give her to the minister with the sharpest intelligence. Saying, "I will give her to whoever can pass this silk thread through this piece of turquoise the size of a shield that has a hole in the center and a hole on one edge," he showed them the turquoise. The other ministers tried many schemes for a number of days, but they could not thread it. Gar tied a silk thread around the waist of a large ant, put it near one of the holes, and by blowing on it threaded the turquoise. Nevertheless the princess was not given to him.

Soon after that the emperor presented the ministers with one hundred mares and one hundred foals and said, "I will bestow the princess on whoever knows which foal belongs to which mare." The others did not know how to figure it out. Gar put the foals into an enclosure and did not give them any water. The next day he let them out and each one went to its mother to nurse. Thereby he knew which was which. Yet again the princess wasn't given to Gar.

Then the emperor presented the ministers with one hundred hens and one hundred chicks and said, "It will be the one who can distinguish each pair of mother and chick." The others did not know how to figure it out. Gar scattered grain kernels on a spacious flat and knew which chick belonged to which hen because they ate in pairs of two. Again the princess wasn't given to Gar.

Then the emperor presented the ministers with logs of wood and said, "I will bestow the princess on the one who can tell the top from the bottom of the log." The others did not know how to figure it out. By throwing the logs into water, Gar knew the top from the bottom. Again the princess wasn't given to Gar.

Again, one day the emperor presented each of the ministers with a hundred sheep and said, "I will bestow the princess on the man who can eat all the mutton and tan every hide in a single day." [222] The others were not able to do even one. The Tibetan minister and his attendants made individual piles of the meat and hides, cut the meat into little pieces, mixed them with salt, and ate it all. And each hide was cured by the men working in rows; the man at the top of a row scraped it with a dagger and then passed it down to be scraped by the next man in the row. Again the princess wasn't given to Gar.

The emperor said, "I will bestow the princess on the one who can drink all this by noon and not become drunk," and he presented each of the ministers with pitchers of beer. The others became drunk and vomited. Because the Tibetan minister and his men drank it sip by sip from tiny cups, they drank it all and did not become drunk. Again the princess wasn't given to Gar.

One night a great drum was beaten to summon everyone to the palace. The emperor said, "I will bestow the princess on the one who finds his way back to his own quarters without a mistake tonight." The other ministers got lost and did not find their residences. Gar had marked the doors through which he had come. Bearing a lamp, he could see the marks, and by following them easily got back to his residence. Nevertheless the emperor did not want to give the princess to the Tibetans.

Then from the emperor came the announcement, "Tomorrow there will be three hundred girls in rows in the square. I will give the princess to whoever recognizes her." Gar gave a gift of gold to a Chinese woman with whom he was intimate. Using a means that could not be detected by Chinese divination, he asked her how to recognize the princess. He made sure he would recognize Wencheng's figure and dress. The next morning the other ministers each led out an attractive girl. The Tibetans led the princess by an arrow hooked to the collar of her dress.

Included in the princess's dowry there was a statue of the Buddha at the age of twelve, called Lord Śakyāmuni. Thus the emperor sent this special icon as the princess's object of worship, a statue that is perfect with respect to its donor, material, and artistry, as well as consecration, as described earlier. The princess and a vast amount of various sorts of wealth were to be escorted to Tibet.

Then the emperor said, "Minister Gar must stay in China." Because he was not allowed to return to Tibet, he acted as if he were going to live in China for a while. Then he pretended to become ill. The emperor sent physicians. They did not know what cures to employ. The king said to Gar, "Since you are wise, tell us what would ease your illness?"

Gar said, "I need the ashes made from burning fine silk, a lance made of charcoal made from burning sandalwood, blood from the spleens of goats, and so forth." He made them do many unproductive things, such as planting parched grain and so forth, thus creating much misfortune in China. [223]

Then he said, "I must make an offering to the gods in a place where I can see the mountains of Tibet." Allowed to go with four guards, he gave them dry meat to eat, then when they got thirsty he poured beer for them. They became drunk and fell asleep. Gar broke their weapons and lamed the legs of their horses. Then he mounted his own horse and fled. He caught up with Wencheng and her entourage on the road at Godong Gomo Tsa.

In this way, the minister Gar employed various creative strategies in the competition of wits set up by the Chinese emperor. When he was not allowed to depart from China, he made them experience much suffering. In this way he achieved victory and obtained the princess Wencheng as a queen for the Tibetan king. Together the king and queen launched the building and inauguration of a new main cathedral. They made the teachings of the Buddha shine like the sun over Tibet.

The slightest setback completely destroys fools:

46 When fools experience a single problem
they are extinguished like a butter lamp.

> Look at the king who attacked the sage Kṣāntivādi;
> his state of mind was instantly wrecked.

This verse means that fools are ignorant of the way to accomplish things. Their decline begins if they experience a single moment of misfortune; their well-being and happiness are extinguished just like a butter lamp that has run out of oil. For example, look at the way a king who argued with and harmed a great man, the sage Kṣāntivādi, immediately experienced the result of his own bad actions. His well-being was destroyed.[260]

Long ago a son was born to Brahmadatta, the king of Vārāṇasī, and given the name Kāśīsundara. After he grew up he saw that living in society is the source of many problems and that being a renunciate avoids those problems and has many benefits. So he left his home and became a homeless renunciate. He lived in a marvelous spot in a secluded and delightful forest grove. [224] He kept his personal vow of patience. And because he taught religion in accord with his vow and in a way that was comprehensible and pleasant to hear, both gods and men developed faith and reverence. He became known as Kṣāntivādi, "proponent of patience," a name in accord with his actions.

At one point during the spring when the tree branches had sprouted leaves, flowers blossomed, bees hummed and cavorted, and birds sang sweetly and flew in a soaring dance, a king with his queens and court came to the forest grove for relaxation. After enjoying the pleasures of the forest grove, the king became tired and lay down to sleep under a tree. The queens, entranced by the forest's beauty, wandered about to see more. Going farther and farther they eventually came to where Kṣāntivādi was practicing austerities. When they saw the supreme sage sitting beneath a tree, his countenance blazing with the splendor of a peaceful and disciplined mind, the queens approached him with faithful respect and venerated him. In turn, the great man gave easily understandable religious discourses on the value of a human life, death and impermanence, abandoning sin and creating virtue, and patience.

Then the king woke up. His queens were not there and his mind was overcome with desire for them. He went in pursuit. When he saw the sage Kṣāntivādi surrounded by his queens, jealousy greatly agitated the king's mind. He said, "Who is this evil hypocrite looking at my harem of queens?"

Smiling and recollecting their manners, the queens went before the king. At that point they realized the king was angry. In apprehension and fear the queens and eunuchs said, "O Lord, this sage is the great man Kṣāntivādi. Please do not do anything rash."

Although they tied to dissuade him, the king did not listen. He raised his sword and advanced. The queens scattered in despair. Then although the great man spoke conciliatory words, the sinful king remained under the influence of anger and said, "Now we will really see if you like patience." With his sword he cut off the sage's right hand at the wrist. [225] He did the same to his left hand, his two shoulders, ears, nose, and also his two legs. He chopped until the sage's body collapsed to the ground. The great man's mind never became disturbed and he felt great compassion for the king. He made prayers of compassion for him:

> Even if my body is chopped
> into sesame-seed-size bits,
> hacked to dust, and cast on the ground,
> I will not forsake patience.

Then, owing to the power of the king's horrible actions, his body instantly blazed with a fever like fire. Before he could leave the forest, the earth cracked open and he fell down into the Avīci Hell.

The ministers were frightened of being cursed by the sage. With pathetic prostrations they begged his pardon. The great man reassured them, and by proclaiming the vast waves of the bodhisattva deeds and by teaching them the Dharma of the great vehicle, they developed faith and aspiration. Then he died, passing to another realm.

This story appears in a slightly different version in the sutras; here, however, I have presented it in accordance with how it is found in *Garland of Birth Stories* and its commentarial texts.

* * *

A wise person's helpful attitude creates harmony between others:

> 47 A wise person's helpful attitude
> restores harmony when others quarrel.
> Because Prince *Śraddhā caused two nāga kings
> to become friends, look at the auspicious signs!

This verse means that a wise person is good-natured. Thus his positive attitude of helpfulness is the means to establish harmony between others who are quarreling and arguing. For example, when *Sthiraśraddhā, the son of the king of Bhagala, was on the road to the land of the rākṣasas, he came across the nāga kings Śankhapāla and *Bahuhasta, who were fighting. The prince's helpful attitude caused them to break apart and become friends. Look at the auspicious signs that arose from that. This tale will be explained below.[261] [226]

Fools ignore the quarrels of others:

48 A foolish person's warped mind
takes pleasure in others' quarrels.
Look how the mouse came to ruin
by ignoring the elephant and the mongoose.

This verse shows that fools are crooked and hard-hearted. Their warped dishonesty makes them enjoy it when others quarrel and argue. For example, consider that because a mouse remained neutral while watching an elephant and mongoose fight and hurt each other, the fighters became his ruination.[262]

* * *

Showing how the wise are happy to give away their wealth:

49 The wise give away their accumulated wealth,
so it increases like water welling up in a spring.
Look how the youth *Kṣipratuṅga—"quickly exalted"—
created merit by making an offering to the Buddha.

This verse means that the wise give whatever wealth they have accumulated to both supreme and lower objects of offering. The power of that causes their wealth and possessions to increase the same way that water wells up in a spring. For example, a young man who got the nickname Trela Tho, which means "quickly exalted," used his saved wages to make offerings to the Buddha and the sangha. Look how the merit of that action caused him to be put in charge of the merchants right away.[263]

Long ago a married couple in Rājagṛha had a son. The householder went to sea in search of wealth and died. His wife raised the boy with the help of relatives. By studying literature he became a master of traditional tales. He and a friend went to the main temple in Bamboo Grove. In the vestibule they saw a drawing of the wheel of life with five sections. They asked a monk about it; he explained each part. The young man wanted to be reborn as a god and so asked, "Venerable, is there a way to be born as a god?"

The monk replied, "There is. As a renunciate, you must practice sexual abstinence for as long as you live." [227]

The youth said, "I can't do that. Is there another way?" The monk responded, "Offer a meal to the Buddha and the sangha. For that you will need 500 silver coins."

To get the silver coins, the young man worked as a laborer building the house of a leading merchant. When the other workers slacked off, the youth told stories and worked quickly. The others liked hearing the tales, so they worked in order to keep up with him. Because of that the work was quickly completed.

The homeowner recognized what happened. He was pleased with the young man and gave him double wages. However, because he did not receive 500 silver coins, the youth cried.

"Boy, why are you crying?" the homeowner said.

The youth said, "In order to be reborn as a god, I need 500 silver coins to offer a meal to the Buddha and the sangha. I do not have it."

Because the householder was a religious man, he added the rest of the needed silver coins. Happily, the young man invited the Buddha and the sangha to the leading merchant's house. He distributed the delicious food with his own hands and asked them to accept the midday meal. The Teacher taught the young man the Dharma and departed.

Then the youth generously gave the remaining food and drink to five hundred traders who had returned from the great ocean. He did not charge them anything. The traders were pleased with the youth and said, "Whose son are you?"

"I am the son of so and so."

In reply the leading merchant said, "Well! You are the son of my childhood friend," and he gave him a precious gem. Then he said to the other traders, "Come here and give him something." The treasure piled up. They said to the youth, "Because you are happy to be generous, please take these things."

The youth wondered, "If I take this will I be reborn as a god or not?" So he went to ask the Teacher.

"Accept it. It is but a flower. There will be other fruit."

So he accepted the jewels. Then the leading merchant of Rājagṛha died without an heir. The merchants got together and said, "We must appoint as our chief merchant someone with great merit." To make the decision, they put a variety of colored seeds into a pot. Whoever took out seeds of just one color would be appointed. The others picked out seeds of various colors. When the youth picked up seeds of just a single color, [228] they said, "He is just a laborer, how can he be appointed as our chief merchant?" They did the drawing of seeds three times. Each time the youth drew out seeds of only a single color, so he was appointed chief merchant.

They adorned the daughter of the former chief merchant with every kind of ornament and presented her to him as a wife. Through that union the youth's household wealth increased and his possessions quickly piled up. Therefore they gave him the nickname Quickly Exalted.

Quickly Exalted and his wife remembered the kindness of the Teacher. After offering him a midday meal, they listened to the Dharma and thereby saw the truth.

Fools enjoy hoarding:

50 Being stingy, fools do not use their possessions,
so they waste away like the waning moon.
Look how the honey hoarded by bees
is enjoyed and consumed by others.

This verse means that fools do not see the disadvantages of sensory pleasure. Under the power of stinginess they do not utilize their possessions. Therefore their wealth does not increase, and in addition it dwindles like the waning moon. For example, it is pointless for bees to hoard their honey, using so little of it themselves. Look how others enjoy eating it!

* * *

The wise shun disputes:

51 The wise shun disputes at first,
but in battle they show their power to the foe.
Look how the king named Arjuna
overwhelmed the opposition's forces.

This verse demonstrates that a noble, wise person first avoids engaging in disputes and arguments with others. But later, out of necessity, they will reveal their power and completely bring down an enemy who attacks them. For example, look how the famous son of Pāṇḍu, King Arjuna, [229] who was known as the best archer in the world, conquered all the hosts of his enemy rivals, the Kaurava.[264]

Long ago when a human lifespan was eighty thousand years, the sage king Vyāsa had two sons: Pāṇḍu and Dhṛtarāṣṭra. King Pāṇḍu had two queens: Mādrī and Kuntī. Kuntī received a mantra from the sage Durvāsa enabling her to have a child. From the union of Kuntī and the sun god, a boy adorned with an earring was born, so he was known as Karṇa—"having an earring." The child was put in a box and the Ganges River carried it off. The rākṣasa Adhiratha picked him up and raised him as a son.[265]

By joining with the god called Dharma, Kuntī had a son named Yudiṣṭhira; by joining with the wind god she had a son named Bhīma; and by joining with Indra she had a son named Arjuna, who became known as the best archer in the world. By joining with the divine twin doctors, the Āśvina, Mādrī gave birth to the twins Nakula and Sahadeva. Thus Kuntī had three sons and Mādrī had two sons. They were known in the world as the five sons of Pāṇḍu, the Pāṇḍavas.

Dhṛtarāṣṭra's holy queen Gāndhārī gave birth to a ball of flesh. By cutting it into a hundred pieces, a hundred sons were born, the Kauravas—Duryodhana and so forth. Then when Pāṇḍu died because of a sage's curse, his body was cremated. Queen Mādrī jumped into the funeral pyre and died too. Thereafter the five sons of Pāṇḍu lived under the protection of the Kaurava kingdom.

Jealous of the five brothers, the Kauravas had evil thoughts and plotted to kill them. The five brothers realized this and fled. They went to the land of rākṣasas and killed the rākṣasa men. Bhīma married a rākṣasa woman, and they had a son named Ghaṭotkaca.

Then the five brothers jointly married Draupadī of Pañcālā. Once again the Kaurava king became jealous. Karṇa, the first son of Kuntī who later had been taken in by the Kauravas, the one hundred Kaurava brothers, and the twelve divisions of a worldly army drew up for war. [230] At that point Viṣṇu took the side of the Pāṇḍavas.

When they reached the shore of the ocean they prepared for battle. When Arjuna saw all his relations, he was distraught about going into battle. So he turned back. At that point Viṣṇu exhorted him to have fortitude and go into battle. Then Arjuna and his five brothers, and with Viṣṇu on their side, fought. Arjuna killed most of the Kaurava forces and defeated them. Yudiṣṭhira ruled the world with his brothers. This story is famous.

Fools incite quarrels:

52 Fools are the first to incite disputes,
but in a fight they give victory to their foes.
It is well known that by wearing a mirror,
the king ceded victory to his minister.

This verse shows that fools are the first to incite disputes. But after entering into arguments and quarrels they give victory to their opponents. For example, it is well known that the Tibetan king Drigum Tsenpo emphatically pressured his minister Longam. Giving him no choice, the king said, "You must challenge me." Because they fought after the king attached a mirror to his forehead, carried a fox corpse over his shoulder, and so forth, the king ceded victory to his minister. Longam killed the king and made the kingdom his own.[266]

To expand on this summary, the son of Siptri Tsenpo, who was the last of first seven Tibetan kings, was King Drigum Tsenpo (literally, "the emperor who died at a sword's end"). He was persuaded by a demonic spirit to say to his minister Longam, "You must challenge me in battle."

Longam said, "I am a servant. How can it be right for me to contest my ruler?" Although he said this, he was powerless to go against the king's command. The king and his minister agreed to fight.

The king had a magical female dog. He sent it to listen at Longam's feet. Longam recognized the dog and said, "Tomorrow the king will come to kill me. If that is to happen, he will come unaccompanied by his army, he will wear a black silk turban on his head, [231] have a mirror tied to his forehead, bear a fox corpse on his right shoulder and a rat corpse on his left, brandish a sword over his head, and bring an ox loaded with a sack of ashes. Then it will be impossible for me to live."

The dog heard this, went back to the king, and told him. The next day, the king did exactly that and went to kill Longam. At that point Longam whistled, making the ox shy. That tore open the sack of ashes. The dust filled the king's eyes. The fox corpse made the king's warrior spirit disappear. The rat corpse made the king's personal protective deity disappear. When the king circled his sword overhead, he cut the rope to heaven that made the emperor unslayable. Then the minister Longam aimed at the mirror on the king's forehead, shot an arrow, and killed the king. Then the king's three sons fled to the regions of Kongpo and so on. Longam soon seized the kingdom.

Here is another example of how fools incite pointless quarrels and are their own ruination. Long ago in a mountainous area there was a large lotus pond.[267] An elephant lived nearby and a fox lived in another nearby spot. One time the elephant went to the pond to drink water; the fox came too and they met. The fox said to him, "Fight me or step aside!"

The elephant thought, "This foul-mouthed creature is rotten. If I kill him with my tusks, trunk, or feet, I'll become unclean. That would not be good." So he stepped off the path and hastened away.

The fox thought, "With just a few words I conquered him; he ran away quick as can be." The fox pursued the elephant.

The elephant knew when the fox came near. The elephant said, "Because the rotten are killed with decay, I will kill you with foulness." Then with great force he defecated on top of the fox's head. The blow killed him.

* * *

The way to create benefits and avoid harm:

53 At the outset, the wise impose an agreement
on enemies who are able to harm them.
It is well known that when going to sea,
a captain kills the sea monster at the outset. [232]

This verse means that a wise person knows the difference between things that are beneficial and those that are harmful. So after subduing an enemy who could harm him in the future, the wise person forces them into agreement or reduces their status. For example, it is commonly said that before a sea captain casts off and departs on the ocean to get jewels, he prepares a means to kill the great sea monsters that could impede his voyage.

To expand, when one goes to get jewels in the ocean, there are sea monsters with bodies like fish many leagues long. They are very terrifying: they can destroy boats, devour them, and so forth. So the captain takes pigeons and live conchs along in his boat. If on their voyage they see what seems to be a mountain, the captain lets loose a pigeon to investigate. If it is a mountain the pigeon will land on it. If it is a sea monster the bird will return because it found no place to land. If the sea monster is too close to avoid, should it be necessary when looking for an escape route, the captain throws the conch overboard. It will burrow deep into the sea monster's body and kill it.[268]

54 Even though something will definitely harm them,
fools are carefree because they desire trifles.
Look at the problems that arose for Bimbisāra
because he made Vaidehī his queen.

This verse shows that fools are ignorant about how to differentiate between things that are beneficial and those that are harmful. Even though they know that something will definitely harm them in the future, they are carefree. They do what pleases them because of their desire for merely temporary and trifling possessions and pleasure. For example, King Bimbisāra lusted for the girl Celā, who was also known as Vaidehī. Look at the problems that arose after he made her his queen.[269]

As the story goes, long ago the king of Videha had a minister named Khaṇḍa who absconded and settled in the land of Vaiśālī. He had two sons: Bhūpāla and Siṅgha. Siṅgha's wife gave birth to a daughter, whom they named Celā. A seer prophesized, "This girl will bear a son who will kill his father and make himself king." Later another daughter was born and they named her Upacelā. It was prophesized that she would give birth to a son with perfect qualities. [233]

At a later time the people of Vaiśālī made Siṅgha their commander. His elder brother, Bhūpāla, became angry and left the kingdom. Bimbisāra installed him as his minister. At a later date when Bimbisāra's primary queen died, Bhūpāla said, "My younger brother Siṅgha has two daughters worthy of my lord. Which would you like to marry?"

The king replied, "Upacelā."

Then Bhūpāla went to take Upacelā. The Vaiśālīs had a law stipulating that a Vaiśālī girl could be given in marriage only to a Vaiśālī man. And if forces opposing them arose against them, they would ring a large bell attached to the neck of a sentry statue in the form of a demon.

Then Celā saw that Upacelā was dressed up to be sent as a bride. "How can you be adorned to go to be married? As I am the elder sister, why shouldn't I go before you?"

The younger sister said, "Well then, you put on the ornaments."

Because the large bell pealed, those who had come with Bhūpāla were startled and panicked. Thinking the girl with the ornaments was Upacelā, they quickly put her in a carriage and fled.

After leaving the palace, they said, "Upacelā, you must come with us."

She said, "Uncle, I am Celā."

Bhūpāla went before the king and said, "Lord, I have brought Celā, mistaking her for Upacelā. It is unfortunate."

The king said, "I will take a look at her." As soon as he saw her he desired her, so he thought, "A son who commits patricide does so in order to get the kingdom. If I give my son the kingdom, what need would there be for murder?" So he took her as his chief queen and she became known as Vaidehī.

Later the king shot an arrow that struck a sage with five supernormal powers who dwelt in a place where animals sought refuge. The sage was angry and accused him of murder. He prayed, "Because you have surely killed me, someone who is without fault, may I be conceived in the womb of your primary queen and later kill the king!" A rain of blood fell the day he was conceived. The queen had cravings, thinking, "How nice it would be to eat the king's flesh. How nice it would be to drink his blood." After nine months passed, a handsome infant was born. On that day too a rain of blood fell. Because he was like an enemy to his father even before emerging from the womb, he was given the name Ajātaśatru—"enemy before birth." [234] When he grew up he killed his father, Bimbisāra, and made himself king.

* * *

Explaining the difference between those imbued with faults and those imbued with good qualities.

55 Whenever a wise person is praised
he shares the credit with others.
Look how Gö obtained acclaim
for the king's establishment of the doctrine.

This verse means that a wise person considers himself and others to be equal. However much he is acclaimed, he shares the credit with other people, knowing he did not accomplish anything alone. For example, look how the religious minister Gö Trisang and others gained approbation for King Tri Song Detsen's promotion of the good principles of the precious teachings of the Conqueror.[270]

To expand, during the reigns of the first twenty-seven Tibetan kings—

beginning with the first Tibetan king, Nyatri Tsenpo, through the seven heavenly kings, the six excellent earthly kings, the eight kings with Lha ("deity") in their name, as well as King Tori Longten, Tri Tsenam, Tri Dra Pungtsen, up to Tri Tok Jeten—the state was ruled through stories, symbolic language, and Bön rituals. After them, the holy Dharma first came to Tibet during the reign of Lha Thothori Nyentsen. Then during the reign of his fifth descendant, the Dharma king Songtsen Gampo, the holy Dharma spread. Then after five generations, Tri Song Detsen was born.

Soon after his birth his father, the king, died. Because the new king was very young, the evil minister Mashang Drompa Kyé and others destroyed the religious laws and drove out the monks. They buried the statue Jowo Śākyamuni underground. They made the central cathedral a slaughterhouse.

When the prince grew up and had just reached the age of thirteen, Mashang and the others blocked his wish to practice the Dharma. The minister Ba Salnang had gone to India. He met the scholar bodhisattva Śāntarakṣita in Nepal and invited him to Tibet. [235] Śāntarakṣita accepted the invitation. Then Salnang returned to Tibet and told the prince all about the scholar bodhisattva.[271]

Out of fear that Mashang would kill him, the prince made Salnang hide for a while. The prince secretly conferred with other ministers who liked the Dharma. Nyamsang said, "Mashang is very powerful and he dislikes the Dharma, so what can we do?"

Gö Trisang said, "Here's what we do. We will trick him." They gave bribes to many fortunetellers and had them proclaim, "Because he is very devoted to the king and the nation, as a ritual for their protection, a great minister should stay in a rock crypt for three months." Employing many strategies, Gö made Mashang Drompa Kyé hear the prophecy in Tölung and go into a cave crypt. Immediately they threw boulders into mouth of the tomb and blocked it.

Then they sent Salnang to invite the great scholar bodhisattva to Tibet. Subsequently the master Padmasambhava was invited. He bound all the gods and demons to a vow. The main temple of Samyé was erected along with all its contents. Throughout central Tibet and Kham, the light of both the teachings and practices of the precious Conqueror shone like the sun.

Thus although the establishment of the Teacher's practices depended on the king, those who carried out his orders, the ministers Gö and so forth, also accrued merit and great acclaim. This story should also be used to understand the following lines (from verse 94) that will appear later:

Look how Mashang Drompa Kyé
was put into a deep pit.

56 Fools insistently attribute
their own shortcomings to others.
Look how the deceitful one left
a bloody sword in front of Gautama.

This verse means that fools are prejudiced against others. They insist that others are guilty and, through various deceits, shift the blame and so forth for their own faults onto other people. For example, look at the trouble that occurred when the deceitful man Mṛṇāla left the blood-stained sword that he had used to kill the courtesan Tārā in front of the hut of the sage Gautama.[272] [236]

Long ago Karṇa, the son of King Kṛkī, was the last of the hundred kings in the lineage of Sujātā to hold the country. He had two sons: Gautama and Bhāradvaja. The latter ruled the kingdom. Gautama took monastic vows from the sage Asita, "the dark-skined one," and lived in a leaf hut that he built near a village.

At that time a deceitful man called Mṛṇāla gave lovely garments to the courtesan Tārā in order to enjoy her favors. He could not bear it when she wore those clothes to give pleasure to other men. He went to the forest and killed Tārā. Then her servants let forth a clamor: "Our lady has been murdered!" Mṛṇāla dropped his bloody sword in front of the sage Gautama's hut and ran off.

When the people saw it they said, "You, a monk who wears the clothes of a sage, did you commit a murder?" Without listening to him they tied his hands behind his back and presented him to the king, saying, "This man enjoyed the favors of Tārā and killed her."

Without any investigation of the facts, the king had him impaled on a pointed stake. Then the sage Asita came and asked, "Son, what has befallen you? Are you hurt?"

He replied, "My body is damaged but my mind is not. Because these words are true, may my abbot's black skin turn to gold!" As soon as he spoke, the sage became a golden color. And everyone believed him.

Then the sage said, "Because it was said that if this brahman has no son there will be no transmigrator who attains enlightenment in the future, I will create a means for your sons to be born." Then through his magic the rain fell and soft breezes touched Gautama's body, so he was oppressed with pain. Because it made him remember sexual desire, his own semen and blood mixed, fell, and became two eggs. The sunlight caused the eggs to develop. They hatched and two infants came out. They lived in a sugarcane field near there.

When the sage saw the two infants he gave them various names: Arkabandhu—relatives of the sun because they matured after being nursed and nourished by sunlight; Gautama because they were Gautama's sons; and Ikṣvāku—sugarcane—because they were found in a field of sugarcane.

King Bhāradvaja died without an heir. The ministers conferred and appointed the Ikṣvāku youths as kings. Ikṣvāku Virūḍaka was the last of the hundred kings of that dynasty. [237] The Śākya dynasty came from his four sons.

* * *

How advantages arise from skillful means and how problems arise from unskillful means:

57 Through the power of their skillful means
the wise bind even the mighty to servitude.
Even though the garuḍa was extremely strong,
look how the golden-clad one rode on him.

This verse says that because the wise have sharp intelligence, they can through the power of their skillful means make even extremely powerful beings act as their servants. For example, the garuḍa, the foremost of birds, is extremely powerful. Yet look how Viṣṇu, the golden-clad one, travels by riding on him.[273]

Long ago Viṣṇu and the garuḍa were adversaries. Viṣṇu wasn't able to overcome the garuḍa's power when they fought. He thought, "After I appease him with a strategy, I will trick him." Assuming a nonantagonistic visage, Viṣṇu sat down as if he were calm and at peace. He said, "Hey! I am pleased with how you subdue adversaries. Ask me for a boon and I'll give it to you."

The garuḍa was arrogant and said, "Hey! How can the great ask for something from the small? You should ask for a boon from me and I'll give it to you!"

Viṣṇu said the same thing again. After the third time Viṣṇu said, "If that is how it is to be, because you are very swift and extremely powerful, you shall be my mount. In this way you will be the best at suppressing adversaries."

The arrogant garuḍa was confused and tricked by Viṣṇu's cunning method. And to this day, because the garuḍa carries Viṣṇu, he is known as Viṣṇu's mount.

58 Because they are not skilled in strategy
fools become the servants even of the weak.
Look at the behavior of the haughty lion
who was made to carry a load by a fox. [238]

This verse means that because fools are dull-witted they are not skilled in strategy. Not only the very strong but even the weak can make fools their servants. For example, a fox who had very little strength used cunning strategy to shift to the nape of a lion a great load that he could not lift. Look at the behavior of the lion: he carried the load with pride, self-satisfaction, and shameless conceit.[274]

Long ago a fox habitually trailed after a lion and ate the leftover meat of the lion's kill. One time the lion killed an elephant and said to the fox, "Carry this! If you don't carry it, hereafter do not expect to eat my meat."

The fox thought, "I can't lift the elephant's corpse, but it is necessary for me to eat meat." He mulled this over and said, "O lord! I would carry this, but I cannot do two things at once. Please, lord, will you do one task?"

The lion said, "What are the two tasks?"

The fox said, "It is customary that when someone travels bearing a great load, someone else must trail at his heels, grunting. One of us must be the bearer of the elephant and one of us must be the grunter."

The lion thought about that and said, "I am the king of the beasts. How could I follow a vulgar creature like this while grunting!" So the lion carried the elephant, and following behind him the fox made grunting sounds to sing a happy and humorous song.

* * *

Showing the benefits of having fine intelligence and the faults of lacking it:

59 The wise use the power of their astute intelligence
to skillfully clear away nasty rumors about themselves.

Look how a sage used skillful means
to purify the mind of the king.

This verse says that a person who is skilled in the means to safeguard himself and others uses the power of his subtle and clear intelligence to adroitly clear away nasty rumors of infamy about himself. Look how a sage called the wanderer Mahābodhi used skillful means to dispel offensive reports about him that were spread by the king and his ministers. [239] And look how he purified the wrong views that contaminated the minds of the king and his ministers.[275]

Long ago the bodhisattva was a man known as the wanderer Bodhi. He was skilled in the various arts and sciences. Grieved by the disadvantages of the householder's life, he became a renunciate. Because of his mastery of the highest religious subjects and his efforts to help those in the world, the king, his ministers, and his subjects respectfully honored him. For the sake of his disciples that great man left his forest wandering and went near the realm of a king. The king was very pleased to hear about the vast power of his good qualities, so he had the renunciate dwell in a delightful spot in his pleasure gardens. With proper worship and respect the king made offerings and served him. Every day the great man benefited the king and his court by giving them pleasant, easy-to-listen-to discourses on the Dharma.

One day an evil demon and the many ministers on whom the demon had conferred blessings felt unbearable jealousy. They said, "Lord! It is not right to have great faith in the wanderer Bodhi. There is no doubt that he was sent by some neighboring king to ruin you through milord's inclination for the Dharma and delight in good qualities. We do not trust him because he associates with envoys from neighboring kings who go back and forth." Again and again they slandered the sage, thus causing dissension. Even the king became distrustful, and his love and devotion lessened.

The great man recognized this and picked up his belongings—a trident and a water pot—in preparation to leave. The king feigned a show of respect and asked, "Why are you so suddenly leaving me? Please forgive me if I did something wrong."

When the sage said, "The time has come for me to go," the king was ashamed, hung his head low, and prostrated to the great man.

"If you definitely must go, please return here at a later date and watch over me with your compassion." The sage accepted his request and went to his hermitage. [240]

There, through striving in single-pointed concentration, Bodhi came to possess the five supramundane powers. When he could see with clairvoyance he observed that the king was influenced by his ministers' wrong views, such as permanence, nihilism, and so forth. Because of his compassion and love he wished to negate these wrong views and clear away the former spiteful rumors. In order to do that he magically conjured up the pelt of a great ape. Putting it on he went to the king's palace.

There, in the presence of the ministers and court, the king asked him, "Who gave you this great ape's pelt?"

The sage said, "I did it. I saw the great ape, killed it, and flayed it." The king was embarrassed and sat there with his head down.

The minsters with the wrong views took this opportunity to find fault. They sarcastically criticized and abused him, "Oh my! A religious practitioner able to do that is amazing! May your practice of asceticism be successful."

Then one after another the great man refuted the ministers' evil views with stainless logic. He refuted the one who asserted that things have no cause, the one who asserted theism, the one who asserted determinism, the one who asserted that causes and effects do not exist, and the one who asserted that sacrificing living creatures is a religious action.

"If everything has no cause, then killing the ape is also without cause, so what sin is there in that? If god does everything, then the monkey was killed by god, so why disparage me? If everything is predetermined and not dependent on any incidental conditions, the ape's death was predetermined and it is not right to say that I killed him. Also, if there are no causes and effects, what is the crime in killing an ape? If it is right to say that sacrificing a living creature is a religious act, then killing the ape is religious and your scriptural tradition is not able to ascribe the slightest fault to killing an ape."

He said this and more. He logically refuted these evil views and made it impossible for the ministers to make an intelligible response. And then he made the magically created ape pelt disappear.

The king and his court became faithful and developed religious aspiration. The great man extensively taught them the Dharma: the necessity of abandoning wrong views and evil friends, of relying on those with good qualities, of governing the realm with religious principles, and so forth. Then he returned to his hermitage. [241] The following two lines from verse 87 should be understood to refer to this story as well:

Look how the wandering sage
made the king become free from sin.

60 Because fools do not have sharp minds,
they admire their own disrepute.
In a petty kingdom of Cūta, they beat drums
for those who become king through patricide.

This verse means that fools are free from embarrassment and have no shame. Because they lack the sharp intelligence that finely distinguishes what should be done from what should be avoided, they mistake their disrepute to be good qualities, show off to others, and are self-satisfied. As an example, in the petty kingdom in the region of Cūta, where people have only one leg, a boy killed his father to gain the kingdom, after which drums were beaten to proclaim that he had made himself king.[276] It is said that the people of Cūta region have only one leg and that once a prince of that region murdered his father and made himself into king. And to proclaim this to others he had the drums beaten, so it is said.

To flesh out this incident: There was a king named *Naravati in the southern region of Kāñcī. Their law was that when a prince reached the age of twenty, he was no longer allowed to go into the presence of his father, the king. He would be put into an iron cage and made to study treatises on the country's customs. When the king died the eldest son inherited the kingdom.

At that time the king had a son who had reached the age of eight. The boy gave his fine clothes to his mother and asked her to care for them. "I will wear these when I become king," he said.

His mother said, "You are a younger son, so you will not inherit the kingdom." The boy cried and asked her if there was anything that could be done.

She said, "You can obtain the kingdom if the royal drums beat after you kill your father."

There is nothing that is not done when in the throes of desire. His mother gave the little boy a sharp dagger. Hiding it, he went near the king, who was sitting on the throne. With smiles and little games he charmed the king. He climbed into his father's lap. Then he stabbed his father in the stomach with the dagger and killed him.

Then he said, "From today on, I am the king." The drums were beaten and the new king was proclaimed. When the populace saw that this little boy was able to commit such an act, they had no doubt that he was very courageous. [242] It is reported that they even said, "Make him king."

* * *

Showing the difference between doing and not doing an inappropriate action:

61 Avoiding extremely dangerous situations
is a sign of a wise person's courage.
It is known that when killing a prime bull
a lion will avoid its horns.

This verse means that a wise person has intelligence and is not confused about whether to engage in a task or avoid it. It is a sign of their skill and courage that they avoid and step away from inappropriate actions in extremely dangerous situations. It is unwise to have qualms about refraining from doing something as a brave and strong person. For example, there is a well-known saying that when a lion kills a purebred bull its technique is to avoid the bull's horns. If the lion were overly confident of its strength and skill, how could it avoid the horns?

62 Thoughtlessly fighting with an enemy
is a sign of a foolish man's stupidity.
Look at the nature of moths
that battle with the light of a flame.

This verse reveals that fools are not sensible about which actions to take and which to avoid. It is a sign of their ignorance and stupidity that without investigation they engage in inappropriate actions, such as fighting and battling, against those who seem to be enemies and who can do them harm. For example, look at the nature of a moth that fights and struggles against the light of an oil lamp. Is it heroic? And so you see. Moreover, engaging in actions that should not be done or that cannot be accomplished is foolish, and it becomes the cause for your own ruin.

Long ago a fox from the charnel ground went to a village in search of food.[277] There two rams had been fighting each other for a long time. The fox went to lick the blood dripping from their horns. The fox stuck his head between the two rams, who were bashing their heads together with great force, and his head was broken into many pieces like an *arjaka* seed pod. [243] So it is widely known.

* * *

Explaining the difference between the ease of knowing the worth of the wise and the difficulty of knowing the worth of fools:

63 Because the wise do what is admirable
it is easy for anyone to grasp their worth.
Look how the desperate people knew
that the elephant had sacrificed his body.

This verse shows that because the wise do not act contrary to the manners of the holy ones, all their actions are appropriate. Therefore it is easy for anyone, no matter who they are, to grasp and understand their worth. For example, the bodhisattva in his life as a king of elephants sacrificed his body in order to save some suffering, destitute exiles from a remote, fearsome desert. Look how those destitute people completed what he intended after they realized that he had given up his life.[278]

Long ago the bodhisattva was a solitary roaming elephant in an attractive, remote mountain and forest region adorned with medicinal plants and ponds. One day he wandered near the edge of the forest. There he heard the voices of people in distress. Wondering what was the problem, he quickly came out of the forest and saw many people stricken with hunger, thirst, and exhaustion coming toward the forest.

Seeing the elephant, the people were very afraid, thinking, "Now as we have no strength to flee, he will kill us."

Realizing this, the bodhisattva felt great pity. He said in a human voice, "You have nothing to fear from me. Do not be afraid."

The people were relieved. They joyfully bowed to him, and said, "We ran afoul of the law and were exiled by the king. Of the thousand of us, some have died from hunger and thirst, so now seven hundred remain." Their eyes filled with tears. They joined their palms together and said in pitiful voices, "O king of elephants, please show us the way out of this place that is a remote wasteland of misery!" [244]

The bodhisattva elephant felt unbearable compassion and thought, "There is nothing in the forest that can help these people who are weakened and emaciated by hunger and thirst. How can they cross this remote wasteland many leagues across? There is no way for them to escape other than for them to use my flesh as provisions for their journey and to use my entrails as water bags." He lifted his trunk to point and told them, "At the foot of those mountains there is a large lake. Not far from there, there is the corpse of an elephant who fell from a mountain cliff. You can use its flesh as provisions for your journey and its intestines to collect water. Then continue in this direction and you will get out of this remote wasteland."

The elephant went there via another path. After ascending to the mountain peak, he made a prayer and threw himself off the cliff. At that point the earth shook. The gods and beings on the side of goodness made prostrations and oceans of offerings.

The people followed the path shown to them by the elephant. After seeing the lake and the elephant's corpse, they thought it through and understood that the great being had given his body out of unbearable compassion for them. Feelings of misery and faithful respect made their eyes fill with tears. Some said, "How could we dare to eat the flesh of a great being like this? It is appropriate to honor and respect it." Other men with great intelligence said, "If we do not do what this great being intended, his sacrifice of his body and life would be in vain. Fulfilling his intentions will be a deed of honor and respect." So they gathered up the meat and used his intestines as bags to collect water. Then by going the way he had indicated they escaped from that remote wasteland.

64 Because foolish people act wantonly
it is difficult for anyone to grasp their worth.
Look how in some barbarian countries
men take their own mothers as their brides.

This verse means that fools act contrary to civilized behavior. They act wantonly and do all kinds of inappropriate things. Therefore everyone finds it difficult to see their worth. For example, in some barbarian countries that have customs mistaking virtue and sin, sons take their own mothers as brides voluntarily and without coercion. [245]

As for the term "barbarian," it refers to Turks. On the far side of the ocean to the west of India there are many barbarian countries: Balkh, Makha, Multan, and so forth. They do not adhere to either Hinduism or Buddhism; they go for refuge to the asura lords and follow teachers like Madhumati, Artola, and so forth.[279] They will not eat meat that has been butchered by anyone who is not of their tradition. They wear white clothes. Also, northwest of India there are barbarians called Tartars, Afghans, and Persians. It is said that these people take their own mothers as their brides.[280]

* * *

How happiness comes from following good customs of the past and unhappiness comes from not following them:

65 The wise nurture the good traditions of the past,
so they achieve irrevocable happiness.
Look how Emperor Yongle, like his ancestors,
honored the teachings of the Conqueror.

This verse says that because the wise follow the noble ones they preserve the way things were done well in the past. So they obtain enduring happiness and good fortune for all regions in the present day. For example, look at the auspicious signs that arose because the Chinese emperor Yongle of the Ming dynasty followed the traditions of his ancestors by worshiping, honoring, and attending to the precious teachings of the Conqueror.[281]

Moreover, in general the sixteen emperors of the Mongol dynasty, starting from Genghis Khan down to Timur, and in China from the start of the Ming dynasty through nine reigns down to Emperor Chenghua, honored and respected the Three Jewels. In particular, Emperor Yongle, who was the khan of the great tribe of the Mongols for thirty-five years and then was the third emperor of the Chinese Ming dynasty for twenty-two years, ruled the realm in accord with the Dharma. Because of his great esteem for the monastics of Tibet and India, the gifts he offered to them were difficult to imagine. So if you rejoice in the merits created by these kings, [246] you will obtain what is known as equivalence of merits through other's deeds. This is what the *Blue Annals* says.[282]

66 Fools abolish good customs from the past
and as a result they obtain intense suffering.
Look at the negative consequences for King Langdarma
because he suppressed the doctrine.

This verse says that because fools are rash and do not follow the noble ones, they suppress good customs of the past. They thereby destroy themselves and suffer intensely in the present and throughout the future. For example, after Langdarma Udumtsen became king, he abolished the teachings of the Conqueror. Look how even in that life he experienced the misfortune of losing his cherished life.

Muné Tsenpo was the eldest of the Tibetan king Tri Song Detsen's three sons. A year and seven months after his ascension to the throne, his mother murdered him by poisoning. Then when the youngest son, Mutik Tsenpo, was killed Lekzing Yön seized the kingdom. He had five sons: Tsangma, Lhajé, Lhundrup, Darma Udumtsen, and Tri Ralpachen. The youngest of these five, Tri Ralpachen, was installed on the throne. He established a new translation system for the religious texts that had been translated in the time of his ancestors. He rebuilt the old main cathedral and restored its contents and so forth. He assigned seven laymen for the support of each monk. He displayed his unexcelled reverence by spreading his braided hair on a cushion and placing his head at monks' feet.

The sinful ministers who liked the black side could not bear this. They drove out Prince Tsangma, who had become a monk, and they caused the religious minister Drenka Payön and the queen to slander each other. Because the queen committed suicide, the great minister Drenka was executed. They twisted the king's neck and murdered him.

Then Langdarma Udumtsen was entrusted with the kingdom. He and the ministers used the occurrence of frost, hail, famine, disease, and so forth as a pretext to break up the Dharma translations. Most of the scholars and translators escaped to other lands. [247] Those who did not go were killed. All the monks were made to drop their vows; they were made to cast off every sign of ordination and become hunters. Those who defied these edicts were killed. Most of the religious scriptures were buried in the mountains around Lhasa and some were flung into fires or rivers. The two Jowo statues were hidden in sand. The door to the main cathedral was sealed up, and over it the regime installed a picture of a monk drinking alcohol. The teachings were abolished.

At that point Lhalung Palgyi Dorjé was meditating and living in the most sacred place on the divine Yerpa Mountain. He heard about what was happening. He felt extraordinary compassion for the sinful king and decided to liberate him—that is, kill him. He applied charcoal dust to a white horse's coat, making it black. He donned clothes that were white on the inside and black on the outside. Carrying iron arrows, he rode to Lhasa. There, at the right moment, when the king was reading out edicts on the obelisk, Lhalung

Pal pretended to prostrate before the king. He pulled back his bowstring and shot an arrow into the king's chest, saying, "When the evil slaughter they are killed like this," and then fled.

He was not caught because he washed the horse in water until it became white and he turned his clothing inside out. Then Lhalung Palgyi Dorjé went in stages in the direction of Domé (Amdo) via Lhokham.[283]

* * *

Showing the advantages of there being many wise people and the disadvantages of there being even a few fools:

67 Even if wise men blanket the great earth
we feel pained that there are too few.
Look how merchants are never satisfied
even though the ocean is filled with jewels.

This verse says that even if wise people enhance every place in every direction and seem to cover the great earth, embodied creatures still feel the mental pain of there being too few of them. For example, even though the ocean islands are filled with precious jewels that are desired by sovereign kings and so forth, look how merchants are never content nor satisfied. [248]

68 There may be no more than a single fool,
but it is as disastrous as if there were many.
Because one frog had an infectious sore,
look how he brought ruin to his friends.

This verse means that there is no need to say that many unseemly fools bring ruin everywhere. Even if there is just one fool, he is a defect that causes bad luck to increase and multiply. He is an extremely great blemish that brings suffering to himself and others. For example, when one frog in a colony has an infection it will spread to all the frogs who live with him and all will decline and be destroyed. When a single frog in a colony has an infection, it is said that the infection spreads to all other frogs in the colony and they will come to rot.

* * *

The wise and fools have different degrees of error:

69 Even if a wise person is mistaken,
the degree of error is very slight.
If a builder who understands measurement errs,
it is well known that it will be just a smidgen.

This verse asserts that it is impossible for a wise person to err in any task if he acts while knowing what to do and what to avoid. If a mistake occurs, it will be very slight and will fall within the margin of error. For example, it is well known that if a builder who is well versed in the texts on measurements and understands their intent accidently mistakes a measurement in a plan, it will be by merely a smidgen.

70 When a foolish person makes a mistake
its magnitude is beyond measure.
Look how when a deer walks into a trap
there is the terrible consequence of losing its life.

This verse says that because fools lack the intelligence to differentiate right from wrong, when they err the magnitude of their mistake far exceeds quantification. For example, when deer and so forth make a mistake and end up in a trap or snare, there is the gravest consequence. [249] There is no misfortune greater than losing one's life.

* * *

The difference between being able or unable to subdue enemies:

71 The wise bring together their own realm
and have success over odious enemies.
Look how the cannibal ogres kept their vows
and then ate the flesh of their human opponents.

This verse means that those who are skilled in ruling their subjects create harmony between people in their realm. Owing to this accord they can elicit the power to suppress any enemy that is inimical to their own side. For example, it is said that on specific dates—the fifteenth of the month and so forth—the cannibal ogres of Laṅkapūrī properly maintained their vows to not kill and so forth. At other times they ate the flesh of their human opponents.[284]

Laṅkapūrī, the abode of the evil demons of southwest India, was encircled by a metal wall made of seven successive layers: copper, iron, bronze, brass, silver, gold, and lacquer. Beyond each side of the wall the demons possessed everything as far as a fast horse could travel in eighteen days. Within the wall the palace of the demon king and all the residences of his court were constructed of lacquer and shellac. Inside the palace the demon king with eleven heads, called Ten-Throated Laṇkā, sat atop a carpet of human skin on a jeweled throne.

Inside the vast and high fortress were 1,000 towers: 991 plus 9 in succession on the summit. To reach the summit there were 360 stairs. Inside the city there was a huge charnel ground called Śītavana where savage nonhumans lived. Many terrifying, horrifying, and weird illusions were on display there: human corpses emitted groans and sighs, corpses of horses neighed, dog corpses barked, skulls banged and ribs rattled, immaterial ghosts threateningly raised their arms and howled, and vultures, jackals, and so forth made varied unpleasant noises. [250]

The dreadful demon king and his court of vicious demons were all very ugly. There were male demons, female demons, and demon children having from one to ten heads. They wore no clothes and their two breasts were twisted back over their right and left shoulders. Their upper eye-teeth extended down to their chests, and their lower eye-teeth extended up to their foreheads. Just seeing a human made their teeth gleam and clack in the desire to eat.

Inside the metal wall were swirling lakes of human blood, canopies of human skin, and walls made of heads and flesh. Many humans were staked out with limbs extended. Some had already been killed, and some were just about to be killed, their veins dripping a stream of blood. It was terrifying and horrifying.

Our compassionate Teacher went to that city of Laṅka and expounded the *Sutra on Going to Laṅka* in order to tame the demon king and his court.[285] In the sutra he explained the disadvantages of eating meat. He bestowed on the demons the one-day vows and made them keep them on the days of the full moon, new moon, and the eighth and fifteenth of the month. Only on those particular days did they strictly keep the vow of not killing. At other times as soon as they saw humans they ate them. They prepared the food by mixing human flesh with rendered human fat in boiled human blood.

It is explained that these demons should be counted as a type of harmful spirit.

72 Fools are craven before their enemies
but cause various disputes among themselves.
Look how a cur wags its tail for people
but chases away other dogs.

This verse says that fools have little valor and a lot of impudence. They are cowardly and timid in front of opponents who could harm them, but in their own homes they create all kinds of purposeless disputes. For example, in front of a human a cur will display all sorts of pleasant behavior, wagging its tail and so forth. But look how it welcomes other dogs that come into its territory: it chases them off by viciously fighting, barking, and so forth. [251]

* * *

The disadvantages of quick retaliation and the advantages of not doing so:

73 The wise take a long view regarding their enemies,
so in the end they have control over their foes.
See how the ascetic's patience
gained him control over the king.

This stanza means that wise people know the advantages of assisting others and the detriments of harming them. Even if a foe causes them harm, they do not engage in instant retaliation. Instead, by taking a long-term perspective they eventually pacify their enemy's hatred with gentleness, gain their respect, and so forth. By those means they gain control over them. For example, because the bodhisattva ascetic habituated himself to love and patience, he eventually gained control over the king who abducted his wife, and the king came to have faith and respect.

The *Cānakya Treatise on Kingship* says:

> Gentleness subjugates the gentle;
> gentleness also subjugates the rough.
> There is nothing not accomplished by gentleness.
> Thus, the nature of gentleness is sharp and acute.[286]

Long ago the bodhisattva was a very learned brahman.[287] He was revered as a god by all ordinary beings. When he recognized the disadvantages of desire, he left his home and became a homeless renunciate. He tried to dissuade his wife, but owing to the force of her love she did not listen. Her eyes brimming with tears, she persisted in following him and becoming a renunciate. The two dedicated themselves to meditation, living in a pleasant and very isolated forest grove.

One afternoon during the spring the ascetic rose from his single-pointed concentration and began sewing rags into robes. The female ascetic, his wife, was practicing meditation under a tree nearby. That day the king of that region came to ramble in the attractive forest. Seeing the female ascetic, he felt lust and wanted to abduct her. He questioned the great man in order to determine whether he had any powers and capabilities.

"Hail ascetic. Is it proper for you to be here with your wife in this isolated, uninhabited place? [252] If your wife were to be abducted and harmed by someone, it would bring dishonor to me and to you too. If that were to disturb your mind, it would go against your practice. So what use is this woman? Thus it is right to send her to the city."

The great man said:

> If someone were to do this injury to me
> through arrogance, pride, or thoughtlessness,
> just as rain always forces down thick dust,
> I would not let it occur for as long as I live.

The king thought, "He doesn't have any powers from his ascetic practices because of his attachment to this woman." He had the female ascetic put on a horse. Lamenting and tearful from fear and dread, she was taken off to the palace.

Watching that, the great man extinguished the power of anger and without any mental agitation sat still and meditated on forbearance.

The king queried, "You said, 'If I were to be harmed, I would not let it occur for as long as I live.' You are not displaying any powerful skills as you vowed. Are you just a sedentary coward?"

"Just as I vowed, I have not given in to the influence of anger, the thing that harms."

> No matter what happened, it did not manifest.
> And when it does not arise, virtue manifests.
> Anger is what harms me;
> I did not fall under its sway.

Saying this and more, he explained in great detail the disadvantages of anger.

> Anger is the internal foe.
> I recognized it to be like that.
> Anger steals one's power and virtue.
> What living being can bear that?
>
> Thus for as long as I live,
> even if anger stirs I will not be swayed.
> Who would not forswear
> this enemy of embodied beings?

When the great man demonstrated that he was accustomed to the manner of forbearance that gives no thought whatsoever to that which causes harm, the king developed faith and respect.

> The succession of your explanation
> is concordant with pacification.
> There is no need to say much;
> but had I not met you, I would be lost.

After lauding the great man, the king prostrated to his feet, begged his pardon, and confessed. He also apologized to the female ascetic and had her returned. The king promised to do whatever service the great man required.

Furthermore, long ago Brahmadatta, the king of Vārāṇasī, coveted the kingdom of Videha.[288] [253] Although the king of Videha was more powerful, he lived in peace and compassion and did not covet others' lands. Brahmadatta prepared an army to seize Videha and set off to give battle. Hearing of this, the king of Videha had the roads cleared for three and a half leagues. He had excellent food and beverages prepared and welcomed Brahmadatta with great deference. Brahmadatta's anger dissipated and he became happy. He thought, "I will reverse course."

The king of Videha invited him in with copious honors and satiated him with wonderful victuals. Brahmadatta begged his pardon, saying:

> From the bent bow of your forbearance
> came a single arrow with the attribute

of conquering anger and pride.
With that you have completely defeated me.

The two kings developed love for each other.

74 Because fools retaliate against their enemies
they have difficulties continuously, without cease.
Look at the constant antagonistic behavior
between the two creatures—the crow and the owl.

This verse means that fools immediately retaliate against their enemies because they are blind to the benefits of helping others and the disadvantages of harming others. As a result, they ruin themselves and unceasingly experience misery that is difficult to endure. For example, look how the crow and the owl live miserably because they think resentfully about their prior disputes and fight continually.[289]

It is said that long ago all the birds convened and discussed who should be appointed their king. Some said, "It should be someone who can protect us during the night because each one of us can see during the day but cannot see at night. Therefore it makes sense to appoint the owl as our king because he is splendid, powerful, and knows the night."

A crow said, "In addition to taking on the duties of rule, a king must be a source of gratification for others. The owl is blind during the day and is unable to do anything for others. Also, he has yellow eyes in a catlike head and emits an unpleasant sound. If he is this ugly even when he isn't in an angry mood, [254] what can be said about him when he's angry? Who would appoint someone as unattractive as this to be king?"

The other birds said, "True," and dispersed.

Because the crow wrecked the owl's chance to become king by exposing his defects and denigrating him before the multitude, the owl felt it deeply. Because they offend each other unceasingly, they fight continuously.

* * *

Showing the benefit of quelling arrogance:

75 Through power that comes from quelling pride
the wise serve the holy and get good advice.

Look at the story of how Kumāra Sudhana
sought for a spiritual teacher.

This verse means that the wise see the defects of the mental afflictions. By the force of having quelled the pride of thinking "I am the best," they treat their holy spiritual guide as a crown jewel and thus can receive the nectar of good advice. For example, it is said we should look at the bodhisattva Kumāra Sudhana, who searched insatiably for spiritual masters. After serving one thousand teachers, he received good advice from their lips and became truly liberated.

In the south a merchant of Dhanyākāra named Dṛṭadhana had a son who was named Kumāra Sudhana—"prosperity."[290] He was given the name Sudhana because while he was in his mother's womb, magical fruit trees that were one of the seven royal treasures of a universal monarch sprouted around the house, all sorts of wealth filled five hundred precious vessels, and a rain of wealth and grain fell, filling every home and storehouse, as soon as he was born.

When the Bhagavān was staying in Jetavana, the noble Mañjuśrī and his many attendants went south to a large town called Dhanyākāra to work. They set many beings into the form of liberation most appropriate for them. Since Kumāra Sudhana was also there, [255] he made this request to Mañjuśrī: "Hail noble one. Please teach me how to practice the bodhisattva deeds."

Mañjuśrī said, "O noble child! Never weary in your search for a spiritual guide. South of here there is a bhikṣu named Meghaśrī. Go to him and ask about the bodhisattva deeds. He will teach you." Sudhana bowed down to Mañjuśrī's feet and left.

When he met the bhikṣu Meghaśrī, he prostrated at his feet and circumambulated him many times. Then coming in front of him, Sudhana asked how to practice the bodhisattva deeds.

Then as it was prophesized, in the same way one spiritual guide after another gradually sent him wandering further and further south. He encountered the noble Avalokiteśvara on the mountain of Potala and asked how to practice bodhisattva activities.

He went to the central land of Magadha, the cities of Kapila, and so forth one after another. Wandering south, he met the bodhisattva Maitreya on the shore of the ocean at Mahodyāna. Sudhana threw himself on the ground and prostrated to Maitreya with great faith and respect. Lord Maitreya greatly praised Kumāra Sudhana for his good qualities among his followers. Sudhana respectfully bowed and, with his hands in prayer, asked how to practice bodhisattva deeds.

"It is good, O child of the lineage. Your striving to attain complete buddhahood in order to benefit all worldly beings in this way is good. O child of the lineage, bodhicitta is like a seed for all the Dharmas of the Buddha." Saying this and more, Maitreya lauded bodhicitta and gave him extensive spiritual instruction.

Thus Sudhana served a thousand teachers from Mañjuśrī up to Maitreya and received spiritual advice on bodhisattva practices. Then he returned and went before the venerable Mañjuśrī. Mañjuśrī placed his hand on top of Sudhana's head, and through his blessing Sudhana obtained limitless memory, courage, concentration, direct perception, and so forth.

Then he had an audience with the bodhisattva Samantabhadra. As soon as Samantabhadra placed his hand on top of Sudhana's head, [256] he obtained countless entries into meditative concentration. For Sudhana and the vast assembly, Samantabhadra gave instructions concerning how to engage in the bodhisattva practice. Thus to Sudhana and the large circle of people gathered there, Samantabhadra taught the noble *King of Prayers: The Vows of Good Conduct*, which opens with the line "To as many of you as exist in the ten directions of the world," ending with the line "May I greatly benefit living beings."

An elaborate version of the story of the bodhisattva Sudhana is found in the *Marvelous Array Sūtra*, which is part of the *Flower Ornament Sūtra*.

The great disadvantages of arrogance:

76 Owing to the force of the great arrogance of fools,
they have no opportunity to serve the holy.
It is well known that someone pompous
put on insignia without a preceptor or teacher.

Fools are ignorant of the disadvantages of the mental afflictions. Through the force of their great arrogance—believing that they are the best—they do not have the good luck and opportunity to serve holy spiritual friends. For example, there is a well-known story that a pretentious pedant put on the robes and paraphernalia of a monk without having any preceptor or instructor whatsoever [ordaining him].[291]

Long ago a householder of Śrāvastī wanted to become a renunciate, so he went to Jetavana grove. There he saw some of the elder monks performing a ritual of the sangha: they were making expiation after confessing their remaining downfalls. The householder thought, "Their religion and livelihood are good, but following their rules lacks dignity."

So he asked a group of śrāvakas, "If I become a renunciate among you, will I have to perform these ritual acts?"

In reply they said, "Even someone vastly superior to you has to do these ritual acts when they become a monk, so what needs to be said about you!"

Because the householder was conceited about his competence, he thought, "I have a way to do it." Staying near the monks, he studied their behavior. Then he went to an outlying area, cut off his hair and whiskers, [257] put on saffron-colored robes, and remained there.

Some monks saw him and said, "The leader of the Dharma is living in Śrāvastī. Religion and even worldly possessions are to be had there, so why not go?" Because they urged him repeatedly, he went to Śrāvastī. There he saw nice carpets spread out and food offerings arranged.

He thought, "If I am seated first in line I will have to give a sermon about the benefits of the offering." So he gave up the first seat and sat in the second one.

The omniscient Kauṇḍinya came up and thought, "Who is this?" Recognizing that he was an imposter, Kauṇḍinya drove him off with the sound of snapping his fingers.

Likewise the elder monks Śāriputra, Maudgalyāyana, and so forth drove him off with the sound of snapping their fingers.

He went up to a group of śrāvakas. They asked him, "How long have you been a monk?"

He said, "If you calculate it roughly, sixty years."

They wondered, "Even the Bhagavān hasn't been a monk for sixty years, so how could he be?"

They asked, "Old man of the Dharma, who was your preceptor?"

He said, "Who was the preceptor of the renunciate Gautama?"

One of the group of śrāvakas said, "This man put the emblems of monkhood on himself." They seized his arms and legs and dragged him before the most senior elders.

"Reverend monks, please listen. In the world, when the sole self-produced monk is the Bhagavān, this old man claims to be the second. Please do something about this."

They threw him out.

* * *

The difference between the wise and fools in terms of the difficulty of causing conflict and the ease of reconciliation:

77 It is difficult to initiate disunity among the wise,
but if they are estranged reconciliation is easy.
It is difficult to cut a fruit tree,
but look how it knits together when grafted.

The meaning of this verse is that it is difficult at the outset to cause division between a wise person who has a positive attitude of helpfulness toward others and those with whom he has long been intimate. However, if they do split apart, it is easy and there is no difficulty in reconciling them once again. For example, look how a hard and solid tree is extremely difficult to cut at first. [258] However, when you graft it after it is cut, it easily knits together.

78 It is simple to initiate disunity among fools,
and after an estrangement reconciliation is difficult.
Look how when a lump of charcoal shatters,
there is no chance of pasting it back together.

This verse means that because fools think that others are as worthless as grass, it is easy to immediately turn them against even people they know well. After they have become estranged, it is difficult for them to reconcile once again. For example, although a piece of charcoal appears to be a single thing, it will shatter into little pieces. Observe that after it is broken, no matter what you do, there is no chance of fusing the pieces back together.

* * *

The difference between how the wise and fools benefit or harm in the long run:

79 A wise person may become very angry,
but in the end his actions are only helpful.
Deities and protectors may be wrathful,
but look how they protect you from all obstacles.

This verse means that wise people know the disadvantages of anger. Even if they become very angry owing to temporary conditions, in the long run whatever they do will only benefit others. For example, both meditational deities who grant supranormal powers and Dharma protectors who safeguard the teachings may display wrath out of necessity. However, look how they act to safeguard the teachings and living beings from all obstacles and hindrances.

80 A fool may smile broadly,
but his actions are only harmful in the end.
Look how the lord of death displays a smile
and then slays the living creatures.

This verse shows that a fool with a ferocious disposition may display a smile and seem to have a pleasant external demeanor. But in the long run, when the syrup drips away, his actions are nothing but harmful. For example, the lord of death, who takes the life of all living beings, may display a smile as if he were nice, but look how in the long run [259] his nature is to slay living creatures one after another by stealing their life-force.

* * *

Explaining the good qualities of a wise person's affluence:

81 As soon as a wise person becomes affluent,
he lives happily without harming others.
When the king of beasts' hunger is sated,
look how he reclines on his right side to sleep.

This verse says that a wise person who has merit from the force of former generosity will live happily with a calm mind and without harming others as soon as he acquires some money and possessions. Consider, for example, the king of beasts. When a lion sates his hunger by eating, he doesn't harm another creature. After lying down on his right side, he cheerfully goes to sleep and stays put.

The disadvantages of a fool's affluence:

82 When a fool becomes a bit rich,
all he does is injure others.
Look how when a fox is full of food
it yaps, proclaiming bad omens.

This verse means that a fool has little merit. As long as he is impoverished, his character is pleasant. But if he should become a bit affluent, he is arrogant, disparages others, and only causes harm. For example, when a fox is suffering from hunger and thirst he appears to be tame. But when his stomach is full of food he becomes arrogant and yaps. See how its howling is felt to be an evil portent for others. The glorious protector Nāgārjuna said:

> Inferior people become arrogant
> if they have wealth or education.
> Both of these two states
> make the wise very humble.[292] [260]

* * *

Explaining the good qualities of perseverance:

83 When the wise work to develop good qualities,
they have fortitude even when it is difficult.
Although it is difficult to cross the ocean,
look how gratifying it is to obtain treasure.

The meaning of this verse is that wise people do not desire mere temporary pleasure. They practice in order to develop good qualities, and no matter how difficult the circumstances, they do not give up. They persevere with endurance and fortitude. For example, the vast ocean is difficult to traverse because of its many terrors: it is broad, there are huge waves, there are sea monsters of various sorts, and so on. However, those who go to sea and endure the difficulties enjoy wish-fulfilling riches by obtaining whatever treasure they desire.

Thus if you are attracted to mere temporary pleasure, you will not obtain any good qualities. The *Staff of Wisdom* says:

> If you crave pleasure, you throw away knowledge.
> When you crave knowledge, you cast pleasure away.

> How can the happy become learned?
> How can those who strive for knowledge be happy?[293]

And the *Jewel Treasury of Wise Sayings* says:

> The wise endure hardship while studying;
> it is impossible for a hedonist to become learned.[294]

The disadvantages of laziness:

84 Fools addicted to pleasure indolently pass their time,
but without training how can good qualities arise?
If laymen are unable to trade or farm,
look how most of them are poor.

This verse acknowledges that fools are addled by temporary, superficial pleasure. They desire only happiness and pleasure, but they spend all their time indolently and do not study the causes for happiness. Thus, because they do not practice, how could any resultant good qualities arise? They cannot. For example, we can see that laymen who are unable to employ any means of earning a living—such as trade, farming, and so forth—are for the most part poor and destitute. If you are under the sway of sloth, you have no chance for religious or worldly success. It says in the *Great Passing into Nirvana Sutra*:

> The sole foundation of afflictive delusions
> is laziness; and whoever is lazy
> is indolent in whatever they do.
> There is no Dharma for them.[295] [261]

* * *

The wise benefit from seeing their own faults:

85 The wise see their own shortcomings,
so they are careful and obtain excellence.
King Ajātaśatru saw his own faults,
so look how he saw the truth.

This verse means that the wise always watch their physical, verbal, and mental activities. After identifying their imperfections, they see them as faults and eliminate them. Because they are careful to turn away from negative behavior, they will obtain the supreme true happiness that is the result of virtuous causes. For example, King Ajātaśatru committed one of the most heinous sins: murdering his father and so forth. He recognized that this fault was nonvirtuous. See how he directly saw the truth because of his strong remorse.[296]

In general "seeing the truth" is a direct perception of selflessness that is obtained on the path of seeing. There is no account in the vinaya texts that Ajātaśatru obtained the ārya path. But in the sutra *Dispelling Ajātaśatru's Remorse* it says that through the power of single-pointed concentration on emptiness, he purified most of his karmic obstructions. Later, the instant after taking rebirth in the hells, he was freed and immediately reborn in a high buddhafield. There are various interpretations of his favorable rebirth: Some say that Ajātaśatru attained the fruit of being a stream-enterer, or that he attained arhatship, or that after death he took rebirth in hell for merely an instant and then was freed from that to be reborn as a god, and then by listening to the Dharma teachings of the Ārya Śāṇavāsi he obtained the state of a stream-enterer. You should investigate whether these have sources in the sutras.

As the story goes, King Ajātaśatru did extremely terrible deeds: Incited by his evil friend Devadatta, he killed his father, Bimbisāra; he set loose an elephant to trample the Teacher; he cut off support for the male and female sangha; he forced the female arhat Kapilabhadrā to become his wife against her will; and so forth. He felt intense remorse for those actions. [262] He could not enjoy the taste of food nor could he sleep. Tortured continually by mental unease, he asked the Teacher what to do.

The Teacher said, "No one, except for Mañjuśrī, will be able to alleviate your regrets and doubts."

So the king invited Ārya Mañjuśrī and his entourage to the royal palace and presented him with superb offerings. Then Mañjuśrī said to the king, "Look at the nature of your sins and regrets." Thanks to Mañjuśrī's teaching of the Dharma in conjunction with the ultimate truth, Ajātaśatru obtained the forbearance that accords with emptiness—the third level on the path of preparation. As a gift of thanks to Mañjuśrī, the king offered the amount of money it would take to purchase a hundred thousand robes. But Mañjuśrī was nowhere to be seen. From the sky came the sound of the words, "Give it to whomever you see." Although the king offered the money, he did not see anyone. Finally, because he did not even see himself, he was freed from the conception of a self. His regrets were dispelled, and he went into single-pointed concentration on emptiness. Rising from that concentration, he actually saw the Ārya Mañjuśrī and so forth.

Then Śāriputra asked the Bhagavān, "How much karma did King Ajātaśatru purify?"

The Teacher said, "He has cleansed evil karmas the size Mount Meru. Those that remain are merely the size of white mustard seeds. After death he will transmigrate and fall into the hell in which your body is split open like a white lotus flower. But he will be immediately freed from that and take birth in a high buddhafield."

The disadvantages of how fools concentrate on others' faults:

86 Fools see other people's shortcomings,
so they are careless and become miserable.
Tiṣya saw the Buddha as having faults;
look at the inevitable consequences of that!

This verse means that fools hold themselves to be superior. They see the shortcomings of others and therefore carelessly do whatever they please. They are miserable in the present and in the future. Although the monk Tiṣya was in the presence of the Teacher for twenty years, [263] he saw all the Buddha's actions as fraudulent and faulty. His wrong view cut the roots of his virtue. Consider how the consequences of his attitude matured in that very lifetime—he fell through a crack in the earth down into hell.[297]

As the story goes, King Śuddhodana's brother, Śuklodana, had a son born under the constellation puṣya, so he was called Puṣya or Tiṣya. When he grew up he become a monk and lived with the Teacher for twenty years. Although he could recite the twelve collections of the sutras and had attained the four dhyānas, he was under the sway of wrong views. He saw all the Buddha's actions as only faults and frauds to confuse others.

Once while the Bhagavān was staying in the king's palace he gave Dharma teachings to the lord of the gods, Indra, on a promenade during the first part of the night. In that region, if children cried they were threatened: "The preta *Vakula will come!" At that time the monk Tiṣya was the Teacher's attendant. He was annoyed because he had to wait a long time in order to perform his duty of assisting the Teacher to retire. So he threatened, "Quickly! Go to bed! The preta Vakula is coming!" The Teacher said, "As for me, I am without fear." Indra asked, "Is a person like this even included among those listening to the Buddha's Dharma?"

Although Tiṣya attended the teachings of the Buddha, he did so in order to show him to be a nonvirtuous spiritual friend. No matter how much Dharma the Teacher taught, Tiṣya never had any faith or comprehension. Although he could recite the entire twelve collections of the sutras, he did not understand even a single verse, so he did not obtain any benefit.

One time the Teacher went into the city of Kāśī to collect alms. Countless numbers of beings wanted to see the Teacher's footprints. Tiṣya followed him and tried to rub out his footprints. However, he was unable to do so and became hostile. Nearby he saw a naked ascetic who had finished his self-mortification and was eating an alcoholic mash. Tiṣya said to the Teacher, "If there is an arhat in the world, this man is the best. He hasn't created any causes and hasn't any results."

The Teacher said, "How could this fool be an arhat when he eats alcoholic mash and has even killed his parents? There is no doubt that he will fall into the hell for beings who have committed heinous sins."

Tiṣya said, "The nature of the four great elements may possibly change, but it is not possible for this man to fall into hell." [264] And he continued, "In the king's palace there is a naked ascetic called Dukhita, who has fixated on the innermost mind and is an arhat."

The Teacher said, "How could someone with sinful views be an arhat?"

In response Tiṣya said, "Why are you jealous of the arhat?"

"I am not jealous. But you have generated evil, sinful views. Seven days from now the ascetic will die from indigestion and be reborn as a preta who eats vomit."

Tiṣya said to him, "But I will tell him that the monk Gautama said this about him. He will not eat food for seven days and will show your prophesy to be false."

After not eating anything for seven days, the naked ascetic ate some coarse brown sugar and drank some water. Because he couldn't digest it, he died. At the charnel ground, Tiṣya went near his corpse and asked, "Are you dead or not?"

The corpse said, "He died of indigestion and was reborn here as a preta who eats vomit."

Then Tiṣya said to the Teacher, "The ascetic Dukhita passed away and was reborn in the Heaven of the Thirty-Three."

The Teacher said, "Fool! Do arhats take birth again?"

Then, debased by his meditation on wrong views, such as the Buddha and even the Dharma do not exist and ultimately there isn't even causality, Tiṣya went to live on the banks of the Joyful River. There from far off he saw the Teacher with his entourage approaching. Because evil, nonvirtuous thoughts arose, not even a single strand of his roots of virtue was left. At that moment the earth cracked open and he fell to the Avīci Hell.

The Teacher said: "Tiṣya lived with me for a full twenty years. If he had not done that, he would have led countless beings into performing sinful, nonvirtuous actions. Because my younger brothers, Nanda and Upnanda, and my son, Rāhula, and so forth became monks, if Devadatta and Tiṣya had not become monks they would have obtained the kingdom, harmed many Śākyas, and destroyed the teachings of the Buddha. Therefore after they became ordained I had them become my attendants."

The above story appears in the *Great Passing into Nirvana Sūtra* translated from the Chinese. [265]

* * *

The wise repay the kindness of others:

87 The wise acknowledge and repay the kindness
of those who have acted to help them.
Look how the wandering sage
made the king become free from sin.

This verse says that a wise, great man acknowledges even a small helpful action that another person does for him and he repays that kindness. Consider, for example, that when a king adhered to sinful views because of foolish wrong ideas, the great being called the wanderer Bodhi used skillful means to free him from those evil views because of what the king had done during the course of their earlier relationship.[298]

Fools repay kindness with ingratitude:

88 Fools do not repay kindness;
in return for help they do harm.

Look at the behavior of the evil man
whom the monkey rescued from the abyss.

This verse reveals that fools are without shame and modesty. They do not reciprocate the kind actions of others. In return for assistance they inflict harm. For example, the bodhisattva monkey felt great compassion for a man who had fallen into a deep abyss and rescued him. Look at the behavior of that evil man. He was prepared to kill the monkey in return for the kindness of saving his life.[299]

Long ago the bodhisattva deliberately took rebirth as a monkey in a solitary place near the mountains, in a deep forest riddled with yawning gorges, ravines, and so forth. He had a compassionate nature. He sustained himself with only fruit and leaves and never harmed another creature.

At one time a man's cow strayed and he went in search of her. He became confused, wandered about, and came to this area. There, because he was tired and tormented by hunger, he ate a ripe *tinduka* fruit that he found. It was very tasty, so he looked all around in search of more. [266] He saw a tinduka tree that was hanging over the mouth of a deep ravine. Desiring to eat the fruit, he climbed out on a branch of the tree that was bent over the ravine. The branch broke as if it were cut by an ax. He and the branch fell into the deep, narrow defile encircled by rock faces like the sides of a well. But because there were thick bushes and deep water in the ravine, he was not wounded and his bones were not shattered.

He investigated and saw that there was no path of egress in any direction. Despairing that he would die, his eyes filled with tears and he wailed. After a while the monkey, the Great Being, came in that direction in search of food. He looked down into the ravine and saw the miserable man. Feeling great compassion, he said in a human voice:

You who are in this ravine
that men cannot escape,
kindly please tell me who you are
and why you have come here.

The man bowed, put his hands together, and said:

Glorious god, I am a man.
Wandering, I got lost in the forest.

Seeking the fruit of this tree,
I got into this terrible fix.

Furthermore, I have no friends or relations
to help me out of this great trouble.
You who are the protector of hosts of monkeys,
please come to my rescue too.

Hearing this, the monkey felt great compassion and said, "Do not be afraid or despair. I will do everything and anything that your relatives would do for you." Having eased the man's mind, the monkey practiced with a rock the weight of a man. Having tested his strength and seeing that he would be able to carry the man out, he went down into the ravine and put the man onto his back to carry him. Oppressed by the man's great weight, it was very difficult. But the monkey generated great courage and fortitude. Enduring severe pain, the monkey brought the man up.

There, very tired and weary, the monkey charged the man, "Guard us both for a while, for there are many dangers here in the forest."

The man said, "You may sleep well. I'll stay on guard." So the monkey went to sleep on a large boulder.

Then that evil man who had cast away any embarrassment and shame, without a thought of the monkey's kindness, reasoned, [267] "If I kill him and eat his flesh, I can build up my body and it will not be difficult to escape from this isolated place." So he picked up a large stone and threw it at the head of the Great Being, the monkey. It was a glancing blow and, not hitting him directly, wounded his head. Startled and in haste the monkey swiftly got up and looked around. He saw the evil man standing there with his head hanging in embarrassment. Certain that the man had acted that way, the Great Being was saddened and felt even greater compassion. His eyes filled with tears and he said:

Dear friend, because you are a human,
you should distinguish right from wrong.
How could you do this evil action
that will hurl you into a life of intolerable misery
when it was proper for you to turn away
anyone who might come to harm me?

> I will lead you to a village;
> from now on abandon sinful deeds.

Giving him compassionate and loving advice, he led the evil man to a village and turned back, going into the forest.

Then, immediately in this very lifetime, that man was struck with a severe case of leprosy. His body became ugly and very frightful. As soon as people saw him they thought, "This person is obviously evil," and they threw stones at him and drove him away with staffs. When he was wandering around like a hungry ghost in remote, uninhabited places, a king who was out hunting game saw him. The king gasped in fear, exclaiming, "Are you a hungry ghost? Or are you a demon? What are you?"

The man replied, "O great king, I am a man. This happened to me because I did an extremely evil deed."

Thus if you cherish and care only for yourself you will accumulate extremely evil karma and you will weep while experiencing the unbearable results. As it says in the *Collection of Aphorisms*:

> Because you desire happiness just for yourself
> you engage in frivolous and sinful activities.
> You will weep while experiencing
> the results that will arise because of these sins.[300] [268]

* * *

Showing how happiness comes from a wise person's wealth and possessions:

> 89 When a wise person becomes prosperous
> a wealth of enjoyment naturally arises.
> Look how the lords of the gods are honored
> with heavenly silk garments and ambrosia.

This verse shows that someone who knows the disadvantages of miserliness is naturally happy and joyous. When a wise person comes to possess a perfect abundance of things and capital—such as the silk garments and ambrosia of the lords of the gods—he gives it away. Using possessions so they will benefit oneself and others results in joy and happiness naturally arising in this and future lives. For example, look how the lords of the gods Brahmā, Śiva, Indra, and so forth make religious offerings of lovely garments made of divine silk that is soft and light, and of food with a hundred marvelous tastes that is ambrosia and that satiates the body and mind with happiness as soon as it is tasted. And they freely enjoy using these things.

Misery arises from a fool's wealth:

90 Even if a fool is rich and wealthy,
as if starving, he does not use or enjoy it.
Look how the fox who found some meat
came to ruin by eating a bowstring.

This verse says that fools are tied up in miserliness. Even if they have a wealth of provisions and riches they do not use it. They live as if they are tortured with hunger and thirst and, unwilling to give, they only hoard. Consider, for example, the fox who came upon the flesh of hundreds of dead men but out of miserliness didn't eat that food. Because he just gnawed on the sinew of a bowstring, he lost his precious life and came to ruin.[301]

Long ago in a time of famine a hunter critically wounded an elephant with a poisoned arrow. The elephant drew the arrow out and hurled it back at the hunter. Both lost their lives and died. A band of five hundred robbers came there and saw the elephant's corpse. Two hundred and fifty of them chopped up the elephant's flesh to cook. Two hundred and fifty of them went to fetch water. [269]

The men cooking the meat thought, "After we eat as much as we need to satisfy ourselves, if we poison the leftovers then the others will die and we'll get all the stolen goods." So they put poison into the leftover meat and waited.

The men who were gathering the water had similar evil thoughts. After drinking what they needed, they put poison in the rest of the water and came back. They exchanged the food and water and consumed it. They all died.

At that point a fox came running there as if freed from being caught in the snare of the death lord. After seeing all those corpses, greediness made him very happy. He thought, "I have found inexhaustible property! I will claim it as mine and eat it over time." Unwilling to eat the good things, however, he gnawed a section of bowstring made of sinew that was attached to the tip of a bow. The bowstring snapped, the bow hit him on a tender point of his head, and he died. A local deity said:

Although they were being saved for use,
the saved leftovers were not used.
Look how the fox blinded by greediness
to hoard came to be killed by the bow.[302]

* * *

Showing how the wise hold illustrious good advice to be best:

91 Disdaining ordinary amenities,
the wise esteem good advice.
A hero does not focus on anything else;
look how he emerges from battle as the victor.

The meaning of this verse is that because the wise are modest and have a sense of shame they disdain merely increasing their standard of living. They respect and esteem illustrious good advice. For example, look how a courageous hero pays no heed to any threats to his body and life. He engages in only the measures necessary to become victorious in battle with his enemies.

Showing how fools hold mere wealth to be best:

92 Scorning a good reputation,
fools prize the littlest bit of wealth.
Look how even people who are thieves
adorn themselves to look attractive. [270]

This verse shows that because fools lack modesty and a sense of shame they disdain the good repute of having an excellent character and the esteem of others and marvel at the acquisition of a bit of money and a few possessions. For example, sneak thieves, violent muggers, burglars, and bandits do not care about bad repute. They adorn themselves with jewels and garments they have taken from others.

* * *

The wise cannot be destroyed by others:

93 Because the wise are always careful
others can never destroy them.

> Look how King Pradyota the Ferocious
> found no opportunity to harm *Bhūdhara.

This verse explains that because the wise have intelligence they always act carefully and prudently. Therefore coarse people are unable to destroy them. For example, look how in the past the very ferocious king of Ujjayinī, Pradyota, sought to annihilate Bhūdhara but never found the chance.[303]

Long ago in the kingdom of Ujjayinī, a king named Pradyota, who was the same age as the Buddha, was afflicted with insomnia. Because he hated butter and liked alcohol he would not drink his physicians' concoctions of medicinal ingredients if they contained butter. When his queens gave him something with butter in it he became furious and ordered that anyone who uttered the word "butter" would have their head cut off. Because he could not sleep, during the first watch of the night he consorted with his harem of queens. In the second watch he inspected his elephants and horses. During the third watch he asked the night watch, "Who is waiting on me tonight?" He tolerated it when there was no response the first two times he asked, but when there was no response from the nightwatchmen the third time he asked, he cut off their heads and hurled them to the ground. Thus he became known as Pradyota the Ferocious (Caṇḍapradyota).

Then he said to the queens, "When I need an attendant at night, why don't you perform that service for me?"

They said, "Your Majesty, we will." After they had attended him for a short time, they said, "Your Majesty, not only has watching you at night not helped your mental state, [271] but it is also not our job."

"Well then, whose job is it?"

"It is the princes' job," they said.

The princes, the ministers, and the army troops each did night watch for a short time and then said, "We are unable to help you. This is a job for your subjects." One by one his subjects served as night attendants for the king. It was now the turn of a young incense seller. He was afraid that the ferocious king would kill him. A friend saw his anxiety and said, "Bhūdhara lives near you. Seek him out."

Upon being asked, Bhūdhara said, "If you give me five hundred silver coins I will do it. I will take half, 250, now and get the other half when I come back alive." With the 250 silver coins he bought a lot of meat, wine, and sweets. He invited all the king's household to a banquet. He gave them as much as wine as they wanted to drink and asked about the king's behavior. They explained in detail.

Then Bhūdhara said, "I, Bhūdhara, will be the night attendant, but if I fall asleep wake me up when the king comes." He stood watch, and when he fell asleep the king approached and a minister woke Bhūdhara up.

The king asked, "Who is my night attendant?" After the first and the second query Bhūdhara gave no answer. After the third, Bhūdhara said, "I, Bhūdhara."

"Who do you think you are?" the king said.

"I am a master of lore, so consider these ordinary notions:"

> An owl, a swan, Tartary grass,
> and a black female, a partridge, a pot,
> and salt, flour, a corpse,
> and a pit, cloth, a clay vessel, and a scorpion.

"Your majesty, an owl weighs exactly the same with or without its feathers. It is very amazing. How can that be? Your majesty, shall I demonstrate this for you?"

The next day Bhūdhara brought an owl before the king. He weighed it with all its feathers. When he weighed it after having removed the feathers it weighed exactly the same.

The king said, "What is the reason for this?"

Bhūdhara answered, "It is because the feathers catch the air."

The king said, "You are a wise man."

Bhūdhara responded, "Your majesty, you are very kind," and left.

And so the other men of the realm paid Bhūdhara five hundred silver coins too. Bhūdhara stood night attendance for all of them. All the notions prompted by the master of lore were elaborated on. "If you mix water and milk and offer it to a swan, the swan drinks the milk and leaves the water." [272] The next day, just as before, the king asked, "How can this be?" And Bhūdhara answered, "As it sours in his beak the milk turns to curds."

And so on: "Tartary grass weighs the same whether beaten by a hammer or not." The king: "How can that be?" Bhūdhara: "Beating it with a hammer consolidates the air." And one time Bhūdhara said, "The body of a female black-faced monkey and its tail are the same length. When she mates in springtime we see her tail reaches her head." And, "Partridge wings are the same whether colorful or not. I accounted for that before." And, "There is room in a pot filled with sand to pour in a pot full of water. This is because sand comes from water." And, "When you put a measure of salt into an equal measure of water, the measure of water remains the same. It is because salt comes from water." And, "If you mix a measure of flour into an equal measure of water, the consistency will be just right, as we have seen many times." And, "If you weigh a live person and his corpse they are unequal in weight. Because a corpse is not a living person, it has lost its vitality." And, "The amount of earth dug from a pit is not the right amount to fill it up again because nonhumans have stolen its vitality." And, "Although a weaver weaves cloth night and day, no one knows where it all went."

The king said, "This is true. Where is it?"

Bhūdhara answered, "It is spread over the ground."

On another occasion Bhūdhara said, "Although a potter makes pots night and day, no one knows what happens to them."

The king said, "Very true. So where do they go?"

Bhūdhara said, "They turn into earth."

The king said, O Bhūdhara, you certainly are a wise man. If you know everything, what is the cause of my insomnia?"

Bhūdhara said, "If you give me assurance that I will not be harmed, I will tell you."

The king said, "Granted. Tell me without fear."

Bhūdhara said, "Your majesty, you were sired by a scorpion."

"What! Are you insulting me?

"No, your majesty, I will make it apparent." Bhūdhara had a pit dug and filled with dried cow dung. On top of that he had a bed constructed. The next day he said to the king, "Your majesty, please sleep on this bed." He lay down and immediately fell asleep. He woke up and Bhūdhara said, "Your majesty, do you see?"

The king understood and went to question his mother. "Tell me truthfully, who is my father?"

"Give me assurance that I will not be harmed and I will tell you," she said.

"So be it," he said.

His mother said, "When your father and his large harem went into a pleasure grove, I was menstruating. [273] I saw a scorpion and I thought, 'If this became a man, I would have intercourse with him.' It became a man, and from intercourse with him you were born."

The king thought, "That Bhūdhara knows about me. I granted him freedom from fear, so it would not be right to kill him. But I can give him a reward and banish him from the realm." The king gave him five hundred silver coins and banished him.

Thus although King Pradyota was extremely ferocious, he did not find it possible to harm Bhūdhara in the least.

Others can destroy fools:

94 Because fools always are incautious,
others will definitely destroy them.
Look how Mashang Drompa Kyé
was put into a deep pit.

This verse says that fools rashly do whatever they please. They are always heedless and not cautious. Thus others surely will harm them. For example, during the time of King Tri Song Detsen, the evil minister Mashang Drompa Kyé destroyed religious law and so forth. Because he did many things rashly and heedlessly, he was executed by being buried alive in a pit.[304]

* * *

Showing how the wise make those who harm them their friends:

95 Even though others may harm them,
the wise respond with helpfulness.
Look at the story about the monk nicknamed Footpath:
he helped the twelve even though they harmed him.

This verse means that wise persons who engage in meritorious actions appropriate to their station will benefit even those who have done harmful things to them. For example, twelve nuns motivated by humiliation undertook preparations to harm the monk nicknamed Footpath. Nevertheless, that very act [274] became a condition that later brought them benefit. This story appears in the ancient sources.[305]

Long ago in Śrāvastī there was a brahman. Every time a child of his was born, it died. He was instructed by a crone: "Carry the newborn baby to a large crossroads. When the Teacher approaches, prostrate to his feet and make requests for the baby."

Because they did that, the Teacher said, "May you live well. May you live long. May you accomplish your parents' religious wishes." Seeing that the child was still alive at sundown, the brahman carried him home and named him Mahāpanthaka ("highway"). Again a child was born and this time they carried him to a minor road. They did as they had before. The child survived and was named Panthaka ("byway").

Mahāpanthaka grew up. He became a scholar of the Vedas and read the sacred words to around five hundred brahman youths. Panthaka studied the alphabet, but when he recited the syllable *sid* he would forget the syllable *dham*. When he uttered *dham* he would forget *sid*. His teachers said he was incapable and sent him back to his father.

Then Panthaka started learning to recite the Vedas. When he remembered *oṃ* he forgot *hūṃ*. When he remembered *hūṃ* he forgot *oṃ*. Again his recitation teacher turned him away. Since Panthaka was extremely slow-witted and small in stature, they called him Footpath and sent him back to his father's house.

Mahāpanthaka went to Jetavana. There a monk was explaining the Dharma of the way dependent origination arises and reverses. Mahāpanthaka developed faith, renounced, and took ordination. He studied, listened, contemplated, and abandoned nonvirtue. By striving in meditation he attained the state of an arhat.

Panthaka's fortunes diminished, and when he had great difficulty making a living, Mahāpanthaka influenced him to renounce and take ordination. In three months he could not learn this verse:

> Do not engage in misdeeds of body, speech, and mind.
> Become free from desire for entanglements to the entire world.
> Become someone who has mindfulness and introspection,
> and who refrains from relying on anything that is harmful
> suffering.

But the cowherds and so forth who listened to him trying learned it.

Mahāpanthaka said to him, "Why did you take ordination?" and drove him out of Jetavana.

Panthaka thought, "Now I'm not even a Buddhist monk. But I'm not a brahman either." And he began to cry. Then although Ānanda tutored him in reading, he could not learn to read. Although the Teacher bestowed on him the two phrases "Eliminate dirt. Eliminate stains," [275] he could not remember them. So the Teacher thought that his karma must be purified and had him take care of the monks' shoes. After learning just those two phrases, Panthaka thought, "I wonder if the Buddha intended this to be external or internal dirt?" Three verses came to his mind:

> This dirt is desire; it is not earthly dirt.
> Dirt is a word for desire; it is not dirt.
> The wise who definitely abandon that dirt
> will be heeding the teachings of the Bhagavān.

He followed the same pattern, inserting the words "hatred" and "ignorance." He persevered and through practice achieved arhatship.

At that time it had become common knowledge that Panthaka was a Buddhist monk. Heretics slanderously said, "It is said that Gautama's religion is profound and difficult to understand, but if even Panthaka can be a monk, how profound can it be?"

The Teacher thought, "They are sarcastic about this great disciple, but I shall proclaim his good qualities." So he appointed him to be the teacher of the nuns.

After learning of this, the nuns said, "Sisters, look how he despises the status of women. He appointed as our teacher someone who could not learn a single verse in three months."

A group of twelve nuns said, "We should make known our displeasure with that son of a demoness." Six of them set up a throne with legs twelve feet high. Six of them went to Śrāvastī and on all the streets of the city proclaimed, "Tomorrow a great disciple will teach the Dharma to us. Those of you who do not see the truth on this occasion shall have to wander in samsara for a long time."

Many thousands of beings came there. Some to see a show and some urged by the roots of their virtue. The next day Panthaka came there along with another monk who followed behind him. Most of the people were asking, "Which is the nuns' teacher, the first one or the one behind? How could a Dharma teacher follow behind? It is the first one. But how could this one be the Dharma teacher if he is the one who could not learn even a single verse in three months? These vixens have tricked us into coming here. Let's go."

Others said, "Let's wait for a while to see."

Then Panthaka came through the crowd. Extending his hand like an elephant's trunk, he pressed down the throne that was intended to humiliate him and settled on it. While sitting on the throne he went into the meditative equipoise of stabilization and displayed various magical emanations in the four directions. [276]

"Sisters! For seven nights I shall explain that single verse it took me three months to grasp." He taught that speaking of the body, there are three physical negative actions. Speaking of speech, there are four verbal negative actions. Speaking of the mind, there are three mental negative actions. The dictum "Do not engage in misdeeds" means that you should not do any of the evil deeds of body, speech, or mind. "To the entire world" refers to the five appropriated aggregates. "Entanglements" indicate the three entanglements of desire, hatred, and ignorance.

After explaining the meaning of merely half that verse, twelve thousand people saw the truth and thereby actualized the four fruits. After developing the desire to attain enlightenment for the sake of everyone, they became devoted to the Three Jewels.

Then the Teacher revealed his prophecy: "This Panthaka is the best of the wise ones at changing listeners' minds."

Even helping a fool becomes a cause of harm:

96 Although others try to assist them,
fools just respond harmfully.
Look at the negative consequences
when Ajātaśatru honored Devadatta.

This verse shows that fools ruin themselves and others. Even attempts by others to help them become a condition for retaliatory harm. For example, because King Ajātaśatru had faith in and honored the monk Devadatta, negative consequences arose that ruined both of them.[306]

Once when the Bhaghavān was living in Rājagṛha there was a dreadful famine. The monks who had attained magical powers collected alms and nectar from other lands, the god realms, and so forth. They divided up their own livelihood to share with the others. Devadatta saw that and thought, "I too should master magical powers." And he went and asked the Teacher and the other monks. [277]

They saw that he had sinful thoughts so they did not teach him the way to attain magical powers. He asked the brahman Mahākāśyapa, the principle disciple of the Teacher, and Mahākāśyapa taught Devadatta without investigating his motivation. Devadatta made an effort to practice and actualized magical powers.

Then when trying to gain influence over Ajātaśatru, Devadatta thought, "How can I achieve the object of my desire?" When he entered Ajātaśatru's palace he made the bodies of the horses, elephants, birds, and so forth that were coming and going into the form of monks sitting on cushions. Sometimes he transformed himself into a radiantly golden infant and rolled about in Ajātaśatru's lap. Although Ajātaśatru spit into his mouth, the infant swallowed it.

Therefore the king thought, "Devadatta's magical powers are even greater than the Teacher's!" So when Devadatta came in the morning and departed at night he was given an entourage of five hundred people, conveyed and escorted in five hundred carriages, and offered food in five hundred vessels.

Then to create dissent, Devadatta said the following and more to Ajātaśatru: "Although your father's hair has gone white three times over, even now he desires sensory pleasure and has not given you the kingdom. So now you must overcome your opponent." Devadatta said, "Ajātaśatru, I will get a *mandārava* flower for you." So Devadatta went to the Heaven of the Thirty-Three and asked the gods to give him one. Because Devadatta had used up his merit, no one gave him a flower. Then he thought, "I'll get one myself." As soon as he began to take it, his magical powers degenerated, and he found himself back in Rājagṛha. He was embarrassed and could not face Ajātaśatru.

He went to see the Bhagavān and said, "Give me leadership of your entourage."

The Teacher said, "As I don't give it even for a short while to the likes of Mahākāśyapa and the supreme pair, Maudgalyāyana and Śāriputra, I would never give it to you who are like a gob of spit."

Because extremely evil thoughts arose in Devadatta's mind, the earth shook six times and cracked open in front of him. From the crevice a high wind came up and covered him in dust. These evil omens disquieted his mind and sapped his vitality. When he went before Ajātaśatru, the king asked what had happened to him. "I am unhappy because local people insultingly call you 'enemy from before birth.'"

Ajātaśatru said, "Who gave me a name like that!"

"They call you that because before you were born soothsayers prophesized, 'After this child is born he will kill the king.' [278] Your mother, Queen Vaidehī, threw you off a high rooftop as soon as you were born. You lost a finger but did not die. Therefore in order to protect your feelings, the court called you Sudarśana, 'vision of virtue.'"

Ajātaśatru couldn't bear it. He threw a scepter at his father, the king. Because Ajātaśatru was injuring the local people, his father, the king, said soothing words to stop him. But Ajātaśatru did not listen. When opposed with harsh words, Ajātaśatru got angrier. He had his army surround and seize his father, the king. Queen Vaidehī tried to stop him. He seized her topknot, and when he was about to stab her with a sword, Jīvaka stopped him. Ajātaśatru put his father, who had attained the fruit of a stream-winner, into prison and stopped those who would bring him food.

Then boils erupted on the fingertips of Ajātaśatru's son, Udayanabhadra. The boy cried and Ajātaśatru took him into his lap and put the boy's fingers in his mouth. The boils burst and pus and blood flowed to the ground. Seeing this the boy cried even more.

Ajātaśatru's mother, Vaidehī, said, "This is hereditary. The same thing happened to you too in the past. Out of concern for your crying, your father swallowed the bloody pus."

Ajātaśatru's hatred was gone. And he said, "Since my father loved me like that, I order that my father shall live. I will give him half the kingdom." Therefore many people raced toward the prison, making a great clamor. In that instant the king died. He was reborn in the western continent of Aḍakavatī as Vaiśrāvaṇa's son Jinarṣabha.

Having killed his father, Ajātaśatru was oppressed with unbearable regret and misery. He became extremely ill. Around seventeen surrounding vassal states rebelled, and their armies surrounded the king's palace. Famines and epidemics occurred all over the land. He was terrified and begged the Bhagavān for forgiveness. Because he took refuge the epidemics and the war subsided on their own. Because of that his faith increased, and he offered the Buddha and the sangha everything they needed for three months. He felt extreme regret for killing his father the king and for the other evil deeds he committed because he had associated with an evil friend. [279] He wept for a long time. The Teacher taught him the Dharma and established bottomless faith within him. He went for refuge to the Buddha and the sangha. He closed his door to Devadatta and his disciples.

Devadatta wanted to make himself the Buddha. So he summoned a goldsmith and had him spread gold over his body and had the soles of his feet branded with a wheel. From doing these and other foolish things he experienced unbearable pain. He said, "I myself will kill Gautama." He hurled a catapult stone at the Bhagavān, and he incited Ajātaśatru's wild elephant, Dhanapāla, to attack him. Also he feigned asking forgiveness. He put poison under his fingernails and, pretending he was bowing down to the Teacher's feet, spread the poison on him. But no matter what he did he was not able to harm the Buddha.

Then Devadatta thought, "Although I committed three deeds of immediate retribution—I caused dissent in the sangha, with evil intent I caused the Buddha to bleed, and I killed the female arhat Utpalavarṇā by beating her up with my fists—I didn't achieve a single thing. Now I'll be born in hell." He became very depressed.

The heretic Pūraṇa Kāśyapa said, "If you think that among the Śākyas you alone are wise, you must be just a fool. How can you say there are future lives? It is like this example." He broke a round pot in front of Devadatta and asked, "Is it possible to get it back? There is no reason to be distressed. Come now, you must go to Kapilavastu. I will have you made the chief minister." Because of this wrong views arose, and his remaining roots of virtue were annihilated.

Not long after that, when Devadatta went for a walk, little hell flames came out of crevices in the ground with each step. Because the flames touched his feet, he cried, "It's hot. It's hot!" and ran quickly. Instantly the earth cracked open, and the tops of the flames of the hell fires enveloped his body, burning him severely. He cried out, "Ānanda! I am burning!"

Ānanda said, "You must go for refuge to the Buddha."

Having seen the reality of the fires of hell, Devadatta was convinced. He said, "Even down to my bones I go for refuge to the Buddha." After he spoke his body fell into Avīci Hell.

The Buddha prophesized, "Because Devadatta took refuge in the sangha, his roots of virtue will be restored. After being in Avīci Hell for an eon, he will become a pratyekabuddha named *Astivāna." [280] A prophecy in the *Lotus Sūtra* reads, "In the future this very Devadatta will become a buddha named Devarāja."[307]

* * *

The way happiness naturally arises for those close to the wise:

97 Those who are close to the wise
are granted a carefree, cheerful mind.

Look how the lion brought relief
to all of the wild animals.

This verse says that a carefree mind, mental happiness, and physical pleasure are naturally bestowed on those who rely on and stay close to an intelligent, wise person. For example, we will see how a lion, the king of beasts, relieves many prey animals and predators from terror and nervousness.

Suffering arises naturally for those close to fools:

98 Those who are close to fools
are naturally granted undesired misery.
Look how the rabbit who heard the sound
"chal" agitated all his animal friends.

This verse says that harm and unwanted misery are naturally bestowed on those who stay near fools who lack wisdom. For example, let us see look at how their animal friends became agitated just by observing the rabbits who heard the sound "chal" when a bilva fruit fell into pond.

A legend illustrates these two verses.[308] Long ago there was a grove of bilva trees on the banks of a pond. Six rabbits lived there. When a bilva fruit fell from a tree into the pond, there was the sound "chal." Hearing it, the six rabbits bolted in fear. [281]

A fox seeing them flee, asked, "Why are you running away?"

"There's a chal!" they said. So the fox ran away.

In the same way monkeys, deer, buffalos, rhinoceroses, elephants, brown bears, grizzly bears, leopards, tigers, and lions also fled.

On a nearby mountain there was a lion with a mane like a royal crown. He saw the lions running away, and said, "You have strong claws and fangs, so why are you running away?"

They said, "A chal! Something called a chal is coming!"

He asked, "What is this thing called a chal? Where is it coming from?"

"We don't know," they said.

"Don't run off! Let's look into this. Who told you?"

"A tiger said so," they said. The lion asked each one in turn.

The tiger said, "A fox told me."

The fox said, "The rabbits told me."

When asked, the rabbits said, "We clearly saw that scary thing. Come back with us and we'll show you the thing called a chal." They led the lion and showed him the bilva grove. "The thing called chal came out of there," they said. Once again a bilva fell from a tree in the grove and there was the sound "chal."

The lion said, "This is the sound of a bilva falling into the water. Relax, do not be afraid."

A god said:

> Do not run off because of popular rumors.
> You should see matters clearly for yourself.
> Look how the thumping splash of a bilva
> emptied the forest of four-legged creatures.

* * *

Showing the advantages of the wise who conceal their education:

99 The wise hide their knowledge inside,
so masses of people gather around them.
Look how many sea traders gather
to get the gems that are in the ocean.

This verse means that a wise person who has amassed a massive treasure trove of learning does not show off in front of other people but keeps his education hidden inside. Therefore he does not encounter harmful spirits or obstacles, and intelligent people naturally gather around him in pursuit of knowledge. For example, even though the precious gems in the ocean are distant and difficult to reach, sea traders who have seen the good qualities of those precious things gather them, [282] paying no heed to difficulties.

The disadvantages of fools who show off their accomplishments:

100 Fools blab about their good qualities,
so people do not gather around them.
Look how no one ever picks up
chaff that is floating on water.

This verse means that fools have minimal learning. Their education is limited but they show off, blabber, and brag. Therefore intelligent people will not gather around them. For example, no intelligent person picks up the chaff of wheat or other grains that float or are carried along on the water's surface.

* * *

The wise speak little and appropriately:

101 The wise have vast intelligence and do not chatter:
this indicates their trait of profundity.
Look how very difficult it is to fathom
the depths of a gently moving ocean.

This verse says that the wise behave appropriately. Their intelligence is vast and they do not chatter—that is, speak for no reason. Their behavior indicates and makes comprehensible their particular quality of profound intelligence, the depth of which is difficult to ascertain. For example, look how difficult it is to fathom the depths of the vast ocean, which looks calm and moves slightly only on the surface.

Fools talk indiscriminately and in error:

102 Fools are full of themselves and talk a lot:
this indicates their limited intelligence.
Look how very easy it is to fathom
the depth of a babbling brook. [283]

This verse indicates that fools are shameless and impetuous. They are very conceited and a lot of what they say is babbling, unconnected nonsense. This indicates their limited intelligence and feeble understanding. For example, look how very easy it is to fathom the depth of a constantly babbling brook.

* * *

The ease of pacifying the ire of the wise:

103 Even if a wise man is deeply offended,
he will be appeased if you pay proper respect.
Silver and gold are very strong,
but look how they can be melted.

This verse reveals that a wise person knows the right way to do things. Even if his mind is deeply aggravated by immediate circumstances, his resentment will immediately dissipate if you properly clarify matters and are deferent. For example, just as the normal state of gold, silver, and other metals appears to be hard and strong, look how easy and simple it is to melt them with fire.

Fools hold on to their resentment:

104 Whether or not a fool is offended,
he is rigid when you pay proper respect.
When you melt a pile of dog shit,
look how it emits only a foul odor.

This verse means that a fool mistakes what should be done and what should be avoided. Whether or not he is offended by others, his abrasive attitude becomes increasingly rigid when others act with deference toward him. For example, if you burn a heaping pile of filthy dog shit in a fire, thinking that you will get rid of it, look how a nauseating stench is emitted and spreads. [284]

* * *

The good quality of a wise person's honesty:

105 Because the wise are honest,
whatever they do is done sincerely.
Look how Kumāra Jīvaka's medical treatments
all came out satisfactorily.

This verse explains that a wise person has an honest attitude that is without deceit. So whatever he does is done in a straightforward way. For example, because King Bimbisāra's son, *Kumāra Jīvakabhṛtya, had a good attitude of wanting to assist others, whatever medical treatments he performed were immediately helpful. Thus he and everyone else became happy and satisfied.[309]

King Bimbisāra engaged in sexual intercourse with the wife of a merchant. From this union a boy was born. The king adopted him and named him Kumāra Jīvakabhṛtya. He grew up and went to Takṣaśilā to study medicine.

From the king of physicians, Ātreya, he learned how to perform surgery that opens the cranium surrounding the brain. So Kumāra Jīvaka became well known as a specialist.

After that he paid his respects to Ātreya, and on the road back to his homeland he learned the language of all the spirits. In a bundle of wood that he had purchased he found a jewel called Making the Spirits Become Clear. When it was put in front of a sick person, Kumāra Jīvakabhṛtya could see what ailed the patient. He traveled in stages back to the king's palace. Using the power of this jewel and his knowledge of the spirits' language, he helped many sick people along the way with his medical treatments.

At that time, although his younger brother Ajātaśatru welcomed Jīvaka home, he did not accept Jīvaka as his own family.

A while later when Jīvaka was very distracted by his work, a brahman with an eye disease demanded, "Give me medicine!"

Becoming annoyed, Jīvaka said, "Put some ashes in it." Because Jīvaka was trustworthy, the brahman put ashes in his eyes and was cured.

That brahman told another person with an eye disease, "I know about eye medication." But by putting ashes in his eyes as the brahman told him, the man went blind.

After an abscess erupted on King Bimbisāra's head, the king said, "Treat this!"

Jīvaka said, "I shall wash it and do so." He poured five hundred jugs of water infused with various substances over the abscess to make it come to a head. When it swelled up, Jīvaka pierced it without the king being aware of it. Then he poured five hundred jugs of water infused with healing substances on it. [285] The king's sore, his skin, and even his hair recuperated.

After the king had eaten, he again said, "Treat it."

He could not believe it when Jīvaka told him, "It's all done."

He rubbed his head with his hand and couldn't find the abscess. He looked in a mirror. Even when the queens looked they couldn't find the place where the sore had been. Amazed, the king said, "Appoint Jīvaka to be the king of physicians."

Then the man who had gone blind said, "If he is so skilled, why didn't he cure my eyes?"

Jīvaka said, "I have never even seen you, so how could I cure you? Because you have a different constitution, do this and this and you will see."

He did as he was told, his eyes recovered, and he was pleased. So he said, "Please appoint this man to be the king of physicians."

Jīvaka was seated on an elephant, endowed with much fabulous wealth, and installed as king of the physicians.

All the other physicians had given up on a householder afflicted with a cancerous tumor. He showed it to Jīvaka, who said, "The medicine for you is very difficult to obtain."

So the man thought, "Now I'm going to die." He went to the charnel ground. There a hawk and a vulture were fighting and fell into a burning funeral pyre. Because the man was hungry he ate their flesh. Then he drank rainwater from a ditch. He drank a gruel of millet and fat-free yogurt. All this made the tumor rupture. Because it was excreted and vomited out, the disease was cured.

Then boils erupted on Queen Vaidehī's genitals. The king said to Jīvaka, "Cure this lady."

Jīvaka mixed some substances that make boils come to a head into some dough and gave it to a lady-in-waiting. He instructed the lady-in-waiting, "Have the queen sit on this poultice. When the boils come to a head, conceal splinters of red ocher in the poultice." As she was told, she had the queen sit on the poultice and then later stand up again. As soon as the boils came in contact with the red ocher splinters, they burst open. Then Jīvaka had her wash the queen with water infused with medicines for fostering health, and she was cured.

The king said, "Did you or did you not remove her clothes and examine her naked body?"

"I did not examine her," Jīvaka said. The king was amazed by the way the queen had been treated.

The man who had earlier recovered from cancer said, "He didn't cure me."

In response Jīvaka said, "Didn't I say medicine for you would be difficult to obtain? My remedy would have been like this," and he related how the man should have gone to the charnel ground and what he should have done.

The man said, "Your knowledge is excellent. That is exactly what I did." [286] Pleased, the man continued, "Please appoint this man king of doctors." And for the second time Jīvaka was appointed king of physicians.

Then Ajātaśatru had a tumor develop. "Cure me!" he said.

Jīvaka thought, "There are two things that will destroy this tumor: extreme anger and excessive joy. This sinful man will not become joyful, so he must be angered." So he said, "Your majesty, if you eat the flesh of your son Udayanabhadra you will be cured."

The king became angry. "Right! I have killed my father. You will have me slaughter Udayanabhadra. And if I too were to die from this illness, you indeed would become king."

"Your majesty, nothing else can cure you." Because he did not care about anything but himself, the king agreed to eat his son's flesh.

Then Jīvaka hid Udayanabhadra in a secluded place. He brought the king some flesh taken from the charnel ground. The king was about to eat it when Jīvaka snatched away the bowl and hit him on his head with it. "Sinner! You killed your father and now are you going to eat your son?"

The king became incensed and said, "Well then, why did you kill my son!" His extreme rage ruptured the tumor, and he vomited and excreted it out along with some blood. Thus he was cured.

Then Jīvaka produced the boy and said, "Since I won't even kill an ant, how could I kill the prince? This was the way to cure your highness's illness." The king was amazed and once again Jīvaka was appointed king of physicians.

Thus he was appointed king of physicians three times: twice by his father, the king, and once by his younger brother, King Ajātaśatru. Then Jīvaka thought, "No other physician is my equal." And he became very conceited and did not see the truth.

The Teacher, desiring to alleviate his arrogance, led him to a snow peak and showed Jīvaka many medicines that he had not known about. The Teacher's explanations of their names, flavors, and efficacies quashed Jīvaka's conceit. Then the Teacher taught him the Dharma and Jīvaka saw the truth. [287]

Explaining the disadvantages of the deviousness of fools:

106 Because fools have devious minds,
most of their actions backfire on themselves.
Look how, because of a woman's deviousness,
Udayana was slain after he escaped.

This verse indicates that because fools' minds are devious, they dissimulate and deceitfully mislead others. Whatever actions they undertake backfire on themselves. For example, although King Udayana escaped execution after being captured by King Pradyota the Ferocious, afterward he was slain by a woman's devious actions.[310]

King Pradyota the Ferocious of Videha thought that because his harem of queens was so large, he could not take care of them all. So he informed his queens, "You can go and make love to any man you want, but you must be back here at daybreak when the palace drums beat. If you have not returned, I will chop off your head." And he rang a bell.

King Udayana of Kauśāmbī was a man who lusted for women. When he learned of King Pradyota's decision, he said to his minister *Yogadhāraṇa, "I'm going to have sex with the queens of King Pradyota the Ferocious."

The minster said, "Doing that will be trouble."

"O Yogadhāraṇa, indeed you are the most senselessly cautious man among men. You stay here and I'll go," the king said, and left for Videha. He saw the royal queen named Tārā and said, "Prepare a bed for us to have sex."

The queen said, "You make the bed!" Out of arrogance, by daybreak neither one had set up a bed, so Tārā took King Udayana's ring and left. After she told the king what happened, he said to his minister *Poṣaṇa, "No one was aware that King Udayana had come here. If he departs it will be unacceptable. Do not let him leave!"

However, although Udayana was prohibited from leaving, he did not listen, and led by Yogadhāraṇa, he left Videha and went into an inn. Poṣaṇa had the building surrounded by men wielding swords and ordered, "If the women come out, let them go free. But don't let the man go!" Yogadhāraṇa heard that and had Udayana put on women's clothing. [288] Carrying a water jug and clutching a staff, he went outside, saying, "Why can't I go fetch water?" Thinking he was a maidservant, the guards let him go. He threw down the water jug and fled.

King Pradyota became infuriated and said, "You better bring Udayana here! If you don't, you will be condemned to the ultimate capital punishment!"

In fear, Poṣaṇa ordered a craftsman to build a mechanical elephant in which he could hide five hundred men. Then he sent the elephant to the environs of Kauśāmbī. Udayana saw it. In order to capture the elephant for himself, he went toward it playing a lute sweetly. The five hundred men emerged, stuffed him into the machine, and swift as the wind went back to Videha. The king ordered, "Execute Udayana!"

Some ministers advised, "Since he is a master of training elephants with music, have him teach us his methods with elephants and then kill him." They made him teach Princess Vāsavadattā from behind a silk screen.

Then Yogadhāraṇa disguised himself as a madman and had his sister *Kāñcanamālā transform her appearance to be like an ascetic sage. The two went to Videha. Employing various trickeries, they managed to meet with Udayana and with Vāsavadattā. They mounted King Pradyota's elephant *Nalagiri and fled to Kauśāmbī. Because Udayana escaped alive, they held a great feast, and he and Vāsavadattā lived together.

At one point Udayana said to Vāsavadattā, "Summon your father here. If he doesn't learn how to weave, I am not King Udayana!" She related that matter to Yogadhāraṇa. The minister disguised himself as a caravan leader and prepared trade goods. He bribed a beautiful prostitute to act as the caravan leader's wife. Then they went to Videha. King Pradyota the Ferocious learned that a caravan leader had come and went to his house to assess the wares for himself. The caravan leader went outside and disappeared. Seeing the caravan leader's wife, the king desired her. He went to bed with her.

At that point Udayana's men broke down the door, forced the king and the prostitute into a palanquin, and it was hauled off by four men. Some people clapped their hands. [289] Some laughed. Some sang this song as they ran off to Kauśāmbī:

> Bees are eating the moon.
> A shopkeeper herds Vaiśravaṇa.
> The earth with its forests is above the sky.
> A harlot leads King Pradyota.

Udayana had him tied up and made him learn to weave. At one time Udayana was on the palace roof along with Vāsavadattā when Pradyota came out of the weavers' hut. Udayana said to Vāsavadattā, "See that man. Do you know who it is?"

She looked carefully and recognized the bald man was her father, the king. Choking with tears, she thought, "This evil king has turned my father into this. If I don't kill this evil king, I am not Vāsavadattā!"

Udayana said to Yogadhāraṇa, "My revenge on my enemy is complete. Now release Pradyota the Ferocious, give him some food, and with great fanfare escort him back to Videha." They escorted him as they were told.

Vāsavadattā deceived the king by seeming to be happy for a while. Then she pretended to be ill and lay in bed. When questioned by the king she said, "Your majesty, I am worried. When my father had captured you and we two joyfully escaped to Kauśāmbī, I vowed that together we would fast for seven days. When the seven days were over, you would be garlanded from head to toe with flowers and rest on the top rung of a high fence. And you would feed, make offerings, and greatly honor a thousand brahmans."

Udayana said, "Since it is for my sake, get up and it all will be done."

Then Vāsavadattā shut two hounds who could only eat human flesh into an enclosure surrounded by a high fence. She stayed and fasted with the king for seven days. But she ate at night. The king wasted away from not eating and out of lust for his wife. After the seven days elapsed, he was garlanded with flowers and rested on top of the high fence of the pen containing the hounds. While all sorts of music and dancing were going on, Vāsavadattā said, "Your majesty, from gazing on the lovely city from the top of the fence you may fall." With a shout she pushed him off the fence. As soon as he fell the two dogs ate him. Only bare bones remained.

Yogadhāraṇa investigated and realized the king had been killed by subterfuge. He was furious. [290] He had Vāsavadattā put into a lacquer house and set it on fire.

* * *

The wise are wary of random encounters:

107 The wise trust only people they know;
they are wary of random acquaintances.
Wild animals are not used to humans,
so look how they flee as soon as they see them.

This verse says that the wise have discernment. Except for people whom they already know from a prior relationship, they are wary of—that is, do not place their trust in—the seeming friendliness of people they casually encounter. For example, animals in the wilderness have no experience of relating to humans. So they turn and run as soon as they see a human.

The disadvantages of a fool's trust in new acquaintances:

108 Fools immediately trust random associates
even though they had no prior relationship.
Look at what happened to the king of Bhaṅgala,
who was deceived by a demoness.

This verse teaches that fools lack discernment. Even though they have no knowledge of someone through a former relationship, they seem to enjoy random encounters and immediately trust those people as friends. For example, in the past when the blessed queen of King Bhaṅga of Bhaṅgala passed away, the king, because of lust, took as his queen a girl of demonic lineage who came from somewhere unknown. Look what happened when she separated him from his bodhisattva son.[311]

Long ago in eastern India, in the country of Bhaṅgala, there was a king named Bhaṅga. A bodhisattva son was born to him and his queen, *Dhanadā. Even when held back by his parents, if he saw representations of the Three Jewels he would not listen to his parents and would go in the direction of the Three Jewels. Because he had a very respectful and devoted manner, people would say, "Here comes someone with steadfast faith," so he came to be called *Sthiraśraddhā, "steadfast faith." [291] In like manner the king, his wife, and son made offerings and honored their spiritual teachers and the Three Jewels. They ruled the kingdom religiously with love and compassion for all beings, primarily the populace.

The demon couple Kāmeśvara were displeased to see the spiritual and temporal welfare of the land increase steadily, so they prepared to interfere. They transformed themselves into an extremely large black boar and a magnificent sow. They went inside the fence surrounding the tree-of-life of the king and queen and damaged it. Around five hundred ministers surrounded the boar and the sow. The royal prince himself shot an iron arrow and slew the black boar. The sow escaped. Queen Dhanadā became ill and died.

Then, brandishing weapons, the prince along with his ministers went into the forest to hunt for the sow. Although they searched, they could not find her. Then the prince saw a vision of a beautiful and enticing girl, the likes of whom he'd never seen before. Her body radiated five colors and her clothes similarly glittered like beautiful chain mail. The prince thought, "This girl is most likely that wild sow herself. Because my mother has already passed away, it would be pitiful if I were to kill her." So he let her be.

Once the ministers saw the gorgeous girl they could not stop looking at her. They asked the prince if it would be acceptable to make the girl his or the king's consort, since such radiant beauty is rare in the world. The prince said:

> If in the past a nine-headed tigress
> were never found in all the world,

> if one appears now it is a bad omen.
> And in the future it will be the same.

"How can it be right to unhesitatingly consort with something like this that comes from who knows where?" The prince did not accept the glittering girl.

The ministers told the king the prince's decision. The king said, "The prince wasn't pleased, but it surely couldn't be this lovely girl. There may be some problem in the future, but for now I shall make her my queen." And he married her. When the prince saw the girl in the presence of the king he said:

> A mountain lion living
> as a city watchdog bitch
> still has the arrogance of a lion.
> How can a bitch be made a pretty girl?

The demoness thought, "The prince's manner of speaking indicates he has decided that I am not of a good family. [292] I must employ some means to banish him to another realm."

The demoness feigned dire illness. The king wondered what treatment she required, so he asked her. The queen said, "Because I truly am a goddess, I will be helped when you obtain heavenly medicine and a divine doctor. Nothing else will help me."

The king said, "How can we find a god? What shall we do?"

"This way," she replied. "In the southwest where the rākṣasas roam, there is a flower called a *kuśanā* that is medicine for deities. Since Prince Sthiraśraddhā is no different than the gods, send him to get it."

The king thought, "The prince is surely a magical incarnation, so he could definitely get that medicine. I must entreat him to do so." So he went to the prince and explained the matter.

The prince said, "You erred in making a demoness your queen, and now you are banishing a young son, from your body born, to the frightful, terrifying place of the rākṣasas."

The prince thought, "I could destroy that demoness in an instant, but my kind father's unhappiness would be on my account henceforward. It would not be right if I sinned so."

So he said, "I'll go. There is nothing paining the queen but her being sick of me. She will recover as a consequence of my departure without relying on medication."

The king loved his son very much, but because he lusted for the queen, there was no other recourse. So he sat there and cried.

Then the thirteen-year-old prince mounted a good horse and rode out of the city. Many of the ministers and populace followed him wailing like camels that had lost their calves. The prince made a religious speech and sent them back. The prince relinquished any pride in being venerated and traveled to the southwest for three years and three months. The road ended when he reached an unpleasant, forsaken place in black, rocky mountains where many ferocious beasts and birds roamed.

He encountered the yellow guard of the rākṣasa road. He had iron claws and wielded a golden sword. The guard questioned him and the prince answered honestly, explaining what had happened in the order that it had occurred.

The guard's ferocity was pacified. As happy as a father gazing on his son, he said, "Your father is an idiot. A flower isn't medication. Kuśanā is actually the name of the daughter of the rākṣasa king of Laṇkā. [293] And 'flower' is an epithet for pretty.

"The region called Laṇkā is a place of vicious rākṣasas and is ringed by seven iron fences. The gates are secured by rākṣasa sentries that have from one up to seven heads. Their king, called the ten-throated Laṇkā, is extremely terrifying and horrific. The place is filled with male and female rākṣasas eating human flesh and drinking blood.

"In the center of the citadel, atop a thousand-storied building with 360 stairwells, lives the girl named Kuśanā. She looks as if she has just reached the age of sixteen. She can be gazed at insatiably. She outshines even the sun. She is surrounded by girls numbering seven times seven: forty-nine.

"Now if you go there you must go on the fifteenth of the month when the rākṣasas take one-day precepts. At that time they won't harm others. Because this horse of yours can't get there, take whichever of my horses you wish and ride there." And he sent him off.

When the prince had gone fifty leagues along the southwestern border, he saw two snakes, a black one and a white one, yoked together in a fight, each one consuming half the body of the other. Feeling great compassion, he separated them and let them go. The white snake was the nāga king Śaṅkhapāla and the black snake was the nāga king Bahuhasta. Because their savagery was pacified and their bodies recovered, there were a vast number of auspicious signs: rain fell when needed, fruit ripened on the trees, and food, wealth, prosperity, and offspring increased. Both nāga kings invited him to their palaces on his travels. Honoring Sthiraśraddhā lavishly, they both gave him five pieces of turquoise and begged him to visit when he was traveling through again.

Then he entered the region of Laṇkā. He answered the questions of the guards at the gates of the seven iron fences, and after giving them each a turquoise, he had an audience with the rākṣasa king. After many questions and answers he was allowed up to the peak of the citadel and met the goddess Kuśanā. He made lavish offerings, venerated, and honored her. And there he stayed.

Then he conferred with the rākṣasas. They entrusted him with a hundred successive keys to the great cemetery Śītavana. Having opened the hundred doors, he could go everywhere within the iron fence of the demon realm without harm. In that way he tamed the rākṣasa host and lived there quite a few years. [294]

As a farewell gift, the rākṣasa king gave him a jeweled vessel that would produce whatever one needed or desired. When he went, taking with him the goddess Kuśanā, the demons living there were angered. They lifted up the valleys, flattened the high peaks, and picked up and hurled the mountains and boulders. However, Prince Sthiraśraddhā and Kuśanā were not hurt in the slightest. Then the black nāga king hailed them on the road. They stayed in his palace for seven days. The nāga king had daughter whose complexion was like the color of a blue crystal. Along with other parting gifts, he gave the prince his precious daughter and a black goatskin. Similarly, the white nāga king, Śaṅkhapāla, invited them to his palace and they stayed for seven days. He had a daughter whose complexion was like a clear white crystal. He gave the prince that precious girl and a wooden chest.

Then they went on. The road guardian from before greeted and hosted them. They petitioned the jeweled vessel and gave him all the provisions he would need for life: food, clothing, dwellings, and so forth.

In this way, over the course of thirteen years the prince tamed the hosts of rākṣasas and the savage nāgas. When he was twenty-six years old he, Kuśanā, and the two nāga girls and their lovely precious gifts arrived in the kingdom of Sahora.

Then he went before his father, the king, and said, "I have come bringing Kuśanā and more. Now let me assist the queen."

The king asked the queen and she became even more displeased. She said, "In that case, in the middle of the great iron mountains encircling the kingdom of Bhaṅgala there are nine hundred and ninety-one fortresses surrounding nine citadels, making a thousand in all. I will recover from my illness if they make a concoction of the water from the many springs and the many types of birds from the tops of the trees within the iron boundary." This was explained to Kuśanā and she said:

> There is nothing that cannot be accomplished
> in the illusory sphere of emptiness and appearance.

She petitioned the vessel that provided everything wanted and needed. The two nāga girls shook the goat skin and opened the wooden chest. They made something even better than what the queen had requested.

However, after that the queen said, "The strong cover of the interior of the king's spirit mountain is but an overturned clay vessel filled with water. A great sandalwood tree grows above the center. Rising above and around it there are thousands of renunciate dwellings. Many birds are on the treetops of the vast forests on the slopes of the spirit mountain. I'll recover if you make a concoction of all that." [295] The three girls, Kuśanā and the nāgas, made something far, far better than even what she had described.

Considering that, the demoness thought, "They have made all these impossible things possible. I shall stop them before they hurt me." So she said, "Now the prince must stay with me for three days."

Kuśanā said, "I myself am the medication for demons. I'll go." Together with the two nāga girls, she went near her. The queen was abashed. Unable to bear Kuśanā's brilliance, she couldn't raise her eyes.

Kuśanā brought her before the king and said, "I came in response to this queen saying she was ill. Now I will make the appropriate medicine for your sort of being, but what sort of creature are you?"

"I am a goddess," said the queen.

Kuśanā said, "I am the foremost female of all the gods. But I've never seen or heard of anyone like you in any god realm."

"As a female nāga, I am called a goddess," said the queen.

The black and white nāga girls said, "Every nāga is classified as one of us—either black or white. We have never seen or heard of anyone like you among us."

The king said, "There isn't anyone like this among we humans either."

Kuśanā said, "Well then, isn't a demon what you are? Regardless, you must bathe in the medicinal water that I have made." After that they brought her to the shore of king's spirit mountain lake and made her bathe in the water.

When the demoness called out to the black nāga girl, "Don't you have a sibling?" the nāga girl cried out, "Brother Bahuhasta!" And from below the water a red ox with a single horn rose up. Its horn tore open the demoness from the top of her head down to her toes and dragged her down to the watery depths.

Then Kuśanā transformed herself to look exactly like the demoness and went before the king and said, "I killed your previous queen. Moreover, because your son killed my husband and my heart was pained, I had him sent to the rākṣasa realm. However, not only did he not die but what he did was helpful. Although I enjoined many impossible tasks, they were done without difficulty. Because you made her my superior, I think I will destroy this entire realm or at least not allow this prince to live."

Then she transformed herself into the extremely terrifying and magnificent sow that seemed to be about to devour the king. Terrified and hoping to create good karma before he could be eaten, the king's lustful desire was gone instantly. He reached for the prince and ran out. [296]

Then King Bhamga, the father, felt disgust for all samsara and became a monk.

Prince Sthiraśraddhā was an emanation of Avalokiteśvara. Kuśanā was an emanation of Tārā. The black nāga girl was an emanation of Bhṛkuṭī and the white nāga girl was an emanation of Vasudā. These four, as if they were parents, religiously ruled Bhaṅgala for one hundred and one years and greatly benefited all beings.

* * *

It is difficult for others to suppress the wise:

109 A wise man doesn't let harmful words out of his mouth,
so his real enemies are unable to suppress him.
Look how even when a lion is asleep
the other animals are terrified.

This verse shows that the wise have broad intelligence. Even if they have thoughts about harming someone else, no hurtful words come out of their mouths. And because they do not speak, others do not know how they feel, so their enemies are unable to suppress them. For example, even when a lion, the king of beasts, is sleeping like a log and doesn't make a peep, look how all the animals are frightened and terrified of him.

It is easy for others to suppress fools:

110 A fool lets harmful words out of his mouth,
so his real enemies are able to suppress him.
Even though dogs constantly bark,
look how they are terrified of wolves.

This verse says that fools have limited minds. Whenever they dislike the slightest thing about someone else, they immediately say harmful things. Because it is easy to assess their feelings, their true enemies are able to suppress them. For example, dogs always make noise to scare others. But even though they bark, it is easy to suppress them. Look how they are terrified of ordinary wolves. [297]

* * *

The wise do not depend on others:

111 Because of the force of their vast intelligence,
the wise act independently without relying on others.
Look how the king of those making ritual sacrifices
made them into religious offerings of the Dharma.

This verse means that the wise have penetrating discernment. Because of the power of their deep and profound intelligence, they undertake or shun actions using their own strength and without relying on others. For example, a king was urged by his ministers and brahmans to sacrifice cattle in order to reverse the harmful effects of a drought. But the king, a great being, listened to their words and then used skillful means to establish his people in the virtuous Dharma. His marvelous actions were praised as an object of veneration and offerings.[312]

Long ago a lovely ornament existed on this planet because of the bodhisattva actions of an incomparable king who was esteemed for his merit by every surrounding principality. Although the king ruled his kingdom in a religious manner, because of the karma of the beings living there rain did not fall and there was a drought.

The king asked the senior brahmans and his ministers what should be done. They said, "If we perform a ritual sacrifice as described in the Vedas, the gods will be pleased and rain will fall."

The king was uncomfortable because he knew that ritual sacrifices according to the Vedas would kill many creatures. He thought of another method. In order to lead the people to virtue through skillful means, he acted as if he had listened to his advisers' words and then said, "I agree to sacrifice one thousand people. You must all make preparations."

That frightened the brahmans and ministers, and they said, "If we seize a thousand people all at once, the populace will revolt."

The king said, "You should not worry. Done like this, the populace will not be repulsed." Then having gathered together all the people of the city, the king announced, "I wish to sacrifice one thousand people, but I cannot sacrifice those who are without sin. Know that anyone among you who is breaking the law and [298] harming his compatriots will be seized as a sacrificial creature by the very great examiners I have sent out."

Then the king dispatched honest, reliable ministers to every inhabited town and city in order to seize those who were doing wrong. They couldn't find anyone committing a sin. All the people were living according to the ten rules of virtuous conduct. This delighted the great being, the king. He praised those possessing virtue as objects worthy of offering and respect. He opened his treasuries and sent gifts to all the people of the Earth, delighting them with whatever property they desired.

In this way he made the people content with the Dharma and material things. Through the force of actions according to the Dharma, rain fell at the right time and crops and animals flourished. Epidemics and disputes were pacified. It became a time of complete peace and happiness. The ministers and the people acquired deep faith in the practice of generosity, and they offered oceans of praise and auspicious speeches for the skillful means employed by the king.

Fools do what others say:

112 Because a fool's intellectual strength wavers,
he follows others' suggestions without control.
Look how Śrīgupta was convinced
to prepare poisoned food for the Buddha.

This verse means that a fool's eye of discernment is blind. Because his intellectual strength regarding what to do and what to avoid vacillates, he can be made to do whatever others say without any independent volition.

For example, the lay-devotee of naked ascetics Śrīgupta listened to the words of the naked ascetic Pūraṇa. He was made to invite the Buddha and his disciples to his home and prepared poisonous food out of a desire to kill them.[313]

In Rājagṛha there lived a devotee of naked ascetics, [299] a novice named Śrīgupta who was the husband of Jyotiṣka's sister. Jyotiṣka said, "Give donations and offerings to the Buddhist sangha. That will become merit." Śrīgupta said to Jyotiṣka, "I will, if you first offer victuals to Pūraṇa and the other naked ascetics."

"I will do it," Jyotiṣka promised him.

Then Jyotiṣka bade Pūraṇa come for an offering of food. Accompanied by many naked ascetics, Pūraṇa put a foot on Jyotiṣka's threshold and whinnied like a horse. Another naked ascetic asked him why he laughed so. Pūraṇa said, "Oh! On the bank of the *Viśeṣā River a male monkey thought, 'I'll cross over to the female monkey.' Because he was hurrying, he fell from the top of a tree and died."

Jyotiṣka heard this and thought, "I'll play a joke on him." He completely covered the vegetables in Pūraṇa's begging bowl with rice and gave it to him.

Pūraṇa said to the householder, "I don't have any vegetables." The householder said:

> He sees that which is unseen
> and doesn't see what ought to be seen,
> sees the monkey on the bank of the Viśeṣā
> but doesn't see the vegetables in the bowl.
>
> The one who doesn't see should see;
> the one who will see isn't seen.
> For the one seeing a monkey of the bank the Viśeṣā
> there are no vegetables in his begging bowl.

Pūraṇa was humiliated and couldn't remain in the presence of the householder. After eating his food he dedicated the merits of the offering:

> For benefactors it is the time to give,
> for religious practitioners it is the time to eat.
> When it's time to give the leftovers to others,
> there is no such thing as virtue and nonvirtue.

The doorkeeper heard that and thought, "What sort of a dedication is that! I will play a trick on him." In front of the door he poured the water in which the rice had been cooked, drew the dead bolt halfway out, and waited. When Pūraṇa came out, he slipped on the rice water, struck his head on the dead bolt, and began to bleed. When the doorkeeper saw that he said:

> The time to throw the deadbolt arrived;
> because it is time to spill the rice water
> it is time for a head to be wounded,
> but there isn't any time of virtue and nonvirtue.

Dripping with blood, Pūraṇa went before Śrīgupta and said, "Jyotiṣka injured me like this." Śrīgupta said:

> You escaped with your life. May you live long.
> I will kill Gautama and his disciples.

Then Śrīgupta had a huge pit dug in front of his door. He had it filled with burning coal and covered with earth. He prepared food and drink laced with poison. After saying, "Come to see me kill your enemy," [300] he seated Pūraṇa and his retinue on the roof.

After spreading a mat, he invited the Teacher and his followers. As soon as the Teacher placed his foot on the hot coals, they all turned into pond lotuses and so forth. Water birds of all sorts uttered their calls. The gods threw down a rain of flowers. Śrīgupta was astonished and said to Pūraṇa, "Look at the Bhagavān's miracles!"

Pūraṇa said, "Do you have faith in these illusions of Gautama?"

Śrīgupta said, "Well then, you do the same." Pūraṇa was embarrassed and snuck out.

Śrīgupta said, "I was deceived by an evil friend and made food and drink laced with poison. Shall I throw it away and make fresh victuals?"

The Teacher said, "Since I have completely abandoned the three poisons, what can this ordinary poison do. Bring it here." Śrīgupta brought the prepared food.

The Buddha uttered the words "May there be abundance and wealth," and the food became free of poison. Śrīgupta's faith intensified. When he finished consuming the offerings the Teacher taught him the Dharma. Śrīgupta saw reality and became the door opener for the fourfold assembly.

* * *

Showing how good actions immediately result in experiencing good effects:

113 Because the wise do positive actions
they immediately experience good results.
Look how the man named Siṅghala
immediately obtained the kingdom.

This verse says that because wise and holy people only engage in positive actions, they immediately experience the auspicious results of those actions in this very life. For example, the merchant captain Siṅghala immediately obtained the kingdom because he engaged in positive actions that benefited others without falling under the influence of deception.[314]

Long ago, when King Siṅghakeśari ruled the fortress city of Siṅghakalpā, a merchant captain named Siṅgha had a son who was given the name Siṅghala. When he grew up he went to sea with five hundred companions to obtain jewels.

At sea a sea monster, having a fish-like shape, [301] broke up the boat. Some of the men got onto the ship's planks, some got on cotton cushions, some got on floats made of dried gourds, and some rode on inflated goatskin bags. Owing to the force of their karma, a wind rose and carried them south to a shore. On the subcontinent of Tāmradvīpa, there lived female rākṣasas, called young crane women, who went to the shore to deceive shipwrecked merchants. The rākṣasas transformed themselves into attractive women, adorned themselves with jewels, and said, "Sirs, please take this wealth and this food and be our husbands." When they took pleasure in each other, boys and girls were born.

When they were living there the rākṣasa women ordered, "No one among you should go on the southern road." The merchant captain Siṅghala wondered why they were protective of the southern road. When the women were sleeping he tucked a sword under his arm and went down the southern road. There he saw a huge iron city. He went all the way around it and did not find an opening in the city walls that even a mouse could slip through. On the northern side of the city there was a very tall acacia tree. He climbed up and looked around.

Inside the city he saw crowds of men uttering lamentations. When Siṅghala asked why, they said, "We are shipwrecked merchants. Those women are demons and tricked us. We are the remaining few of the merchants who have come here and have not yet been eaten."

The merchant captain said, "Is there no way to escape?" They replied, "There is no way for us to escape. But all of you should go along the northern road on the fifteenth of the month. The horse king named Powerful Cloud is there. We heard the gods say that if you hold on to him you will escape."

The next day the merchant captain gathered all the merchants together in a deserted woods and told them this. They were all frightened and terrified. They went on the northern road on the fifteenth of the month. The horse king said, "Even if you are riding my back, any one of you who thinks of his rākṣasa wife, little boys, or little girls will fall, dropping like a ripe fruit. Those of you who don't think of them will easily get to Jambudvīpa merely by holding onto a hair of my coat."

The merchants mounted up, some holding the horse king's coat, and they rose up into the sky. The rākṣasa women transformed themselves to be even more beautiful than before. They came holding their boys and girls. When they came near they said, "Please be our husbands. If you refuse, you must take these boys and girls." [302] Those who thought lovingly, "My wife and so forth," fell and the women ate them. Only the merchant captain Siṅghala escaped.

Then Siṅghala's rākṣasa wife came before him carrying their son and said, "I, the daughter of the king of Tāmradvīpa, was given to be the wife of Siṅghala. Therefore I forswear being bad luck for those who were shipwrecked. So it is proper for you to forgive me."

When the masses of people and even his parents said, "Son, you should be tolerant," he said, "This is a rākṣasa woman!" and threw her out.

After that she was brought to King Siṅghakeśari by his ministers. Due to lust the king took her as his queen. One night when the king was sleeping with his queen, she told the rākṣasas how to get in and they ate the king and his court. Because the palace doors didn't open at dawn, Siṅghala took his sword, climbed a ladder, and looked in. He saw rākṣasa women running off carrying human legs, arms, and heads.

Then, because they had no king, all the people came together and anointed the merchant captain Siṅghala as their king. King Siṅghala gathered his wizards and his army to kill the rākṣasa women of Tāmradvīpa. Some fled to another land. Because Siṅghala established a city there, it became known as Siṅghala Island.

Showing how bad actions immediately result in experiencing bad effects:

114 Because fools engage in negative actions
they immediately experience unpleasant results.
Mākandika incinerated Śyāmāvatī and her retinue,
and look at what happened to him.

This verse means that fools are ignorant and have inferior minds. Because they engage in negative actions that are nonvirtuous and sinful, they immediately experience the unbearable suffering of the awful results of that bad karma. For example, a minister of King Udayana named Mākandika used deception to kill Queen Śyāmāvatī and her retinue of five hundred women [303]—all of whom had seen the true nature of reality—by burning them in a fire. The immediate result of that evil deed was that Mākandika was put in a house of resin and burned alive.[315]

King Udayana of Kauśāmbī had a queen named Śyāmāvatī. She was the daughter of King Udrāyaṇa's minister Bhiruka. She was a devout Buddhist laywoman who had obtained the fruit of being a nonreturner. Her retinue of five hundred women had all seen the true nature of reality.

Now Sākali, the wife of the wandering ascetic Mākandika, gave birth to a fine-boned girl of unparalleled beauty, so she was given the name Anupamā, "unparalleled." When Anupamā grew up Mākandika brought her to Kauśāmbī and had her stay in a pleasure garden. When King Udayana saw the girl he lusted for her. He took her as his queen and made Mākandika a minister.

The king would eat in the quarters of Queen Śyāmāvatī and Anupamā on alternate days. Anupamā was continually jealous of Śyāmāvatī, so she became vindictive and incited slanderous things to be said to the king. One time the king became angry. He drew his bow and shot an arrow toward Śyāmāvatī and her retinue, who were meditating on love. The arrow fell when it was halfway there. The second arrow he shot reversed course and fell in front of the king. When he was ready to shoot a third arrow Śyāmāvatī said, "My lord, do not shoot. Do not completely destroy yourself."

The king was terrified and said, "Are you a goddess or a nāginī?"

Śyāmāvatī said, "I am neither. But because I am a disciple of the Buddha I have obtained the fruit of being a nonreturner." The king became faithful, and thereafter he considered her as a sister and gave her every manner of necessities, even the choicest food and drink.

At a later time the king ordered Mākandika, "You must stay and provide Śyāmāvatī with whatever she needs," thus demoting him to the level of a mountain peasant.

Then Anupamā said to Mākandika, "Father, it is jealousy and miserliness that most harm women. So kill Śyāmāvatī."

Mākandika said, "What! Do you think I am that two-faced?"

Anupamā said, "If you kill her, things will go well. If you don't kill her, I'll reduce you to your former state."

Mākandika became fearful and thought, "I'll find a way." Because Śyāmāvatī and her retinue [304] studied the Buddha's words at night by the light of oil lamps, they had a need for thin twigs, lamp oil, black ink, and wool. Mākandika piled a lot of these things by the entry of her house. He put a lit oil lamp in the last bundle of twigs, and the fire spread in the house's entryway. Many people came running to put out the fire. Mākandika said, "How can you go inside the queen's quarters!" And he sent them away.

A magical emanation of Śyāmāvatī rose up in the sky and said, "Sisters, this is the result of our karma." And like moths falling into a candle flame, she along with five hundred women were burned up.

The king was petitioned. He ordered that Mākandika be repaid by placing him in a lacquer house and setting it on fire.

* * *

The wise are not pleased by a mere semblance of knowledge:

115 It is difficult to please the wise;
they take no pleasure in those lacking good qualities.
Look how Mālikā never took the time
to venerate non-Buddhist tīrthikas.

This verse means that the wise have extensive and profound intelligence. Because they are not pleased with persons lacking genuine good qualities, it is difficult for anyone with a mere semblance of knowledge to please them. For example, the noble queen of King Prasenajit named Mālikā had a wise and discerning nature. Through understanding the Buddha's teachings she obtained faith. Thus she never had occasion to venerate the non-Buddhist tīrthikas.[316]

Mahānama Śākya had a brahman servant in his summer residence who had a daughter named Candrā. She was clever and her behavior and comportment were proper, so people liked her. The brahman died and the girl was made a personal attendant to an elderly wife of Mahānama. Candrā would go to the gardens and gather flowers. Because she was skilled in chaining flowers together into lovely garlands she became known as Mālikā.

One day she took her meal to the garden. [305] There she saw the Teacher begging for alms. She had faith and offered him her food. Dedicating the merit of this act, she prayed, "May I not be a servant and not be poor."

King Prasenajit went hunting for game. Because his horse bolted and ran off, the king found himself alone in the gardens of Mahānama in Kapila. The girl drew water from the edge, middle, and depths of a pool, offering him water that was warm, tepid, and cool in succession. The king washed his feet and face and then drank. Then the girl massaged the king's legs. Because of her superb touch, he quickly fell asleep. The girl thought, "These kings have many enemies," and she shut the pavilion door.

The king was very pleased with all that and thought, "This girl is wise." And he asked Mahānama, "Who is this girl of yours?"

"A servant," he replied.

The king said, "This is no servant. She is your daughter. Please give her to me." And he made her his queen.

King Prasenajit had two noble queens. Varṣākārā was known to be the best of beauties. Mālikā was known to have the best touch. From then on Varṣākārā studied the Buddha's words with Śāriputra and Mālikā studied with the monk Udayi. Influenced by Udayi's instruction, recitations, oral transmissions, and so forth, she became learned. She obtained firm, unwavering faith in the Bhagavān's teachings. No matter what the non-Buddhist tīrthikas did, on no occasion were they venerated and honored by Mālikā.

Showing that it is easy to please fools:

116 It is easy to please fools;
a mere semblance of good qualities pleases them.
Look how most Tibetan lamas and officials
paid homage to the Chinese abbot.

This verse says that fools have limited minds and it is easy to please them and make them happy. They are amazed and delighted to see a mere semblance of good qualities. For example, thousands of the common people, [306] and nearly every Tibetan lama and official, paid supreme homage and had faith in the theories and practices of the Chinese master Hashang Mahayana.[317]

In the time of the religious King Tri Song Detsen, a man named Hashang Mahayana came to Tibet from China. He taught that since acting virtuously or nonvirtuously causes one to take a high or low rebirth, actions will not liberate one from samsara and are an obstruction to the obtainment of buddhahood. It is like this: it doesn't matter if a cloud is black or white, a cloud will obscure the sky. He said that one attains enlightenment by not engaging in any conceptualization: in other words, staying free of all activity—not thinking, not conceptualizing, and not doing anything at all. Most Tibetans were delighted with his teaching of nihilistic meditation. The system spread, and all manner of physical and verbal religious actions were abandoned. Even the king's decrees became difficult to enforce.

So the king invited the great scholar Kamalaśīla to come from India and had him debate Hashang. Using logic and scripture, the great scholar vanquished Hashang. The religious king Tri Song Detsen circulated a decree: "From now on everyone must practice the ten virtuous actions and the perfections by adhering to the system of Nāgārjuna's views. I shall condemn to death anyone who adheres to Hashang's system." Hashang was deported.

However, later the king's laws degenerated. Many monks pretending to be Nyingmapas and practitioners of Mahāmudrā held the Chinese master's ideas as the pillar of their own system. Nyingma and Mahāmudrā were just other names for Hashang's views. Even most of the lamas and officials had faith and preferred Hashang's system. Thus the lord of the Dharma Sakya Paṇḍita said:

> Although they solely rely on the words
> of the Chinese master's system,
> they keep his name a secret
> and change their name to Mahāmudrā.
> So present-day Mahāmudrā
> is primarily that Chinese system.[318]

* * *

The third part of the second main section of the text, the summation and conclusion, has six parts: (1) a summary of what it means to be "wise" and to be "foolish," (2) how to put into practice this differentiation of the wise and the foolish, (3) praise of the wise, (4) the way in which this text of wise sayings was composed, (5) an exhortation to those who possess good fortune to listen, and (6) a dedication of the merits of composing this text. [307]

* * *

First, a summary of what it means to be "wise" and to be "foolish":

117 The wise have every good quality.
A fool is someone with only faults.
Look how a gem yields everything desired
and a poisonous snake causes harm everywhere.

This verse says that the wise have good qualities that are beneficial to themselves and others in the present and in the long term. Fools are a locus of only faults that bring disaster to themselves and others. For example, look how everything wished for and needed comes from a precious wish-fulfilling gem, whereas a poisonous snake causes all sorts of calamities and harm.

Second, how to put into practice this differentiation of the wise and the foolish:

118 Therefore you must properly differentiate
the distinguishing features of wise men and fools.
It is right to hold the wise as an ornament
and throw away the foolish like straw chaff.

This verse instructs that right after the good qualities of the wise and the faults of fools have been explained to you, you must properly and without error differentiate between the the wise and the foolish. It is right for those who want what is good for themselves to hold on to and use the wise as a crown ornament. And it is right to cast fools far away as if they were bits of chaff.

Moreover, the master Amoghavarśa said:

> If you ask what is it to be wise,
> it is to differentiate things precisely.
> If you ask what is it to be foolish,
> it is not learning the compass of skillful actions.[319]

And as Lord Nāgārjuna said:

> Only a wise person
> will achieve the best sought-for goal.[320]

And:

> Two-legged creatures who see clearly
> should completely forsake the foolish.[321]

Third, praise of the wise, has two parts. First, to praise those who are wise in ways of the world, the text reads:

> 119 The wise stand out in the world
> like a trumpeting elephant in a herd.
> The charm of someone skillful and valorous
> is the greatest of ornaments in this world.

This verse says that elephants are the most supreme of creatures, but not every elephant in a herd of a thousand will trumpet. Similarly, the allure of an intelligent person who is brave, intrepid, skilled, and wise is a great ornament that beautifies wherever that person is in the world, even among those already skilled in knowing what to do and what to avoid.

Second, to praise those who are wise in the Dharma, the text reads:

> 120 Just like a wish-fulfilling jewel among gems,
> among those learned in the Dharma too,
> whoever possesses all three—learning, virtue, and goodness—
> is a great ornament of the Buddha's teaching indeed.

This verse says that a wish-fulfilling jewel that increases whatever possessions one wishes for or desires is a precious gem that eliminates poverty. Similarly, even among persons wise in the holy Dharma, those who combine all three qualities—an unvarying clarity of knowledge of the internal and external sciences, the morality of restraining from the negative actions of the three doors, and having good intentions to benefit others—are the greatest of the ornaments that maintain, protect, and increase the precious teachings of the Conqueror in both teaching and practice.

Fourth, the way in which this text of wise sayings was composed, has three parts: (1) how former masters wrote wise-sayings texts, (2) how this tradition deteriorated with the passage of time, and (3) how, once again, this wise sayings text came to be composed. [309]

First, how former masters wrote wise-saying texts:

121 Although Sakya Paṇḍita, lord among the learned,
gave us *A Jewel Treasury of Wise Sayings,*
which differentiates the wise and the foolish,
to be used as eyes to view the world . . .

This verse indicates that the glorious Sakya Paṇḍita Kunga Gyaltsen Palsangpo, an emanation of the venerable Mañjuśrī and the lord of the multitude of the wise of the land of snows, condensed the valuable teachings of many great Indian treatises: the three works by Ārya Nāgārjuna, *A Hundred Stanzas on Wisdom, Staff of Wisdom,* and *A Drop to Nourish a Person,* and master Sūryagupta's *Treasury of Verse,* master Vararuci's *Hundred Stanzas,* the *Cāṇakya Treatise on Kingship,* and Masūrakṣa's *Treatise on Norms.* These distillations appear in the glorious Sakya Paṇḍita's compositions *A Jewel Treasury of Wise Sayings: A Treatise Differentiating the Wise and the Foolish* and *A Necklace for the Youth: Differentiations of People.* His intention was to open the eyes of persons of good fortune to see what should be done and what should not be done in the world.

Second, how this tradition deteriorated with the passage of time:

122 Nowadays the beaming sun of the wise
has set over the western peaks and gone elsewhere.
The rise of ignorant fools in the form of the moon
has made the flowers of wise sayings mostly close.

This verse acknowledges that the beaming sun of the wise ones who had impartial minds has set. Influenced by disciples they have gone to another realm, an invisible place beyond the peaks of the western mountains. Swayed by the rise of the moon—fools with biased minds and arrogant scholars who are ignorant—the lotuses of wise sayings have mostly closed, and endeavoring bees have few opportunities to enjoy the honey to which they aspire. [310]

Third, how, once again, this wise-sayings text came to be composed:

123 Once again in the garden of my mind
the white lotuses of wise sayings blossom
because the sunlight of discernment shines
and it is moistened with rain of perseverance.

This verse says that when the lotuses of the wise sayings of former masters had mostly closed, once again various flowers of wise sayings appeared in the pleasure garden of this writer's mind. The white lotuses of wise sayings, containing the essence of the honey of excellent meaning, grow from the combined causes and conditions of the vivid, shining light of the sun that completely discerns the Dharma and analyzes its profound points, and from being moistened again and again by the good rains of perseverance that takes joy in virtue.

The fifth section of the summation and conclusion is an exhortation to those who possess good fortune to listen:

124 By having beautiful bodies of modesty
and far-seeing eyes of wisdom,
may the bee-like fortunate ones
enjoy and frolic here from now on.

This verse states that those who have bodies beautified by the ornament of modesty that shuns unwholesome actions because of feeling shame before others, and who have the far-seeing eye of intelligence that sees what to do and what to avoid, are like fortunate bees enjoying a superb feast of wise sayings. So the text exhorts them to always relish this feast of wise sayings with dedication and constant effort, just as honeybees playfully engage with flowers and enjoy the honey-like essence of flowers. In the last three stanzas, the similes are used in such a way that their corresponding references take the form of the metaphors themselves.[322]

Furthermore, the good conduct of wordly norms does not contradict the practice of the holy Dharma. Therefore if you enact wordly norms in accord with the holy Dharma, then with the attainment of a series of fortunate human births or god rebirths, you will near the state of the definite goodness of liberation. As it says in *A Hundred Stanzas on Wisdom*:

> If you properly practice human ethical behavior,
> the journey to the god realm will not be long.
> If you thus ascend the stairs of men and gods,
> even the liberation of nirvāṇa will be close by.[323] [311]

Sixth, a dedication of the merits of composing this text:

125 Therefore, owing to the merit of these wise sayings,
may every living creature now and in the future
have the wisdom to differentiate wise men from fools
and thus have unerring faith in the wise.

The meaning of this verse is that through the merit of composing this text of wise sayings in the manner of former teachers, may all beings alive now and in future come to understand the distinction between the wise who should be followed and fools who should be avoided. And therefore with strong aspiring faith that does not err, may they rely on supreme wise men.

* * *

The third major section of the text is "the concluding points." This refers to a discussion of the colophon of the root text:

> I, Sönam Drakpa Namchö Chokgi Dé, an eloquent speaker from central Tibet, composed this treatise examining the wise and the foolish entitled *Ganden Wise Sayings: A Bouquet of White Lotuses* at the request of some of my learned students who had interest in wise sayings. It was written at the victorious place of Ganden Monastery and was scribed by the expounder of wise sayings Ngawang Chökyi Drakpa.

The colophon indicates five particulars: the text that was composed, the ones who requested for it, the author, the place of composition, and the scribe. Once again, the author prays that the text may be of benefit to others, when he writes:

> Through this may all people be able to easily differentiate between the wise and the foolish.[324]

To sum up:

The superb behavior of holy and respectable people
brings together the norms of religion and society.
Utterly marvelous wise sayings
clearly teach this without confusion.

The method of the holy Dharma is subtle and profound.
Because those with inferior minds cannot handle it,
there are many conceited scholars without learning
and counterfeit religious teachings that deceive. [312]

Therefore fortunate people with clear minds
should hold up this lamp of good advice,
and without being deceived by false friends,
seek out holy wise men with much learning.

After those who aspire to be wise properly rely on wise men,
the wealth of proper learning accumulates with interest
and good qualities increase like lakes in summer rains.
Then how can the fame of being wise be far away?

Being able to precisely distinguish
fools who brag about being wise men
from the wise who hide what they know
is also from the force of virtue accumulated previously.

This method is set forth in an abbreviated fashion
based on texts of absolute reliability:
the previous-birth stories of the Buddha
and the illustrative stories of the Vinaya and so on.

As a result of the merits of my endeavor herein,
may all beings rely on a wise, ethical, and kind spiritual friend
and thus perfect their study, contemplation, and meditation
on the vast ocean of spiritual texts and practice.

This work entitled *Rays of Sunlight*, a commentary on *Ganden Wise Sayings: A Bouquet of White Lotuses*, which is a treatise examining the wise and the foolish, was written in response to a persistent urging by the learned spiritual friend Naimang Lharampa Geshé Ngawang Tenzin. It was composed by the lazy monk Yangchen Gawai Lodrö, whose head rests on the dust below the feet of many eminent scholars and practitioners.

6. A Pearl Garland of Advice[325]

The Fifth Dalai Lama, Losang Gyatso

1 O Mañjuśrī, the lord of eloquence,
Sarasvatī, goddess of splendid wish-granting sciences,
glorious Brahmā, treasurer of the four aims of life,
and lords of the earth, please bestow your blessing.

2 Profound and unvarying words of religious and secular ethics
played as a song on the strings of the lute of poetics
are sweet to the ears of discerning youths who have the wisdom of their elders.
However, most people do not like it: the music is like a thorn in their ears.

3 Therefore here are pearls of straightforward verses
that can be understood by everyone, both high and low.
It is a necklace to beautifully adorn the throat of the emperor
who descends from Chingis's lineage of heaven.[326]

4 Nowadays in India, China, Mongolia, Tibet, and so forth,
the noble nature of both ancient codes of ethics has declined.
Now when bad behavior is accepted as admirable,
even if norms are explained well, it is like having two feet in Tsuta.[327]

5 Rays of sun do not penetrate a cave facing north;
that is the genuine nature of things. Nevertheless,
because light can shine into cavities facing other directions

I decided to produce something to clear away enveloping
darkness.

6 Setting aside religion, progress even
in ordinary affairs depends on merit.
So worship the holy, give generously to the poor, and so on
to amass the great collection that is increased by good deeds.

7 Because you are not clairvoyant it is difficult to sift through
all advice and counsel. Categorize the importance of situations
by analyzing place, time, occasion, and whether friend, enemy, or
neutral party.
Doing that and then taking action is the height of manliness.

8 There is no end to the ideas that arise in the mind,
but it is wise to hold them back in your throat and not speak.
It is astute to welcome your heartfelt enemy
with a feigned smile and not be belligerent immediately.

9 People may tell you things that you find disagreeable,
but take care to conceal your feelings so they are not apparent.
A shrewd man fulfills even his desire for food or wealth
with the subtle power of clever speech and crafty means. [314]

10 Do not bear grudges against evildoers; it is possible they will
change.
Do not praise good men; it is hard to know what they will
become.
It is improper to deliver an edict based on what others say
without having critical information about what has befallen
them.

11 As there is no certainty that any activity can be completed,
do not be quick to volunteer, keep your thoughts hidden inside.
If you love your children and relatives too much, they develop
bad habits.
If you hate your enemies too much, they will do the same to you.

12 If you tear down your friends a lot, they will resent it eventually.
If you scold your servants a lot, attendants will be hard to find.
If you are very harsh to your followers, they will be heartsick.
If you are often contemptuous of your friends, they will be vindictive.

13 If you set a bad example to others, it cycles back to you.
Do not quickly express hostility; keep enmity in your thoughts.
Do not praise your friends; keep your love in your mind.
You may think badly of someone, but externally speak nicely.

14 It is difficult to subdue enemies with direct confrontation,
so resolve to complete your objective in various ways:
On meeting, speak with a smile and the rest will go smoothly.
Speak of significant matters appropriately and gracefully.

15 It is difficult to amass resources through avarice;
so expend a hundred to get a thousand. Increase the scope of your love.
If you point out children's faults, they benefit later.
If you stop craving acclaim, you are sought after in the end.

16 It is noble to hold your desires inside and act for the common good.
Make your own decisions; do not be influenced by women's advice.
Do not make ignorant men advisers or grant power to evil men.
Do not explain discussions to men unauthorized to confer.

17 Do not put those who stir up trouble into your council.
Query those who are wise, aged, experienced, and sympathetic.
Do not present your final position for a while; things may change.
Give a lot of careful thought to advice to reduce lapses and gaps.

18 Using others' lives as an example, analyze them closely.
Three things lead to disaster: refraining from risk on seeing minimal gain,

not paying attention to disrepute, and craving pleasure.
Nobles adapt to the times, so it is not right to demean them.

19 If a vulgar man is promoted, he becomes inflexibly pompous.
Do not discount a wise man; those with good qualities are rare. [315]
Do not make the populace your enemy; attract them as friends.
Neither promise nor begin something that cannot be achieved.

20 Be discreet; do not reveal yourself to men greedy for wealth.
Do not trust those who are intemperate or promote intrigue.
Keep private matters secret from those who talk too much.
Avoid ties to short-tempered men who have no sense of humor.

21 Do not insist on arguing with someone who is dishonest.
Do not delegate to someone who does not listen or carry through.
Do not assign undoable tasks. Do not be frustrated with the ignorant.
If you demand too much thanks, you will lose the affection of others.

22 Even relatives stop liking you if their losses are too great.
Do not take pleasure in the suffering of others, it will come back to you.
Do not flaunt your happiness, others will pay that back.
Do not regret how bad advice turned out; henceforth be careful.

23 Pointless antagonistic speech draws forth enemies.
Think for a while to understand the intentions of others.
A clever person has great ability to attain his goals independently.
When you attain a high estate, reduce your arrogance and pride.

24 Make your subordinates happy when they are utterly obedient.
Do not do just anything; measure and reflect on the pros and cons.

When in charge, minimize personal desires and have regard for the collective.
Protect your dependents with imperceptible force.

25 Do not start whatever you think of; take it up later.
Employ lenient and harsh measures to achieve your goals.
Do not believe whatever is said is true; analyze it well.
Give people tasty food; hold choice treasures for yourself.

26 Restrain your tongue from speech that cuts men to the quick.
Do not focus on your enemies' wealth, but do not forget it either.
Stop wrinkling your nose at bad smells, grabbing for delicious treats,
and pursing your lips and averting your eyes as soon as something is unpleasant.

27 Effort in pointless activities will tire you out.
Do not shrink from killing or beating when really necessary.
Do not shy away from levying taxes and spending.
Do not undertake things that torture your subjects for no reason.

28 Assuming you know someone as soon as you meet,
trusting someone as soon as you are acquainted,
smiling immediately when something pleasant comes to mind,
and grimacing when it does not are all naïvely childish.

29 Angry men carried away by anger are unwise and end up in ruin.
Loving people carried away by love are unwise and end up resentful.
Scholars carried away by learning are unwise and end up being foolish.
Monks carried away by respectability are unwise and end up irresolute.

30 The exalted carried away by greatness are unwise and end up low.
There may be truth in the remarks of others, so investigate their words.

Charm others by relaxing them and speaking nicely and pleasantly;
after this method uncovers their faults you can defeat them. [316]

31 No one understands without an explanation: speak slowly.
Even children will not listen if you are not intense: scold appropriately.
Who can know anything without being taught: instruct properly.
Even relatives will not attend you if you are not generous: give a few presents.

32 Always going back to get more will exhaust benevolence;
it is smart to not annoy a benevolent person.
Do not provoke a foe whose neck is already in your yoke.
Do not cast off the weak, for you do not know who will help you.

33 The best servants always do what they are requested to do.
Someone who knows naught of lies or deceit is sought after in the end.
Speaking little and being trustworthy are the best good qualities.
If you boast too much of what you have done, your work is little appreciated.

34 Allying with tight-fisted men who have big mouths is disastrous.
Do not expose the shortcomings of conceited men in high positions.
Do not consult mercurial men who have evil thoughts.
Be wary of the danger posed by soft-spoken malevolent men.

35 Forsake repeating groundless rumors again and again.
The rich who know how to use their wealth prosper in future.
Economizing a little, without deprivation, reduces your misery.
Being able to endure suffering, even poverty, makes you a man.

36 A wealthy man should not pretend to be poor; everyone will know.
A thug should not proclaim his magnificence; he will be ridiculed.

It is better to have enemies who feel embarrassed and chagrined
than to put your hopes in relatives who never blush with shame.

37 Intelligent friends and neighbors who can keep secrets
are better than relatives and consorts who cannot be trusted.
It is more satisfying to teach one intelligent student
than to be the instructor of many who lack good qualities.

38 It is nicer to have one servant with dignified good behavior
than to be the lord over many who do not listen to what you say.
Do not let an inveterate thief join your inner circle.
There is a risk of mistaking cautious, smart people for baffled men.

39 There is a risk of mistaking those of little intelligence for clever men.
There is a risk of mistaking the incapable for those concealing their excellence.
There is a risk of mistaking the overly confident for those with little gravitas.
There is a risk of mistaking the good-natured for those lacking discrimination.

40 There is a risk of mistaking honest men for simpletons.
There is a risk of mistaking a hypocrite for a virtuous person.
There is a risk of mistaking a true renunciate for a charlatan.
There is a risk of mistaking a good faker for a skilled person.

41 Thus in order to accomplish your goals in this life
know the pros and cons of what should be done and avoided
and then take care to embrace the strategies of governing
through various courageous, skillful, and heroic ploys. [317]

42 However, after you have finished enjoying all the heavenly
and human luxuries of Brahmā, Indra, and world emperors,
are you confident that you will not be born once again
as kindling for hell fires on scorching iron ground?

43 Even though the sun and moon illuminate the world,
after your good karma from the past is used up
you will rise from bed in impenetrable darkness.
Groping about with your hands, your tears will flow.

44 They touch you with cloth soft as lotus petals,
but lovely girls cause irritation to your body.
Who can bear to be burned by the blazing fires
of a crematorium along with their corpse?

45 A great merchant may have rivaled Vaiśravaṇa
with goods from his travels to the land of jewels,
but he sighs *alas* after rebirth in the realm of hungry ghosts,
where it is natural to starve for food and thirst for drink.

46 Life is but a lightning flash, even for someone counted
among the brilliant and courageous who is amassing
increasing wealth and power to subdue enemies and protect
friends.
What is the use of happiness that is just a dream?

47 Our spiritual teacher, the son of Śuddhodana,
who never even considered telling a lie,
taught that the nature of life and death in samsara is misery.
If you think about it this way, your heart will shatter into bits.

48 The method to enter the abode of liberation,
never to return again to this misery that is difficult to bear,
is to act appropriately after considering actions and their effects.
A wise man takes up the practices of the three trainings.

49 It is hard to see buddhas and bodhisattvas directly.
So offer clouds of various offerings—flowers, incense,
lamps, heavenly food, sounds, hanging banners, and so on—
to representations of their body, speech, and mind.

50 It is very important to collect a vast amount of merit.
Merit is greatly increased by the three spheres of action

encompassing the ten Dharma activities—venerating the sangha,
possessing the three trainings, studying the Buddha's teachings,
and so on.[328]

51 Give aid to all beings living in destitution: [318]
sustain the poor and ill with clothing, food, and medicine,
and give the gift of protection from fear by saving the lives
of animals bound for slaughter and evil men condemned to
death.

52 The primary causes for obtaining a good life as a god or human
are the easy, undemanding eightfold ethical rules of the path.
You should take and correctly keep these commitments and vows
on the full moon, new moon, and eighth days of the month.

53 Your mind will not be disturbed if you put on the armor
of not caring a bit about harsh words used as weapons.
Strive to practice this technique that prevents the destruction
of your roots of virtue and increases virtues accumulated earlier.

54 It is difficult to accomplish any virtuous action properly
when under the influence of indolence, laziness, or apathy.
If you make an effort with intensity and great determination,
even extremely difficult actions will be accomplished effortlessly.

55 If you practice uninterrupted, continuously stable concentration
that remains fixed without distraction on your focus of
attention—
for example the Buddha's form—first you suppress the manifest
afflictions
and then you acquire the concentration uniting a serviceable
body and mind.

56 No phenomenon is ultimately found to be anything other than
a mere conceptual designation dependent on its basis of
designation.
The Mādhyamika path of dependent origination
is the weapon of wisdom that cuts the root of cyclic existence.

57 Always rely on Guhyādhipati (Vajrapāṇi), who eliminates Māra and
his hordes,
and on the indivisible guru and protector Six-Armed
(Mahākāla).
They are your refuge for this life, the bardo, and your next life.
Remembering them destroys the army of death and grants
immortality.

58 Moreover, great kings of men with dominion over
the sky, the earth, and all in between are praised as supreme
for enacting the means to benefit the teachings and living beings
rather than doing their own solitary religious practice.

59 The great lords of everything under the sun
with good intentions of mutual affection and love
augment good government to make all their subjects happy
and bring contentment to the provinces over which they rule.

60 The Buddha's boundless compassion extends to all beings.
Likewise the perfect Dharma is completely impartial.
The tenets of Buddhism that our forebears spread
from ancient times are extremely propitious.

61 The Dalai Lama with the name Sönam,
who went to the great Mongolian empire of the north
as the religious preceptor for the Dharma king Altan,
made the Yellow Hat sect prevalent to this day.

62 For that reason, if you esteem the precious teachings
of Tsongkhapa, who is inseparable from Mañjuśrī,
you will always be guarded by Dharma protectors—Mahākāla,
Kālarūpa, Palden Lhamo,[329] and so forth—
and your power and happiness will increase. [319]

63 Your paternal ancestors united the two forms of ethics
suppressing thousands of kings to make the nature of this vast
realm soft as silk.
By doing what is necessary to practice the six perfections

your ultimate aims for this life and the next will naturally be
achieved.

64 I have no skill in what to do and avoid religiously or temporally,
so in that way my words are like a parrot's chatter.
Although my speech is scorned by scholars, my good intentions
are faultless and as brilliantly white as the autumn moon.

65 From the merits thus created, O lord of men clad with heavenly
garb,
may your queens, sons, ministers, and subjects be loyal and
steadfast;
may your dominion, glory, and wealth be like Vaiśravaṇa's;
and may your reign be equivalent to a golden age.

Thus when Khalka Tüśiyetü—the adamantine king who is a descendent of Genghis, the mighty lord empowered to rule by the mandate of heaven—came to the land of snows to make offerings to the Three Jewels and take them as his supreme refuge, he requested that I compose this garland of pearls of advice that brings together the two norms of spiritual and wordly conduct.[330] In compliance with that entreaty, I, Ngawang Losang Gyatso Jikmé Gocha Thupten Langtso Dé, a custodian of the Three Baskets born in the lineage of Sahor kings, composed this text at the great palace of Potala. The scribe was Terapa Phuntsok Wangpo from the Chongyé region.

7. A Treatise on Trees[331]

Gungthang Tenpai Drönmé

May there be true happiness!

1 I bow to the Buddha, a wondrous tree:
the root of your precious mind is firm,
your two magnificent collections are expansive branches
bending under the excellent ripe fruit of the three bodies.

2 For yogis to whom every perception appears as a metaphor,
there is an abundance of spiritual instruction.
In clearings within densely forested valleys,
there is no end to the masses of leaves.

3 When you depend on a wish-granting tree
everything you need and desire showers down like rain.
Similarly, when you rely on a holy spiritual friend
the excellent collections are completed naturally.

4 A person who has no respect for his teachers
may know a hundred texts, but they will be of no use.
A dry branch may be put in water and left for a hundred years,
but it can never sprout leaves.

5 Even just a single verse will benefit
someone with faith and a good nature.
Even just a sprinkle of rain
causes a tree seedling to flourish.

6 Thorn bushes and poison plants
are unwanted but cover the ground.
Those born in lower rebirths bereft of freedom
are beyond count, like particles of earth.

7 A white sandalwood is a wondrous tree;
to find one in the world is mere chance.
An excellent life with complete leisure and fortune
is found once in a million; this just cannot be denied. [322]

8 If you do not extract the essence of being human,
your life is no different than the life of an animal.
If you do not taste the fruit of the mango tree,
how is it different from a castor-oil bean?

9 The color, leaves, fruit, flowers, and so forth
of even a single plant change over time.
The drama of birth, aging, sickness,
and death changes moment by moment.

10 Leaves may be on a tree for a long time,
but once scattered they cannot be rejoined.
Lovers may have been together for a long time,
but one day they will part forever.

11 Chopping, cutting, and sawing a tree
quickly tires out a woodsman.
Even though they work for eons,
the hell guardians never get tired.

12 Until you have eliminated nonvirtue
you will experience misery without cease.
As long as there are poisonous seeds
poisonous leaves will grow; it is a natural law.

13 Someone who goes for refuge to the Three Jewels
is not enervated by samsara or nirvana.

A person who takes shelter up a large tree
cannot be harmed by vicious carnivores.

14 Sheltering under a tree with rotten roots
is a sign of being a fool.
Alas, those who take refuge in people
who are sunk in samsara are deluded.

15 There is never confusion about the fruit
grown from poisonous and medicinal seedlings.
It is impossible for virtuous and nonvirtuous actions
to give rise to each other's result.

16 Karma accumulated since beginningless time
does not wither away even after a hundred eons.
A palm seed may be dry for a hundred years
but will grow if it comes in contact with moisture. [323]

17 A banyan tree matures from a tiny seed
into a leaf canopy spreading over a league.
The result obtained by giving just a morsel of food
can be to become a universal monarch.

18 The gorgeous things here in cyclic existence
have not a bit of meaningful essence.
A plantain tree trunk is suffused with water
but has no core anywhere from top to bottom.

19 Even a tree that has grown for a hundred years
will topple down when its time has come.
After ascending to the peak of existence
you can go once again to miserable lower realms.

20 You can eliminate the bitter taste of gentian
if you douse it with sugarcane juice.
By really practicing the truth that is the path
you eliminate the origin that is the root of misery.

21 A delightful arbor house is made
by uniting pillars, beams, and rafters.
The holy palace of liberation comes to be
by uniting the three higher trainings.[332]

22 From time immemorial a *jandu* has grown from
a *jandu* seed and produces another such seed.
If you have been born in samsara beginninglessly,
is there anyone who has not been your parent?

23 The heavy packs of a hundred horses and oxen
can be hauled in one great wagon.
None of the śravakas and pratyekabuddhas[333] can lift
the load gracing the shoulders of bodhisattvas.

24 An ordinary tree's fruit is gone after it is harvested;
but a wish-granting tree's fruit is inexhaustible.
Ordinary virtues are used up by enjoying their results;
but the virtue of bodhicitta increases ever more.

25 People are attracted to a tree
that is laden with ripe fruit.
The glorious ones who give selflessly
fulfill the wishes of everyone.[334] [324]

26 The foundation of high rebirth and liberation
is nothing other than ethical discipline.
The foundation of branches bent low with fruit
is simply the trunk of the tree.

27 Responding to a thorn that has pricked you
by hitting it with your fist is a cause for ridicule.
Responding in anger to someone who harmed you
is nothing but the cause for your own ruin.

28 If you do not slacken your effort on the causal stage
every good quality will arise on the resultant stage.

If you do not deprive its roots of moisture
leaves and fruit will flourish at the treetop.

29 When a tree is shaken by a great wind
its fruit falls down to the ground. Likewise,
a mind that wavers because of lethargy and agitation
will lose its object of meditative concentration.

30 From perfect meditative absorption
qualities like clairvoyance and so forth arise.
When a tree trunk endures without damage
flowers in full bloom sway as its crown wreath.

31 Brandishing a wooden sword in battle
will make your enemy joyfully celebrate.
Alas, it is astonishing to want to sever
samsara's root with wrong and limited views.

32 Excellent white sandalwood
relieves the physical suffering of fever.
The right view with the nectar of compassion
eliminates the manifold illnesses of the three poisons.

33 Insects that are born in trees
consume that very same tree. Likewise,
wisdom that is born from attachment
will pacify the ill effects of desire.

34 Treating a dry plank with moisture
changes it to the color of lapis. Similarly,
clear light purifies ordinary appearances,
and they arise as heavenly pure forms. [325]

35 Trees with fully leafed-out boughs
offer completely cooling shade.
Buddhas have attained every good quality
and so are the protectors of all living beings.

36 Thus, from the *Treatise on Trees*,
the section presenting the Dharma is complete.
Now I shall explain some worldly norms,
so please listen with ears wide open.

37 The glory of righteous rulers
brings even enemies under their sway.
The fragrance of trees growing in Malaya[335]
is a messenger that summons bees.

38 One day even servants will not rally around
an evil ruler who torments his subjects.
A wooden staff can scatter a heap of peas,
but peas will never stick to the staff's edge.

39 How can a great king remain in power
if he is not respected by officials and citizens?
How can a royal palace come into being
if its beams are not supported by pillars?

40 A good ruler's kindness increases
his subjects' influence and power.
When supported by a huge tree
a vine's tip can reach for the sky.

41 If you lean on a thorn tree for support
the pain of being deeply pierced arises.
When you rely on a wicked person
only misery will arise in the future.

42 Increasing happiness among the populace
is the mark of a truly great ruler.
A wide crown of spreading branches
is the lovely ornament for a tree's root.

43 A ruler whose people's prosperity wanes
is a source of shame even if he is rich himself.

No matter how thick a tree trunk may be,
it is naked if there are no branches and leaves. [326]

44 People who rest at the base of a rotten tree
have no ease throughout the day and night.
The servants and retinue of a wicked chief
are also constantly tormented by anxiety.

45 Servants and retainers flee from an evil ruler
but are drawn to a good leader even if he sends them away.
Honey bees that avoid thorn trees
circle around mango trees even if driven away.

46 A ruler may act kindly when he is new
but later impose taxes that are hard to pay.
Although a tree may protect you from rain,
later heavy streams of water drip from it.

47 A tree shades everyone equally.
The sun and moon illumine everything alike.
Rain from a cloud falls on everyone the same.
A king's laws are the same for everyone.

48 A ruler may be good, but if his court is malicious
it is difficult to come into his presence.
Who would stay near a sandalwood tree
if a venomous snake is coiled around it?

49 There are said to be four types of mangos:
ripe or unripe with respect to inside and outside.[336]
There are many divisions of humans too:
decent or indecent in both thought and deed.

50 A wise person with every good quality
is self-disciplined, peaceful, and without conceit.
Resplendent with its load of clusters of fruit,
a tree stands with its crown bent down.

51 Why do people without any good qualities
hold their heads high with pride?
Trees that have no ripe, juicy fruit
stand erect; it is a natural law.

52 If someone has no innate good qualities,
what use are their external pretensions?
Can a desiccated tree without boughs and leaves
be pretty even if crowned with a diadem? [327]

53 Someone who is idle when it is time to study
has ambitions for mastery that will bear no fruit.
When blossoms are carried off by frost
there is no hope for fruit on the trees.

54 If someone lacks the aptitude of intelligence,
even high status is a source of embarrassment.
A lion that is carved out of wood
may look terrifying, but is inconsequential.

55 If wood has no sweet fragrance,
saying "It is sandalwood" is but a lie.
If someone's actions do not accord with pure behavior,
their claims of holiness have no significance.

56 A rogue will engage in low-class behavior
even if he is placed on a king's throne.
A banana tree grows upright
but its leaves hang downward.

57 Teak wood can be cut into a hundred small pieces
but will not lose its naturally sweet fragrance.
No matter what problems weaken a holy person,
can he ever lose his natural goodness?

58 When you put juniper needles in a fire,
their sweet scent intensifies and spreads.

Inflicting harm on holy people
elicits their greatness in response.

59 Even if a holy person lives in seclusion,
the gods will proclaim his high repute.
Sandalwood grows on the southern mountains,
but its fragrance spreads on the wind.

60 Even if you straighten a crooked board,
it will warp when exposed to moisture.
Even if a bad-natured person reforms,
in certain circumstances he reveals his true nature.

61 A person with few brains and a bad character
is of no use even if he has knowledge.
Flowers on plants with poisonous roots
may be lovely, but who needs them? [328]

62 Pillars made of sandalwood and juniper
are equally able to support crossbeams.
People with fortitude, whether rich or poor,
are the same when it is time to take action.

63 Even if people have equal power and wealth,
their character is known when they are assigned a task.
Even if a log is equally thick throughout its length,
when thrown into the water you can tell top from bottom.

64 Even in foreign lands a knowledgeable person
is in demand and will be honored by everyone.
A tree that has grown in a forest
will function as a tree elsewhere too.

65 Cotton fluff borne off by the wind
settles in valleys, not on mountain tops.
An unintelligent person roaming distant lands
falls to a debilitated state in the end.

66 It is very easy to become enveloped in flaws;
developing good qualities is not the same.
It is easy to set fire to a tree;
dividing a river into many streams is hard.

67 When two disreputable people become friends
eventually they ruin themselves and each other.
Rub dry sticks against each other
and both will be burned in the end.

68 Even a magnificent tree
is uprooted if submerged in water.
Even virtuous people of high quality
are dragged down by evil friends.

69 By grafting two fruit trees
hybrid fruit will grow. Likewise
when two smart people become friends
unprecedented good insights arise.

70 An elephant tears up a tree's roots
when it shelters in its shade.
Keeping evil servants and retainers close
damages the roots of your integrity. [329]

71 A bird may be honored by a treetop perch,
but it will cast droppings when it flies off.
You may support a wicked companion,
but he will leave evil behind when he goes.

72 No matter how much you help a bad person,
there is no hope for assistance in return.
Wood always nourishes fire,
but fire turns that wood into ashes.

73 Every person of intelligence and strength
will fulfill the needs of everyone, both high and low.

Just a single bow made of bamboo
can be used to shoot a thousand arrows.

74 Just having good ancestry is of little use
if you do not have wealth and prestige.
What use is a tall treetop
when it provides no needed shade?

75 If you have no roots of virtuous karma,
even hoarding will not reduce your poverty.
If a tree's trunk is without any moisture,
what's the use of wiping water on its branches?

76 You may wish to increase your wealth
by charging interest on loans, but the principal is often lost.
After you remove a tree from where it was grown
and replant it elsewhere, it usually dries up and dies.

77 Like the fruit on a mango tree
that grows hanging over a high precipice,
vast wealth that is not used to benefit
oneself or others is just a strange excrescence.

78 Those who desire to increase their fortune
are counseled to give a part of it away.
If you want a fruit tree's boughs to spread,
trimming off the top is a good method.

79 The vulgar do not gain even though they hoard;
the virtuous get rich even though they are charitable.
A tree will grow in a damp place even if you cut it;
but how can it grow in a dry place even if you plant it? [330]

80 The fruit on a tree next to a road
invites a shower of children's stones.
An evil businessman may have wealth,
but it is usually a summons for enemies.

81 Becoming wealthy is life threatening
for a person of meager merit.
Fruit on the top of a bamboo tree
is a sign of its imminent decay.

82 Sugarcane is cut down for its taste;
foxes are killed for their pelts;
merchants come together to get rich;
rebellions against kings are for the people.

83 Mark wood with lines first;
it cannot be changed after it has been cut.
You must consider what to do at the outset;
regretting afterward is the mark of a fool.

84 Who would boast of their cleverness
after achieving a goal just through luck?
Asserting that a dormant tree with shriveled leaves
is sentient is a doctrine of non-Buddhist traditions.[337]

85 Everyone tramples the dirty fallen leaves
of a tree that stands at a crossroads.
A person whose utterances are confused nonsense
is of little importance to anyone.

86 Even when an inferior person does something minor,
he lambasts others with boasts of his great kindness.
Even a small fire made from wet kindling
fills the entire kitchen with black smoke.

87 A tree where a snake had lived just once
inspires fear when it is seen later.
A person who steals and lies just once
is always doubted thereafter.

88 Even if a thorn is sharp,
its tip is blunted when it stabs a rock.

Envious criticism of superior people
is just a diminishment of yourself. [331]

89 In this degenerate era everyone will belittle you
if you are too submissive to someone unworthy.
Doesn't everyone use cotton wool for their cushions,
saying, "This is so soft and smooth?"

90 Although trees growing straight are beautiful,
a crooked one is better for a saddle-form.
Although a straightforward nature is good,
sometimes the Buddha taught in paradoxes.

91 Shooting an arrow without an arrowhead
is to send an inviting message to your enemies.
If you haven't the strength to conquer your enemies,
why make purposeless heroic speeches?

92 Having too much affection for your friends
often becomes a cause of resentment.
If you consume too much sweet sugarcane
it causes indigestion and sour belches.

93 An ax is the enemy of a tree,
but its handle is made from wood.
Although your enemies bring devastation,
frequently your friends created the root cause.

94 If you use the wrong technique to fell a tree
it will fall down on top of you.
You may excessively hate your enemies,
but this hatred often becomes your own nemesis.

95 You cannot bend dry wood,
but it becomes flexible if treated with moisture.
Your enemies may have abrasive attitudes,
but with skillful techniques you can pacify them.

96 The sun and moon cannot make an aśoka bud unfurl,
but the touch of a maiden's anklet makes them blossom.[338]
Some vulgar people who do not listen
to good advice can be subdued by insults.

97 Those living in jungles want nice houses;
those in nice houses prefer lovely groves.
The impoverished want to be monastics;
monastics drunk on luxury turn into householders. [332]

98 Even monkeys who are raised in a forest
will go elsewhere when the fruit is all gone.
When people become impoverished
even their cherished children run away.

99 Even the birds of the sky will circle
a marvelous forest grove for no reason.
Wherever peace and happiness abound
people gather even when not summoned.

100 If the fruit on a tree is well cared for,
it follows that the foliage is looked after too.
If you make an effort to practice the holy Dharma,
success in worldly affairs comes as a byproduct.

101 This discourse on all the ethical behavior
included in the two norms
using just the attributes of trees as similes
is an unprecedented feast for the wise.[339]

102 On an ocean of milk
Sarasvatī on her swan frolics in full voice.[340]
Waves of good advice from her mouth
swirl everywhere like vines.

103 This text is based on the path
of the wise sayings of glorious Sakya Paṇḍita;

the jeweled lasso of his renown
ropes around the lands of China and Tibet.

104 You may find lopsided texts in which
a simile key as long as a forearm
is used to unlock a point the size of a fist.
But for whom were they written, the wise or foolish?[341]

105 Those wishing to understand the two norms
should not focus on the simile—that is just a pointing finger.
They should look instead at the moon that is the reference
and see the wonderful pattern of an animal there!

106 May the merit of having worked well on this text
mature like the seed of a ficus tree,
with branches spreading over the ten directions,
bringing about the welfare of all beings.

This *Treatise on Trees: A Hundred Branches of Wise Sayings on the Two Norms* was composed by the Gungthang monk Könchok Tenpai Drönmé, spurred by impressions brought about by various sights while on the road to visit a medicinal hot spring.

8. A Treatise on Water[342]

Gungthang Tenpai Drönmé

1 May the ocean of the Buddha's teaching be triumphant!
Its depth of knowledge is beyond comprehension,
it is filled with wish-fulfilling jewels of compassion,
and it has successive undulating waves of supreme deeds.

2 Clear, untainted streams of water
ease the suffering thirst of creatures.
Likewise the nectar of fresh wise sayings
gives relief to people who are intelligent.

3 Pure water infused with perfume
is good however you use it: drinking,
bathing feet, sprinkling for purification, and so on.
Similarly, wise sayings please everyone.

4 Those who know the ethics of the two norms
accomplish their immediate and final objectives.
Similarly, captains who venture across the seas
are masters of everything requiring observation.

5 How can someone who cannot cross a small river
possibly swim across the ocean?
If you are ignorant of the norms of civility
how can you understand the truth of the Dharma?

6 Someone who is impartial and wise
picks up the good qualities of others.
A clean brook in a grassy meadow
gurgles along collecting flowers.

7 Even if evil people travel far and wide,
they collect only imperfect things.
Water flowing through eroded ravines
is tainted by the mud it drags along. [334]

8 Knowledge is difficult to master at first,
and if you are not attentive it easily declines.
It is hard to fill a vessel one drop at a time,
but when it spills it is all lost instantly.

9 If you can bear the burden of hardship,
nothing you undertake poses any difficulty.
Rain does not cause any additional problems
for someone who is already in the water.

10 Anything can be accomplished if you work gradually
and continuously strive without giving up.
Slowly but surely a flowing river
circles vast areas and moves on.

11 Large tasks are accomplished over time;
impatient efforts do not get you to the end.
A river flows slowly but goes great distances;
waves may be powerful but do not go far.

12 Even if others urge you to engage in a task,
if it is beyond your capacity it is not right to do it.
Why would someone who does not know how to swim
jump into the water even if others exhort him?

13 Water is for everyone to drink;
the sun and moon shine their lights for all;

the excellent ones are crown jewels for everyone;
the sublime Dharma is nectar shared by all.

14 A ship with large sails is the ocean's ornament;
a cloud-free moon is the sky's ornament;
a learned person is the teaching's ornament;
a heroic leader is an army's ornament.

15 Rulers and subjects with principled behavior
mutually promote each other's well-being.
The great ocean and rivers
come to assist each other in turn.

16 Evil masters and bad servants
cause each other to degenerate.
If you pour water into an unfired pot
both will be spoiled and ruined. [335]

17 Many clever, conceited, and powerful men
will wreck a realm's ruling council.
It is impossible for a house to be stable
on land that is waterlogged on all sides.

18 When a ruler and the populace are in harmony,
it is hard for foes to defeat them, but not if they are disunited.
Horses may find it difficult to ford a river,
but even sheep can cross one branched into many streams.

19 Although righteous kings collect taxes,
the revenue is for the care of the populace.
Huge clouds draw water from the great ocean
and with gentle rainfall sustain the earth.

20 A bad ruler seizes all the food and wealth of his subjects,
and yet he feels destitute and hungers for more.
The mare's mouth—an undersea volcano—
drinks in ocean water and is constantly ablaze.

21 You may constantly honor a bad ruler,
but he gets angry if he misses out on a single bribe.
Even if water has been boiling for many days,
it cools as soon as you take it away from the fire.

22 Does anyone enjoy being dependent
on an extremely brutal and arrogant ruler?
Fish and so forth do not dwell
in a very turbulent whirlpool.

23 All beings naturally congregate around
kind people who are able to help them.
All creatures seek to stay close by
the shore of a wish-granting sea.

24 You may obtain glory by associating with powerful men,
but even greater danger may develop from that.
The ocean is the source of precious gems,
but it is also the home of ferocious sea monsters.

25 New friends whom you do not know well
can cause your ruin if you trust them.
Even the bodhisattva, when he was a leader of geese,
was caught in a snare because of certainty about a new lake.[343] [336]

26 A dear friend with sensitive ears
is soon driven away by slander.
Water inextricably mixed with milk
can be separated by a swan's beak.[344]

27 The wise act after determining what is true or false,
whereas fools run after popular opinion.
The sound of a splash in the water
caused most of the wild animals to flee.[345]

28 The increase or decrease of someone's good behavior
determines whether they are virtuous or sinful friends.

Similarly, clear drinks are deemed to be medicinal or poisonous
based on whether they are helpful or harmful.

29 The angry frown of someone who loves you
is better than the bright smiles of evil friends and harlots.
White clouds may signify a drought,
but black rain clouds give life to farmers.

30 An intelligent, good-natured person
is sought after by everyone, whether high or low.
All creatures joyfully approach
a pond that has accessible banks.

31 Even people who have no reason to do so
rise up as enemies of coarse, arrogant people.
The proud and wild Ganges River
enraged Jahnu, so he drank her in one gulp.[346]

32 If you overconfidently bully the lowly
you will fall into an abyss of wretchedness.
Fish conceited because they swim in water
will die if they are up on dry land.

33 When ill-bred people become a little bit rich
they have as much arrogance as a king.
Small streams passing through narrow gorges
make roaring noises like the ocean's surf.

34 Unaware of the vast empire,
a provincial fool is self-important.
Haughty about the water in his spring,
the turtle died when he heard of the ocean. [337]

35 Common people are easily pleased,
but even when joyful they are easily shamed.
The headwaters of a small, short stream
can rise or fall in just moments.

36 Even if you lovingly care for coarse people
they are unappreciative and get hostile.
Even if lava is sprinkled with cool water
the molten rock boils even more and stays hot.

37 Even though good people may be maltreated
they are happy because they are calm and forbearing.
Water that has been treated by a mantra for scalding
may seem to be boiling, but when sprinkled is cool.

38 Even if you help shameless people
they will forget it as soon as the action is done.
When people reach the other side of a river
they abandon their boat without a qualm.

39 The actions of just one bad person
can bring a great empire to ruin.
It is said that the jump of a malevolent sage
split the Sita River into a hundred streams.[347]

40 People who have been misled by rough brutes
will not trust even holy beings.
Geese fooled by the moon's reflection on water
will not eat lotus roots even during the day.

41 Even if a bad person seems to reform,
when conditions are right their true colors show.
A river's channel may be altered,
but when it floods it reverts to its former course.

42 A noble person's nature does not change
whether they are high or low, rich or poor.
Whether water is cold or hot,
how can it eschew being wet?

43 Unruly people are more easily subdued
by firm insistence rather than advice.

Washing soda works better than plain water
to rinse stains out of your clothing. [338]

44 The flaws and virtues of embodied creatures
are revealed by their external behavior.
Similarly, hovering water fowl signify water,
and from smoke you know there is fire.

45 It is easy to see the flaws and virtues of others
but hard to see your own manner of behavior.
A lake reflects the moon and all the stars in the sky,
but its own depth cannot be seen.

46 Deceitful and hateful actions
may seem expedient but will end in ruin.
Even the course of a meandering river
flows downward, going lower and lower.

47 The birth of a wicked child assures the end of your line;
bad thoughts promise the exhaustion of your merit;
wild, desirous ideas guarantee self-destruction;
too much sediment promises to dry up a spring.

48 A fool may succeed by enduring many hardships,
but someone intelligent will get the credit.
Even if a lotus is grown on a mountain
water gets the credit for growing it.

49 Some men have no knowledge from scriptures or realizations,
but they deceive others by boasting of their sanctity.
The sound of thunder in the clouds is an ominous portent
of a dearth of life-giving seasonal rains.

50 The self-styled omniscient ones of this degenerate era
are duller than ordinary folk when they are learning.
Water from a natural hot spring is already hot
but takes longer to bring to a boil than cold water.

51 An indolent person may be a skillful religious orator,
but his mind is worse than a butcher's.
A mist that arises in winter
makes the area it envelops even colder.

52 Even if holy beings become destitute
they never act contrary to the Dharma.
Even if birds caught in a rainstorm are thirsty
they will not drink water that is on the ground. [339]

53 Engaging in a wrong means of livelihood conflicts
with a desire to strive to do spiritual practices.
Does irrigating with hot water from a hot spring
help people who want to grow flowers?

54 A great person may have trouble at one time,
but his grandeur will increase in the future.
A lake that is covered by a sheath of ice
will gradually emerge in the spring.

55 People with feeble intelligence and weak determination
may become prosperous, but it quickly vanishes.
A small pond whose inflowing water is cut off
will quickly dry up once again.

56 Lacking wealth but wanting expensive clothes and food;
not knowing the scriptures but assuming the role of a scholar;
not knowing how to swim but going across a lake;
such people knowingly purchase their own misery.

57 The magnitude of your power and intelligence
can never exceed the extent of your merit.
If a small pond exceeds the extent of its basin
its banks will break and it will naturally drain.

58 Before something of great importance occurs,
gather the means and make preparations.

If you have not built dikes beforehand,
it is hard to channel a river overflowing its banks.

59 You ruin yourself and it is not heroic
to daringly plunge into pointless activities.
To do so is to be like the lion who died
because he lunged at his reflection in a well.[348]

60 Act in a gentle and easygoing manner
even when you wish to subdue your enemy.
Look how herons move stealthily
to catch fish and other creatures.

61 Ill will toward others more fortunate
will destroy your own store of merit.
If you jump into a powerful torrent
you commit suicide but do not hurt the water. [340]

62 Therefore strive to cultivate good qualities
if you want a way to overcome your enemies.
The way to cross a great river
is to build a boat while still on land.

63 If your merit and karma have not degenerated,
enemies alone cannot vanquish you.
If a spring does not dry up on its own,
it cannot be stopped even if buried under earth.

64 Wealth and poverty, success and failure, high and low status:
these differences are the result of prior karmic deeds.
From the churning of the great circle of ocean
the strata of peaks, valleys, and other environs were formed.[349]

65 Very often wise people are poor
and fools are endowed with wealth.
Ponds filled with muddy sediment
teem with frogs, tadpoles, and insects.

66 A hero is one in a hundred;
a wise man is one in a thousand.
Gold comes from Lake Manasrovar's water;
and jewels come from the great ocean.

67 People who do not have intelligence
may acquire wealth but not know how to use it.
They are like dogs; even if they are thirsty
they lap stream water but do not drink in gulps.

68 Wealth that is not used to help yourself or others
is the same as not having any assets at all.
If an extensive plain has no water,
everyone shuns it, saying, "It is a desert."

69 Those who wish to increase their possessions
must know how to give a little bit away.
If you draw water from a well its flow increases;
if left alone, the well silts up and becomes dry.

70 Ignorant fools may have tremendous wealth,
but it is nothing but a cause of misery.
Lakes surrounded by golden mountains
are always under cover of gloomy shade. [341]

71 The wealthy must accrue merit;
it is easy to decline when merit decreases.
Even if a tree has extensive branches
it will dry up when deprived of water.

72 Powerful merit and a virtuous mind
are mutual causes for good fortune.
Water increases rain, and rain increases water;
they enhance each other in turn.

73 Whether someone talks a lot or says little,
you know its significance when put into practice.

Whatever the extent of a river's width,
you will know its depth when you go across it.

74 A master establishes a tradition of good deeds
so it is easy for others to follow in his footsteps.
Once an excellent horse has created a trail
even dogs can follow it along later.

75 Wise people have equanimity toward all others;
desire and hatred fill the eyes of the prejudiced.
It is easy to carry a full vessel
but those half full often wobble.

76 Someone who says whatever comes into his mind
is said to lack credibility and is belittled by all.
Even children can go across
a stream that babbles along.

77 Everyone should deal carefully with people
who smile, say little, but cut to the quick.
It is difficult to assess the depth of a river
that is in full and silent flow.

78 Dispel evil thoughts as quickly
as lines drawn on water disappear.
Virtuous promises should be held
as firmly as if carved in stone.

79 When your intent is good
worldly actions become the practice of Dharma.
Water drawn up an aqueduct by a waterwheel
can reach the peak of a high mountain. [341]

80 If the Three Jewels and karma are your primary focus
you will accomplish whatever you desire.
When the king of gods makes it rain
the harvest will be marvelous.

81 We have now reached the end of the chapter
of worldly norms, wandering through Brahma's matted hair.[350]
In order to wash away the stains of the two obscurations,
I will guide you along the path of holy Dharma.

82 The best of the seven varieties of water
is water from snow on mountain peaks.
Likewise, the unmistaken, faultless Dharma
must come from the speech of the Conqueror.

83 Complete and error-free instructions
that are organized as three successive paths
of vast and profound practices come from him.
This is refreshing water offered to the fortunate.

84 Nevertheless, when it degenerated over time
the guru Mañjuśrī illuminated it,
just as Viṣṇu in the form of a fish drew forth
the four Vedas that were submerged in the ocean.[351]

85 Who would enter a counterfeit path
when they encounter teachings like this?
Who would dig a well for brackish water
right next to the heavenly River Ganges?

86 Unfortunate people with little intelligence
are duped by claims of profundity and go wrong.
Animals confused by a mirage of water
experience pointless suffering.

87 To enter the path of the Dharma,
you first rely on a spiritual friend.
The first task of those wishing to cross the sea
is to seek out a skilled sea captain.

88 Your guru is the root of all good things:
both mundane and supramundane.

All the vegetation and grain in the world
stem from the kindness of Lake Manasarovar's nāgas.[352] [343]

89 You become a suitable vessel for the holy Dharma
by eliminating pride and pacifying yourself.
Rivers do not stay on high ground,
they meander through valleys below.

90 You may not understand all the Dharma at once,
but whatever you do understand will be useful.
Even though you do not drink up a whole river,
whatever you drink will slake your thirst.

91 If you do not put your vast learning into practice
it will not benefit your mind.
Although a rock may be in water for a hundred years,
the essential nature of stone remains dry.

92 A float is used in the process of learning to swim:
first held always, then sometimes, and then never.
Study, contemplation, and meditation are taught
as the three ways to rely on words and concepts.

93 Now that you have found the ship of human existence,
rely on the sails of study, contemplation, and meditation
to cross over the ocean of cyclic existence.
It will be difficult to find such a boat again.

94 There are infinite doors to birth in the six realms,
but a life with all eight types of leisure is very rare.[353]
Countless rivers may flow downstream,
but a mere few have eight special qualities.[354]

95 From the very moment of your birth
you approach the death lord's jaws without pause.
Rivers flow down to the sea,
never reversing even for an instant.

96 How can you expect to prosper and live happily
while in the grip of the demon of impermanence?
There is no chance at all for happiness
when you are caught in the jaws of a sea monster.

97 Resolutely stop mundane activities;
they never end no matter how you try.
One water ripple pushes and another one follows;
they never cease no matter how many go by. [344]

98 You may be very intelligent, strong, and skillful,
but time's messenger binds you against your will.
The dancing waves of a great body of water
are trapped below ice during the winter.

99 Negative physical, verbal, and mental behavior
will definitely result in a bad future rebirth.
Water falling from a mountain basin
continuously tumbles and surges off cliffs.

100 Then for hundreds and millions of years
you will roast and burn, but cannot die.
Continuous rain falling on volcanic magma
will boil for eons on end.

101 The refuge that saves you from that fearsome fate
is none other than the unerring Three Precious Jewels.
Surely someone swept away by a river
can be rescued only by a boatman.

102 The blessings of the Three Jewels are limitless,
but how can they protect you if you have no faith?
Although the ocean is vast, it cannot slake
the thirst of little birds sheltering from rain.

103 Do not rely on an ordinary person
who has not gotten across the swamp of samsara.

If you grab on to someone being swept away
by a river, both of you will drown.

104 It is important when relying on the precious Three Jewels
to strive to act in accord with the laws of karma.
If you trust the ship captain but do not get in the boat,
how can he ferry you across?

105 All the joy and sorrow experienced in the world
arises unerringly from the previous karma of beings.
It is taught that a bowl of water appears differently
to each of the four classes of migrating beings.[355]

106 Little acts of virtue and nonvirtue
add up to pervade your mind.
A boundless ocean circle is formed
by gathering together drops of rain water. [345]

107 Something may temporarily appear to be virtuous
but is often corrupted by motivation or dedication.
The supremely sweet water of the Ganges River
becomes bitter when it merges with the ocean.

108 Those blinded by the darkness of ignorance
and bound by the snares of karma
are swept away by torrents of desire,
moving through oceans of unbearable rebirths.

109 The salt water of desire is never satiating
no matter how much of it you drink.
So, like what a swan feels about a frozen lake,
feel disgust for samsara and resolve to become free.

110 You will journey to the land of liberation
by taking the ship of the three trainings
that liberates you from samsaric misery—
an ocean filled with the sea monsters of karma and afflictions.

111 In particular, the commitments of ethical discipline
should never be soiled by the stains of downfalls and infractions.
Always protect your vows with stable mindfulness,
just as the ocean is never compatible with corpses.

112 However, it is unworthy to work for your own aims
and forsake all living beings, your aged mothers.
Abandoning friends and relatives on a desert island
is not proper conduct for a ship captain.

113 The reflection of the moon in water has three qualities:
being on the water, unsteadiness, and unreality.
Likewise the three types of compassion for living beings
constitute the living core of the Mahayana path.[356]

114 The virtues held by the altruistic awakening mind
are inexhaustible and become the cause of great enlightenment.
Rose apples that fall into Lake Manasarovar
come to have the characteristics of pure gold.

115 Although a bodhisattva's actions are limitless,
they can be categorized as the six perfections.
Similarly, hundreds of streams flowing from mountains
merge into a single river down below. [346]

116 Bodhisattvas engage in superb generosity,
giving all their possessions along with that merit.
Rainfall nourishes all plants, protecting them
without any expectation of a return.

117 Pure ethical conduct removes all the impurities
of the moral downfalls and infractions.
Sand mixed with a *ketaka* gem[357]
cleanses the impurity of polluted water.

118 Anger is what incinerates all your merit;
patience is what will destroy that enemy.

Water is the corrective that destroys
the tongues of flame of an all-consuming blaze.

119 There is nothing that cannot be accomplished
if you do not cease consistently persevering.
We can see that mountain crags are eroded
by the constant dripping of droplets of water.

120 All good qualities shine in the clarity of concentration
free of the faults of lassitude and excitement.
Everything is plainly reflected by a clear lake
that is like a mirror of polished lapis lazuli.

121 All the suffering of samsara is cleared away
by meditating on the emptiness of all things.
Because the sage Agastya assessed all the rivers
by sipping them, they all became nectar.[358]

122 The vast ocean of Nāgārjuna's insight
robbed the realists of their self-confidence.
The awesome, dark ocean terrifies the childish
with its unfathomable depth and breadth.

123 To investigate profound ultimate reality
you must first identify the object of refutation.
To retrieve precious gems from the ocean
it is important to know what dangers there are.

124 In confusion you imagine "I am"
on the basis of designation—the group of aggregates.
A river may seem to have always been a torrent,
but it is just a collection of many small streams. [347]

125 When you logically analyze a referent object
you find nothing has any substantive existence.
When a stream is diverted into hundreds of canals
not even a droplet remains left behind.

126 Everything that was taught by the Teacher
leads to emptiness and dependent origination.
All the rivers on the vast earth
flow to and converge in the great ocean.

127 Bodhisattvas who have matured their own minds
care for disciples with the four ways of gathering.[359]
A captain experienced in traversing the ocean
leads others so that they too can obtain wealth.

128 Although the causal vehicle is a lengthy process,
you progress quickly with the methods of secret mantra.
A huge boat is difficult to draw across the land,
but when in the ocean it moves swiftly.

129 The secret mantra well taught by Vajrapāni
has powers that cannot be conceived of.
Just by uttering the invocation "Mother Ārti"
you can summon the water of the heavens.[360]

130 Union is the abode of the nāga king
amid the vast ocean of the Vajrayāna.
The stairway of the precious four empowerments
is a set of convenient steps leading to its portal.

131 Nevertheless it is the vows and commitments
that are the foundation of the two types of attainment.
If an ocean completely dries up,
where can a series of waves originate?

132 A yogi who has realized suchness
may enjoy sensuality but has no attachment.
Fish move in the depths of the ocean,
but the water does not drown them.

133 The faulty mental afflictions, desire and so forth,
are destroyed by taking the afflictions into the path.

Water removes water that has gotten into your ear;
the pain of something burned is alleviated by fire. [348]

134 The subtle and coarse generation-stage practices
purify life, death, and the intermediate state.
Similarly, the water offering of Bhagīratha[361]
washed away all the poisonous pollutants.

135 The conate great bliss of the four joys
intensifies the gnosis of the four emptinesses.
The continuous flow of the four rivers
makes the undersea volcano, Aśvamukha, blaze.

136 From the subtle innate mind and prāṇa
the body manifests like an illusion,
just as bubbles rise in pure water
and clouds appear in the clear sky.

137 Just as a reflection of the moon appears
in the dewdrops on every blade of grass,
every successive simile can exemplify
all the phenomena of samsara and nirvana.

138 Good worldly behavior up through
the stages of the paths of sutra and tantra
have been exemplified by a single analogy:
this is an ocean that transforms into good advice.

139 In the lake of the sambhoga-cakra
a swan with a melodious voice plays;
from her mouth come waves of wise sayings
roiling and moving in every possible way.

140 The new moon of wise sayings born from the lake of my thoughts
purges the darkness of worldly ignorance, and its cooling touch
relieves heartache.

May its virtue spread a lovely cloth of white light through the three realms,
increasing the reservoir of teachings and the good deeds and thoughts of beings.

Previously, to help plant good propensities in my own mind, I had written various treatises that might be counted among the works on sutra and tantra appropriate for our time. However, my *Treatise of Trees* spread widely, and it appeared to have attracted the esteem of many people. [149] Thus the Mongolian religious official Kalsang Dargyé, who comes from Barön Sunyi, is praiseworthy, and wears a garland of many good qualities, said that it would be wonderful if I could write a commentary on that treatise. After being urged again and again, as I began to write I realized the following: when it comes to the chapter on Dharma, there is no need write something separate from what is found in the Stages of the Path (*lamrim*) texts; and as for the rest, the text had been written in an easy language with analogies easily comprehensible by both the learned and the ignorant. So there seemed nothing that required further elucidation. If, however, an explanation were to be offered with quotations drawn from suitable sources, such as glorious Nāgārjuna's three works—*A Hundred Stanzas on Wisdom*, *Staff of Wisdom*, and *A Drop to Nourish a Person*—the *Chāṇakya Treatise on Kingship*, Masūrākśa's *Treatise on Norms*, Sūryagupta's *Treasury of Verse*, Vararuci's *Hundred Stanzas*, Kamalagupta's *Vimala's Questions and Answers*, the *Sakya Wise Sayings* (*Jewel Treasury*), as well as other sources like epistles and advice, such a work will be extremely heavy with words. So here I expanded a bit using the analogy of water that makes trees grow in order to supplement parts of *A Treatise on Trees*, thus making that text more complete. There the chapter on the Dharma is presented first, since the text is organized by hierarchy and importance. Here I wrote as a meaning commentary, so the text is arranged as steps proceeding upward and is organized sequentially.

This text, *A Treatise on Water: A Hundred Waves of Wise Sayings on the Two Norms*, was composed by the monk Könchok Tenpai Drönmé at the retreat site of Yiga Chözin. Bhikṣu Ratna Ānanda, who has the wisdom-eye to see the scriptures, acted as the scribe. May this work be the cause that illuminates the entry to virtuous activity for all living beings.

9. A Treatise on Wind[362]

Kyilsur Losang Jinpa

Oṃ! May happiness and well-being prevail!

1 I praise the wind of faith that stirs
the wish-granting tree—the Buddha—
whose loving compassion provides cool shade
equally and always to all embodied beings in the world.

2 To accomplish the two goals, I will let loose
the winds of the ethics of the two norms,
the means by which the two buddha bodies are actualized,
the state where the two accumulations are perfected.

3 Wise sayings perfectly phrased with good intent
are parables that appeal to others' minds.
Similarly, a breeze wafting over lotus groves
diffuses sweet scents that satisfy the olfactory sense.

4 Cultivate perceiving the positive and be a good friend
in order to be in harmony with all beings.
The moisture-laden chariot of the wind
is a pleasure the world over.

5 Whatever occurs—joy or sorrow, good or bad—
is the result of previously accumulated karma.
Mountains and surrounding lands gradually form
from amid water churned by the wind.

6 A great goal that is ultimately beneficial
can be achieved by patience and perseverance.
A wind blowing for thousands of years
makes the earth into a wind mandala.

7 It is better to shun negative actions
that do not benefit yourself or others.
During the snowstorms of winter
there is no point in planting seeds. [352]

8 No matter what activity you plan to engage in,
analyze whether success is possible or not.
When you plan to separate wheat from chaff,
do so after determining whether it will be windy.

9 If you supplicate and venerate the Three Jewels,
whatever you undertake will turn out as you wish.
The wind in autumn separates wheat from chaff,
accomplishing the goal desired by farmers.

10 Even though words have no weapons
they can slice a man's heart into pieces.
Even though the wind has no wings
our elders say that it flies through the sky.

11 Therefore renounce harsh words
and speak gentle words with a smile.
Please everyone—high, low, and in between—
but do not reveal your thoughts.

12 Do not disparage others, thinking,
"I doubt that they will hear this."
Those who care about us tell us,
"Talk is like a feather carried by the wind."

13 Talking about the faults of others
is the cause for your own ruin.

You can see that you will burn your face
by blowing outward across a fire.

14 Under the sway of these degenerate times
gentle, disciplined folk live among the coarse.
You can see that an evil wind carries off
soft cotton fluff amid clouds of dust.

15 The wicked crowd in and bring disaster
in the middle of those who act ethically.
After an evil wind enters through cracks in a wall
you can see how camphor is ruined.

16 When the low rely on noble people,
they are conveyed wherever they wish.
Similarly, scents carried on a fine breeze
spread to places far away. [353]

17 When an evil person obtains wealth
he displays various manners to others.
The honking of cranes is a bad omen
signaling the rise of a terrible wind.

18 No matter how much a noble person is praised
he does not develop the slightest degree of pride.
No matter how much the wind blows
the great ocean never vacillates.

19 A bad person's pride rises higher than Mount Meru
from the slightest bit of praise.
You can see that wind blowing over a desert plain
swirls up more dust there than elsewhere.

20 Even if the wise are brought low
can they ever cast off their true nature?
The color of a gold nugget will not change
even if it is melted in a fire pumped with air.

21 A minor criticism makes unintelligent people
suffer much more than others.
A candle placed out on an open plain
will be extinguished by a slight breeze.

22 Those with faith proclaim the good qualities
of noble beings among the masses.
The aromatic scent of white sandalwood
is spread near and far by the wind.

23 Most people in these degenerate times
are very hostile toward spiritual practitioners.
It is said that winds blowing from every direction
are inimical to white prayer flags.

24 Those who are studious and absorbed in practice
are wise and live in peace and moderation.
A pleasant breeze that is always cool
eases the misery of heat.

25 Those with intellectual ambition but no learning
have mental continuums even harder than a horn.
Everyone says that the wind from a cloudless sky
is more piercing than an arrow. [354]

26 Not studying when you are a student
but wanting expertise later is laughable.
There is no point in hoping for seasonal rain
from rain clouds dispersed by the winds.

27 What is the point if, no matter how much you study,
there is no improvement to your mind?
The wind always flutters a cloth curtain,
but you see that it never goes anywhere.

28 Even if you seek only happiness and wealth in this life,
if you practice the Dharma you will get them straightaway.

Similarly, wind that brings forth the rains
fulfills the farmer's wishes.

29 Even if you try, it is difficult to attain perfection
through a variety of meaningless actions.
Similarly, the wind pushes water into ripples,
forming and breaking them up over and over again.

30 Wealth and majesty adorn rulers;
teaching and composition adorn scholars;
strength, weapons, and armor adorn heroes;
wind and rain clouds are cooling adornments.

31 Just as most people refer to a last will and testament
as an example of something set forth on the wind,
I write this with purest intentions
to benefit those with clear minds.

32 Having finished a brief explication of advice
regarding the norms of worldly conduct,
now I will write a little about the system
that comes from the divine holy Dharma.

33 By engaging in proper, well-bred behavior,
you may obtain wealth and happiness in this life,
but seeing that their nature is unstable as the wind,
apply yourself to study, contemplation, and meditation.

34 The vehicles borne by the wind come from the activities
of the three secrets of the guru[363] who reveals the path.
He teaches so that others may obtain the ultimate harvest,
but there are many who perceive it as faulty. [355]

35 The noble ones transform others' minds with skillful means
when they exhort them to practice the Dharma.
When driven by the wind even inanimate trees
make various movements of dance.

36 The devout will speak publicly amid crowds
about their teacher's good qualities.
The sweet fragrance of lovely trees
is spread in ten directions by the wind.

37 It is said that a human life is as difficult to obtain
as it is for a tortoise to put its neck
through the hole of a yoke tossed about on the ocean
by winds that come from every direction.[364]

38 Therefore using this boat—a human life of leisure and fortune
adorned by the white banner of practice
and propelled by the wind of perseverance—
you should cross over the ocean of cyclic existence.

39 The supreme ārya Nāgārjuna said that
this fortunate life, a platform found just once,
is just like a butter lamp in a gale,
in that it is very easily destroyed.[365]

40 Like banks of clouds torn apart by the wind,
when we die we will leave behind
all our wealth, possessions, vehicles, and so on.
Then nothing but the holy Dharma can truly help.

41 Once you die you have no control
over where you will be born and where you will go.
You are carried by the winds of karma
to upper or lower realms: it is the same either way.

42 If you are born in the lower realms,
the suffering is having your body carved up into bits
by different types of blazing hot weapons and so forth.
It is like being a parrot overwhelmed by a gale.

43 To become free from that grave danger
you must seek refuge in the Three Jewels.

When a huge forest is engulfed in flames
stoppage of the wind is needed for help. [356]

44 Whatever pleasure and misery there may be
arises from having engaged in good or bad actions.
The wind mandala of the hard and solid earth
comes from the collective karma of living beings.

45 Because even a small virtue or nonvirtue
will yield a result of great joy or sorrow,
the powerful wind of devoted faith
rouses us to avoid evil and practice virtue.

46 The blazing flames of four powers[366]
whipped up by the winds of perseverance
burn the entire forest of downfalls and sins
accumulated from beginningless time until now.

47 Even if your riches in this life
rival the treasures of Vaiśravaṇa,
they have absolutely nothing at their core;
they are like the wind's victory banners.

48 The wise say sensual objects are poison
and the realms of cyclic existence
are like a pit of poisonous snakes
who eat the wind for food.

49 In the sky of the conceptual mind
dense clouds of desire and craving abound.
If a corrective wind does not destroy them
there is no way to freedom from samsara's fortress.

50 Therefore enter the grove of liberation
where wish-fulfilling trees are heavily laden
with the fruit of the three trainings
and are unshaken by the winds of desire for fame.

51 Firmly establish the root of the great vehicle
by having compassion for all mother sentient beings.
The stirring of gentle breezes
forms the wind mandala that supports the world.

52 Then, after casting away selfishness,
whatever you do will be for the sake of others.
The song of the Dharma is proclaimed
by breezes stirring the trees. [357]

53 Be courageous and lift to your shoulders
the huge load of bodhisattva practices.
Hundreds of millions of samsaric realms
are supported by one great wind mandala.

54 When joined with Mahayana aspiration,
your roots of virtue will increase limitlessly.
All the winds of space, on earth, and in between
increase without having any intention at all.

55 Generosity can attract all people:
the high, the low, and those in between.
The fame of someone constantly striving to be generous
spreads in all ten directions like the wind.

56 If you were to summarize all the bodhisattva practices
they would fall into the three precious ethical disciplines.[367]
Whatever has the nature of lightness and movement
is categorized as the element of air.

57 All the beings of the three realms may arise as your enemies,
but they will become friendly if you cultivate patience.
When the winds rise up to battle against a fire,
all the gusts come to be in aid of the fire.

58 When the great fire of perseverance blazes
owing to the strong wind of constant application,

the spreading light of perfect wisdom
consumes every bit of the fuel of laziness.

59 Clear and stable concentration will be achieved
when you are undisturbed by the winds of laxity and excitement.
Similarly, the moon is reflected on a clear lake
that is unruffled by winds from any direction.

60 You will continue to experience suffering in samsara
for as long as you do not stop self-grasping.
Similarly, your life force continues
until you stop breathing.

61 The sharp blade of the realization of selflessness
severs the roots of hundreds of faults.
It is like the fierce gales at the end of an eon
that destroy everything in this world. [358]

62 Then, if after entering the door of secret mantra
you hold as fundamental the protection of your vows,
with a pace as fast as the wind
you will quickly attain the state of union.

63 In order to purify grasping at ordinary appearances,
cultivate the pure appearance of divine pride
in the mandalas of inhabitants and their abodes
that are as beautiful as the wind's victory banners.

64 Through the power of meditation
the wind enters, abides, and dissolves in the central channel.
In the end the extremely subtle wind and mind
arise as the dharmakāya and rūpakāya.

65 Thus this composition of words
exemplifying the characteristics of wind
was produced as a result of seeing
Gungthang's *Treatise on Water*.

66 By churning the great ocean of that treatise of most learned
Könchok Tenpai Drönmé with the winds of critical intelligence,
and through the power of my past merits, I have found this treatise,
which sets forth every stage from the civilized worldly conduct to union.

67 From the power of the merit of endeavoring in this way,
may the advice on the two norms be proclaimed
throughout the entire world, spreading it like the wind,
and may everyone be able to follow these norms.

Having seen with my own eyes the *Treatise on Water* composed by Gungthang Könchok Tenpai Drönmé, and having heard that there are treatises on earth and fire composed by the precious teacher Namgyal Söpa,[368] I thought that if there were to be a treatise on wind in addition to these there would be a treatise on each of the four elements. For this reason I, the monk Losang Jinpa, the abbot of Kyilkhang College of Tashilhunpo Monastery, was motivated to write this *Treatise on Wind: Wise Sayings That Flutter the Flag of the Two Norms*, with the hope that it might give pleasure to those with intelligence and increase their desire to engage in practice by means of studying and contemplating these treatises. For whatever mistakes and errors may exist in this work, I seek the forbearance of the learned masters.

10. A Treatise on Earth[369]

Paṇchen Chökyi Nyima

1 You stand firm amid the ocean of the two collections
at the very top of the staircase of the four buddha-bodies,
jingling sun and moon earrings—the two aims.
Supreme sage, the greatest of mountains, please protect me.

2 I pray that any youth adorned with a garland
of blue lotus flowers—the mark of perfect intelligence—
on the ground of this human life so difficult to find,
will come to listen to this discourse.

3 The eye of intelligence is necessary to sift through
what should and shouldn't be done according to the two norms.
Similarly, a magnet is necessary
to separate iron filings from dust particles.

4 Just as earth's essence can be turned into pure gold
by cleaning away the stains of rust,
even those who have limited intelligence can become
more learned if they listen a lot to wise sayings.

5 No one but someone with great analytical wisdom
can distinguish right from wrong.
Is there any use for stones other than
a jewel that grants all your wishes?

6 Thus those who wish to be learned
should hold on to precious gems of wise sayings,
and, whether they be large or small,
wear them as jewels that beautify the mind.

7 Just as this great earth is the foundation
for every aspect of the world and its inhabitants,
perfecting all the many actions of the two norms
is dependent on meritorious virtue. [359]

8 Therefore the best of all refuges
are the sovereign wish-fulfilling Three Jewels.
Wearing them like a crown ornament
create the causes of merit by making offerings and so on.

9 It is improper to take up any activity
without inquiring and examining its purpose.
How could you purchase a precious gem
without seeing it first?

10 Our friends, whether good or bad,
influence all the behavior of most of us.
Through glasses tinted with color
a display of many varied hues will appear.

11 Therefore properly discriminate
between the types of friends.
Do what you should and shun what you should not,
just as mercury separates gold from iron filings.

12 Some people talk a lot and are very devious;
they act like your bosom friend as soon as you've met.
Discard jealous, rough, and conceited friends
like stones that were used to scrape off excrement.

13 Good friends are upright, sympathetic,
have capacious intelligence, delight in virtue,

have disciplined minds, and are tolerant.
Hold such people close to your heart, like gold.

14 When you first endeavor to do something
do not heedlessly follow the lead of others.
Consider your long-term goal and the effort required,
just as farmers do when they cultivate fields.

15 Things may appear to be similar,
but weigh each one's benefit or harm on its own.
Pure and adulterated gold are the same color,
but their actual natures are not identical.

16 Hold close to your heart and do not speak
about your important long-term goals for no reason.
Similarly, it is not appropriate to reveal
every precious treasure that you own. [361]

17 Just as farmers work hard,
grinding their bodies and speech into dust,
you must renounce fatigue and persevere
when working for an important aim.

18 When something desirable befalls you,
do not get distracted by its slight faults.
If you are unhappy about putting gold in a forge,
how can you engage in craftsmanship?

19 Even if a task is very difficult
it can be accomplished if you try.
You can see that even hard iron is made
into useful items by smelting and beating.

20 Even if someone's external manner is bad,
it is hard to know what good qualities lie within,
so do not hold them in low esteem.
Likewise, gold and silver lie hidden deep in the earth.

21 Do not trust someone greedy and discreditable
even if his external behavior seems proper.
If you befriend him you will quickly fall
like a tree growing over the rim of a crevasse.

22 Do not engage in inconsiderate behavior,
insulting people lower and worse off than yourself.
You can see that a man could lose his life
from being wounded by a small stone.

23 If you act without examining and investigating
whether the words of others are tainted by deceit,
you will come to ruin, just as we've heard in fables
that the three worlds were lost by a few steps.[370]

24 A person who merely aspires to fill his belly
without differentiating help from harm or good from bad
will be derided and rejected by everyone and
left behind like ground on which someone vomited.

25 Poor soil will not bring forth a harvest
even if you plow it many times. Likewise,
anything undertaken by someone lacking
courage and perseverance will come to naught. [362]

26 Some people display hostile behavior
immediately upon seeing their enemy.
Like children playing in the dirt,
their manners reveal a brainless, weak mind.

27 Instead, respond even to your enemies
with pleasantries and appropriate skillful means.
Even huge chunks of iron ore
can be broken down by controlled smelting.

28 However, when the right time arrives
you must dauntlessly do what is necessary.

Similarly, in order to split open a rocky mountain
you must put dangerous substances into use.

29 Moreover, if you disparage, revile, and so forth
everyone you meet—whether they be high or low—
they will be like boulders that are above you:
when pried loose they will fall on your head.

30 You will become hardened if you are too deferential
to inferior people with coarse minds and evil natures.
Similarly, you will be harmed if you walk on ground
where you might trample on poisonous snakes.

31 Just as you must prepare the ground
that will be the foundation of a new house,
to accomplish your goals you must rely
on a leader with courage and skill.

32 You will be virtuous if you stay close to the wise;
nothing but faults will come from the wicked.
Wish-granting jewels grant all you desire;
snake-infested ground will reduce you to ruin.

33 Even if you kindly help malicious people
they repay your kindness with harm in the end.
Although mice live in the ground,
look how they throw dirt around.

34 It is difficult to destroy mountains from the outside,
but they are easily damaged by springs from within.
It is amazing how sickness, faults, and deception
instantly bring down even powerful people. [363]

35 Someone wise, intelligent, and good-natured
repays those who gave them just a little help
with something far greater in return.
Like radiant gold they become ever more lovely.

36 You should ask for advice and place your trust
in no one but the intelligent, learned, and upright.
How could anyone argue that pure gold
is the same as other types of earth?

37 If someone is your enemy, even if they weaken
you must remain attentive and careful.
Look how irregular streams in little gullies
gradually erode the mountains.

38 You must be careful of swindlers
with impenetrable external disguises
that conceal their intent within:
they are brass with a veneer of gold.

39 Too much affection leads to ruin
even if it is for your beloved friends and family.
It is said that Rāvaṇa's head fell to earth
because he lusted for Sītā.[371]

40 No one will seek your company
if you continually say cruel words to others
because you are under the sway of anger.
Who likes rough and hard ground?

41 Even if a task is assigned to you by others,
commit yourself only after analyzing its feasibility.
In other words, who can successfully cultivate
fields that do not produce any crops?

42 It is unsuitable to heedlessly squander
even small items that you possess.
Similarly, even vast lands come to be
from a gradual aggregation of atoms.

43 When you are working toward an important goal
give freely without being chained by miserliness.

If you fill a treasury with precious things
but do not use them, they are someone else's riches. [364]

44 The various actions you engage in
owing to excessive scheming and great ambition
will be the basis of your own ruin,
just as it was for King Māndhātṛ.[372]

45 It is easy to see the faults of others, but to see your own
is as hard as finding treasure hidden underground.
Therefore examine yourself properly:
it is important to distinguish faults from good qualities.

46 Thus, on the basis of having engaged
in mundane activities without error,
assiduously cultivate the soil of the holy Dharma
for the sake of this life and your future lives.

47 Who would be willing to exchange for money
a jewel that fulfills all your needs and desires?
This human life that can bestow permanent happiness
will be a loss if you are distracted by minor pleasures.

48 Just as the five sorts of precious materials
are brought forth from the treasury of the earth,
the realizations of the ten grounds and five paths
are accomplished through this good human life.

49 Just as the roots of wish-granting trees
rest in the foundation of strong ground,
the door to access the precious Dharma
is only the art of poetic composition.

50 Good qualities cannot arise in those
who do not know to read and write.
How can fruit trees, flowers, and other plants
grow without the earth as a foundation?

51 Thus all who desire to become learned
should dispel fatigue and strenuously endeavor
to become literate, just as one must work hard
smelting and working ore to get refined gold.

52 You must rely on an experienced guide
when you venture into unfamiliar regions.
Similarly, properly rely on a spiritual friend
who teaches the Dharma's essence without error. [365]

53 Just as you examine the distinguishing features
of any place that you wish to travel,
never be satisfied with your effort to acquire learning
that discerns the ways to practice the Dharma.

54 Ground that is soaked in water
will soon collapse. Similarly,
this life does not last long, and then
we go on a path to one of the five realms.

55 Each step you take going down a road
gets you closer to your destination.
Likewise, as years, months, and days pass
you approach nearer to the Lord of Death.

56 It is difficult for anyone to help you
when the messengers of the Lord of Death
drag you away without your volition.
When the earth quakes, who can hold firm?

57 The only thing that helps at that time
is the precious gem of the holy Dharma.
It is the treasure that grants all your wishes:
focus on nothing other than that.

58 Therefore do not be entrapped
by superficial, adulterated muck.

Develop perseverance in the refined pure gold
of the excellent Dharma of the Ganden tradition.

59 If it's hard to complete even the smallest task
under the influence of laziness and procrastination,
how could you take into your hands the gem
that produces beneficial, lasting happiness?

60 Therefore from a young age
you should forsake frivolous things
and endeavor only in the holy Dharma.
Be like a firm mountain that never wavers.

61 You may think you will try when youth is past,
but a weakened body and faculties
cannot complete things properly.
It is hard to cultivate an overgrown thicket. [366]

62 When you proceed to the world beyond,
as a result of your former black deeds
you fall into a huge chasm miles deep
and experience the suffering of the lower realms.

63 You will be born amid tongues of flame
whose blaze encircles all four directions;
dragged to a red-hot iron ground,
you will be tormented by being scorched.

64 Some experience the feeling
of having flesh torn from their bones
in a place so frigid that the excruciating cold
even causes stones to crack open.

65 In a place in between the hell realms
some alternate between pleasure and pain, day and night.
The types of misery in the occasional hells
are akin to what you have done before.

66 Think about the state of being tormented
by the suffering of hunger and thirst
with no chance to enjoy even an atom of food
for a period of many long years.

67 How could you bear being an animal?
They are tormented in many ways:
wretchedly living in filth, underground, and in swamps,
eating one another, exploited, beaten, and so forth.

68 The precious Three Jewels are definitely
the refuge for all the beings who fill the three worlds;
they save us from the unbearable misery
of the lower realms as mentioned above.

69 It is unrealistic to expect that crops will grow
even in well-watered fields if you do not plant seeds.
Thus it is difficult to be saved if you do not create
the conditions of faith, admiration, and respect.

70 Thus if the sprouts of properly done good deeds
are nourished by the warmth and moisture
of prayers made with strong faith,
the fruits of high rebirth and liberation will ripen. [367]

71 Even the most marvelous treasures
of gods and men, on earth and in the heavens,
are sullied by the dust of birth, aging, sickness, and death.
How could they be anything other than that?

72 Craving for mundane affluence and power
becomes the cause for suffering to arise.
We hear that excessive desire for the earth's honey
is the way that leads to the pain of being stung.

73 Contemplate the twelve links of dependent origination
that are the way we revolve and go without control

through the vast expanses of the three worlds—
from the peak of existence to the lowest hell.

74 Recognizing that every place in samsara's three realms
is a platform on which hundreds of shortcomings arise,
become diligent about accomplishing the supreme path
that leads to the expansive space of liberation.

75 You should light the lamp of compassion
for all beings who have been your mother,
kindly nurturing you from beginningless time,
and who, because of suffering, live in the depths of darkness.

76 Even animals desire their own happiness;
but just having that is not sufficient.
Take up the practice of equalizing self and other;
it is the ground for accomplishing definite happiness.

77 Make an effort to produce bodhicitta;
it is the excellent alchemical elixir
that transforms the earth element of the impure body
into the precious gold of the three kayas.

78 Do not be tied up in knots of stinginess
for your piles of illusory property.
With the four precious types of generosity[373]
set out a treasure for the totally destitute.

79 Cultivate lasting happiness in the field
of pure ethical discipline. It is the foundation
from which every excellent thing grows:
high rebirth and the definite goodness of liberation. [368]

80 Even when pierced by the blazing weapons
of unending harsh words and beatings,
protect the state of your basic consciousness
by erecting the iron fence of patience.

81 Conjecturing that the thieves of distraction and laziness
will carry off the supreme wealth of your virtue,
you should bind shut the doors of your senses
with the long metal straps of perseverance.

82 When you focus your mind, do not stray from
whatever virtuous object you have chosen;
with mindfulness as stable as a mighty mountain
hold tightly to meditative stabilization.

83 Strive in the method that smashes into dust
the mountain of egoism—the view of the perishing collection—
with the thunderbolt of knowing the lack of true existence
that is free from all elaborations of dualistic appearance.

84 Although dreams do not truly exist,
they show signs of happiness and suffering.
Look how crops of dependent origination
ripen in the field of emptiness in the same way.

85 After training your mind on the common path,
be diligent in the means to establish
the stable pillars of the vows and pledges
that rest on the foundation of perfect empowerments.

86 Completely block ordinary conceptions
of the vast earth and all the things that it supports.
Strive in the supreme yoga of the generation stage
that makes every appearance arise as a mandala.

87 On the surface of the wall of pure ultimate reality
the brush of concentration brings into being
the Buddha's form, vividly glowing with the noble marks.
So endeavor single-pointedly to establish union.

88 Then pray to lead all sentient beings
who live on the ocean-clad earth

to the grounds of omniscient wisdom
by emanating in various ways. [369]

89 Even though my effort is not worthy of holy beings,
I composed this jewel garland of wise sayings
glowing with manifold lights of the two norms,
thinking it would be useful as an ornament for beginners.

90 From the merits of this action
having the power of a wish-fulfilling jewel,
may the stainless teachings of the Victor
flourish on earth until samsara ends.

In general, the recommendations assembled in collections of advice for mundane activities can be a cause for nonvirtuous actions; therefore offering such advice can become a basis for downfalls among those holding vows. Such activities are something to be largely rejected. Nevertheless I am following the model of past masters who wrote treatises conjoining the two norms. Specifically, most people seem to find it difficult to devote themselves to study and contemplation of the great treasuries of precious advice that are vast and deep—such as the *Stages of the Path to Enlightenment* and so forth—because of the pressures of this degenerate era and because they are influenced by their own mistaken actions that are contrary to those treatises. Because of their preoccupation with concerns of this life alone, most people appear to value texts belonging to this wise-sayings genre that present matters of worldly norms. So I was motivated by the thought that it would be possible to gradually shift their minds from that toward the Dharma. And on top of that, my attendant, bearing the name Lakṣmī, also made a request, saying, "Something like this is needed." Thus I, the Buddhist monk Dharmasūrya, composed this *Treatise on Earth: A Jewel Garland That Glows with a Hundred Lights of Wise Sayings on the Two Norms*. It was written at the temple at Wutai Shan, the pure land of glorious Mañjuśrī.

11. Khaché Phalu's Advice[374]

Oṃ svasti!

If you were to ask and I were to tell you about the omens, marvelous events, and actions of countless righteous miracle-makers that occurred in the past throughout the world and especially throughout the holy land of India from the time the Buddha was ten years old, one life, and perhaps not even many lives, would not be sufficient.[375] To be brief, the Buddha offered five things: a treasury of uprightness, a source of law, an ocean of modesty, a king of generosity that is the door to victory, and religious teachings and so forth. His religious and worldly advice is like a root from which grew the scriptures that are like the leaves of a large tree. The gems of advice that he gave regarding causality, shame and modesty, love and compassion, a system of the path, and so forth are as many as the water drops in the ocean. From this I, Khaché Phalu Ju, threading words together like pearls on a string, composed some verses of advice as a wellspring of realizations.

Chapter 1

1 The source of religion is the adamantine throne above.
Behind are the summits of the rocky crags of religion.
In front is an ocean of compassion filled with light.
There is no summer or winter; days and nights are the same duration.

2 Summer is not hot and winter is not cold;
it is a temperate place throughout summer and winter.
When the sun reaches the middle of the sky
there are no dark shadows surrounding the houses.

3 These are the characteristics of the center of the world.
There is a path that goes from that center to the center.
I bow down to the center of the center.[376]

4 I bow down to the one called Supreme Precious Jewel in Tibetan,
and in my language called Godā.[377]
If you wish to go to the land of noble India,
eliminate every trace of ignorance from your mind. [372]

5 Send black desires to the depths of the ocean;
burn craving and hatred in red-hot fire;
think of the one. Meditate on and recollect the one.[378]

6 When you can say, "I think of this, not anything else,"
O son, prepare what you need for pilgrimage.
While traveling on and on, many sights will be seen:
whatever you do will be pious; whatever you give will further your path.

7 Whatever you think you'll get; whatever you need will fall into your hands.
Whatever you say will be proverbial; whatever you intend will hit the mark.
When you say, "I have the desire to go to such a place,"
there are three essential necessities.

8 First, your mind must be as clear as a mirror.
Second, your commitment must be as pure as the Bhramaputra.
Third, your fidelity must be as great a lion's.
When you have all three, you will have arrived there.

9 When the young men who arrive at such a place
do not put on their own protective armor,
they will drown in the cycles of this world.

10 Having an attitude of procrastination,
you say, "I'll do it tomorrow or the day after."

Then when the one who calls you to death arrives
you will be thrown into a state of remorse.

11 A date tree on barren rock
suddenly sprouts branches and leaves.
Every leaf grows bearing a word:[379]
the vast knowledge of the learned will not deteriorate.
I offer my petition to go the center, directly to the center.[380]

12 Behind the seal and beneath the stamp of a passport
are words of essential import, a crown jewel
for me, a great sinner, and other worldly beings.

13 Held from afar with your great compassion, may I never:
be without permission to set forth on the righteous path,
be apart from my source of hope for this life and the next,
be separated from the sanctuary for my mind and heart.

14 Look upon me with your wisdom-eye and hold me in mind.
Protect me with love and compassion and guide me on the path.
Having envisioned the great star's paradisiacal garden of light,[381]
I am a little star amid a hundred and fifty-two smaller stars.

15 Have you understood this exposition written by my pen?
These black lines filled with white virtuous words
are Khaché Phalu's unforgotten recollections offered to you. [373]

Chapter 2

16 The religious and the worldly are two different things.
The mind and the body are two separate things.
After engaging in ascetic practices, the mind wants to continue
on.
After eating tasty food, the body really wants to stay put.

17 Physical bliss lasts but three days;[382]
you will endure mental suffering in the end.

If you desire mental joy, practice physical austerities.
If you wish for physical pleasure, consign your mind to misery.

18 If you would listen to me, keep your mind and body separate.
A man who exchanges gold for brass is insane.
Someone mistaking a green rock for turquoise is a fool.
If you don't know the rewards and hazards of this life and the
hereafter,
I say you will waste your life in the transient world.

19 Maybe not in a year or two, but after a hundred years
this bundle of flesh and bones will dissolve into earth.[383]
A king who sits atop a golden throne
and a beggar boy sheltering under a barrel
are both ephemeral; when death comes they are the same.

20 Tasty food is sweet on your tongue until swallowed.
Worldly happiness and suffering last but three days.
A pauper suffers, but his life will come to an end.
A king is happy, but he too will die in the end.

21 The number of those who have gone before is not known.
Who can know precisely how many are going now?
People are coming and going, coming and going,
The fact is, all those who come will depart.

22 There isn't a thing in this world that is permanent.
Since there is no permanence, who has the truth?
This human life has no permanence or stability;
it is like the sun rising and setting over a mountain pass.

23 There is only passing through; there can't be any staying.
Now do not be childishly distracted by appearances.
If you are wise you must seize the essential meaning.
If you grasp the real meaning, you will be the best of heroes.

24 Actions in this transitory world have no core.
This world is not a place you live forever.

You are a traveler; a guest for three nights in an inn.
It is best that each person make up his own mind.

25 When a traveler doesn't make provisions in advance,
he cannot travel carrying an inn on his back, and
the innkeeper's wife can't be taken along to serve.
Think about your wealth while you have it;
when you lose the key to someone else, it is a cause for regret.
[374]

26 There probably are many whose parents have died;
you've probably seen many children left behind.
Can the little son follow his mother? Of course not!
Can the little daughter follow her mother? Of course not!
Everyone passes on having lived out their allotted time.

27 You need to think about your own fate.
As for provisions on the road for this solitary journey,
send your wealth in advance in beggars' hands;[384]
train your horse—that is wealth—to go in a swift gait;
be ready to depart on the road that leads to the next life!

28 If you aspire to wealth and prosperity in the hereafter,
it is best to look after the conditions of paupers here and now.
If you want to eat apricots when you've been buried underground,
it is best to plant an apricot tree now while you are above ground.[385]

29 It is best to plant the root of happiness for all.
The root of religion is nothing but the focus on humankind.
The essence of religion is to make yourself fit to help others.
If you only wish to fulfill your own desires
then there is nothing better than beer and arak.[386]

30 A conceited person says, "Me, me! I'm the best."
"I deserve all the money and fame."
"The tasty food is for me; the softest clothes are for me."

"I am wonderful; I am beautiful."
Even if such a person goes on pilgrimage, there is little sincerity.

31 Even if he travels to a hermitage, there will still be a noisy clamor.
He may see twisting swirls in the air, but they are nothing.
Subsisting on mineral alchemy is to purchase misery for himself.[387]

32 Elders with manners and traditional ways
are superior to a hundred selfish monks.
People with selfish desires have no shame.
Shameless people are classed as animals.

33 A girl may be adorned with jewelry and clothes,
but there's no way she's fit to be Prince Norsang's wife.[388]
Someone whose mind is not separate from sin may do a religious practice,
but there is no way a mirror can reflect in the dark.

34 The eyes of an ox working a water mill are covered by blinders.
It walks all day but is in the same place at night.
If you do not free yourself from the noose of desire,
saying "I've practiced religion" is but empty words.

35 If his wings are tied with silk thread,
there is no way even a vulture can fly though the sky.
You must have sincere commitment and perseverance;
whatever is encountered is dependent on the mind.
As for this path, it is a path set forth for the mind.
You must sweep the mind clean again and again.

36 Check whether you are worthy of others' admiration. [375]
Check whether you are worthy of a good reputation.
Check whether you have established a good legacy.
If you have done all three you are the best of the best.

37 I, Khaché Phalu, have offered my heartfelt advice.
Whether you listen or not is your own choice.

Whatever the case, I have filled up this paper with lines.
The yellow bamboo quill has worked to its heart's content.

Chapter 3

38 The canopy made by the sun and moon are the sky's ornaments;
clearing away darkness, they fill the four continents with light.
Hollyhock flowers are a garden's ornament;
when they bloom the garden is extremely lush.

39 A great king is a kingdom's ornament.
If he rules according to law, his realm will be powerful.
If he enforces the law, his goals are naturally met.
If he upholds the legal system, there will be happiness and prosperity.

40 When a lake roils, of course the fish are disturbed.
When a realm is poor, of course the king is impoverished.
A ruler's prosperity manifests as royal lands and serfs.
A ruler without lands and serfs is a joke.

41 A lord for his subjects is like a doctor for his patients.
A doctor applies salve to incisions he made with his lancet.
A lord rules kindly after he enforces reprimands.

42 First offense: impose the law on the criminal according to the situation.
Second offense: in addition to imposing the law, have the criminal flogged.
Third offense: it is appropriate to kill such an evil man.
There is no need for compassion toward such people.

43 Guard a lamb before it is carried off by a wolf.
Banish evildoers before the country is roiling in blood.
When a king has congealed like yogurt and stays in his bed,
he will not know when his lands are convulsed in blood.

44 If a shepherd is addled by food and drink,
it is certain that a wolf will carry off the lamb.
Commission a task to someone who is skilled at it:
someone may be a skilled carpenter but cannot paint icons.

45 A wolf may be pleasant, but it doesn't heed the shepherd.
Appoint as chief a man who understands the consequences of actions;
otherwise the lamb will be put in the jaws of the wolf.
Essential matters should be entrusted to those with good qualities.

46 When you want jewels you'll find they are in the depths of the sea.
Depend on a man who really keeps his commitments. [376]
How could a diamond-hard rock ever change?
So, whether day or night, act in accord with men who are wise.

47 A dog's corpse in a salt pit turns to salt in the end.
Caring for dear friends is reciprocated in the end:
when the consequences of that deed arise your desires will be met.
Do not disappoint those who have done things for you.

48 Then many will help you when you are faced with things to do.
Support to the utmost those who depend on you,
and good accounts of you will fill this world.

49 While you have the leisure, take care of those who are brave;
there will be a time when you need them to confront an obstacle.
You should continually fill your storehouse with valuables,
for dire conditions will increase and enemies will spring up.

50 Two things are indispensable for subduing enemies:
wealth and an army to utterly strike down the foe.
Without wealth and property, you are helpless and lack allies.
To find allies, you are helpless without wealth and property.
When you have both of course your enemy will be destroyed.

51 Parents should bring up their sons to acquire wealth.
Listen to an old man who has lived many years,
for old men have experienced much joy and sorrow.

52 When you reach the border with the iron fence,
an old man's tactics are better than the strength of youth.
If you want to conquer your present enemies right away,
it is best to draw them in as your friends for now and wait.

53 If you say you'll achieve your main objective strategically,
to brandish arrows, swords, and lances is the act of a fool.
It is better to desist from war with invincible enemies;
you can't grab hold of a sword blade with your bare hand.

54 Even for Gesar himself, not to mention General Denma,[389]
an accord was paramount if a compromise were possible.
Heroic charges into enemy ranks endanger the realm;
the skillful shoot their guns from a distance.

55 Try peaceful tactics the first ninety-nine times;
at the hundredth try, you have no choice if there's demand for a fight.
A man who doesn't understand this is worse than a dog.
If you encounter an aggressive dog, hit it on the nose with a stick.

56 If someone says, "I will leave," see him off on his way.
If someone says, "Let's fight!" let him move three steps forward.
If you don't remember to refrain from anger when it arises,
when you recall it later, slap yourself on the mouth.

57 If you say you'll attain your main objective peacefully,
pride and anger are pointless and meaningless.
Bringing anger under control is the mark of a wise man. [377]
A person who follows his anger is a simpleton.

58 If you think things through in advance, you are wise.
Anyone can see situations that are right in front of them.

Anyone can see when a right-twisting white conch shell is
broken.
When it must be mended the repair will be painfully hard.

59 When an enemy surrenders and comes before you
expunge heartfelt anger from the depths of your mind.
A submissive enemy should not be humiliated;
however, you must be wary of his cunning and deceit.

60 If a river that flows around a fortress
is left undammed, it will destroy the castle in the end.
Protecting evil people is like beating up the good ones;
aiding thieves is like killing merchants.

61 If you ignore a poisonous snake, it will harm people.
If you ignore a wolf, it will be bad for the sheep.
Don't say, "The dog has bitten someone";
it is the person who owns the vicious dog that is bad.

62 A man who subjugates his enemies must defend his allies.
If you are too gentle, your enemy will be stubborn.
If you are too harsh, you risk dangerous revenge.
Your demeanor to all should blend gentleness and harshness;
this method induces every ally and foe to be friendly.

63 If you wish to possess both the present and ultimate kingdoms,
rule impartially from atop your golden throne
with the intent to bring happiness to your land and people.
At night descend to the ground and apply yourself to religion.[390]

64 Offer prayers of homage with body, speech, and mind.
Supplicate the precious Three Jewels, the eternal source of help.
Live in accord with the word of the Master of the Precious Star.[391]
If it is important to you to be exalted in both this life and
hereafter,
do not forget impermanence and death. Fix them in your mind!

65 The counsel and advice of the most earnest Khaché Phalu
are meaningful suggestions strung together like pearls on a string.
I offer this up to the sovereign of the three worlds.
When you compute its value it will be in the hundreds.

Chapter 4

66 This world has many high plateaus and valleys.
With countless differences in wealth, status, and strength, [378]
clearly no two people are the same,
so it's best to find your own contentment.

67 You may scrub, but you can't rub the lines of fate off your forehead.
So instead it is best to conform to your fate.
A donkey from the rocky valleys suffers, but that's its sad fate;
it cannot choose not to carry a load on its back.

68 If you are capable of reason, it doesn't matter how rich you are.
A king who is never satisfied is a destitute beggar.
If a beggar can think, he is superior to that king.

69 A king may still be ravenous after eating up his land and people.
A beggar does a backflip for joy after filling his food bag.
If you do not make yourself content with the fate laid out for you,
you are senselessly bringing misery onto yourself.

70 If you are content, it doesn't matter if you are rich or poor.
If it is fated, your enemies' treasures will be yours.
If it is not fated, it is difficult for a son to inherit his father's fortune.
Vegetation can't grow on bare rock;
what is the use of shaking with anger?

71 If you must admire somone, admire the son of a good father.
If you make yourself content, you will be physically and mentally happy.

You should give up the practices of the inferior classes.
Think about what makes a father happy and brings joy to the son.

72 Your reputation in this life and the next is in the palm of your hand.
Khaché Phalu's heartfelt advice spilled from his mouth.
Dear children, listen sincerely with unobstructed ears.
If you can comprehend, I have written what you need to comprehend.
Though there is not a lot in quantity, it is potent and tasty.

Chapter 5

73 In summer take care of your iron plow; in winter take care of your slate roof.
Take care of your red tongue no matter what the season.
Gauge how many secrets to tell your dear friends;
friends in the morning often become enemies by nightfall.

74 You may need to trust someone and leave your money in their charge;
even if the custodian gives it to someone else, you'll find it after a search.
However, if you trust others too much with your secrets,
you will surely live with your hand clapped over your mouth.

75 Confine devilish tales to the depths of your heart:
padlock your mouth and bolt your tongue.
If a demon escapes from those depths, a man may die.
What help is it to be remorseful later?

76 If you say too many things too many times,
you will have to live saying, "Don't tell anyone."
If you do not guard your oblong tongue, [379]
your round head might find itself in trouble.

77 When is it time to divulge that untold secret?
It will be too late if you come to regret revealing it.

You control your secrets so long as you do not disclose them.
Tell them and you put the person you've told in control.

78 The good have a risk that evil people will gossip.
The wicked take good peoples' advice as inimical.
The good protect themselves from all good or bad.
A good man creates harmony by averting an enemy's evil intent.

79 A man whose speech is straightforward is sincere.
If you are sincere, you have entered the righteous path.
From now into the future joy will lead to yet more joy.
Your wishes for both this life and the next will be fulfilled.

80 Khaché Phalu's wishes met with pen and ink;
the black lines written on white paper are clear.
The writer may be dead and underground, but the writing lives on above.
May these ideas be remembered and the world not forget.

Chapter 6

81 This world is like a mirror reflecting back and forth.
Samsara is like a rocky cliff sending back echoes.
Whatever you have seen is reflected in the mirror.
Wherever you say is echoed by the rocky hills.

82 Good is repaid by good; bad is repaid by bad.
This is what will be. This is the karmic law of the world.
If you say, "They can't all have what they want,"
be cautious for your own sake; do not say that to others.

83 Everyone will act in accord with their own nature.
Whatever is done is as clear as the palm of your hand.
The things that please others may be unpleasant for you;
however that may be, good comes to good and bad to bad.

84 A poisonous tree cannot bear apricots.
If you must have apricots, go to an apricot tree.

If you say, "I want gold and jewels,"
don't go to a worthless region of darkness.

85 If you say, "I must have due respect from others,"
you must treat others with that much respect.
It is difficult for those with ambition to become great;
it is better to set ambition aside as the means to attain it.

86 If you act kindly, even your enemies become your friends.
Unmitigated harshness annuls even a child's affection.
A person whose forehead lines point upward [380]
and has a nice smile with bright teeth is skilled in pleasing others.

87 Do good deeds and go on the path to liberation.
O son, go forth bearing a good reputation.
A man whose forehead lines point downward is evil.
He has all the signs of being a poisonous snake or a mad dog:
whether day or night they do nothing but bite.
People with bad behavior will get what they deserve.

88 A good reputation will follow a good person.
Good men's deeds mature into positive fruit.
The fruit of evil weighs down a bad man's neck.
A bad reputation and evil omens follow bad people.

89 The subject of these words written with an Indian bamboo quill
will be clear on the white Indian paper of the mind.
I have translated these from the Indian language into Tibetan.
Khaché Phalu's intent is now finalized.

Chapter 7

90 Be humble and, whatever befalls you, practice forbearance.
Always keep your essential goal in mind.
Always speak words that charm others.
Always use strategies appropriate for your goal.

91 Pursue things that are meaningful without bravado;
in such a pursuit, it is better to be humble.
People who are humble are liked by many.
Many are disposed to be helpful to such a person.

92 You will pass through life enjoying tea and beer;
there will be many who will say, "Come here! Sit here!"
The wild horse of passion is reined in by judiciousness.
Whatever the situation, exercise appropriate self-control.

93 Some people know how far to go, how long to stay,
how much to say, how much to do,
how much to please others, how much of another's sorrows to bear,
how much good food to eat, and how much finery to wear.
Such people are counted as the most competent of mankind.
People like that find favor with the Lord of the Stars.

94 Future experiences are dependent on present causes.
First, there are those who let their passions go unbounded.
Second, there are those who lack parameters for regulating the mind.
After consorting with such people you will become just like them.
People like these lead you into calamity.

95 Actions without due measure are the basis of destruction.
Business without due measure is the basis for great loss.
Talk without due measure is the basis for getting your ass whipped. [381]
Hilarity without due measure is the basis for tears in the end.

96 The world is filled with crevasses and cliffs.
If you slip, you will fall; if you trip, you will tumble.
You must live skillfully to navigate such a path.
The world is six-sided, like a nomad's dice:
there is no certainty which side will face up.
Keep profit and loss in mind and play the game.

97 Look for ways to open the door to profit.
Look for strategies to block the path to loss.
When there is a disparity between profit and loss
it is better to suppress hard feelings and be restrained.

98 I, immoderate Khaché Phalu, who has gone beyond moderation,
let slip onto paper jewel nuggets of advice.
When calculating the value, do not mistake the cost.
My son, I remain here holding what I have found.

Chapter 8

99 Do not eat only fine food and wear only fine clothes:
your appetite and desire will consign you to misery.
Even though the space inside of your body is large,
it cannot all be just a place to store food.

100 Neither your eyes nor your stomach can ever be sated,
so it's best to set limits on your food and eating.
If you cook too much too often in the belly's oven,
when it becomes painful, look how the hearth grows cold.

101 The taste of your own grass and water is sweeter
than copious food and liquor hoped for from others.
When you crave red meat, it is better to eat your own lice
than to eat the filthy residue of a butcher's evil deeds.[392]

102 Eating and sleeping are what cows and donkeys do.
Can someone who acts that way be happy, my son?
If a dog and your stomach's appetite get out of hand,
you risk them going after horse and donkey carcasses for food.

103 If you do not control the door to your stomach,
you risk losing the jewel of your reputation to a thief.
If you want to be draped with a good reputation,
it is good to make your stomach's appetite as small as your fist.

104 Pond fish come to ruin because they trust the bait.
Mice and birds get caught by eating a trail of laid-out grain.
Because a hungry mouse wants to eat a few crumbs,
its neck is caught in a trap. That's the problem with craving food.

105 If the northern steppes fox does not control itself
its body will be skinned. That's the problem with craving food.
This childish greediness is like a bloodthirsty tiger; [382]
old tigers get beaten like dogs that pounce on sheep.

106 Although indeed I have no claim to be a scholar,
my few black lines on white paper are clear.
Even when Khaché Phalu is long underground,
may these lines of black ink on white Indian paper
last for a long time above the ground.
May auspiciousness prevail so this advice appeals to all.

Chapter 9

107 There are two ways to see a life in this one world:
from one perspective, only your ancestral heritage is primary.
A father has been a son; a son becomes a father.
If you think like that, how could a lineage be short?

108 If you don't think that way, generational bonds deteriorate.
Those with debased bonds may become fierce enemies.
It is impossible for children to exist without parents;
however, both are alive for just a short time.

109 You may have them early in life, but not have them later in life.
It is better to strive to preserve generational bonds.
Seasons and time never tarry, they rush onward;
without wasting any time, educate your children.

110 The root of all good qualities is education.
The king of all good qualities is education.
Place someone with an elementary education on a golden throne.
Place someone with an advanced education on a tiger-skin seat.

111 In the lama's court education is the mirror.
In the king's court education is what yields results.[393]
Education and discernment create a lineage of the wise.
A lack of education and discernment creates a lineage of fools.

112 Twisty letters may look as crooked as a bow,
but their meaning, like an arrow, strikes the target in the mind.
An education is a precious wish-fulfilling jewel.
Nothing impedes a person whose aim is this wish fulfillment.

113 In fact there ought to be education for everyone.
Wealth and possessions sometimes come and sometimes go.
There is a risk that wealth may be lost, wasted, or stolen.
A precious education is an inexhaustible treasure.

114 You should begin teaching children when they are young.
It is pointless to teach them when childhood is past.
A willow sapling can be straightened to espalier.
If you straighten an old willow too much, you risk it breaking.
[383]

115 When you associate with and befriend evil people,
you become poisoned when you contact that poison.
Evil people are like black coals:
when afire you risk being burned; cold, they are dangerous fuel.

116 At every juncture you have to weigh profit and loss;
you must continually discuss the pros and cons.
Lauding the good points is the cause for getting praise;
criticizing the bad points will drive shortcomings away.

117 If a mother keeps her mouth locked shut too much,
there's great risk her children will open the door to calamity.
The result of polishing a stone is a precious gem.
The result of buffing iron is a reflective mirror.

118 If you perfect your education, you are my dear child.
If you act improperly, you are worse than my enemy.

These things I've said are my sincere thoughts;
O parents with children, keep them in mind just so.

Chapter 10

119 Now listen, you darling of your mothers.
A mother is benevolent, loving, and adoring.
When children are young they are their mother's primary focus.
If a child is overindulged, the mother is the one doing it.

120 When a child is fed to excess, it is the mother doing it.
When a child is dressed to excess, it is the mother doing it.
A child who is spoiled by his mother when little
doesn't bring his mother happiness as a result of that pampering.

121 Often children like that become murderers and are executed.
Often children like that become horse thieves and run off.
If a mother raises her children without controlling her affection,
she will be throwing her children to the wind.

122 When they steal it is good to give them a beating.
When they lie it is good to set things straight.
If you can't bear to correct them when they steal an egg,
after filching chickens they will steal horses.

123 Don't give them too much tasty food or too many nice clothes.
Teach them their duty, good manners, and deportment.
Should they have no manners, it was you who taught them to eat.
Who is crazy enough to want a senseless result like that?

124 There is no reason for fox kits to trip on flat, smooth ground.
It is a pity when vulture chicks fall off a precipice.
It is the fate of beggars' children to wander the land begging.
A rich man roaming as a beggar will become a foe.

125 If you care to listen, I have explained the implications.
If you care to see, I have shown what should be seen. [384]

These lines from my pen contain the real essentials;
hold them in your hearts, O mothers!

Chapter 11

126 Therefore listen, children!
When children emerge from their mother's womb,
they are like tigers and leopards coming forth from the forest.
Connected to their mother by an umbilical cord when born,
except for mewling cries they are like a lump of meat.

127 The breast is put to their mouth, but they do not know how to drink.
They have legs but do not know how to take a step.
They have ears but do not understand any spoken words.
They have two eyes but see nothing but their mother.

128 They have a mind but think of nothing but their mother.
They do not know how to drive away the flies circling their faces.
They do not know how to remove dust from their eyes.
They cry when they're cold; they cry when they're hungry.

129 Babies disrupt their parents' sleep at night.
The dry spot is for their baby; the parents take the damp.
The soft spot is for their baby; the parents take the rough.
It cannot be a time like that for you now.

130 When children are young they mainly follow their parents' lead.
Parents teach their children their duty, good manners, and deportment.
Whatever success children attain is due to their parents' kindness.

131 Parents judge what to say for the sake of their child.
Throwing caution to the wind, parents act for the sake of their child.
Nothing but their child is to be thought of and considered.
Nothing but their child's needs are to be met and supported.

132 Both your mother and father, who are so kind,
do you not see that they are now growing old?
Isn't it right to want to repay their kindness?
This is where you need conscience and a sense of shame.

133 Repaying them is the root of accumulating wealth and merit.
God is in heaven and your mother and father are on earth.
Nothing is more precious than these three.
Whether day or night, heed your parents' words.

134 Whether morning or evening, kneel at your parents' feet.
Offer them tasty food and take into consideration whether they like it.
Lay out nice things and take into consideration whether they like them.
Speak pleasantly and take into consideration whether they are pleased.
Speak well and take into consideration whether they are pleased.

135 Pleasing your parents will serve you in this life and the next.
Not pleasing your parents is ruinous in this life and the next. [385]
If you aren't grateful to your parents while they are alive,
ultimately, when they are no longer here, you will feel remorse.

136 That remorse will consume you throughout time.
Other regrets are just temporary feelings of remorse.
Therefore children who have both their parents
should store this jewel of advice deep in the recesses of their hearts.

137 Women's dishonesty and deceit are the basis of quarrels.
Abetting their deceits will divide fathers and sons.
Such actions will cast you to the depths of hell.
Consorting with such people, you will be drawn to follow them.

138 You have probably heard that the plains are covered with goats.
You probably know the saying that the choicest grass is dew-covered.
What need be said about a human female, even if her ancestry is divine;
if she is female, she is a limb of the devil.[394]

139 If you listen to what such a woman says, you will be brought to ruin.
If you let her have her way, you cast all caution to the wind.
You should be suspicious of a man who consorts with a demon.

140 If you are befriending an evil spirit, you can meditate on your guru.
If the clothes you wear get old, you can have new ones made.
Even if you haven't a wife, you can bring in a bride.
But you cannot find new parents even if you search in need.

141 You cannot replace your parents with a wife.
To consort with people who do so is shameful.
Such a man may seem competent, but what capability has he?
If you don't know the difference between your parents and your wife,
you may look like a human, but you are worse than a dog.

142 Even if a bad dog becomes rabid, it knows its master.
The man who is worse than a dog is more self-centered.
Someone like that can turn into a malicious enemy.

143 One evil person can cast a hundred into the winds of chaos.
Even if he has a human form, he is exiled to the ocean depths.
Setting others a bad example, he brings the world to destruction.
When a single cow eats the grain in a man's field,
all other cows find the right of way for them blocked.

144 Know that you should give up bad actions like the examples given here.
O my son, take these essential points to heart.
O dear brother, may you think straight.

145 From summer's hopes and winter's fears
may you be elevated to the place of liberation.
When you aspire to good and fear evil,
O fortunate ones, that is the true path.

146 Stuck deep in the well of this life, samsara is unimaginable.
In this physical lifetime, karma and afflictions are unimaginable.
Integrate these important points; then when you set out on your
final journey
call only on God, the repository of all hope.

147 Bearing cause and effect in mind is the way to proceed.
Keeping good and bad in mind is the way you should act.
There are many who blab about cause and effect,
but those who practice accordingly are rarer than gold.

148 When I look at that, contrition rises from my heart.
When I contemplate that, worry rises from deep within.
These few black letters that were written today
are the crazy musings of the madman Khaché Phalu.

149 This man has ignorance running riot in his heart.
He doesn't know anything himself but advises others.
He doesn't see his own faults but points out the flaws of others.
It's as if he is proud of something cracked and broken.

150 May the lama hold me from afar with kindness.
May my words and actions accord with enlightened activity.
May everything that appears be auspicious.

151 Gems were drawn forth to cover this paper
from the ocean of Khaché Phalu's thoughts.
I place this in the public market square.
May this sweet cuckoo song in the body of a peacock
fill every direction with the sound of happiness and joy.

This concludes *Khaché Phalu's Advice.*

Table of Proper Names

This table includes Tibetan, Sanskrit, and Chinese names. Names prefixed with an asterisk (*) indicate an unattested Sanskrit reconstruction.

Name in Translation	Tibetan Transliteration
Abhayadattaśrī	'jig me sbyin
Aḍakāvatī	lcang lo can
Adhiratha	lhag pa'i shing rta
Ajātaśatru	ma skyes dgra
Ājīvaka	kun tu 'tsho ba
Akaramatiśīla	a ka ra ma ti shī la
Akṣapāda	rkang mig
Akṣobhyavajra	(jo bo) mi bskyod rdo rje
Akya Yongzin Yangchen Gawai Lodrö	a kyā yongs 'dzin dbyangs can dga ba'i blo gros
Amitābha	a mi de wa
Amoghavarśa	don yod 'char
Ānanda	kun dga' bo
Anāthapiṇḍada	mgon med zas byin
Aṅgulimāla	sor mo'i phreng ba
Aṇśuvarma	'od zer go cha
Anupamā	dpe mod mo
Arjaka	ardza ka
Arjuna	srid sgrub
Arkabandhu	nyi ma'i gnyen
Āryadeva	ārya de wa
Asita	mdog nag
*Assana	nye thung bzhin
*Aśthabhuti	a sha tha bhu ti
*Astivāna	rus pa can
Aśvajit	rta thul
Aśvarūpa	rta gzugs
Aśvathāma	rta'i shugs
Āśvina	lha'i sman pa
Aśvinī	tha skar
Ātreya	rgyun shes kyi bu
Avalokiteśvara	spyan ras gzigs

*(Ṣaḍbhuja) Avalokitśvara	myur mdzad phyag drug pa
Avīci	mnar med
Ba Salnang	sba gsal snang
*Bahuhasta	'dzin pa lag mang; lag mang
Balahāka	sprin gyi shugs can
Balāka	gser can
Bāli	stobs ldan
Barön Sunyi	ba ron sun yid
*Bhadrāchara	bzang byed
Bhaga Brāhmaṇa	bha ga'i bram ze
Bhagala	bha ga la
*Bhakanbha	bha kanbha
Bhaṅga	bham ga
Bhaṅgala	bham ga la
Bhāradvaja	bha ra dhva dza
Bharata	'jig sde
Bhīma	jigs sde
Bhīmasena	bhi na si na
Bhiruka	bhi ru ka
Bodha	rtogs ldan
Bhojadeva	bho dza de wa
Bhṛkuṭī	khro gnyer can
*Bhūdhara	sa 'dzin
*Bhūmija	sa la skyes
Bhūpāla	sa skyong
bilva	bil ba
Bimbisāra	gzugs can snying po
Bodhi	byang chub
Bodong Choklé Namgyal	bo dong phyogs las rnam rgayl
Brahmā	tshangs pa
Brahmadatta	tshangs pas byin, tshangs byin
Brahmadeva	lha tshangs pa
Butön Rinchen Drup	bu ston rin chen grub
Camara	tsa ma ra
Caṇḍālikā	tsaṇḍalika
Candra	zla ba
Candraprabha	zla 'od
Cāru	mdzes pa
Cārumanta	mdzes ldan
Celā	gos can
Chapel Tseten Phuntsok	chab spel tshe brtan phun tsogs
Chenghua	ching hwa
Chongyé Terapa Phuntsok Wangpo	'phyongs rgyas bkras rab pa phun tshogs dbang po
Cūta	tsu ta
Dānaśūra	sbyin pa la dpa' ba

Darma Udumtsen	dar ma 'u dum btsan
Demo Ngawang Gelek	de mo ngag dbang dge legs
Devadatta	lhas sbyin
Devarāja	lha'i rgyal po
Devī Kṛṣṇā	lha mo kṛiṣṇa
*Dhanadā	nor 'byin ma
Dhanapāla	nor skyong
*dhandhaka	dha na dha ka
Dhanyākāra	skyid pa'i 'byung gnas
Dharmakīrti	chos kyi grags pa
Dharmapāla	dharmā pa la
Dhṛtarāṣṭra	yul 'khor srung
Domé	mdo smed
Doring Tenzin Paljor	rdo rings bstan 'dzin dpal 'byor
Draupadī	dro pa ti
Drenka Payön	bran kha dpal yon
Drigum Tsenpo	gri gum btsan po
Dromtön Gyalwai Jungné	'brom ston rgyal ba'i 'byung gnas
Drongtsé Losang Tsultrim	rdzong rtse blo bzang tshul khrims
Dṝṭadhana	nor brtan
Drukpa Kunlek	'brug pa kun legs
Dukhamātṛka	ma la gnod
Dukhita	sdug nsngal 'gyur
Durāgata	nyes 'ongs
Durvāsa	gnas ngan
Duryodhana	'thab dka' ba
*Eḍaka	lug
Gampopa	sgam po pa
Ganden	dga' ldan/ dge ldan
Gandhārī	dri za mo
Gar	mgar
Gauḍa	go ḍa
Gautama	go'u ta ma, gō ta ma, go ta ma
Gendun Chöphel	dge 'dun chos 'phel
Gendun Drup	rgyal ba dge 'dun grub
Genghis	jing gi
Ghaṭotkaca	bum sgra
Gö	'gos
Gö Lotsāwa Shönu Pal	gos lo gzhon nu dpal
Gö Trisang	'gos khri bzang
Godong Gomo Tsa	sgo gdong sgo mo'i rtsa
Guhyādhipati (Vajrapāni)	gsang ba'i bdag
Gungthang	gung thang
Gungthang Könchok Tenpai Drönmé	gung thang dkon mchog bstan pa'i sgron me
Hanumān	ha nu mantha

Hashang Mahayana	hva shang mo ho yen
Hiraṇyakāśyapa Balāka	gro skyob gser can 'od srung chu skyar
Horkhang Sönam Palbar	hor khang bsod nams dpal 'bar
Ikṣvāku	bu ram shing pa
Indra	brgya byin
*Indraketu	rgyal ba dbang po'i tog
Jahnu	dza hū
*Jālika	nya pa ru tol
Jālin	dra ba can
Jambudvīpa	dzam bu gling
Jamgön Anyé Shab	'jam mgon ah myes zhabs
Jampal Rölpai Lodrö	'jam dpal rol pa'i blo gros
Jé Tsongkhapa	rje tsong kha pa
Jetavana	dze ta'i tshal / rgyal byed tshal
Jikmé Chin	'jigs med sbyin
Jikmé Gocha Thupten Langtso Dé	'jigs med go cha thub bstan lang tsho'i sde
Jinarṣabha	rgyal ba khyu mchog
Jīvaka	tsho byed bo, 'tsho byed
Jonang Tārānātha	jo nang tā rā nātha
Jyotiṣka	khye'u me skyes, me skyes
Kailaśparvata	ri bo gangs can
Kālidāsa	nag mo'i khol po
Kaliṅga	ka lin ka
Kalmāṣapāda	rkang khra
Kalyāṇa	dge ba
Kamalaśīla	ka ma la shī la
Kāmeśvara	dga' rab dbang phyug
*Kāñcanamālā	gser phreng can
Kāñcī	kanyach'i; kanyitsa
Kapila	ser skya
Kapilabhadrā	ser skya bzang mo
Kapilavastu	ser skya, ser skya'i gzhi
*Karmadeva	karma lha
Karmapa Rangjung Dorjé	karma pa rang byung rdo rje
Karṇa	rna can, rna ba can
Kārtika	karti ka
Kāśi	ka zhi, ka shi
Kāśīsundara	kā shī mdzes dga'
Kāṣṭhavāṭa	shing thags can
Kātyāyana	ka tyā ya na
Kauṇḍinya	kōṇḍinya
Kaurava	dgra ngan, sgra ngan
Kauśala	ko sa lī
Kauśāmbī	ko'u shāmbhī
Khaché Phalu Ju	kha che pha lu 'ju

Khalka Tüśiyetü Khan	khal kha thu she ye thu khan
Khaṇḍa	dum bu
*Khapara	kha pa ra
Khenpo Sangyé Tenzin	sangs rgyas bstan 'dzin
Khepa Deu	mkhas pa lde'u
Kongpo	kong po
Kṛkī	krī krī
Kṛṣṇā	kṛṣṇa 'dzin
Kṣāntivādi	bzod smra
*Kṣipratuṅga	'phral la mtho
Kulīraka	bu ler ka
Kumāra Jīvaka	'tsho byed gzhon nu
*Kumāra Jīvakabhṛtya	'tsho byed gzhon nu gsos
Kumāra Sudhana	gzhon nu nor bzang
Kumbhakarṇa	kumbha karṇa, bum sna
Kuntī	kuntī, kun ḍi
Kuru	ku ri
Kuruvamśe	skyu ru ra
Kuśanā	ku sha na
Kyilkhang	dkyil khang
Kyilsur Yongzin Losang Jinpa	dkyil zur yongs 'dzin blo bzang sbyin pa
Kyishö	skyi shod
Lakṣmaṇa	lakṣ man
Langdarma	glang dar ma
Langdarma Udumtsen	glang dar ma 'u dum btsan
Laṅkapūrī	lang ka pu ri
*Latrotala	la tro ta la
*Lehuducha	le'u du cha
Lekzing Yön	legs mdzing yon
Lha Thothori Nyentsen	lha tho tho ri gnyan btsan
Lhajé	lha rje
Lhalung Palgyi Dorjé	lha lung dpal gyi rdo rje
Lhokham	lho kham
*Liśī	li shi
Longam	lo ngam
Losang Chödrak	blo bzang chos grags
Losang Palden	blo bzang dpal ldan
Mādrī	ma tri; mā tri
Magadha	ma ga dha
Mahācandra	zla ba chen po
Mahādeva	lha chen
*Mahākāla	phyag drug mgon
Mahākāśyapa	'od srung chen po
Mahānama Śākya	shākya ming chen
Mahāpanthaka	lam chen pa
Mahāraurava	'bod sgrog

Mahāsaṃmata	mang pos bkur ba
Mahauṣadhi Dāraka	khye'u sman chen po
Mahiṣavarda	mchog sbyin
Mahodyāna	bza' shing gi ra wa rgya chen po
Maitreya	byams pa
Maitribala	byams pa'i stobs
Mākandika	ma du
Mālikā	phreng ldan ma
*Mallaputra	gyad bu nor
Mandārava	man da ra ba
Māndhātā	nga las nu
Mañjuśrī	'jam dpal
Māra	bdud sdig can
Martön Chögyal	dmar ston chos rgyal
Mashang Drompa Kyé	ma zhang grom pa skyes
*Masūrakṣa	ma su raksha; ba yu ra sha
Mātali	mā ta li
Mathurā	bcom brlag
Maudgalyāyana	mo'u 'gal, mōnggal
Megavāhana	sprin la zhon
Meghaśrī	sprin byi dpal
Meru	ri rab
Ming dynasty	ta'i ming gi rgyud pa
Mongol dynasty	hor gyi rgyal
Mount Malayagiri	ri bo ma la ya
Mount Vaṇka	ri bo bang kar
Mṛṇāla	padma'i rtsa lag
Muné Tsenpo	mu ne btsan po
Mutik Tsenpo	mu tig btsan po
Naḍaparvata	dam bu'i ri
Nāgārjuna	klu sgrub
Naimang Lharampa Geshé Ngawang Tenzin	na'i mang lha rams pa geshe ngag dgang bstan 'dzin
Nakpa Tsering	nag pa tshe ring
Naktso Tsultrim Gyalwa	nag tsho tshul khrims rgal ba
Nakula	na ku la, rigs med
Nālada	na la da
*Nalagiri	bzang ldan
Namgyal Söpa	rnam rgyal bzod pa
Namri Songtsen	gnam ri srong btsan
Nanda	dga' bo
*Naramatima	na ram ti ma
*Naravati	na ra ba ti
Ngawang Chökyi Drakpa	ngag dbang chos kyi grags pa
Ngawang Losang Gyatso	ngag dbang blo bzang rgya mtsho
Nyamsang	nyam bzang

Nyangshap	nyang shab
Nyatri Tsenpo	gnya khri btsan po
Nyethang Or	snye thang 'or
Pāla	pa la
Pañcālā	lnga len
Paṇchen Chökyi Nyima	pan cheṇ chos kyi nyi ma
Paṇchen Losang Palden Yeshé	pan cheṇ blo bzang dpal ldan ye shes
Paṇchen Sönam Drakpa	paṇ chen bsod nams grags pa
Pāṇḍu	skya seng
Panthaka	lam phran pa
*Pāpaja	sdig byung
*Pāpārtha	sdig don
Parivrājaka	kun tu rgyu
Pāṭaliputra	pa ṭa li pu ta li
Pawo Tsuklak Trengwa	dpa' bo gtsug lag phreng ba
*Poṣaṇa	gsos pa
Potala	ri bo gru 'dzin
Pradyota	rab snang
Prasenajit	gsal rgyal
Pūraṇa	gang po
Pūraṇa Kāśyapa	rdzogs byed
Purgyal	pur rgyal
Rāhula	sgra gcan 'dzin
Rājagṛha	rgyal po'i khab
Rāma, Rāmaṇa	ra ma ṇa
Rāmapāla	ra ma pā la
Rāṣṭrapāla	khor bsrung
Ratna Ānanda	rin chen kun dga
Rauruka	sgra sgrog
Rāvaṇa	bod sgrogs
Ravigupta	nyi ma sbas pa
Rinchen Kunga	rin chen kun dga
Rinchen Pal	rin chen dpal
Roca	'od mdzas
Rudra	drag po
Ruru	ru ru
Sahadeva	lhur bcas, sa ha de ba
Sahora	za hor
Sākali	phur ma
Sakya	sa skya
Śākya	shā kya
Sakya Paṇḍita Kunga Gyaltsen Palsangpo	sa skya paṇḍita kun dga' rgyal mtshan dpal bzang po
Śākyamuni	shā kya mu ni
Samantabhadra	kun tu bzang po
Sāṃkhya	grangs can

Śāṇavāsi	sha na'i gos can
Sañjaya	kun tu rgyal ba
Śaṅkhapāla	Dung skyong dkar po
Śāntarakṣita	zhi ba 'tsho
śarabha	(ri dvags) sha bha
Sarasvatī	dbyang can ma, dbyangs ldan ngang mo
Śāriputra	shā ri'i bu
Sārthavāha	ded dpon mdza' bo
Shangshung Chöwang Drakpa	zhang zhung chos dbang grags pa
Śibi	shi pi pa
Śikhī	gstug phud can
Siṅgha	seng ge
Siṅghakalpā	pho brang seng ge
Siṅghakeśari	seng ge ral pa can
Siṅghala	sing ga la
Siptri Tsenpo	sribs khri btsan po
Sītā	si ta
Śītavana	bsil ba'i tshal
Śiva	dbang phyug
Sönam Gyaltsen	bsod nams rgyal mtshan
Songtsen Gampo	srong btsan sgam po
*Śraddhā	(rgyal bu) ded pa
Śrāvastī	mnyan yod
Śrīgupta	dpal sbas *or* dpal sbed
*Sthiraśraddhā	ded pa brtan pa
Subhadra	rab tu bzang po
*Śubhārtha	dge don
Sudarśana	dge mthong
Sudāsa	bran bzangs, su dā sa
Śuddhodana	zas gtsang; gtsang
Sugrīva	mgrin bzang
*Suhṛt	mdza' bo
Sujātā	legs skyes
Śūka	ne tso
Śuklodana	zas dkar
Sumāgadhā	ma ga ta bzang mo
Sumukha	bzhin bzang
Supāraga	legs par pha rol tu phyin pa
Suparṇa	dab bzang
Supriya	rab dga'
Surapāraka	su ra pā ra ka
Sūryagupta	nyi ma sbas pa
Suvarṇākṣa	gser mig
Suvarṇottamā	gser mchog ma
Svāgata	legs 'ongs
Śyāmāvatī	sngo bsangs can

Taizong	seng ge btsan po
Takṣaśilā	yul rdo 'jog
Tāmradvīpa	zangs gling
Tārā	bzang mo, sgrol ma
Tashilhunpo	bkras shis lhun po
Tattvakaumudī	de nyid ko ma ḍi
Timur	thi mur
Tiṣya	legs pa'i skar ma
Tö	stod
Tö Drompa	stod grom pa
Tölung	stod lung
Tori Longten	to ri long bstan
Tri Dra Pungtsen	khri sgra dpung btsan
Tri Ralpachen	khri ral pa can
Tri Song Detsen	khri srong lde'u btsan
Tri Tok Jeten	khri thog rje bstan
Tri Tsenam	khri btsan nam
Tsang	gtsang
Tsangma	gtsang ma
Ü	dbus
Udayana	u tra ya na, shar pa, shar ba'i bu
Udayana Kañcī	u ta ya na kanyci
Udayanabhadra	char byed bzang po
Udāyī	'char ka
Udrāyaṇa	u tra ya na
Ujjayinī	yul 'phags rgyal
Umā	u ma
Upacāru	nye mdzes
Upacārumanta	nye mdzes ldan
Upacelā	nye gos can
Upananda	nye dga', nye dga' bo
Upoṣadha	so sbyong 'phags
Utpalavarṇā	utpa la'i mdog
Vādisiṃha	smra ba'i seng ge
Vaidehī	lu phags ma
Vaiśālī	yangs pa can
Vaiśravaṇa	rnams thos kyi bu, rnam thos sras
*Vakula	ba ku la
Vālī	bha ling
Vālmīki	grog mkhar ba, grog mkhar
Varakalyāṇa	dge mchog
Vārāṇasī	'kor mo 'jig, 'khor mo 'jig, wā rā ṇa sī
Vararuci	mchog sred
Varṣākārā	dbyar tshul ma
Varuṇa	wa ru na
Vāsavadattā	nor lha'i byin

Vasudā	nor 'byin ma
Vāsuki	nor rgyas
Videha	lus 'phags, lu 'phags
Vikramāditya	bhi ka ma a ti ta
Vikṛti	bi kri ti
Virūḍaka	'phags skyes po
Viṣṇu	khyab 'jug
Viśvakarmā	bi shā karma
Viśvantara	thams cad sgrol
Vyāsa	rgyas pa
Wencheng	kong jo
*Yama	las gshin
Yarmo	yar mo
Yerpa	yer pa
Yiga Chözin	yid dga' chos 'dzin
*Yogadhāraṇa	sbyor ba 'chang
Yongle	ye dbang
Yudhiṣṭhira	g.yul ngor bstan pa, g.yul ngor brtan pa
Zemey Rinpoché Losang Palden	dze smad rin po che blo bzang dpal ldan

Notes

1. Ludwik Sternbach, "*Subhāṣita-saṃgrahas,* A Forgotten Chapter in the Histories of Sanskrit Literature," *Indologica Taurensia* 1 (1973): 170.
2. Sir Monier Monier-Williams, *Sanskrit-English Dictionary* (New Delhi: Munshiram Manoharlal Publishers, 2nd reprint, 1981), 565.
3. For the range of meanings of the Sanskrit word *nīti*, see Chandra Rajan's introduction to her translation of the *Pañcatantra*. Viṣṇu Śarma, *The Pañcatantra*, trans. Chandra Rajan (London: Penguin Books, 1993), xxvii–xxviii.
4. Khepa Deu, *Extensive History of India and Tibet* (Lhasa: Tibet Nationalities Press, 1987), 236. For a detailed analysis of this trio of stories, symbolic languages, and Bön rituals, see Namkhai Norbu, *Drung, De'u, and Bön: Narrations, Symbolic Languages, and the Bön Tradition in Ancient Tibet*, trans. Andrew Likianowicz (Dharamsala: Library of Tibetan Works and Archives, 1995).
5. Tibetan: (1) *ba mo dbyar 'jo dgun nas gso* and (2) *mar rdo la zhu na mar gyong rag / rdo mar la zhu na mar ngyong rag.* A useful collection of these coded Tibetan sayings as well as other types of proverbs can be found in Kyabjé Zemey Rinpoché's *Collected Works*, vol. 6 (Delhi: Tashi Gephel House, 1997), especially 583–620. For those who can read Tibetan, see my introduction to the Tibetan edition of this volume, where I discuss the different categories of Tibetan sayings and reference interesting new research published in Tibet on ancient Tibetan stories and proverbs.
6. For detailed information on the texts and other archeological items discovered in the Dunhuang caves, and the current locations of these finds, see the International Dunhuang Project's website: http://idp.bl.uk/.
7. There is only one known commentary to Dromtönpa's text, which was written by the nineteenth-century Geluk author Shangtön Tenpa Gyatso (1825–97) and will be featured in volume 26 of *The Library of Tibetan Classics*. The *Garland of Jewels* (*Nor bu'i phreng ba*) is not a typical commentary but more of an interwoven comparative analysis, again written in verse.
8. *Phu bos nu bor gtams shing bstan pa'i mdo.* The Chinese region of Dunhuang came under Tibetan rule in 786 CE. Even after the end of Tibetan rule in 848, people in the Dunhuang area seemed to have used the Tibetan language and followed Tibetan Buddhism for some time. See, for example, Christopher Beckwith, "The Tibetans in the Ordos and North China," in *Silver on Lapis: Tibetan Literary Culture and History* (Bloomington, IN: The Tibetan Society, 1987).
9. I have used the Tibetan text along with a helpful word commentary by the twentieth-century Tibetan scholar Chapel Tseten Phuntsok, *Sutra Extracted from Dunhang on an Elder Brother's Advice to His Younger Brother: A Word*

Commentary, featured in volume 1 of the four-volume *Anthology of Wise Sayings Treatises* (*Legs bshad bstan bcos phyogs bsgrigs*) (Xining: Kokonor Nationalities Press, 2006).

10. Ibid., 15.
11. Ibid., 18–19.
12. Ibid., 20. Space prevents us from exploring this ancient Tibetan text in greater detail here, but the text and its central concept of *mi chos* certainly deserves an in-depth study.
13. Sam van Schaik, "The Naming of Tibetan Religion: *Bon* and *Chos* in the Tibetan Imperial Period," *Journal of the International International Association for Bon Research* 1 (2013): 236.
14. One curious fact is that a cognate of *mi chos—mi yi chos lugs*, literally "the system of human dharma"—occurs in two of the Indian wisdom texts translated into Tibetan. One is from Nāgārjuna's *Hundred Stanzas on Wisdom*, where we read: "If you properly practice human ethics, / the journey to the god realm will not be long (98a–b). The other is in the concluding verse of the *Drop to Nourish a Person*, where the text reads: "For those who do not sustain the holy Dharma in their mind / yet uphold in their mind the excellent human values, / I have composed this work to help them." Since no original Sanskrit remains of these two texts, it is difficult to determine which Sanskrit words are rendered here as *mi chos* by the Tibetan translator. Even harder to determine is whether this term is being used in the technical sense in which Tibetan authors like Dromtönpa came to use it. My own feeling is that the technical sense is more of an indigeneous development than an import from Indian sources. R. A. Stein, by contrast, opines in *Tibetan Civilization* (Stanford, CA: Stanford University Press, 1972), 259, the *mi chos* aphorisms as bearing "the stamp of Chinese ethical and Buddhist religious ideas" while retaining a purely Tibetan flavor.
15. This system of enumeration is based on Pawo Tsuklak Trengwa's *Feast for the Learned: A History of Buddhism* (Beijing: Nationalities Press, 1989), 1:192, where he also lists an alternative system of enumeration.
16. To date, several English translations have been made of the *Jewel Treasury* (see under Sakya Paṇḍita in the bibliography). The one by John T. Davenport includes a translation of the extremely helpful twentieth-century commentary by Khenpo Sangyé Tenzin.
17. Michael Hahn has convincingly demonstrated that this work cannot be by Nāgārjuna, especially since it contains verses from texts that are as late as the seventh century. See Michael Hahn, "The Tibetan *Shes rab sdong bu* and Its Indian Sources (1)," *South Asian Classical Studies* 24 (2009): 1–78.
18. For a complete list of Indian wisdom literature available in Tibetan translation and a detailed description of these texts, see Suniti Kumar Patak, *The Indian Nītiśāstras in Tibet* (Delhi: Motilal Banarsidass, 1974), part 4; and also Ludwik Sternbach, "Indian Wisdom and Its Spread beyond India," *Journal of American Oriental Society* 101.1 (1981): 103. Sternbach identifies six known versions of the *Cāṇakya Treatise* and states that the one translated into Tibetan is the *Cāṇakyarājanītiśāstra* version, which, though not so well known today, must have been popular in the

ninth century when it was translated into Tibetan. According to Sternbach this same version is included as the *Bṛhaspatisaṃhita* in the *Garuḍapurāṇa*.

19. On modern Western scholars' study of the parallels between verses in the *Jewel Treasury* and Indian wisdom literature, see Sternbach, "Indian Wisdom and Its Spread beyond India," 105. See also the introduction by John Davenport in Sakya Paṇḍita, *Ordinary Wisdom* (Boston: Wisdom Publications, 2000), 15–17.
20. On the importance of Daṇḍin's *Mirror of Poetics* and its influence on Tibetan literature, see the introduction to Thupten Jinpa and Jas Elsner, *Songs of Spritual Experience: Tibetan Buddhist Poems of Insight and Awakening* (Boston: Shambhala, 2000).
21. Many versions of the *Pañcatantra* exist, with variations in the selections of stories, because it has been disseminated widely since ancient times. On the problems concerning the dating of the *Pañcatantra*, see Patrick Olivelle's introduction to Viṣṇuśarman, *The Five Discourses on Worldly Wisdom*, Clay Sanskrit Library (New York: New York University Press, 2006); also, Chandra Rajan's introduction to Viṣṇu Śarma, *The Panćantantra* (London: Penguin Books, 1993), liii–liv. The *Hitopadeśa*, though popular in India, seems to have been completely unknown to the classical Tibetan authors. It was finally translated into Tibetan in the twentieth century and published in 1966 as *Gzhan la phan pa'i ngag las mdza' grogs thob pa*.
22. Shang Gyalwa Pal, *Biography of the the Great Sakya Paṇḍita* (Sichuan: Nationalities Press, 1995), 7.
23. An English translation of this sutra from the Mongolian version by Stanley Frye was published as the *Sutra of the Wise and Foolish* by the Library of Tibetan Works and Archives, Dharmsala, 1981.
24. In the endnotes of our Tibetan volume, the editors (myself as the chief editor) have identified the sources of the stories alluded to in the *Jewel Treasury* and spelled out in the commentary, as well as those found in Paṇchen Sönam Drakpa's *Ganden Wise Sayings* and its commentary.
25. On the popularity and the spread of the *Jewel Treasury* in Mongolia, see James E. Bosson, *A Treasury of Aphoristic Jewels: The Subhāṣitaratnaniddhi of Sa Skya Pandita in Tibetan and Mongolian*, Uralic and Altaic Series 92 (Bloomington: Indiana University Press, 1969).
26. In the multivolume *Collected Works of Bodong Choklé Namgyal*, an early fifteenth-century profilic Tibetan author, there is a text titled *Bodong Wise Sayings* (*Bo dong legs shad*). Closer inspection revealed that this is essentially a copy of the *Treasury* in its entirety, with a slight modification of chapter organization and the addition of few new verses. So I did not include this particular text in the present anthology. On the influence of the *Treasury* on subsequent Tibetan wise-sayings literature, including parallel passages between some of the well-known texts and the *Treasury*, see also the introduction by John Davenport in Sakya Paṇḍita, *Ordinary Wisdom*, 8–17.
27. *Skyes bu'i rnam 'byed bshad pa gzhon nu'i mgul rgyan*. Although I know of no commentary on this work, Yangchen Gawai Lodrö mentions it as a source and inspiration for Panchen Sönam Drakpa's *Ganden Wise Sayings: A Bouquet of White Lotuses*, alongside the *Jewel Treasury*.
28. *Legs par bshad pa shing gi bstan bcos kyi 'grel pa lung zung blang dor 'char ba'i me*

long, in the *Collected Works of Kyabje Zemey Rinpoché* (Mundgod: Tashi Gephel House, 1997). First published separately as a book under the same title by Drepung Loseling Printing Press, Mundgod, in 1980. I have also heard of the publication of commentaries on Gungthang's two treatises in Bhutan by the country's Department of Education in 1984 but have not been able to locate a copy of this book.

29. These treatises on fire and on metal, as well as other wise-sayings Tibetan texts, can be found in volume 4 of the six-volume *Anthology of Wise Sayings Treatises, Legs bshad bstan bcos phyogs bsgrigs* (Xining: Kokonor Nationalities Press, 2006), which also contains similar works of the wise-sayings genre written by authors like the historian Sumpa Yeshé Paljor, Dharmasūrya (possibly Paṇchen Chökyi Nyima), and Nomchi Khenpo.
30. *Rgyal po'i lugs kyi bstan bcos sa gzhi skyong ba'i rgyan.* For a brief description of this important treatise, with reference to existing contemporary studies of the socio-historical context in which the text might have emerged, see Sakya Paṇḍita, *Ordinary Wisdom*, 12. The work is translated and introduced by José Cabezón in *The Just King: The Tibetan Buddhist Classic on Leading an Ethical Life* (Boulder, CO: Snow Lion, 2017).
31. *Lugs kyi bstan bcos dpag bsam ljon pa.* Jampal Rolpai Lodrö's collected works were published in two volumes as part of the series on the writings of Golok authors (Sichuan: Nationalities Press, 2004). According to the brief biography of the author in volume 1, he was a close disciple of the famed Geluk master Drakar Rinpoché, and his own students include Khyenrab Norbu, the official physician of the Thirteenth Dalai Lama.
32. *Rdzogs pa chen po 'jam dpal thugs tig.*
33. Horkhang Sönam Palbar, who was a student of Gendun Chöphel and the compiler of his collected works, asserts that this advice text was actually written by Drongtsé Losang Tsultrim, a tutor to the Paṇchen Lama. See the *Collected Works of Horkhang Sönam Pelbar* (Beijing: Krung go bod kyi shes rig dpe skrun khang, 1990), 504.
34. See, for example, Gendun Chopel, *Grains of Gold: The Tales of a Cosmopolitan Traveler*, trans. Thupten Jinpa and Donald S. Lopez Jr. (Chicago: University of Chicago Press, 2014), 399–400.
35. A translation of this text by Dawa Norbu and a study and review of the work by Tashi Tsering, two of the most prolific Tibetan writers in English in the twentieth century, appeared in the monthly Tibetan magazine *Tibetan Review* in 1986 and 1988, respectively.
36. *Mi chos gnad kyi phreng ba.* As the basis for this text the Tibetan editors chose the version found in a special anthology printed in Tibet entitled *A Compilation of Requisite Mind-Training: A Collection of Folio Texts on Enlightenment* (*Blo sbyong nyer mkho phogs bsgrigs / byang chub lo mo dpe tsogs*).
37. Dromtönpa is saying that if you are able to resist talking about the faults of those who depend on you—your family, friends, students, and so on—and let it go or "evaporate into thin air," this is wise. If, by contrast, you talk about it to one person, you will start worrying that he might tell others, and when two people have heard, it starts to cause problems. By the time three people have heard it, then it will be reach everywhere as if spread by the wind.

38. Five "degenerations" are said to characterize a given era as being a degenerate age: (1) degeneration of lifespan, (2) degeneration of time, (3) denegeration due to proliferation of afflictions, (4) degeneration of views, and (5) degeneration of the quality of human experience.
39. *Lañca* is a script for writing Sanskrit that was particularly popular in Tibet. For a discussion on *lañca* and its relation to ancient Indian script that was the basis for the invention of Tibetan writing system, see Gendun Chopel, *Grains of Gold*, 191–93.
40. What Dromtönpa seems to be saying here is that, once these words of advice have been penned, Naktso would enjoy reading them as a source of entertainment when he is alone in a hermitage. But if he is able to familiarize himself with these verses, they will be helpful to him more generally.
41. This is a reference to the famous aspirational prayer of the bodhisattva Samantabhadra known as the *Vows of Good Conduct* (*Bhadracaryāpraṇidhāna*).
42. *Legs par bshad pa rin po che'i gter.*
43. These are names of ancient Indian sages who are revered as important figures in the history and mythology of the Indian Brahmanical traditions. Vyāsa is a sage associated with astrology; Vālmīki, the celebrated author of the much-loved epic the *Rāmāyaṇa*; and Akṣapāda Gautama, the author of the influential work on logic the *Nyāyasūtra*. No clear consensus exists on the dates of all of these sages.
44. This story is told in Rinchen Pal's commentary (henceforth referred to as "the commentary") featured in this volume; see pages 99–192. For verses not covered by Rinchen Pal's commentary, a cross-reference is provided to the commentary of Khenpo Sangyay Tenzin translated in Sakya Paṇḍita, *Ordinary Wisdom*.
45. After reading these two lines from the *Treasury*, Drukpa Kunlek (1455–1529), the famous Tibetan mystic and satirist, is said to have quipped: "The great Sakya Paṇḍita had seen so much, he saw ants faster than horses!"
46. "Golden-clad one" refers to the Hindu god Viṣṇu, whose traditional mount is the powerful mythic bird garuḍa. For this story from the Indian myths, see commentary on pages 117.
47. See commentary, page 117–23.
48. A folk legend, probably from Indian sources, says that swans can extract just the milk when it is mixed with water.
49. Drigung Rinchen Pal tells the story behind this allusion in *A Commentary on "A Jewel Treasury of Wise Sayings"* on page 121 of this volume to elucidate verse 25 of *A Jewel Treasury of Wise Sayings*. Yangchen Gawai Lodrö also tells this story in *Rays of Sunlight: A Commentary on "Ganden Wise Sayings"* to elucidate verse 21 of *Ganden Wise Sayings*. See pages 238ff. This is story 5 of book I in Viṣṇuśarma, *Pañcatantra*, according to the numbering in the translation in *Five Discourses on Worldly Wisdom* by Patrick Olivelle, who follows a reconstruction produced by Edgerton in 1924. In Chandra Rajan's translation, this is story 8 of book I.
50. "Malaya" here refers to a mountain range in the southern part of Indian subcontinent thought to be home to sandalwood trees mentioned often in ancient Indian texts. Malaya can also refer to a region that includes parts of modern-day Kerala, Tamil Nadu, and Karnataka states.
51. The Tibetan word *ku ru ra*, rendered here as "sour fruit," is myrobalan fruit, which

is thought to have medicinal properties. See the story below in Rinchen Pal's commentary.

52. In ancient Buddhist sources Mahāsaṃmata is recognized as the first king of the world and the founder of the Śākya dynasty to which the historical Buddha belonged. This story of King Mahāsaṃmata can be read in Sakya Paṇḍita, *Ordinary Wisdom*, 65–66.
53. This is story 11 of book I in Chandra Rajan's translation of the *Pañcatantra*, where she lists it as "The Blue Jackal." It does not appear in Olivelle's translation.
54. Bāli is the lord of the realm of the demigods. In the story Viṣṇu assumes the form of a dwarf who tricks Bāli into offering him the space he can cover with one step, and he thereby secures the entire world under his dominion. See commentary, page 133.
55. See commentary, page 134. The story appears in the *Pañcatantra* as story 2.1 in book III in Olivelle and as story 2 of book III in Chandra Rajan.
56. This echoes a verse from chapter 5 of Cāṇakya, *Cāṇakya Treatise on Kingship* (*Cāṇakyarājanītiśāstra*), Toh 4334 Tengyur, thun mong ba'i lugs kyi bstan bcos, *ngo*, 132a7.
57. This story appears in the *Pañcatantra,* as story 8.1 in book I in Olivelle and as story 16 of book I in Chandra Rajan. There the story involves two flying geese carrying a turtle biting on a stick held in their beaks. Some children, witnessing this spectacle, start shouting about how two geese are carrying a turtle in the air. The turtle, wanting to say "It's me who is flying!" opens its mouth and falls to the earth. A variant of this story also appears in Western folk tradition dating back to ancient Greece, including as one of Aesop's fables.
58. This comes from the same story embedded in verse 64.
59. The wrathful lord Yama personifies death in both Buddhist and Hindu mythology.
60. See commentary, pages 139–40.
61. See commentary, pages 141–43. In Olivelle's translation this is story 1 of book III in the *Pañcatantra*, while in Chandra Rajan it is story 7 of book IV.
62. See commentary, pages 143–44. This is story 3 of book III in Olivelle and story 4 of book III in Chandra Rajan.
63. See commentary, pages 144–47.
64. See commentary, pages 147–48.
65. In Indian and Tibetan folk beliefs, serpentine creatures known as *nāgas* (*klu* in Tibetan) are closely associated with water and trees and are believed to be responsible for rain.
66. See commentary, page 154 and Sakya Paṇḍita, *Ordinary Wisdom*, 125–26. This story appears in the *Pañcatantra*, book IV, story 10, in the Chandra Rajan translation.
67. In the *Pañcatantra*, book III, this is story 2 in Olivelle and story 1 in Chandra Rajan.
68. The author is referring here to a genre of Indian works that focus on the norms of kingship, such as the treatise of Cāṇakya.
69. This is almost identical to Masūrakṣa's *Treatise on Norms* 3.3.
70. In Tibetan culture the right-curling conch is considered auspicious and a harbinger of good fortune. All straight things are not good and all twisted things are not bad, Sakya Paṇḍita is saying, so you should not jump to conclusions based on superficial appearances.

71. In Chandra Rajan (book III, story 5) there is a similar story where ants kill a large snake, not a lion cub.
72. Rinchen Pal's commentary does not cover this verse, though glosses on it can be found in *Ordinary Wisdom*, where the sea monster is identified as a crocodile. My conjecture is that this is a reference to a Hindu myth according to which Krishna is said to have, after rescuing the son of a sage kidnapped by a sea monster, killed the monster and made a powerful conch from its bone.
73. For this story see Sakya Paṇḍita, *Ordinary Wisdom*, 148, where no source is provided.
74. The Malaya mountains are praised as the home of sandalwood trees. See note 50.
75. One of the emblematic symbols of the Hindu god Śiva is the crescent moon that adorns his crown. The "demigod" here refers to Rahula, whose swallowing of the moon is thought to cause the lunar eclipse.
76. See commentary, pages 160–67. This is a reference to the famous story of the five brothers or Pāṇḍavas and their dispute with their cousins as narrated in the *Mahābhārata* epic, referred to briefly in the *Pañcatantra*, book III, story 7, as well.
77. See commentary, page 168. Source of the story not identified.
78. This is the reference to the well-known Buddhist story of Aṅgulimāla (literally "finger necklace"), a serial killer who wore a garland made of fingers and was a source of terror in a region of central India during the Buddha's time. Eventually tamed by the Buddha, Aṅgulimāla joined the monastic order and gained spiritual freedom.
79. According to popular folk belief in Tibet, probably with an Indian source, a unique relationship is said to exist between otters and owls, with the former catching fish and leaving them for owls as gifts.
80. See commentary, pages 169–71. This is story 3.1.1 of book I in Olivelle but does not appear in Chandra Rajan.
81. See commentary, pages 171–72. The source of this exact story remains unidentified, although the frame story of book III of the *Pañcatantra* concerns the ongoing enmity between owls and crows.
82. See commentary, page 170. The source of this story is unidentified.
83. Although a gloss on Śiva's unique attributes, such as why he is called Maheśvara (the great god), wears a necklace of human skulls, and so on are described in Prajñāvarman's *Praise of the One More Perfect Than the Gods* (*Devātiśayastotraṭīkā*, Toh 1113 Tengyur, bstod tshogs, *ka*, 47a5), the exact source of the story embedded here is unidentified.
84. See Sakya Paṇḍita, *Ordinary Wisdom*, 187–89. This is probably a reference to the myth whereby Viṣṇu, in the form of a lion-man (*narasiṃha*), slays the demigod Balāka.
85. See commentary, page 175.
86. See commentary, pages 176–81. This is a reference to the story in the *Rāmāyaṇa* epic where Rāma slays the demon Rāvaṇa, who had lustfully kidnapped Rāma's wife, the beautiful Sītā. In the Buddhist sources, the story is told in Prajñāvarman, *Explanation of Praise of the Exalted* (*Viśeṣastavanāmaṭīkā*), Toh 1110 Tengyur, bstod tshogs, *ka*, 13b3
87. This and a subsequent verse, 449, echo Masūrakṣa's *Treatise on Norms* 4.3.
88. This verse parallels Masūrakṣa's *Treatise on Norms* 6.15.

89. This perceived enmity between crows and owls is part of Indian folk mythology and is extensively featured in the *Pañcatantra* stories, especially in book III.
90. See commentary, page 181. In the Hindu myths, Śiva's son Kārtikeya defeats the demon Tāraka but spares her subjects. In the commentary, there is a conflation of Tāraka with *Karmadeva [*sic*], probably Kāmadeva, "god of love," who awakens Śiva from his deep meditation by shooting "flower arrows" and thereby incurs his wrath and is incinerated. The story is found in Prajñāvarman, *Commentary on Praise of the One More Perfect Than the Gods* (*Devātiśayastotraṭīkā*), Toh 1113 Tengyur, bstod tshogs, *ka*, 48b4.
91. See commentary, pages 182–83. This is probably a reference to the frame story of book II of the *Pañcatantra*, where the crow Laghupatanaka, having witnessed how the mouse Hiraṇyaka had helped rescue the dove Citragrīva, sought the friendship of the mouse.
92. This echoes the first verse of chapter 8 of Cāṇakya, *Cāṇakya Treatise on Kingship* (Tengyur, thun mong ba'i lugs kyi bstan bcos, *ngo*, 134b7), where one reads: "A bad wife and a bad friend, / a bad king and bad company: / these relationships of negative influence, / cast them far away."
93. This echoes Śāntideva's *Guide to the Bodhisattva's Way of Life* 6:14ab, where one reads, "There is nothing that remains hard / if it becomes familiar."
94. This echoes Āryadeva's *Four Hundred Verses* 2.1, where we read: "Though this body might be seen as an enemy, / you should still look after it; / for through living a long life, a moral person / will perform with his body great acts of merit."
95. The three lower realms—the hell realm, the realm of the hungry ghosts, and the animal realm—are the three realms among the six realms of cyclic existence where sentient beings are reborn as a result of their negative karma.
96. This echoes Śāntideva's *Guide to the Bodhisattva's Way of Life* 5.12. Also many of the subsequent verses dealing with the practice of patience, or forbearance, echo lines from Śāntideva's chapter 6.
97. *Legs par bshad pa rin po che'i gter gyi 'grel pa.* This is the earliest commentary on Sakya Paṇḍita's *Jewel Treasury.* Although many people identify this work with Martön Chögyal, an examination of the colophon shows that it was originally written by Rinchen Pal (thirteenth century, TBRC resource ID P5298) and that Martön Chögyal later edited and corrected mistakes in this text, verifying these with Sakya Paṇḍita himself. The commentary offers explanations of only select verses.
98. In this verse Rinchen Pal plays with the meaning of Sakya Paṇḍita's full name, Kunga Gyaltsen Palsangpo. Each line uses one part of his name in various ways: every/all, joyful/festive/delight, victory banner, splendor/glory/perfection, beautiful/elegant.
99. See note 43 above.
100. This story is found also as story 61 in Tenzin, *Selected Anthology of Vedic Myths.*
101. The Buddha instructed his disciples to carefully examine his teachings. Just as jewelers inspect gold to determine its purity before purchase by rubbing, cutting, and heating it, disciples are to determine the obvious meaning of the teachings that is not in conflict with what is observed by the senses, the slightly hidden meaning that

is not contradicted by logic, and the very hidden meaning that at first can only be accepted on faith.

102. *A Hundred Stanzas on Wisdom* (*Prajñāśataka*), v. 98, Toh 4328 Tengyur, thun mong ba'i lugs kyi bstan bcos, *ngo*, 103b4.
103. *Four Hundred Stanzas* (*Catuḥśatakaśāstra*) 7.19, Toh 3846 Tengyur, dbu ma, *tsha*, 8a4.
104. Śāntideva, *Bodhisattvacaryāvatāra* 5.93, Toh 3871 Tengyur, dbu ma, *la*, 13a7.
105. Maitreya, *Uttaratantra* (*Mahāyānottaratantraśāstra*) 1.22, Toh 4024 Tengyur, sems tsam, *phi*, 55a7.
106. This story is in the *Account of the Noble Deeds of Sumāgadhā* (*Sumāgadhāvadāna*), Toh 346 Kangyur, mdo sde, *am*, 291a1–298b6.
107. To count each person included in a group, monks would take a stick out of a set of sticks.
108. Although the legend of Nāgārjuna's practice of alchemy is found in the tales of the eighty-four siddhas, the text does not contain this specific event of Nāgārjuna's offering tree leaves to the sage. Abhayadattaśrī, *Biographies of Eighty-Four Siddhas* (*Caturaśītisiddhapravṛtti*), Tengyur P 5091, rgyud 'grel, *lu*, 19a1.
109. This story appears in Butön's *History of Buddhism* (Tib.), 160, and in Jonang Tārānātha's *History of Buddhism in India* (Tib.), 168, as well.
110. *Rājaśrīvyākaraṇa* (*Rgyal po dpal gyi sgra*). This is not a text in the Tengyur, but a Sanskrit palmleaf manuscript of this name is part of the collection of the Norbulingka Palace, according to an undated catalog in Beijing called the *Krung go'i bod kyi shes rig zhib 'jug lte gnas su nyar ba'i ta la'i lo ma'i bstan bcos (spyin shog 'dril ma'i par) kyi dkar chag mdor gsal.*
111. Nāgārjuna, *Staff of Wisdom* (*Nītiśāstraprajñādaṇḍa*) 171, Toh 4329 Tengyur, thun mong ba'i lugs kyi bstan bcos, *ngo*, 109a6.
112. This story about the great Indian poet Kālidāsa is found also in Tārānātha's *History of Buddhism in India*, 75.
113. This story is in the *Finer Points of Discipline* (*Vinayakṣudrakavastu*), Toh 6 Kangyur, 'dul ba, *da*, 59a2–65b.
114. Source of the story not identified.
115. A similar story, in part, appears in the *Finer Points of Discipline* (*Vinayakṣudrakavastu*), Toh 6 Kangyur, 'dul ba, *da*, 59a2–65b.
116. Source of this story not identified.
117. We find similar lines in the *Pañcatantra* (Olivelle, book 2, v. 75): "Only the good can deliver the good from their misfortunes; / only elephants can pull elephants out of quagmire."
118. See note 46 above. In the Buddhist sources the story is found, for instance, in Prajñāvarman, *Commentary on Praise of the One More Perfect Than the Gods* (*Devātiśayastotraṭīkā*), Toh 1113 Tengyur, bstod tshogs, *ka*, 50a3.
119. Āryaśūra, *Garland of Birth Stories* (*Jātakamālā*), jātaka 31, Toh 4150 Tengyur, skyes rabs, *hu*, 118a6. Yangchen Gawai Lodrö also tells this story in *Rays of Sunlight: A Commentary on "Ganden Wise Sayings"* to elucidate verse 15 of *Ganden Wise Sayings*. See pages 226ff.
120. Āryaśūra, *Garland of Birth Stories* (*Jātakamālā*), jātaka 31, Toh 4150 Tengyur, skyes rabs, *hu*, 125a1.

121. Ibid., 125a4.
122. Ibid., 125a6.
123. Ibid., 125a6.
124. Ibid., 125a7.
125. Ibid., 125b2.
126. Ibid., 125b2.
127. Ibid., 125a4.
128. See note 49 above on the location of this story in the *Pañcatantra*. Yangchen Gawai Lodrö also tells this story in *Rays of Sunlight: A Commentary on "Ganden Wise Sayings"* to elucidate verse 21 of *Ganden Wise Sayings*. See pages 238ff.
129. This tale is in the *Finer Points of Discipline* (*Vinayakṣudrakavastu*), Toh 6 Kangyur, 'dul ba, *da*, 69b.
130. Source of story not identified.
131. The story about *Śubhārtha (Dge don) and *Papārtha (Sdig don) is found in the *Basis of Discipline* (*Vinayavastu*), Toh 1 Kangyur, 'dul ba, *nga*, 186b7; in the *Great Passing into Nirvana Sutra* (*Mahāparinirvāṇasūtra*), Toh 119 Kangyur, mdo, *ta*, 159a3; and in the *Sutra on the Wise and the Foolish* (*Damamūkanāmasūtra*) 33, Toh 341 Kangyur, mdo, *ah*, 137a6.
132. Folk legends in the Tibetan texts, and their Indic predecessors, frequently relate tales of merchants braving the dangers of the great oceans to gather precious jewels.
133. The story of King Mahāsaṃmata is told to elucidate verse 39 of *Ganden Wise Sayings* in *Rays of Sunlight: A Commentary on "Ganden Wise Sayings."* See pages 256–58 of this volume.
134. See note 53 above. This story is found also in the *Basis of Discipline* (*Vinayavastu*), Toh 1 Kangyur, 'dul ba, *nga*, 255b3. Yangchen Gawai Lodrö also tells a version of this story in *Rays of Sunlight: A Commentary on "Ganden Wise Sayings"* to elucidate verse 40 of *Ganden Wise Sayings*. See page 258.
135. This story from the Hindu myths is found in a number of Buddhist sources as well: Prajñāvarman, *Explanation of Praise of the Exalted* (*Viśeṣastavanāmaṭīkā*), Toh 1110 Tengyur, bstod tshogs, *ka*, 10b6; and Prajñāvarman, *Commentary on Praise of the One More Perfect Than the Gods* (*Devātiśayastotraṭīkā*), Toh 1113 Tengyur, bstod tshogs, *ka*, 41a2. See note 54 above as well.
136. Udbhaṭasiddhasvāmin, *Praise of the Exalted* (*Viśeṣastava*) 10, Toh 1109 Tengyur, bstod tshogs, *ka*, 2a3.
137. See note 55 above for the location of this story in the *Pañcatantra*.
138. This legend is found in the *Sutra on the Wise and the Foolish* (*Damamūkanāmasūtra*) 22, Toh 341 Kangyur, mdo, *ah*, 197a4.
139. Source of this story unidentified. Yangchen Gawai Lodrö identifies a verse from Nāgārjuna's *Staff of Wisdom* alluding to this story. See note 212 below.
140. Cāṇakya, *Cāṇakya Treatise on Kingship* (*Cāṇakyarājanītiśāstra*), chap. 3. Toh 4334 Tengyur, sna tshogs, *ngo*, 134a6; also Nāgārjuna, *Staff of Wisdom* (*Prajñādaṇḍa*), Toh* Tengyur, sna tshogs, *ngo*, *
141. This story appears also in *Clear Differentiation of the Discipline* (*Vinayavibhaṅga*), Toh 3 Kangyur, 'dul ba, *ja*, 195b. Another version of this story is told in *Rays of Sunlight: A Commentary on "Ganden Wise Sayings"* on page 324 of this volume to elucidate verse 98 of *Ganden Wise Sayings*.

142. Masūrākṣa, *Nītiśāstra* 6.9, Toh 4335 Tengyur, thun mong ba'i lugs kyi bstan bcos, *ngo*, 14b5.
143. Source of story unidentified.
144. Probably all six are meant to refer to the owl.
145. See note 61 above for the locations of this story in the *Pañcatantra*.
146. See note 62 above for the locations of this story in the *Pañcatantra*.
147. This story appears in Khepa Deu, *Extensive History of India and Tibet*, 98, and Jonang Tāranātha, *History of Buddhism in India* (Sichuan: Nationalities Press, 1976), 51. A variation of this story is translated by Andy Rotman in *Divine Stories: Divyāvadāna, Part 2* (Boston: Wisdom Publications, 2017), 40–49. For a book-length investigation of the many variations of the Mahādeva legend in Buddhist literature, see Jonathan Silk, *Riven by Lust* (Honolulu: University of Hawai'i Press, 2009).
148. Source of story unidentified. This story is also told in *Rays of Sunlight: A Commentary on "Ganden Wise Sayings"* on page 240 of this volume to elucidate verse 24 of *Ganden Wise Sayings*.
149. Source of story unidentified. This story is also told in *Rays of Sunlight: A Commentary on "Ganden Wise Sayings"* to elucidate verse 60 of *Ganden Wise Sayings*. See page 285.
150. This story is Jātaka 33 in Āryaśūra, *Garland of Birth Stories* (*Jātakamālā*), Toh 4150 Tengyur, skyes rabs, *hu*, 131b1. The three verses cited as part of the story come from the same text.
151. This story is in the *Sutra on the Wise and the Foolish* (*Damamūkanāmasūtra*) 24, Toh 341 Kangyur, mdo sde, *ah*, 170b6.
152. This story is found in Āryaśūra, *Garland of Birth Stories* (*Jātakamālā*), jātaka 24, Toh 4150 Tengyur, skyes rabs, *hu*, 89a7. All the verses in this story come from the same text. This story is also told in *Rays of Sunlight: A Commentary on "Ganden Wise Sayings,"* to elucidate verse 88 of *Ganden Wise Sayings*. See pages 309ff.
153. See note 66 above for the location of this story in the *Pañcatantra*. It can be found also in Vasubandhu, *Rules of Exposition* (*Vyākhyāyukti*), Toh 4261 Tengyur, sems tsam, *shi*, 129b5.
154. Āryaśūra, *Garland of Birth Stories* (*Jātakamālā*), jātaka 26, Toh 4150 Tengyur, skyes rabs, *hu*, 95b2. The verses in this story are from the same source. Yangchen Gawai Lodrö also tells this story in *Rays of Sunlight: A Commentary on "Ganden Wise Sayings"* to elucidate verse 18 of *Ganden Wise Sayings*. See pages 233ff.
155. See note 67 above on the lcoations of this story in the *Pañcatantra*.
156. Sources of this and the subsequent verses cited in this story are unidentified.
157. Source unidentified.
158. Source of this story unidentified.
159. This paragraph does not seem to fit here and might be an error in the Tibetan text.
160. See note 76 above. In the Buddhist sources, an abbreviated version of the *Mahābhārata* epic is also found in Prajñāvarman, *Explanation of Praise of the Exalted* (*Viśeṣastavanāmaṭīkā*), Toh 1110 Tengyur, bstod tshogs, *ka*, 33b4.
161. This is reference to Dharmakīrti's explanation of how exclusionary terms function in sentences and their difference in scope. The phrase "Arjuna is an expert archer" is an exclusionary term in that it indicates there to be no better archer than him. In

contrast the phrase "Kṛṣṇa is an expert archer" simply states that he too is a good archer, precluding only that he is not a good archer. See Dharmakīrti, *Thorough Exposition of Valid Cognition* (*Pramāṇavārttika*) 4.193, Toh 4210 Tengyur, tshad ma, *ce*, 147a1.

162. Dhṛtarāṣṭra's hundred offspring are the Kauravas ("those from Kuru"), whereas their cousins the offspring of Pāṇḍu are the Pāṇḍavas.
163. Drigung Rinchen Pal says this is a citation from the Sanskrit work *Tattvakaumudī* by Vācaspatimiśra (eighth–ninth century). The editors and translator were not able to find the source of this quote.
164. Although the exact source of this citation is unidentified, the reference here is clearly to the sermon Viṣṇu in the form of Kṛṣṇa gives to Arjuna at the famous Kurukṣetra battle. This is part of a long sermon in the *Bhagavadgītā*, which is a part of the Hindu *Mahābhārata* epic.
165. Source of story unidentified.
166. *Mahāyānasūtrālaṃkāra* 19.11, Toh 4020 Tengyur, sems tsam, *phi*, 28b5.
167. Ibid, 14.8, 18a1.
168. Source unidentified.
169. See note 80 above on the location of this story in the *Pañcatantra*. In the *Basis of Discipline* (*Vinayavastu*) too there are two lines of a verse concerning two battling rams: "If you see someone smashed / in between two rams . . ." Toh 1 Kangyur, 'dul ba, *ka*, 213a7. Yangchen Gawai Lodrö also tells this story in *Rays of Sunlight: A Commentary on "Ganden Wise Sayings"* to elucidate verse 62 of *Ganden Wise Sayings*. See pages 286–87.
170. It is difficult to determine whether this is a summary verse from Rinchen Pal himself or a citation from another source.
171. Source of story unidentified.
172. The reference to a particular story is unclear.
173. Whether this refers to a particular myth of the Hindu god Śiva is not clear.
174. See note 83 above.
175. Source of story unidentified.
176. Source of story unidentified.
177. This is a note added by Martön Chögyal, a student of Sakya Paṇḍita, who corrected and edited Rinchen Pal's commentary. He seems to be saying that the identification of this old abbot in the story with the historical person by the name of *Bhakanbha is something that he learned from Sakya Paṇḍita himself, who was his stainless savior (*rnam 'dren*), his revered teacher.
178. See note 85 above on the source of this well-known story in the *Rāmāyaṇa* epic. Rinchen Pal is probably drawing also from the *Rāmāyaṇa* itself, for although it was not available in Tibetan translation at that time, Sakya Paṇḍita would have been quite familiar with it.
179. "Mar" here refers to Martön Chögyal, and "the great venerable" probably refers to Sakya Paṇḍita. I am not sure if this clause was added by a later editor or if it is part of the original text. If the latter, it suggests that Martön was Rinchen Pal's teacher.
180. See note 89 above.
181. See note 90 above on this story in the *Pañcatantra*.
182. The source of this quotation was not determined.

183. This story is found in the *Śrīgupta Sutra*, Toh 217 Kangyur, mdo sde, *pa*, 269a1 and 284a2; and *Preeminent Account of Discipline* (*Vinayottaragrantha*), Toh 7 Kangyur, 'dul ba, *pa*, 170a6. The story is also classed as a jātaka in Kṣemendra's *Wish-Granting Vine of the Bodhisattva's Prior Lives* (*Bodhisatvāvadānakalpalatā*), Toh 4155 Tengyur, skyes rabs, *ke*, 79b2.
184. *Clear Differentiation of the Discipline* (*Vinayavibhaṅga*), Toh 3 Kangyur, 'dul ba *ca*, 126a7.
185. The three lower realms—the hell realm, the realm of the hungry ghosts, and the animal realm—are the three realms among the six realms of cyclic existence where sentient beings are reborn as a result of their negative karma.
186. *Ded dpon mdza' bo'i bu mo*. The story referred to was not identified.
187. Śāntideva, *Guide to the Bodhisattva Way of Life* (*Bodhisattvacaryāvatāra*) 5.31–32, Toh 3871 Tengyur, dbu ma, *la*.
188. This verse is often attributed to Dharmakīrti as if it is from *Thorough Exposition of Valid Cognition*; however, it is not found in the extant Tibetan version of the text.
189. Source unidentified.
190. Śāntideva, *Guide to the Bodhisattva Way of Life* (*Bodhisattvacaryāvatāra*) 6.14, Toh 3871 Tengyur, dbu ma, *la*, 15a3.
191. Dharmakīrti, *Pramāṇavārttika* 2.125, Toh 4210 Tengyur, tshad ma, *ce*, 112a5.
192. Ibid., 2.140, 112b6.
193. This story is found in *Finer Points of Discipline* (*Vinayakṣudrakavastu*), Toh 6 Kangyur, 'dul ba, *tha*, 275b2; also *Basis of Discipline* (*Vinayavastu*), Toh 1 Kangyur, 'dul ba, *ga*, 59a1.
194. This is a paraphrase of part of the concluding verses from the root text, *A Jewel Treasury of Wise Sayings*. See page 95 of this volume.
195. This too is part of the concluding verses of the root text.
196. Maitreya, *Mahāyānasūtrālaṃkāra* 12.60, Toh 4020 Tengyur, sems tsam, *phi*, 15b4.
197. Śāntideva, *Bodhisattvacaryāvatāra* 5.100, Toh 3171 Tengyur, dbu ma, *la*, 14a4. The second line of the verse is slightly different in this text.
198. Sakya Paṇḍita Kunga Gyaltsen, *Treatise on Music*, vol. *tha*, 161a3.
199. The Tibetan text reads *shā kya'i dge slong*, which literally means "the Śākya monk," meaning a monk in the order of Buddha Śākyamuni.
200. The full title of the text is *Ganden Wise Sayings: A Bouquet of White Lotuses, being a Treatise on the Examination of the Wise and the Foolish* (*Mkhas pa dang blun po brtag pa'i bstan bcos dge ldan legs bshad padma dkar po'i chun po*). The Tibetan editors chose the root text embedded in Yangchen Gawai Lodrö's commentary, which is translated as the next text in the present volume, to be the basis of their critical edition.
201. Since Gawai Lodrö's commentary includes every verse, please consult the commentary and its annotation for explanation of the stories referenced by the verses and for their sources in classical literature.
202. This is an allusion to Cāṇakya's *Treatise*, chap. 3 (134a6).
203. In some versions of the root text there is the following additional verse after this stanza: "Someone to whom the great bow their heads / is considered by inferior people to be equivalent to straw. / The wise make obeisance to a stupa, / but crows use it as a roost." This verse seems to be in fact a quote from Nāgārjuna's *Staff of*

Wisdom, and Yangchen Gawai Lodrö's commentary treats it as such rather than as part of the root text.

204. In the Tibetan original too this a five-lined stanza.
205. *Dge ldan legs bshad padma dkar po'i chun po'i 'grel pa nyi ma'i 'od zer*. The Tibetan editors made the basic text for this publication the *Commentary on the Good Advice of Ganden* found in the collected works of A kyā Yongs 'dzin. They compared it in detail to the commentary published with root text of *The Good Advice of Ganden* by Mtsho sngon mi rigs dpe skrun khang.
206. Cāṇakya, *Cāṇakyarājanītiśāstra* 6.1, Toh 4334 Tengyur, thun mong ba'i lugs kyi bstan bcos, *ngo*, 132b6.
207. Nāgārjuna, *Prajñādaṇḍa*, v. 170, Toh 4329 Tengyur, thun mong ba'i lugs kyi bstan bcos, *ngo*, 109b6.
208. *Staff of Wisdom* (*Prajñādaṇḍa*) 11, Toh 4329 Tengyur, thun mong ba'i lugs kyi bstan bcos, *ngo*, 103b6. See also Hahn, "The Tibetan *Shes rab sdong bu*," 14.
209. This refers to the passage in the *Questions of Dhāraṇiśvarāja Sutra* (*Dhāraṇīśvararājasūtra*) regarding how a master jeweler cleans a gem with three types of washing and three types of polishing. This sutra surives only in fragments cited in texts such as the *Sūtrasamuccaya*, attributed to Nāgārjuna.
210. Rinchen Pal also tells this story in *A Commentary on "A Jewel Treasury of Wise Sayings"* to elucidate verse 116 of the *Jewel Treasury*. See page 135.
211. This is a gloss on the word "in front of" (*gam*) in the first line of verse 5 in the root text, and the commentary lists two other terms that have the same meaning.
212. Nāgārjuna, *Prajñādaṇḍa*, v. 241, Toh 4329 Tengyur, thun mong ba'i lugs kyi bstan bcos, *ngo*, 112a7.
213. Ibid., 109a4.
214. This is a well-known jātaka. Āryaśūra, *Garland of Birth Stories* (*Jātakamālā*), jātaka 14, Toh 4150 Tengyur, skyes rabs, *hu*, 52a5.
215. Nāgārjuna, *A Hundred Stanzas on Wisdom* (*Prajñāśataka*), v. 69, Toh 4328 Tengyur, thun mong ba'i lugs kyi bstan bcos, *ngo*, 102a4.
216. This story appears in *Clear Differentiation of the Discipline* (*Vinayavibhaṅga*), Toh 3 Kangyur, 'dul ba, *ca*, 7b1; and also in the *Pañcatantra*. This story appeared in verse 93 of Sakya Paṇḍita's *Jewel Treasury* as well; for its appearance in the *Pañcatantra*, see note 57 above.
217. *Basis of Discipline* (*Vinayavastu*), Toh 3 Kangyur, 'dul ba, *ca*, 7b1.
218. Āryaśūra, *Garland of Birth Stories* (*Jātakamālā*), jātaka 6, Toh 4150 Tengyur, skyes rabs, *hu*, 17a2. In *A Commentary on "A Jewel Treasury of Wise Sayings,"* Drigung Rinchen Pal also tells this story to elucidate verse 18 of the root text. See pages 115ff.
219. *Basis of Discipline* (*Vinayavastu*), Toh 3 Kangyur, 'dul ba, *ja*, 7b1.
220. Āryaśūra, *Garland of Birth Stories* (*Jātakamālā*), jātaka 19, Toh 4150 Tengyur, skyes rabs, *hu*, 62b1. All the verses cited as part of this story are also from Āryaśūra's text.
221. Although this story is well known in Tibetan literature, its Indic source has not been identified.
222. *Basis of Discipline* (*Vinayavastu*) 79, Toh 3 Kangyur, 'dul ba, *ka*, 19b3. Disparaging a holy object is seventh in the count of ten downfalls.
223. Āryaśūra, *Garland of Birth Stories* (*Jātakamālā*), jātaka 22, Toh 4150 Tengyur, skyes rabs, *hu*, 43b2.

224. This story is in Kṣemendra, *A Wish-Granting Vine of the Bodhisattva's Prior Lives* (*Bodhisatvāvadānakalpalatā*) 41, Toh 4155 Tengyur, skyes rabs, *ke*, 306b6; and appears also in *Clear Differentiation of the Discipline* (*Vinayavibhaṅga*), Toh 3 Kangyur, 'dul ba, *nya*, 102a7.
225. Āryaśūra, *Garland of Birth Stories* (*Jātakamālā*), jātaka 31, Toh 4150 Kangyur, skyes rabs, *hu*, 112a6.
226. This story appears in *Basis of Discipline* (*Vinayavastu*), Toh 1 Kangyur, mdo sde, *ga*, 28a5.
227. *Sutra on the Wise and the Foolish* (*Damamūkanāmasūtra*), 17, Toh 341 Kangyur, mdo sde, *ah*, 102b4.
228. This is the famous Viśvantara (Vessantara in Pali) story. It is jātaka 9 in Āryaśūra, *Garland of Birth Stories* (*Jātakamālā*), Toh 4150 Tengyur, skyes rabs, *hu*, 30b5.
229. This as well as all subsequent verses in this story are also from the *Jātakamālā*.
230. Jātaka 26 in Āryaśūra, *Garland of Birth Stories* (*Jātakamālā*), Toh 4150 Tengyur, skyes rabs, *hu*, 95a2. The verses in the story are also from the *Jātakamālā*. In *A Commentary on "A Jewel Treasury of Wise Sayings,"* Drigung Rinchen Pal also tells this story to elucidate verse 182 of the root text. See pages 152ff.
231. Āryaśūra, *Garland of Birth Stories* (*Jātakamālā*), jātaka 27, Toh 4150 Tengyur, skyes rabs, *hu*, 99b3.
232. Jātaka 34 in Āryaśūra, *Garland of Birth Stories* (*Jātakamālā*), Toh 4150 Tengyur, skyes rabs, *hu*, 133a1. The verses below are from the same source.
233. This story appears in the *Pañcatantra*, as story 5 of book I in Olivelle and as story 7 of book I in Chandra Rajan. In *A Commentary on "A Jewel Treasury of Wise Sayings,"* Drigung Rinchen Pal also tells this story to elucidate verse 25 of the root text. See pages 121ff.
234. Although the text of the commentary here suggests that the story embedded in this verse is also the same story that is alluded to in a later verse, no such verse exists in the root text itself. These lines bear similarity with verse 48, but there it is the mouse that comes to ruin. The commentator also admits here that he has failed to locate the full story and suggests that more research is required. A story about a herd of elephants fooled by a rabbit is cited by Sakya Paṇḍita in verse 87 of his *Jewel Treasury*. See note 55 above.
235. Nāgārjuna, *Prajñādaṇḍa*, v. 135, Toh 4329 Tengyur, thun mong ba'i lugs kyi bstan bcos, *ngo*, 108b2.
236. The source of the story remains unidentified. In *A Commentary on "A Jewel Treasury of Wise Sayings,"* Drigung Rinchen Pal also tells this story to elucidate verse 153 of the root text. See page 145.
237. This tale appears in *Clear Differentiation of the Discipline* (*Vinayavibhaṅga*), Toh 3 Kangyur, 'dul ba, *nya*, 19a3. The story of Svāgata/Durāgata is also translated in Andy Rotman, *Divine Stories: Divyāvadāna, Part 1* (Boston: Wisdom, 2008), 289–323.
238. Āryaśūra, *Garland of Birth Stories* (*Jātakamālā*), Jātaka 16, Toh 4150 Tengyur, Skyes rabs, *hu*, 57a1. This story appears also in *Basis of Discipline* (*Vinayavastu*), Toh 1 Kangyur, 'dul ba, *kha*, 257b5.
239. Āryaśūra, *Garland of Birth Stories* (*Jātakamālā*), jātaka 16, Toh 4150 Tengyur, skyes rabs, *hu*, 57b3.

240. Āryaśūra, *Garland of Birth Stories* (*Jātakamālā*), jātaka 16, Toh 4150 Tengyur, skyes rabs, *hu*, 57b5.
241. This story is found in *Clear Differentiation of the Discipline* (*Vinayavibhaṅga*), Toh 3 Kangyur, 'dul ba, *ca*, 150b6; and it is elucidated in *Finer Points of Discipline* (*Vinaya-kṣudrakavastu*), Toh 6 Kangyur, 'dul ba, *tha*, 88b5. It appears also in Kṣemendra, *A Wish-Granting Vine of the Bodhisattva's Prior Lives* (*Bodhisatvāvadānakalpalatā*), Toh 4155 Tengyur, skyes rabs, *ke*, folio 12, 113b2.
242. This story as well as the verse cited below as part of it appear in *Basis of Discipline* (*Vinayavastu*), Toh 1 Kangyur, 'dul ba, *nga*, 256b5.
243. Āryaśūra, *Garland of Birth Stories* (*Jātakamālā*), Jātaka 11, Toh 4150 Tengyur, skyes rabs, *hu*, 43a7.
244. Source of this story remains unidentified.
245. This is the famous story of the four harmonious animal friends (*mthun pa spun bzi*) depicted often in temple murals. It appears, for example, in *Basis of Discipline* (*Vinayavastu*), Toh 1 Kangyur, 'dul ba, *nga*, 189b.
246. This story appears in the *Finer Points of Discipline* (*Vinayakṣudrakavastu*), Toh 6 Kangyur, 'dul ba, *tha*, 237b2.
247. Āryaśūra, *Garland of Birth Stories* (*Jātakamālā*), jātaka 8, Toh 4150 Tengyur, skyes rabs, *hu*, 24b4. The story is also found in *Basis of Discipline* (*Vinayavastu*), Toh 1 Kangyur, 'dul ba, *nga*, 123a7.
248. See commentary on verse 28. *Finer Points of Discipline* (*Vinayakṣudrakavastu*), Toh 6 Kangyur, 'dul ba, *tha*, 93a4; also *Clear Differentiation of the Discipline* (*Vinayavibhaṅga*), Toh 3 Kangyur, 'dul ba, *cha*, 161a1.
249. Āryaśūra, *Garland of Birth Stories* (*Jātakamālā*), jātaka 25, Toh 4150 Tengyur, skyes rabs, *hu*, 92a5.
250. This probably refers to the famed *Mahābhārata* epic.
251. This legend appears in *Sutra on Going Forth* (*Abhiniṣkramaṇasūtra*), Toh 301 Kangyur, mdo sde, *sa*, 106b1; and *Clear Differentiation of the Discipline* (*Vinayavibhaṅga*), Toh 3 Kangyur, 'dul ba, *ca*, 48b3.
252. This story is found in *Basis of Discipline* (*Vinayavastu*), Toh 1 Kangyur, 'dul ba, *nga*, 255b3; it appears also in the *Pañcatantra* (Chandra Rajan, book I, story 11). In *A Commentary on "A Jewel Treasury of Wise Sayings,"* Drigung Rinchen Pal also tells a version of this story to elucidate verse 64 of the root text. See page 130.
253. *Basis of Discipline* (*Vinayavastu*), Toh 1 Kangyur, 'dul ba, *nga*, 256b1.
254. Ibid., 161a4.
255. Āryaśūra, *Garland of Birth Stories* (*Jātakamālā*), jātaka 4, Toh 4150 Tengyur, skyes rabs, *hu*, 12a2. The verses in the story are from this same source.
256. This tale appears in *Great Passing into Nirvana Sutra* (*Mahāparinirvāṇasūtra*), Toh 119 Kangyur, mdo sde, *ta*, 137a5; and *Finer Points of Discipline* (*Vinaya-kṣudrakavastu*), Toh 6 Kangyur, 'dul ba, *tha*, 12a4. It is found also in Kṣemendra's *Wish-Granting Vine of the Bodhisattva's Prior Lives* (*Bodhisatvāvadānakalpalatā*) 9, Toh 4155 Tengyur, skyes rabs, *ke*, 86b1. A translation of the Jyotiska story is in Rotman, *Divine Stories, Part 2*, 51–88.
257. Āryaśūra, *Garland of Birth Stories* (*Jātakamālā*), jātaka 12, D 4150, Toh 4150 Tengyur, skyes rabs, *hu*, 45a4. The verses in this story are from the same source.
258. This story appears in various Tibetan historical texts, such as Sönam Gyaltsen,

Clear Mirror (Beijing: Nationalities Press, 1995), 101, as well as Panchen Sönam Drakpa's own *Magical Mirror of History* (Beijing: Nationalities Press, 1989), 13a1.

259. This story, including the various feats achieved by Minister Gar at the Chinese court, when competing for the hand of princess Wencheng, is found in the *Pillar Testament* (Lhasa: Tibetan People's Press, 2015), 161; and also in Sönam Gyaltsen, *Clear Mirror*, 101.
260. Āryaśūra, *Garland of Birth Stories* (*Jātakamālā*), jātaka 28, Toh 4150 Tengyur, skyes rabs, *hu*, 103b2. The verse cited below as part of the story is also from this same source. This story appears also in the *Great Passing into Nirvana Sutra* (*Mahāparinirvāṇasūtra*), Toh 119 Kangyur, mdo sde, *ta*, 159b5 and 103b2.
261. See verse 108 for elaboration on this tale, found in the birth stories of Dromtönpa, which is chapter 7 of the Son Teachings of Atiśa, *Book of Kadam*, 304–35.
262. Source of story unidentified. This is the story mentioned above in the commentary to verse 22. There Yangchen Gawai Lodrö said the source of this story needs investigation.
263. This tale appears in *Clear Differentiation of the Discipline* (*Vinayavibhaṅga*), Toh 3 Kangyur, 'dul ba, *ca*, 115a7.
264. Both the root text and commentary refer to Arjuna as a king rather than correctly as a prince. This tale is a famous part of the *Mahābhārata* where the five Pāṇḍava brothers engage in an epic battle with their cousins the Kauravas, and also the context in which the deeply revered Hindu scripture the *Bhagavadgītā* was taught as a sermon by Lord Kṛṣṇa to Arjuna. In the Buddhist sources, the story is found in Prajñāvarman, *Explanation of Praise of the Exalted* (*Viśeṣastavanāmaṭīkā*), Toh 1110 Tengyur, bstod tshogs, *ka*, 22a1, and mentioned also in Panchen Sönam Drakpa, *Magical Mirror of History*, 11a6.
265. In *A Commentary on "A Jewel Treasury of Wise Sayings,"* Drigung Rinchen Pal also tells this story to elucidate verse 246 of the root text. See pages 158ff. In Rinchen Pal's version of the story, the demoness's name is Aśvarūpa.
266. This is a well-known tale from Tibetan history found in various sources, such as the *Pillar Testament*, 84; Sönam Gyaltsen, *Clear Mirror*, 5; and Panchen Sönam Drakpa's *Magical Mirror of History*, 11a6.
267. This story appears in *Basis of Discipline* (*Vinayavastu*), Toh 1 Kangyur, 'dul ba, *nga*, 245b5.
268. The source of this story is unknown.
269. This story appears in *Basis of Discipline* (*Vinayavastu*), Toh 1 Kangyur, 'dul ba, *nga*, 259b1; *Clear Differentiation of the Discipline* (*Vinayavibhaṅga*), Toh 3 Kangyur, 'dul ba, *ca*, 53b1; and in *Great Passing into Nirvana Sutra* (*Mahāparinirvāṇasūtra*), Toh 119 Kangyur, mdo sde, *nya*, 321na4.
270. This story appears in Sönam Gyaltsen, *Clear Mirror*, 54–223; and in Paṇchen Sönam Drakpa, *Magical Mirror of History*, 17b2.
271. A detailed, supposedly first-person account of how Śāntarakṣita came to Tibet is found in the famed *Testament of Ba* by Ba Selnang. For an English translation and study of this important historical document, see Pasang Wangdu and Hildegard Diemberger, *dBa' bzhed: The Royal Narrative Concerning the Bringing of the Buddha's Doctrine to Tibet* (Vienna: Verlag der Österreichischen Akademie der Wissenschaften, 2000).

272. The story appears in *Clear Differentiation of the Discipline* (*Vinayavibhaṅga*), Toh 3 Kangyur, 'dul ba, *ca*, 48b3; and *Great Passing into Nirvana Sutra* (*Mahāparinirvāṇasūtra*), Toh 301 Kangyur, mdo sde, *sa*, 106b1.
273. This story appears is in Prajñāvarman's *Commentary on Praise of the One More Perfect than the Gods* (*Devātiśayastotraṭīkā*), Toh 1113 Tengyur, bstod tshogs, *ka*, 50a3. In *A Commentary on "A Jewel Treasury of Wise Sayings,"* Drigung Rinchen Pal also tells this story to elucidate verse 17 of the root text. See page 115.
274. This story appears in the *Pañcatantra* as story 10 in book 4 in Chandra Rajan. In *A Commentary on "A Jewel Treasury of Wise Sayings,"* Drigung Rinchen Pal also tells this story to elucidate verse 170 of the root text.
275. Āryaśūra, *Garland of Birth Stories* (*Jātakamālā*), jātaka 23, Toh 4150 Tengyur, skyes rabs, *hu*, 89b5.
276. The source of this story is unidentified. In *A Commentary on "A Jewel Treasury of Wise Sayings,"* Drigung Rinchen Pal also tells this story to elucidate verse 155 of the root text. See page 145.
277. This animal fable appears in the *Pañcatantra* as story 5 in book 1 in Chandra Rajan and as story 3.1.1 in book 1 in Olivelle. In *A Commentary on "A Jewel Treasury of Wise Sayings,"* Drigung Rinchen Pal also tells this story to elucidate verse 277 of the root text. See page 167.
278. Āryaśūra, *Garland of Birth Stories* (*Jātakamālā*), jātaka 30, Toh 4150 Tengyur, skyes rabs, *hu*, 114a1.
279. This is a reference to teachers in the Abrahamic traditions, although the actual names are erroneously rendered in the text.
280. There seems to have been a persistent legend in ancient India that somewhere in the Middle East, "a land where dates grow," there is the abhorrent social custom that permits sons taking their own mother as a bride. Dharmakīrti's *Vādanyāya*, for example, cites the presence of this custom and growing of dates as an example of pure coincidence, not a causal connection. The word *gla glo* (usually translated as "barbarians") in the commentary is the Tibetan equivalent of the Sanskrit *mleccha*. In classical Indian sources, the term appears to refer to followers of all religions and cultures other than those of ancient India, regions where Sanskrit is not used. So, for classical Indian authors, such regions would include Tibet and China as well.
281. This is reference to the Yongle emperor Zhu Di, who reigned in 1402–24 and supported the Buddhist faith in China.
282. Gö Lotsawa Shönu Pal, *Blue Annals*, 1:83.
283. Accounts of Langdarma's activities undermining Buddhism in Tibet in the ninth century, such as his persecution of the monastics and his subsequent assassination by Lhalung Palgyi Dorjé, are found in various historical sources—e.g., Sönam Gyaltsen, *Clear Mirror*, 234, and Pawo Tsuklak Trengwa, *Feast for the Learned*, 1:426.
284. There seems to have been an association between the island of Sri Lanka and man-eating ogres in ancient Indian texts. In the *Rāmāyaṇa* epic, for example, the ten-headed demon Rāvaṇa's palace, where Sītā was confined, is said to be located on the island of Sri Lanka. The source of the story is given later in the commentary as the *Sutra on Going to Laṅka*.
285. *Sutra on Going to Laṅka* (*Laṅkāvatārasūtra*), Toh 107 Kangyur, mdo sde, *ca*, 247b.

286. Cāṇakya, *Cāṇakyarājanītiśāstra* 7.34, Toh 4334 Tengyur, thun mong ba lugs kyi bstan bcos, *ngo*, 134b4.
287. Āryaśūra, *Garland of Birth Stories* (*Jātakamālā*), jātaka 21, Toh 4150 Tengyur, skyes rabs, *hu*, 70a1. The verses cited as part of the story are also from this same source.
288. This story is probably the one that appears in *Basis of Discipline* (*Vinayavastu*), Toh 1 Kangyur, 'dul ba, *nga*, 138b5 or the one on 212a2
289. This story of enmity between the crows and owls appears in the *Pañcatantra* as the frame story of book 3.
290. As identified at the end of the story, this tale of Kumāra Sudhana is told in great detail in the *Marvelous Array Sūtra* (*Gaṇḍavyūhasūtra*), which is part of the *Flower Ornament Scripture* (*Avataṃsakasūtra*), Toh 44 Kangyur, phal chen, *ga*, 324b2.
291. Judging by the story, it appears to be from the Vinaya texts, but its exact source remains unidentified.
292. *Staff of Wisdom* (*Prajñādaṇḍa*) 46, Toh 4329 Tengyur, thun mong ba'i lugs kyi bstan bcos, *ngo*, 105a2.
293. Ibid., 230, 112a2.
294. Sakya Paṇḍita, *A Jewel Treasury of Wise Sayings*, v. 24.
295. *Mahāparinirvāṇasūtra*, Toh 119 Kangyur, mdo sde, *ya*, 128a6.
296. This story appears in chapter 36 of the *Sutra on the Wise and the Foolish* (*Damamūkanāmasūtra*), Toh 341 Kangyur, mdo sde, *ah*, 254a4; in *Dispelling Ajātaśatru's Remorse* (*Ajātaśatrukaukṛtyavinodanā*), Toh 216 Kangyur, mdo sde, *tsha*, 260b5 and 261a7; in the *Great Passing into Nirvana Sutra* (*Mahāparinirvāṇasūtra*), Toh 119 Kangyur, mdo sde, *ta*, 201a1; and in *Basis of Discipline* (*Vinayavastu*), Toh 1 Kangyur, 'dul ba, *nga*, 201b3.
297. *Great Passing into Nirvana Sutra* (*Mahāparinirvāṇasūtra*), Toh 119 Kangyur, mdo sde, *ta*, 187b3.
298. For the story alluded to here, see the commentary on verse 59, pages 282–84.
299. Āryaśūra, *Garland of Birth Stories* (*Jātakamālā*), jātaka 24, Toh 4150 Tengyur, skyes rabs, *hu*, 88b2. The verses cited as part of the story are also from the same source. For an alternative translation of these verses, see Peter Khoroche, *Once the Buddha Was a Monkey* (Chicago: University of Chicago Press, 1989), 168–70. In *A Commentary on "A Jewel Treasury of Wise Sayings,"* Drigung Rinchen Pal also tells this story to elucidate verse 172 of the root text. See pages 148–51.
300. *Udānavarga*, Toh 326 Kangyur, mdo sde, *sa*, 218a1.
301. This story appears in *Basis of Discipline* (*Vinayavastu*), Toh 1 Kangyur, 'dul ba, *nga*, 103b6. This story is found also in the *Pañcatantra*, book II, story 1.1.1, in Olivelle and book II, story 4, in Chandra Rajan.
302. This verse is also from another Vinaya text, *Finer Points of Discipline* (*Vinayakṣudrakavastu*), Toh 6 Kangyur, 'dul ba, *tha*, 272a3.
303. This tale appears in *Finer Points of Discipline* (*Vinayakṣudrakavastu*), Toh 6 Kangyur, 'dul ba, *tha*, 270b2.
304. See pages 278–79, the commentary on verse 55, to read this story. This story appears in Sönam Gyaltsen's *Clear Mirror*, 203; in Sönam Drakpa's *Magical Mirror of History*, 17b2; and also in the *Pillar Testament*, 84.
305. This story appears in *Clear Differentiation of the Discipline* (*Vinayavibhaṅga*), Toh 3 Kangyur, 'dul ba, *ja*, 672a. The verses cited as part of the story are also from the

same source. A translation of this story, the *Cūḍāpakṣa-avadāna*, appears in Rotman, *Divine Stories, Part 2*, 207–46.

306. This story appears in the *Great Passing into Nirvana Sutra* (*Mahāparinirvāṇasūtra*), Toh 119 Kangyur, mdo sde, *ta*, 199b5. See also the commentary on verse 85.
307. *Saddharmapuṇḍarīkasūtra*, Toh 113 Kangyur, mdo sde, *ja*, 97b5.
308. This story appears in *Clear Differentiation of the Discipline* (*Vinayavibhaṅga*), Toh 3 Kangyur, 'dul ba, *ja*, 194a1. The verse cited as part of the story is from the same source. Another version of this story is told in *A Commentary on "A Jewel Treasury of Wise Sayings"* on page 136 of this volume to elucidate verse 117 of *A Jewel Treasury of Wise Sayings*.
309. This story appears in *Clear Differentiation of the Discipline* (*Vinayavibhaṅga*), Toh 3 Kangyur, 'dul ba, *ja*, 60a4 and 66b.
310. This story appears in *Finer Points of Discipline* (*Vinayakṣudrakavastu*), Toh 6 Kangyur, 'dul ba, *tha*, 296a4 and 306b1.
311. The story of Prince Sthiraśraddhā (*ded pa brtan pa*) appears as the seventh of Dromtönpa's former birth stories in Atiśa, *Book of Kadam*, 304–35. However, the story as told here in the commentary in some length as well as the verses cited as part of the story appear to be drawn from a different source, which remains unidentified.
312. Āryaśūra, *Garland of Birth Stories* (*Jātakamālā*), jātaka 10, Toh 4150 Tengyur, skyes rabs, *hu*, 39a6.
313. This story appears in the *Preeminent Account of Discipline* (*Vinayottaragrantha*), Toh 7 Kangyur, 'dul ba, *pa*, 170a6, which also contains the verses cited here as part of the story. However, there is an entire sutra entitled the *Śrīgupta Sutra* (*Śrīguptasūtra*), Toh 217 Kangyur, mdo sde, *pa*, 269a1–284a2.
314. This story appears in *Basis of Discipline* (*Vinayavastu*), Toh 1 Kangyur, 'dul ba, *nga*, 237a2, and in *Clear Differentiation of the Discipline* (*Vinayavibhaṅga*), Toh 3 Kangyur, 'dul ba, *nya*, 174b3. See also Rotman, *Divine Stories, Part 2*, 258–65, where this story appears within the *Mākandika-avadāna*.
315. This story appears in *Clear Differentiation of the Discipline* (*Vinayavibhaṅga*), Toh 3 Kangyur, 'dul ba, *nya*, 158b2. An English translation of the *Mākandika-avadāna* is found in Rotman, *Divine Stories, Part 2*, 247–91.
316. This story appears in *Finer Points of Discipline* (*Vinayakṣudrakavastu*), Toh 6 Kangyur, 'dul ba, *tha*, 86b1 and 77a7.
317. This story of the Chinese Chan master Hashang, who is said to have propagated an antirational and quietist doctrine in Tibet and was later defeated by the Indian master Kamalaśīla in a debate, appears in the *Testament of Ba*, 64–76, and is repeated in subsequent historical texts like Sönam Gyaltsen's *Clear Mirror*, 221, and Pawo Tsuklak Trengwa, *Feast for the Learned*, 1:385.
318. *Clear Differentiation of the Three Codes*, 26a4. In translation by Jared Douglas Rhoton (Albany: State University of New York Press, 2002); see p. 118.
319. Kamalagupta, *Vimala's Questions and Answers: A Precious Garland* (*Vimalapraśnottararatnamālā*), v. 5, Toh 4333 Tengyur, thun mong ba'i lugs kyi bstan bcos, *ngo*, 126b2.
320. *A Hundred Stanzas on Wisdom* (*Prajñāśataka*), v. 69, Toh 4328 Tengyur, thun mong ba'i lugs kyi bstan bcos, *ngo*, 102a4.

321. *Staff of Wisdom* (*Prajñādaṇḍa*), v. 240, Toh 4329 Tengyur, thun mong ba'i lugs kyi bstan bcos, *ngo,* 112b.
322. The commentary is here making a point pertaining to the different uses of similes according to the poetic rules of Indian *kāvya* (poetic) discipline.
323. Nāgārjuna, *Prajñāśataka*, v. 98, Toh 4329 Tengyur, thun mong ba'i lugs kyi bstan bcos, *ngo*, 103a4.
324. This concluding aspiration does not appear in the version of the root text used in this anthology.
325. The full title of this text is *A Pearl Garland of Advice Uniting Spiritual and Temporal Ethics* (*Lugs zung gi bslab bya mi thi li phreng ba*). See under Ngawang Losang Gyatso in the bibliography.
326. The work was composed at the behest of the Tüśiyetü Khan, a Mongolian ruler of Genghis's descent, who met the Fifth Dalai Lama in 1674.
327. Tsuta, or Cūta, is a mythical place where the inhabitants are said to have only one leg. Those who have two legs are considered abnormal, and no one will believe a word they say. See Yangchen Gawai Lodrö's commentary to verse 60 of the *Ganden Wise Sayings* on page 285.
328. The three spheres of action are the sphere of study (*klog pa thos bsam gyi 'khor lo*), the sphere of meditation of the renunciate (*spong ba bsam gtan gyi 'khor lo*), and the sphere of conduct and activity to benefit others (*bya ba las kyi 'khor lo*). The ten Dharma activities are (1) scribing scriptures, (2) worship, (3) giving, (4) listening to discourses, (5) reading the teachings, (6) retaining the teachings in one's mind, (7) instructing others, (8) reciting holy works, (9) contemplation, and (10) meditation.
329. These three are important Dharma protectors in the Geluk tradition, with the first two having special connection with Tsongkhapa himself and Palden Lhamo enjoying a particular connection with the institution of the Dalai Lama.
330. Genghis Khan's empire was divided into four administrative areas, the most important of which was Khalka Tüśiyetü. The proper name of the Khalka khan for whom this text was written is Chakhun Dorji. In his autobiography, the Fifth Dalai Lama says he met the Khalka Khan on February 1, 1674. In contemporary historical records this khan is referred to as Tüśiyetü Khan. Ahmad, *Sino-Tibetan Relations in the Seventeenth Century*, 261.
331. The full title of the text is: *A Treatise on Trees: A Hundred Branches of Wise Sayings on Spiritual and Worldly Norms* (*Legs par bshad pa shing gi bstan bcos lugs gnyis yal 'dab brgya ldan*).
332. The higher trainings in morality, meditation, and wisdom. These three are correlated in the Buddhist tradition as the principal subject matter of the Buddha's teaching enshrined in the "three baskets" of discipline (*vinaya*), discourses (*sūtra*), and higher knowledge (*abhidharma*).
333. Literally "hearers" and "self-enlightened ones," these terms refer to disciples of the Buddha whose primary objective is personal liberation rather than the universal emancipation from suffering sought by bodhisattvas.
334. Stanzas 25–28 pertain to the practice of the first four perfections of generosity, morality, forbearance, and joyful effort. The last two perfections, meditation and wisdom, are presented in two verses each (29–32).

335. On Malaya, a region in the southern part of India, see note 50 explicating a reference in verse 31 of *Jewel Treasury of Wise Sayings,* and page 215.
336. Zemey Rinpoché's commentary (p. 30a) lists the four as the following: (1) unripe both inside as well as outside, (2) ripe outside but not inside, (3) ripe inside but not outside, and (4) ripe both outside and inside.
337. This is an allusion to the assertion in the Jain philosophy about the sentient nature of trees, an object of critique by Indian Buddhist thinkers.
338. According to an ancient folk belief, the touch of a young woman, or even spit from a woman chewing tobacco, can make an aśoka tree unfurl its blossoms.
339. In Tibetan, the single word *shing* covers tree, wood, and timber. Thus, in the Tibetan original, the author is indeed using the attributes of *shing* alone for his metaphors throughout the entire poem, an impressive literary achievement.
340. Sarasvatī is the goddess of wisdom, both in the Buddhist and Hindu iconographic tradition, and is characteristically depicted seated on a swan and holding a sitar. She is also the goddess of poetry and thus invoked here by the author.
341. This verse criticizes some of the Tibetan works in the wise-sayings genre by stating that although the authors employ a profusion of similes, the actual points being made are quite inconsequential. Zemey Rinpoché's commentary does not attempt to identify the specific targets of this critique.
342. The full title of the Tibetan text reads: *A Treatise on Water: A Hundred Waves of Wise Sayings* (*Legs par bshad pa chu'i bstan bcos*).
343. This is a reference to the story of the Buddha's former birth as the king of geese, as told in Āryaśūra's *Jātakamālā*, jātaka 22, Toh 4150, skyes rabs, *hu*, 73b2, and in Khoroche, *Once the Buddha Was a Monkey*, 140–52. In this volume on page 224, this story is told in *Rays of Sunlight: A Commentary on "Ganden Wise Sayings"* to elucidate verse 13 of *Ganden Wise Sayings*.
344. See note 48 explaining this analogy, which is also found in verse 20 of *A Jewel Treasure of Wise Sayings*.
345. A version of this story is told in *A Commentary on "A Jewel Treasury of Wise Sayings"* on page 136 of this volume to elucidate verse 117 of *A Jewel Treasury of Wise Sayings*. Another version of this story is told in *Rays of Sunlight: A Commentary on "Ganden Wise Sayings"* on page 324 of this volume to elucidate verse 98 of *Ganden Wise Sayings*.
346. Source story not identified.
347. Exact source of story unidentified.
348. Drigung Rinchen Pal tells the story behind this allusion in *A Commentary on "A Jewel Treasury of Wise Sayings"* on page 121 of this volume to elucidate verse 25 of *A Jewel Treasury of Wise Sayings*. Yangchen Gawai Lodrö also tells this story in *Rays of Sunlight: A Commentary on "Ganden Wise Sayings"* to elucidate verse 21 of *Ganden Wise Sayings*. See page 238ff.
349. This is probably a reference to a story from the Hindu myths found in various sources including the *Mahābhārata*. In its original context, the story involves the gods and the demigods churning the great ocean using Mount Mandara as the churning rod and the serpent king Vasuki as the rope, and has more to do with the extracting of *amrita*, immortal nectar. See Wendy Doniger O'Flaherty, *Hindu Myths* (London: Penguin Books, 1975), 273–80.

350. "Wandering through Brahma's matted hair" is probably an allusion to the origin myth of the Ganges River, which is said to have been sent down to the earth to help cleanse the ancestral sins of King Bhagīratha. Verse 81c onward presents the norms related to Dharma practice. This is the reverse sequence of Gungthang's *Treatise on Trees*.
351. This is a reference to the story of one of the ten avatars of Viṣṇu, his incarnation as a fish. For this avatar story drawn from various sources, see O'Flaherty, *Hindu Myths*, 179–84.
352. See note 65.
353. The eight types of leisure refer to freedom from eight states of existence that preclude the opportunity to practice Dharma. They are freedom from (1) wrong views, and freedom from birth (2) in a place where the Buddha's teaching is absent, (3) as an animal, (4) as a hungry ghost, (5) as a hell being, (6) in a barbarian land, (7) as a mute or dumb, and (8) as a long-lived celestial being.
354. The "eight special qualities" of water are its (1) crystal clarity, (2) coolness, (3) sweetness, (4) lightness, and (5) softness, and the way it (6) soothes the stomach, (7) is free of impurities, and (8) clears the throat.
355. It is said that, due to their own specific karmic power, when a human, animal, hungry ghost, and god look at a body of water, it appears differently to each—as plain water, as an abode, as pus and blood, and as ambrosia, respectively.
356. This echoes the opening salution verses of Candrakīrti's *Entering the Middle Way* (*Madhyamakāvatāra*), where he pays homage to the three types of compassion—compassion focused on the suffering being, compassion focused on the phenomenal reality of the being, and nonobjectifying or nonreferential compassion.
357. There are variant readings of this line in the various Tibetan editions of the text. One reads "A miniscule piece of a ketaka fruit," while another could be read as "With sand mixed with ketaka fruit." I have read the word *'bras* ("fruit") in the text as an error, which should be read correctly as *'dres* ("mixed"). *Ketaka* is the name of a mythic gem that is believed to have a magical cleansing power.
358. This is a reference to the sage Agastya ("mountain thrower") mentioned in the ancient Hindu myths, although the source of the story about him drinking up all the rivers remains unidentified.
359. The four ways of gathering others are (1) giving what is materially needed, (2) speaking in a pleasant manner, (3) instructing what is righteous, and (4) setting an example through living the advice by oneself. These four are contrasted with the six perfections, the latter being the means by which a bodhisattva cultivates him- or herself.
360. This is probably a reference to the Ganges invocation prayer known as *Gaṅga Ārti*, which is performed regularly by the devout Hindus on the banks of the Ganges.
361 See note 350 on the connection between Bhagīratha and the Ganges River.
362. The full title of the text reads *A Treatise on Wind: Wise Sayings That Flutter the Flag of the Two Norms* (*Lugs zung bad an gyo ba'i legs bshad rlung gi bstan bcos*).
363. The three secrets of the guru's enlightened activity refer to the guru's body, speech, and mind.
364. This echoes *Bodhisattvacaryāvatāra* 4.20.
365. *Precious Garland* (*Ratnāvalī*) 4.17, Toh 4158 Tengyur, spring yig, *ge*, 118b7.

366. The four powers are the essential elements in the practice of confession: (1) the power of the support (refuge in the Three Jewels), (2) the power of regret, (3) the power of the resolve not to perform the act again, and (4) power of enacting the antidote.
367. The three are (1) the ethic of restraint, (2) the ethic of gathering virtues, and (3) the ethic of bringing about the welfare of sentient beings.
368. The author here seems to suggest, though admitting he himself has not seen them, that there are treatises on both earth and fire composed by Namgyal Söpa. This is probably an error. Kyilsur Losang Jinpa is likely referring to Nomchi Khenpo (Bya bral nom chi mkhan po blo bzang bshad sgrub, b. 1756), who wrote a treatise on fire as well as one on iron. However, no treatise on earth is known to have been composed by him. The treatise on earth that is known today and featured in this volume was composed by Paṇchen Chökyi Nyima. See next note.
369. The full title of the text is *A Treatise on Earth: A Jewel Garland That Glows with a Hundred Lights of Wise Sayings on the Two Norms* (*Legs par bshad pa sa'i bstan bcos lugs gnyis 'od brgya 'bar ba'i dbyig gi 'phreng ba*). The author, Thubten Chökyi Nyima (1883–1937), was sixth in the succession of Paṇchen Lamas that began with Losang Chökyi Gyaltsen in the seventeenth century. The Tibetan editors of this volume attributed authorship of this text to Paṇchen Losang Chökyi Nyima (1782–1853).
370. The story of Bāli losing the three worlds is told by Rinchen Pal in *A Commentary on "A Jewel Treasury of Wise Sayings"* to elucidate verse 72 of the *Jewel Treasury*. See page 131 of this volume.
371. Rinchen Pal tells this story in *A Commentary on "A Jewel Treasury of Wise Sayings"* to elucidate verse 321 of the *Jewel Treasury*. See pages 174–75.
372. Māndhātṛ, known also as Māndhātā, is the name of an ancient king mentioned in the Hindu myths. His name, literally "he shall draw sustenance from me," was given by Indra. The story of this mythical king appears also in the Buddhist sources. See, e.g., *Basis of Discipline* (*Vinayavastu*), Toh 1 Tengyur, 'dul ba, *kha*, 169b6; translation in Rotman, *Divine Stories, Part 1*, 348–71.
373. Most of the *lamrim* literature presents three forms of generosity: (1) giving material things, (2) giving the Dharma, and (3) giving protection from fear.
374. The full title of the text reads *Khaché Phalu's Advice on How to Observe the Law of Karma in Everyday Life* (*Kha che pha lu'i 'jig rten las 'bras rtsi lugs kyi bslab bya*). "*Khaché*" in Tibetan can mean Kashmir or Islam, and when used as an adjective it means a Muslim. Ostensibly, the text is offered as an advice from a Tibetan Muslim bearing the name Phalu Ju, although, as mentioned in the introduction, the exact authorship of the text remains hugely problematic. The Tibetan editors have used the version of this text published the Tibet Nationalities Press, prepared by one Losang Tsering, and compared it against other versions, including especially a small old woodblock print in the personal collection of Zemey Rinpoché.
375. This entire text of the preamble, with its reference to the time when the Buddha was ten years old, seems quite obscure.
376. The notes inserted by the translator to point out a few of the Islamic references in the Tibetan text should not be construed as an extensive analysis of this text. Many other passages seem to have clearly Buddhist references, and some allusions could

be related to either religious tradition. In this verse "the center" is likely Mecca. Mecca is conventionally regarded by Muslims as the center of the world and the Kaaba is called "the center of the center."

377. Khuda or Khoda (خدا) is the Persian word for "Lord" or "God." The term is originally from a Middle Persian honorific and can also mean "king." Formerly Persian speakers used it in reference to Ahura Mazda. Today in Islam it is reserved for God. Khuda is occasionally used as a loanword in Bengali, Urdu, Sindhi, Hindi, and several South Asian languages. From http//en.wikipedia.org/wiki/Khuda, accessed January 10, 2014.
378. "The one" is likely a reference to God in Islam.
379. There are Islamic traditions that speak of miraculous trees with leaves bearing the names of Allah. Johan Van Manen, "Khacche Phalu: A Tibetan Moralist," *The Asutosh Mookerjee Silver Jubilee Volumes* 3.2 (1925): 174.
380. The petitioner is perhaps requesting permission to go to Mecca (the center) from the authorities in Mecca or from Allah himself.
381. In some Islamic devotional writing, the phrase "Master of the precious stars" is used as an epithet for Allah. This same phrase occurs again in chapter 7, verse 4. The phrase "Garden of Light" is frequently used in the Qur'an as a metaphor for paradise. Hence the translator read *gling* as a shortened form of *gling ka*.
382. "Three days" (*zhag gsum*)—referring to today, tommorrow, and the day after—is a typical Tibetan expression used for describing the brevity of a particular temporal framework. This expression comes up repeatedly later in the text as well.
383. This may be a reference to Islamic burial practices. Traditional Tibetan Buddhists did not bury the dead.
384. The author is speaking here of the importance of giving away one's wealth as a preparation for one's impending death, the "solitary journey."
385. Dried apricots are highly prized in Tibet as delicacies and they are imported from the Ladakh regions where they are grown. Ladakh and its neighbor Kashmir are also the regions from where Tibetan Muslims historically emigrated.
386. *Arak* is a widely used Arabic-derived word for alcoholic spirits.
387. This is criticism of monks who are self-centered but may have the alchemical practice known as "extracting the stone-like essence" (*lde'u bcud len*), which involves hermits surviving, through their meditative power, on only a few seeds or grains a day for a prolonged period.
388. Likely a reference to the main protagonist of the popular Tibetan opera *The Righteous King Norbu Sangpo* (*Chos rgyal nor bu bzang po*), who was given a musical nymph to be his wife.
389. This is a reference to the famous Tibetan epic of Gesar of Ling, in which King Gesar and his general Denma, a skilled archer, are two of the main characters.
390. This is possibly a reference to the formal salat, during which a Muslim performs a series of prostrations. One of the five daily required prayer sessions is in the evening.
391. This line perhaps references one of the ninety-nine names of Allah: the Eternal, the Protector, the Master, and so on.
392. This might be a reference to the Islamic stricture on eating properly butchered (halal) meat.
393. The author is saying that at the king's court an education is the means to reach decisions whereas for a lama an education is the means to self-knowledge.

394. A hadith, possibly known to the author, contains the saying "The woman advances and retires in the shape of a devil." Sahih Muslim, Hadith 2491.

Bibliography

Kangyur (Canonical Scriptures)

Basis of Discipline. Vinayavastu. 'Dul ba gzhi. Toh 1, 'dul ba *ka, kha, ga, nga.* P 1030, *khe.*

Clear Differentiation of the Discipline. Vinayavibhaṅga. 'Dul ba rnam 'byed. Toh 3, 'dul ba, *ca* to *ja.* P 1032, *che.*

Collection of Aphorisms. Udānavarga. Ched du brjod pa'i tshoms. Toh 326, mdo sde, *sa.* P 112, *shu.*

Dispelling Ajātaśatru's Remorse. Ajātaśatrukaukṛtyavinodanā. Ma skyes dgra'i 'gyod pa bsal ba'i mdo. Toh 216, mdo sde, *tsha.* P 881, *tshu.*

Finer Points of Discipline. Vinayakṣudrakavastu. 'Dul ba phran tshegs. Toh 6, 'dul ba, *tha–da.* P 1035, *de.*

Flower Ornament Sutra. Avataṃsakasūtra. Sangs rgays phal po che zhes bya ba shin tu rgyas pa chen po'i mdo. Toh 44, phal chen, *ga.* P 761, *ju.*

Great Passing into Nirvana Sutra. Mahāparinirvāṇasūtra. Yongs su mya ngan las 'das pa chen po'i mdo. Toh 119, mdo sde, *ha.* P 787, *ju.*

Lotus Sutra. Saddharmapuṇḍarīkasūtra. Dam pa'i chos padma dkar po. Toh 113, mdo sde, *ja.* P 781, *chu.*

Preeminent Account of Discipline. Vinayottaragrantha. 'Dul ba gzhung dam pa. Toh 7, 'dul ba, *pa.* P 1037, *pe.*

Questions of Dhāraṇīśvarāja Sutra. Dhāraṇīśvararājasūtra (aka *Tathāgatamahākaruṇānirdeśasūtra*). *De bzhin gshegs pa'i snying rje chen po nges par bstan pa'i mdo.* Toh 147, mdo sde, *pa.* P 814, *nu.*

Śrīgupta Sutra. Śrīguptasūtra. 'Phags pa dpal sbas zhes bya ba'i mdo. Toh 217, mdo sde, *pa.* P 883, *tsu.*

Story of Sumāgadha. Sumāgadhāvadāna. Ma ga dhā bzang mo'i rtogs pa brjod pa. Toh 346, mdo sde, *am.* P 1015, *u.*

Sutra on Going Forth. Abhiniṣkramaṇasūtra. Mngon par 'byung ba'i mdo. Toh 301, mdo sde, *sa.* P 167, *shu.*

Sutra on Going to Laṅka. Laṅkāvatārasūtra. Lang kar gshegs pa'i mdo. Toh 107 Kangyur, mdo sde, *ca.* P 775 *ngu.*

Sutra on the Wise and the Foolish. Damamūkanāmasūtra. Mdzangs blun zhes bya ba'i mdo. Toh 341, mdo sde, *a.* P 1008, *hu.*

Tengyur (Canonical Treatises)

Abhayadattaśrī. *Biographies of Eighty-Four Siddhas. Caturaśītisiddhapravṛtti. Grub thob brgyad cu rtsa bzhi'i lo rgyus.* P 5091, rgyud 'grel, *lu.*

Āryadeva. *Four Hundred Stanzas. Catuḥśatakaśāstra. Bstan bcos bzhi brgya pa zhes bya ba'i tshig le'ur byas pa* (*Bzhi rgya pa*). Toh 3846, dbu ma, *tsha.* P 5246, *tsha.*

Āryaśūra. *Garland of Birth Stories. Jātakamālā. Skyes pa'i rabs kyi rgyud skyes rabs so bzhi.* Toh 4150, skyes rabs, *hu.* P 5650, *ke.*

Cāṇakya. *Cāṇakya Treatise on Kingship. Cāṇakyarājanītiśāstra. Tsa na ka'i rgyal po'i lugs kyi bstan bcos.* Toh 4334, thun mong ba'i lugs kyi bstan bcos, *ngo.* P 5126, *go.*

Dharmakīrti. *Thorough Exposition of Valid Cognition. Pramāṇavārttika. Tshad ma rnam 'grel gyi tshig le'ur byas pa.* Toh 4210, tshad ma, *ce.* P 5709, *ce.*

Kamalagupta. *Vimala's Questions and Answers: A Precious Garland. Vimalapraśnottararatnamālā. Dri ma med pa'i dris len rin po che'i phreng ba.* Toh 4333, thun mong ba'i lugs kyi bstan bcos, *ngo.* P 5825, go.

Kṣemendra. *A Wish-Granting Vine of the Bodhisattva's Prior Lives. Bodhisatvāvadānakalpalatā. Byang chub sems dpa'i rtogs pa brjod pa dpag bsam gyi 'khri shing* (*Rtogs brjod dpag bsam 'khri shing*). Toh 4155, skyes rabs, *ke.* P 5655, *ge.*

Maitreya. *Ornament of Mahayana Sutras. Mahāyānasūtrālaṃkāra. Thegs pa chen po'i mdo sde rgyan shes bya ba'i tshig le'ur byas pa* (*Mdo sde rgyan*). Toh 4020, sems tsam, *phi.* P 5521 *phi.*

———. *Uttaratantra. Mahāyānottaratantraśāstra. Thegs pa chen po'i rgyud bla ma'i bstan bcos* (*Rgyud bla ma*). Toh 4024, sems tsam, *phi.* P 5525, *phi.*

Masūrakṣa. *Treatise on Norms. Nītiśāstra. Lugs kyi bstan bcos.* Toh 4335, thun mong ba'i lugs kyi bstan bcos, *ngo.* P 5127, *go.*

Nāgārjuna. *A Drop to Nourish a Person. Jantupoṣaṇabindu. Skye bo gso ba'i thigs pa.* Toh 4330, thun mong ba'i lugs kyi bstan bcos, *ngo.* P5822, *go.*

———. *A Hundred Stanzas on Wisdom. Prajñāśataka. Shes rab brgya pa zhes bya ba'i rab tu byed pa.* Toh 4328, thun mong ba'i lugs kyi bstan bcos, *ngo.* P 5820, *go.*

———. *Precious Garland. Ratnāvalī. Rgyal po la gtam bya ba rin po che'i phreng ba,* Toh 4158, spring yig, *ge.* P 5651, *nge.*

———. *Staff of Wisdom: A Treatise on Norms. Nītiśāstraprajñādaṇḍa. Lugs kyi bstan bcos shes rab sdong bu.* Toh 4329, thun mong ba'i lugs kyi bstan bcos, *ngo.* P 5921, *go.*

Prajñāvarman. *Commentary on Praise of the One More Perfect Than the Gods. Devātiśayastotraṭīkā. Lha las phul byung du byung bar bstod pa'i rgya cher 'grel pa.* Toh 1113, bstod tshogs, *ka.* P 2005, *ka.*

———. *Explanation of Praise of the Exalted. Viśeṣastavanāmaṭīkā. Khyad par du 'phags pa'i bstod kyi rgya cher bshad pa.* Toh 1110, bstod tshogs, *ka.* P 2002, *ka.*

Śāntideva. *Guide to the Bodhisattva's Way of Life. Bodhisattvacaryāvatāra. Byang chub sems dpa'i spyod 'jug pa la 'jug pa* (*Spoyd 'jug*). Toh 3871, dbu ma, *la.* P 5272, *la.*

Sūryagupta. (Ravigupta). *A Treasury of Verse. Gāthākośa. Tshigs su bcad pa'i mdzod.* Toh 4331, thun mong ba, *ngo.* P 5823, *go.*

Udbhaṭasiddhasvāmin. *Praise of the Exalted. Viśeṣastava. Khyad par 'phags bstod.* Toh 1109, bstod tshogs, *ka.* P 2001, *ka.*

Vararuci. *Hundred Stanzas. Śatagāthā. Tshigs su bcad pa brgya pa.* Toh 4332, thun mong ba, *ngo.* P 5824, *go.*

Vasubandhu. *Rules of Exposition. Vyākhyāyukti. Rnam par bshad rigs pa.* Toh 4061, sems tsam, *shi.* P 5562, *si.*

Other Works

Ahmad, Zahiruddin. *Sino-Tibetan Relations in the Seventeenth Century.* Serie orientale Roma 40. Rome: Istituto Italiano per il Medio ed Estremo Oriente, 1970.

Anthology of Wise Sayings Treatises. Legs bshad bstan bcos phyogs bsgrigs. 6 vols. Xining, China: Kokonor Nationalities Press (Mtsho sngon mi rigs dpe skrun khang), 2006.

Āryaśūra. *Jātakamālā* or *Garland of Birth-Stories.* Translated by J. S. Speyer. London: Oxford University Press, 1895.

Atiśa (982–1054) (attributed). *Book of Kadam. Bka' gdams glegs bam.* Book 2. Xining, China: Kokonor Nationalities Press (Mtsho sngon mi rigs dpe skrun khang), 1993.

Beckwith, Christopher. "The Tibetans in the Ordos and North China." In *Silver on Lapis: Tibetan Literary Culture and History,* 3–10. Bloomington, IN: The Tibetan Society, 1987.

Bosson, James E. *A Treasury of Aphoristic Jewels: The Subhāṣitaratnaniddhi of Sa Skya Pandita in Tibetan and Mongolian.* Uralic and Altaic Series 92. Bloomington: Indiana University Press, 1969.

Butön Rinchen Drup (1290–1364). *History of Buddhism. Bu ston chos 'byung.* Beijing: Krung go'i bod kyi shes rig dpe skrun khang, 1991.

Catalogue of the Dergé Kangyur and Tengyur. Sendai, Japan: Tohuku University, 1934.

Chapel Tseten Phuntsok. *Sutra Extracted from Dunhang on an Elder Brother's Advice to His Younger Brother: A Word Commentary. Tun hong nas thon pa'i thu bos nu bo la gtams pa'i mdo: 'grel pa.* In *Anthology of Wise-Sayings Treatises* (*Legs bshad bstan bcos phyogs bsgrigs*), vol. 1. Xining, China: Kokonor Nationalities Press (Mtsho sngon mi rigs dpe skrun khang), 2006.

Chökyi Nyima, Paṇchen (1883–1937). *A Treatise on Earth. Legs par bshad pa sa'i bstan bcos.* In his Collected Works, vol. *kha.*

Dromtönpa (1004–64). *A Garland of Essential Advice on Societal Values. Mi chos gnad kyi phreng ba.* Printed in *Blo sbyong nyer mkho phogs bsgrigs / byang chub lo ma dpe tsogs* [*A Compilation of Requisite Mind-Training: A Collection of Folio Texts on Enlightenment*]. Gansu, China: Nationalities Press, 2003.

Frye, Stanley. *Sutra of the Wise and Foolish.* Translated from the Mongolian. Dharamsala: Library of Tibetan Works and Archives, 1981.

Gendun Chopel. *Grains of Gold: The Tales of a Cosmopolitan Traveler.* Translated by Thupten Jinpa and Donald S. Lopez Jr. Chicago: University of Chicago Press, 2014.

Gö Lotsāwa Shönu Pal (1391–1481). *Blue Annals. Deb ther sngon po,* vol. 1. Sichuan: Nationalities Press (Si khron mi rigs dpe skrun khang), 1984.

Gungthang Könchok Tenpai Drönmé (1762–1823). *A Treatise on Trees: A Hundred Branches of Wise Sayings on Spiritual and Worldly Norms. Legs par bshad pa shing gi bstan bcos.* In his Collected Works, vol. *ja.* Delhi: Demo Ngawang Gelek, 1972 (reproduced from the Lhasa edition). English translations of Gungthang's two texts: *Water-Tree Treatises: Hundred Waves of Elegant Sayings and Hundred Branches of Elegant Sayings of rJe-Gung-thang bsTan-pa'i-sgron-me,* translated by Yeshi Tashi. The Dalai Lama Tibeto-Indological Series 33. (Delhi: India Aditya Prakashan, 2011). *The Water and Wood Shastras,* translated by Yeshe Khedrup and Wilson Hurley (Wayne, NJ: Karuna Publications, 2012).

———. *A Treatise on Water: A Hundred Waves of Wise Sayings. Legs par bshad pa chu'i bstan bcos.* In his Collected Works, vol. *ja*. Delhi: Demo Ngawang Gelek, 1972 (reproduced from the Lhasa edition).

Hahn, Michael. "The Tibetan *Shes rab sdong bu* and Its Indian Sources (1)." *South Asian Classical Studies* (Kyushu University, Department of Indology) 24 (2009): 1–78.

Horkhang Sönam Palbar. *The Collected Works of Horkhang Sönam Palbar. Hor khang bsod nams dpal 'bar gyi gsung 'bum phogs bsgrigs.* Beijing: Krung go bod kyi shes rig dpe skrun khang, 1990.

Jampal Rolpai Lodrö ('Jam dpal rol pa'i blo gros, 1888–1944). *Heart Essence of the Great Perfection of Manjuśrī. Rdzogs pa chen po 'jam dpal thugs tig.* In his Collected Works, vol. 1, pages 127–86. Sichuan: Nationalities Press (Si khron mi rigs dpe skrun khang), 2003.

———. *The Wish-Fulfilling Tree: A Treatise on Norms. Lugs kyi bstan bcos dpag bsam ljon pa.* In his Collected Works, vol. 1. Sichuan: Nationalities Press (Si khron mi rigs dpe skrun khang), 2003.

Jinpa, Thupten. "Introduction." *Sngon gleng ngo sprod.* In *Anthology of Advice Texts of Wise Sayings. Legs bshad lugs kyi bslab bya'i dpe tshogs.* Bod kyi gtsug lag gces btus pod phreng 27. Delhi: Institute of Tibetan Classics, 2006.

Jinpa, Thupten, and Jas Elsner. *Songs of Spritual Experience: Tibetan Buddhist Poems of Insight and Awakening.* Boston: Shambhala, 2000.

Jonang Tāranātha (1575–1634). *History of Buddhism in India. Rgya gar chos 'byung.* Sichuan: Nationalities Press (Si khron mi rigs dpe skrun khang), 1976.

Karmapa Rangjung Dorjé (1284–1339). *One Hundred Jātakas. Skyes rabs brgya pa. Gangs can rig brgya'i sgo 'byad lde mig*, vol. 22. Lhasa: Nationalities Press (Mi rigs dpe skrun khang), 1995.

Khaché Phalu's Advice. Kha che pha lu'i bslab bya. Edited by Losang Tenzin. Lhasa: Bod ljongs mi dmangs dpe skrun khang, 2000. English translation: *Kache Phalu's Advice on the Art of Living.* Translated by Dawa Norbu. Dharamsala: Library of Tibetan Works and Archives, 1986.

Khepa Deu (twelfth century). *Extensive History of India and Tibet. Mkhas pa lde'us mdzad pa'i rgya bod kyi chos 'byung rgyas pa.* Gangs can rig mdzod series 3. Lhasa: Tibet Nationalities Press (Bod ljongs mi dmangs dpe skrun khang), 1987.

Khoroche, Peter, trans. *Once the Buddha Was a Monkey: Ārya Śūra's Jātakamālā.* Chicago: University of Chicago Press, 1989.

Kyilsur Losang Jinpa (b. 1821). *A Treatise on Wind: Wise Sayings That Flutter the Flag of the Two Norms. Lugs zung bad an gyo ba'i legs bshad rlung gi bstan bcos.* Delhi: Chophel Lekdan, 1979 (reproduced from the Tashilhunpo edition).

Martön Chögyal. *The Incisive Vajra: Biographies of the Tibetan Lineage of Masters* (*Bla ma bod kyi brgyud pa'i rnam thar zhib mo rdo rje*). This text, also known as *Tibetan Story of the Excellent Masters* (*Bla ma dam pa bod kyi lo rgyus*), is translated by Cyrus Stearns in *Luminous Lives: The Story of the Early Masters of the Lam 'Bras Tradition in Tibet.* Boston: Wisdom Publications, 2001.

Mipham, Jamgön. *The Just King: The Tibetan Buddhist Classic on Leading an Ethical Life.* Translated by José I. Cabezón. Boulder, CO: Snow Lion, 2017.

Monier-Williams, Monier. *Sanskrit-English Dictionary.* New Delhi: Munshiram Manoharlal, 2nd reprint, 1981.

Ngawang Losang Gyatso, Fifth Dalai Lama (1617–82). *A Pearl Garland of Advice Uniting Spiritual and Temporal Ethics. Bslab bya mi thi li phreng ba.* In his Collected Works, zhal gdams, vol. *dza.* Delhi: Namgyal Institute of Tibetology, 1993 (reproduced from the Lhasa Zhol edition).

Norbu, Namkhai. *Drung, De'u, and Bön: Narrations, Symbolic Languages, and the Bön Tradition in Ancient Tibet.* Translated into English from Italian by Andrew Likianowicz. Dharamsala: Library of Tibetan Works and Archives, 1995.

O'Flaherty, Wendy Doniger, trans. *Hindu Myths: A Sourcebook Translated from the Sanskrit.* London: Penguin Books, 1975.

Ohnuma, Reiko. *Head, Eyes, Flesh, Blood: Giving Away the Body in Indian Buddhism.* New York: Columbia University Press, 2012.

Olivelle, Patrick. *See under* Viṣṇuśarma, *Pañcatantra.*

Patak, Suniti Kumar. *The Indian Nītiśāstras in Tibet.* Delhi: Motilal Banarsidass, 1974.

Pawo Tsuklak Trengwa (1504–66). *Feast for the Learned: A History of Buddhism. Chos 'byung mkhas pa'i dga' ston.* 2 vols. Beijing: Nationalities Press (Mi rigs dpe skrun khang), 1986.

Pillar Testament. See under Songtsen Gampo (attributed).

Rajan, Chandra. *See under* Viṣṇuśarma, *Pañcatantra.*

Rinchen Pal (thirteenth century). *A Commentary on "A Jewel Treasury of Wise Sayings." Legs par bshad pa rin po che'i gter gyi 'grel pa.* Lhasa: Tibetan People's Press, 1990.

Rotman, Andy, trans. *Divine Stories: Divyāvadāna, Part 1.* Boston: Wisdom Publications, 2008.

———. *Divine Stories: Divyāvadāna, Part 2.* Somerville, MA: Wisdom Publications, 2017.

Sakya Paṇḍita Kunga Gyaltsen (1182–1251). *Bouquet of Various Flowers. Sdeb sbyor sna tshogs me tog gi chun po. Sakya Collected Works,* 10: 530–69. Dehradun, India: Sakya Centre, 1992–93.

———. *Clear Differentiation of the Three Codes. Sdom gsum rab dbye. Sakya Collected Works,* 5: 297–320 (*na* 1–48). Dehradun, India: Sakya Centre, 1992–93. Translated by Jared Douglas Rhoton in *A Clear Differentiation of the Three Codes.* Albany: State University of New York Press, 2002.

———. *Gateway for the Learned. Mkhas pa rnams 'jug pa'i sgo. Sakya Collected Works,* 10: 325–447. Dehradun, India: Sakya Centre, 1992–93.

———. *A Jewel Treasury of Wise Sayings. Legs par bshad pa rin po che'i gter.* In *Sakya Collected Works,* 10: 199–243. Dehradun, India: Sakya Centre, 1992–93. Several English translations are available. In addition to *Ordinary Wisdom* below, the following two translations are easily accessible: *A Precious Treasury of Elegant Sayings,* translated by Tarthang Tulku (http://mahajana.net/texts/kopia_lokalna/elegant.htm), and *The Precious Treasury of Elegant Sayings by Sakya Pandita,* translated by Nicolas Bommarito (http://www.nicbommarito.com/translation/sakyalegshe/sakyalegshe.pdf). See also the translation from the Mongolian under Bosson above.

———. *Necklace for the Youth: Differentiations of People. Skyes bu'i rnam 'byed bshad pa gzhon nu'i mgul rgyan. Sakya Collected Works,* 18: 289–301. Dehradun, India: Sakya Centre, 1992–93.

———. *Ordinary Wisdom: Sakya Pandita's Treasury of Good Advice. With a Commentary Entitled "A Hive Where Gather Bees of Clear Understanding" by Sakya Khenpo Sangyay Tenzin.* Translated by John T. Davenport, Sallie D. Davenport, and Losang Thonden. Boston: Wisdom Publications, 2000.

———. *Treasury of Words. Mngon brjod kyi bstan bcos tshig gi gter. Sakya Collected Works,* 10: 505–30. Dehradun, India: Sakya Centre, 1992–93.

———. *Treatise on Music. Rol mo'i bstan bcos. Sakya Collected Works,* 10: 309–21. Dehradun, India: Sakya Centre, 1992–93.

———. *Wise Sayings: A Magical Net. Legs bshad 'phrul gyi dra ba. Sakya Collected Works,* 12: 548–55. Dehradun, India: Sakya Centre, 1992–93.

Shang Gyalwa Pal (thirteenth century). *Biography of the the Great Sakya Paṇḍita. Dpal ldan sa skya paṇḍita chen po'i rnam par thar pa*. Printed in *Tshad ma rigs gter rtsa ba dang 'grel pa*. Sichuan: Nationalities Press (Si khron mi rigs dpe skrun khang), 1995.

Silk, Jonathan. *Riven by Lust: Incest and Schism in Indian Buddhist Legend and Historiography*. Honolulu: University of Hawai'i Press, 2009.

Sönam Drakpa, Paṇchen (1478–1554). *Ganden Wise Sayings: A Bouquet of White Lotuses. Dge ldan legs bshad padma dkar po'i chun po*. Mundgod, India: Drepung Loseling Monastery, 1970?. Also in *Dge ldan legs bshad kyi rsta 'grel*. Xining, China: Kokonor Nationalities Press (Mtsho sngon mi rigs dpe skrun khang), 1995.

———. *Magical Mirror of History. Rgyal rabs 'phrul gyi me long*. Beijing: Nationalities Press (Mi rigs dpe skrun khang), 1989. English translations: *The Mirror Reflecting the Dynasties. Rgyal rabs 'khrul ba'i me long (Deb ther dmar po gsar ma)*. Translated by Guiseppe Tucci in *Tibetan Chronicles*, Serie orientale Roma 24. Rome: Istituto Italiano per il Medio ed Estremo Oriente, 1971.

Sönam Gyaltsen (Lama Dampa 1312–75). *Clear Mirror: A Royal Geneology. Rgyal rabs gsal ba'i me long*. Beijing: Nationalities Press (Mi rigs dpe skrun khang), 1995. English translations: *The Clear Mirror: A Traditional Account of Tibet's Golden Age*, translated by Taylor McComas and Lama Choedak Yuthok (Ithaca, NY: Snow Lion Publications, 1996), and *The Mirror Illuminating the Royal Genealogies: Tibetan Buddhist Historiography*, translated and annotated by Per K. Sørensen (Wiesbaden: Otto Harrassowitz Verlag, 1994).

Songtsen Gampo (617–50) (attributed). *Pillar Testament. Bka' chems bka' khol ma*. Gansu, China: Kan su'u mi rigs dpe srun khang, 1989. Lhasa: Tibetan People's Press, 2015.

Stein, R. A. *Tibetan Civilization*. Stanford, CA: Stanford University Press, 1972.

Sternbach, Ludwik. "Indian Wisdom and Its Spread beyond India." *Journal of American Oriental Society* 101.1 (1981): 97–131.

———. "*Subhāṣita-saṃgrahas*, A Forgotten Chapter in the Histories of Sanskrit Literature." *Indologica Taurensia* 1 (1973): 168–219.

Tenzin, compiler. *Selected Anthology of Vedic Myths* (*Rig byed gtam rgyud bdams bsgrigs*). Xining, China: Kokonor Nationalities Press (Mtsho sngon mi rigs dpe skrun khang), 1997.

Tsering, Tashi. "The Advice of the Tibetan Muslim 'Phalu': A Preliminary Discussion of a Popular Buddhist/Islamic Literary Treatise." *Tibetan Review*, part 1 (February 1988): 10–15; part 2 (March 1988): 18–21.

———. "Review of *Kache Phalu's Advice on the Art of Living*." *Tibetan Review* 23 (February 1988): 10–15.

Van der Kuijp, Leonard. "Review: *Dge ldan legs bshad*. By Pan chen Bsod nams grags pa." *Journal of the American Oriental Society* 106 (1986): 617–21.

Van Manen, Johan. "Khacche Phalu: A Tibetan Moralist." *The Asutosh Mookerjee Silver Jubilee Volumes* 3.2 (1925): 147–85.

Van Schaik, Sam. "The Naming of Tibetan Religion: *Bon* and *Chos* in the Tibetan Imperial Period." *Journal of the International Association for Bon Research* 1 (2013): 228–57.

Viṣṇuśarma (attributed). *Pañcatantra.* Translated for the Clay Sanskrit Library by Patrick Olivelle in Viṣṇuśarman, *The Five Discourses on Worldly Wisdom* (New York: New York University Press, 2006). Translated for the Penguin Classics series by Chandra Rajan in Viṣṇu Śarma, *The Panćatantra* (London: Penguin Books, 1993).

Von Schiefner, F. A. *Tibetan Tales, Derived from Indian Sources, Translated from the Tibetan of the Kah-Gyur.* Translated into English from the German, with an introduction, by W. R. S. Ralston. London: Kegan Paul, 1906.

Wangdu, Pasang, and Hildegard Diemberger. *dBa' bzhed: The Royal Narrative Concerning the Bringing of the Buddha's Doctrine to Tibet.* Vienna: Verlag der Österreichischen Akademie der Wissenschaften, 2000.

Yangchen Gawai Lodrö (1740–1827). *Rays of Sunlight: A Commentary on "Ganden Wise Sayings." Dge ldan legs bshad padma dkar po'i chun po'i 'grel pa nyi ma'i 'od zer*. In his *Collected Works*, vol. *ka*. Delhi: Mongolian Lama Guru Deva, 1971. Also in *Dge ldan legs bshad kyi rtsa 'grel.* Xining, China: Kokonor Nationalities Press (Mtsho sngon mi rigs dpe skrun khang), 1995.

Zemey Rinpoché Losang Palden (Blo bzang dpal ldan Dze smad rin po che, 1927–96). *A Commentary on "A Treatise on Trees." Legs par bshad pa shing gi bstan bcos kyi 'grel pa lugs zung blang dor 'char ba'i me long.* In his *Collected Works,* vol. 3 (*ga*). Delhi: Tashi Gephel House, 1997.

———. *Various Tales and Proverbs, Part 4. Gtam dang ngag sgros sna tshogs tshan pa bzhi pa.* In his *Collected Works*, vol. 6 (*a*). Delhi: Tashi Gephel House, 1997.

Index

About the Contributors

Beth Newman received her PhD in South Asian languages and literature from the University of Wisconsin-Madison. Before retiring, she taught at Ringling School of Art and Design in Sarasota, Florida. She is the translator of *The Tale of the Incomparable Prince* and now translates and edits from her home in Madison, Wisconsin.

Thupten Jinpa Langri was educated in the classical Tibetan monastic academia and received the highest degree of *geshé lharam* from Ganden Shartse Monastery. Jinpa also holds a PhD in religious studies from the University of Cambridge, England. Since 1985, he has been the principal English translator for the Dalai Lama, accompanying His Holiness on tours to the West and translating and editing many of his books. In addition to publishing his own books and scholarly articles, Jinpa serves on the advisory board of numerous educational and cultural organizations, and he currently chairs the Mind and Life Institute and the Compassion Institute. He is the president and the editor-in-chief of the Institute of Tibetan Classics, based in Montreal.

The Institute of Tibetan Classics

The Institute of Tibetan Classics is a nonproit, charitable educational organization based in Montreal, Canada. It is dedicated to two primary objectives: (1) to preserve and promote the study and deep appreciation of Tibet's rich intellectual, spiritual, and artistic heritage, especially among the Tibetan-speaking communities worldwide; and (2) to make the classical Tibetan knowledge and literature a truly global heritage, its spiritual and intellectual resources open to all.

To learn more about the Institute of Tibetan Classics and its various projects, please visit www.tibetanclassics.org or write to this address:

Institute of Tibetan Classics
304 Aberdare Road
Montreal (Quebec) H3P 3K3
Canada

The Library of Tibetan Classics

"This new series edited by Thupten Jinpa and published by Wisdom Publications is a landmark in the study of Tibetan culture in general and Tibetan Buddhism in particular. Each volume contains a lucid introduction and outstanding translations that, while aimed at the general public, will benefit those in the field of Tibetan Studies immensely as well."

—Leonard van der Kuijp, Harvard University

"This is an invaluable set of translations by highly competent scholar-practitioners. The series spans the breadth of the history of Tibetan religion, providing entry to a vast culture of spiritual cultivation."

—Jeffrey Hopkins, University of Virginia

"Erudite in all respects, this series is at the same time accessible and engagingly translated. As such, it belongs in all college and university libraries as well as in good public libraries. *The Library of Tibetan Classics* is on its way to becoming a truly extraordinary spiritual and literary accomplishment."

—Janice D. Willis, Wesleyan University

Following is a list of the thirty-two proposed volumes in *The Library of Tibetan Classics*. Some volumes are translations of single texts, while others are compilations of multiple texts, and each volume will be roughly the same length. Except for those volumes already published, the renderings of titles below are tentative and liable to change. The Institute of Tibetan Classics has contracted numerous established translators in its efforts, and work is progressing on all the volumes concurrently.

1. *Mind Training: The Great Collection*, compiled by Shönu Gyalchok and Könchok Gyaltsen (fifteenth century). NOW AVAILABLE
2. *The Book of Kadam: The Core Texts*, attributed to Atiśa and Dromtönpa (eleventh century). NOW AVAILABLE
3. *The Great Chariot: A Treatise on the Great Perfection*, Longchen Rapjampa (1308–63)
4. *Taking the Result As the Path: Core Teachings of the Sakya Lamdré Tradition*, Jamyang Khyentsé Wangchuk (1524–68) et al. NOW AVAILABLE
5. *Mahāmudrā and Related Instructions: Core Teachings of the Kagyü Schools*. NOW AVAILABLE
6. *Stages of the Path and the Ear-Whispered Instructions: Core Teachings of the Geluk School*
7. *Ocean of Definitive Meaning: A Teaching for the Mountain Hermit*, Dölpopa Sherap Gyaltsen (1292–1361)
8. *Miscellaneous Tibetan Buddhist Lineages: The Core Teachings*, Jamgön Kongtrül (1813–90)
9. *Sutra, Tantra, and the Mind Cycle: Core Teachings of the Bön School*
10. *Stages of the Buddha's Teachings: Three Key Texts*. NOW AVAILABLE
11. *The Bodhisattva's Altruistic Ideal: Selected Key Texts*
12. *The Ethics of the Three Codes*
13. *Sādhanas: Vajrayana Buddhist Meditation Manuals*
14. *Ornament of Stainless Light: An Exposition of the Kālacakra Tantra*, Khedrup Norsang Gyatso (1423–1513). NOW AVAILABLE
15. *A Lamp to Illuminate the Five Stages: Teachings on the Guhyasamāja Tantra*, Tsongkhapa (1357–1419). NOW AVAILABLE
16. *Studies in the Perfection of Wisdom*
17. *Treatises on Buddha Nature*
18. *Differentiations of the Profound View: Interpretations of Emptiness in Tibet*
19. *Elucidation of the Intent: A Thorough Exposition of "Entering the Middle Way,"* Tsongkhapa (1357–1419)
20. *Tibetan Buddhist Epistemology I: The Sakya School*
21. *Tibetan Buddhist Epistemology II: The Geluk School*
22. *Tibetan Buddhist Psychology and Phenomenology: Selected Texts*
23. *Ornament of Abhidharma: A Commentary on the "Abhidharmakośa,"* Chim Jampalyang (thirteenth century)

24. *A Beautiful Adornment of Mount Meru: Presentation of Classical Indian Philosophies*, Changkya Rölpai Dorjé (1717–86)
25. *The Crystal Mirror of Philosophical Systems: A Tibetan Study of Asian Religious Thought*, Thuken Losang Chökyi Nyima (1737–1802). NOW AVAILABLE
26. *Gateway for Being Learned and Realized: Selected Texts*
27. *The Tibetan Book of Everyday Wisdom: A Thousand Years of Sage Advice.* NOW AVAILABLE
28. *Mirror of Beryl: A Historical Introduction to Tibetan Medicine*, Desi Sangyé Gyatso (1653–1705). NOW AVAILABLE
29. *Selected Texts on Tibetan Astronomy and Astrology*
30. *Art and Literature: An Anthology*
31. *Tales from the Tibetan Operas*
32. *A History of Buddhism in India and Tibet*, Khepa Deu (thirteenth century)

To receive a brochure describing all the volumes or to stay informed about *The Library of Tibetan Classics*, please write to:

info@wisdompubs.org

or send a request by post to:

Wisdom Publications
Attn: Library of Tibetan Classics
199 Elm Street
Somerville, MA 02144 USA

The complete catalog containing descriptions of each volume can also be found online at wisdompubs.org.

Become a Benefactor of the Library of Tibetan Classics

The Library of Tibetan Classics' scope, importance, and commitment to the finest quality make it a tremendous financial undertaking. We invite you to become a benefactor, joining us in creating this profoundly important human resource. Contributors of two thousand dollars or more will receive a copy of each future volume as it becomes available, and will have their names listed in all subsequent volumes. Larger donations will go even further in supporting *The Library of Tibetan Classics*, preserving the creativity, wisdom, and scholarship of centuries past, so that it may help illuminate the world for future generations.

To contribute, please either visit our website at wisdompubs.org, call us at (617) 776-7416, or send a check made out to Wisdom Publications or credit card information to the address below.

Library of Tibetan Classics Fund
Wisdom Publications
199 Elm Street
Somerville, MA 02144
USA

Please note that contributions of lesser amounts are also welcome and are invaluable to the development of the series. Wisdom is a 501(c)3 nonprofit corporation, and all contributions are tax-deductible to the extent allowed by law.

If you have any questions, please do not hesitate to call us or email us at advancement@wisdompubs.org.

To keep up to date on the status of *The Library of Tibetan Classics*, visit the series page on our website, and subscribe to our newsletter while you are there.

About Wisdom Publications

Wisdom Publications is the leading publisher of classic and contemporary Buddhist books and practical works on mindfulness. To learn more about us or to explore our other books, please visit our website at wisdompubs.org or contact us at the address below.

Wisdom Publications
199 Elm Street
Somerville, MA 02144 USA

We are a 501(c)(3) organization, and donations in support of our mission are tax deductible.

Wisdom Publications is affiliated with the Foundation for the Preservation of the Mahayana Tradition (FPMT).